Joan Littlewood: Dreams and Realities

PETER RANKIN

Joan Littlewood:
Dreams and Realities

The Official Biography

First published in 2014 by Oberon Books Ltd
521 Caledonian Road, London N7 9RH
Tel: +44 (0) 20 7607 3637 / Fax: +44 (0) 20 7607 3629
e-mail: info@oberonbooks.com
www.oberonbooks.com

A catalogue record for this book is available from the British Library.

PB ISBN: 978-1-78319-084-3
E ISBN: 978-1-78319-583-1

Front and back cover images courtesy of Theatre Royal Stratford East.

Printed, bound and converted
by CPI Group (UK) Ltd, Croydon, CR0 4YY.

To bossy women without whom I would have done even less

Contents

Acknowledgements

Philip Hedley and Kerry Michael for getting it going; Jenny King and Emma Jackson for keeping it going; my mother, Gaye Brown, aunt Cecilia, Richenda Carey and Joan Gilbert for general bullying; Peter Everett and Janey Preger for access to BBC archive material and stories of Manchester; Oberon Books for patience.

PROLOGUE

In 1963, aged sixteen, I was taken by my father to see *Oh What a Lovely War*, Theatre Workshop's musical entertainment about the First World War. Even by that early age, the magnetism of the company's name and its director, Joan Littlewood, had been drawing me towards it. Aged eleven and stuck at boarding school, I had read a review of *Fings Ain't Wot They Used T'Be* and, among the stuffy pages of *The Illustrated London News*, the company still looked a jolly lot. Two and a half years later, in 1961, a news item on the TV announced Joan Littlewood's departure from Theatre Workshop, and you didn't normally see stories about theatre directors on the TV news.

When, in the spring of 1963, she returned, there she was on TV again. Huw Wheldon was interviewing her for the BBC arts programme, *Monitor*. Her laughing eyes and warm voice, mocking the formality of a television interview, held me. How would this warmth and mockery translate into a show? That night at the theatre, I was to begin finding out.

On came a jaunty pierrot dressed in black and white, the actor Victor Spinetti. He was the master of ceremonies and he talked to us, really talked to us, so it wasn't embarrassing. When the right moment came, he summoned the company to start the show.

To set the scene, it sang a cheerful song of the period and then, in little scenes interspersed with more songs, explained how the war started. All this happened in a quick, tumbling way that left you almost breathless. It was, at one and the same time, childishly simple, easy to understand and funny. When the band vamped away in preparation for the song 'I'll Make a Man of You' and the actress, Avis Bunnage, walked on in a glittering black gown to eye the audience evilly, it turned daring.

As the pierrots continued to sing and dance, the number of deaths at the various battles began to run across an electronic newspanel at the back of the stage. The audience gasped but, despite things getting worse, it did not sink into depression. It was angry, perhaps; glad to be informed, that's for sure.

Some weeks later, Theatre Workshop announced *The Merry Roosters' Panto*. It was to be performed at matinees during *Oh What a Lovely War*'s run at the Wyndham's Theatre. I rushed to it and there they were again: Victor Spinetti, Avis Bunnage and the actor who had been Field Marshal Haig, George Sewell. This time, Victor Spinetti was Eartha, a bossy Ugly Sister. Avis Bunnage was the Fairy Godmother, and George Sewell was Baron Hardup. Dumpy, the downtrodden Ugly Sister who was forever having her ears boxed by Eartha, was played by the actor who had been Sir John French, Brian Murphy.

Those Merry Roosters had a job to do the show, though, because the manager of the theatre, Mr Redsocks, would have none of it. He wanted an uplifting afternoon of Welsh recorder music, so the audience had to shout: 'Redsocks!' whenever he appeared in order to warn the pierrots. Big Gerry Raffles, in a top hat, frock coat and, of course, red socks, played him. By then, I already knew that he really was the manager of Theatre Workshop. It was the jolliest show I had ever seen.

Although I was watching as a naïve and protected teenager, I had already been to see lots of theatre. Among other things, I had seen John Gielgud in Peter Brook's production of *The Tempest* at Drury Lane; John Osborne's *Luther* at the Royal Court; Shakespeare's York and Lancaster plays turned into *The Wars of the Roses*, at Stratford-upon-Avon; Noël Coward's *Hay Fever* at the National Theatre; and, at the London Academy of Music and Dramatic Art's new theatre in Logan Place, Peter Brook's *Theatre of Cruelty*. *Oh What a Lovely War* was different. Despite the horror of what we were told, a warmth I had never felt before spread out into the auditorium. How this was achieved, what Theatre Workshop was, who Joan Littlewood and Gerry Raffles were, I didn't know, but those two performances were the trigger to finding out and it happened sooner rather than later; in fact only a few months later.

In the spring of 1964, Joan Littlewood, wanting money for her latest project, The Fun Palace, was set to direct a series of commercials for eggs. When my father, who was the agency producer but no longer in the family home, told me, I didn't hang about. On a dull Sunday afternoon, never having been to the East End before, I set off for a two-up, two-down in Plaistow where rehearsals were taking place before the shoot.

Because they had breaks, the actors were easy to talk to – that's Avis Bunnage and George Sewell again, and their stories were smashing – but I could not talk to Joan Littlewood. In that two-up, two-down, she was up and I was down, so I merely watched her appear each morning in her black-and-white-checked raincoat and was thrilled by that alone. When at last I had the opportunity to speak up, I told her I was theatre mad. 'Don't get stage-struck,' she said, the eyes still laughing, the voice still warm, 'Get science-struck.'

Fortunately my experience of science at school was enough for me to state with conviction that I was no good at it. Right then and there, and why, I still don't know, Joan gave me the date and place of the first day's rehearsal for *Henry IV*, her adaptation of Shakespeare's two Henrys, which she was taking to the Edinburgh Festival. I ran up the street, my feet not touching the ground. As starry eyed as that sounds, I am still grateful for that sensation because it doesn't happen again, whatever exciting things come in later life.

I went to the *Henry IV* rehearsals. I went to Edinburgh and the next year, while still at school, I watched Joan rehearsing the most notorious flop of the twentieth century, Lionel Bart's Robin Hood musical, *Twang*.

When I left school, with only a note from Joan saying I could come if I was invisible, I went to the Theatre Royal Stratford East, the home of Theatre Workshop. There, having not been all that invisible, as Joan put me on the stage, I got my first job. In this way, my growing up was combined with learning about Joan and Gerry and their theatre. First Joan, and later Gerry – I didn't like him much to start with – became my theatre parents. With Joan, I watched her disciplined imagination at work and thus was inoculated against what went on in other theatres, where actors learned lines, directors gave moves and that was it. With Gerry, I listened. He had a handful of principles about writing and theatre. They weren't complicated but he was strict about them and that could be painful. Yet, even with this knowledge, and despite having my own play directed by Joan in 1973, I was still only at the beginning because, for those ten years, I thought that she, with her overwhelming personality and phenomenal gift for theatre, was Theatre Workshop all by herself. I was wrong.

In 1975, Gerry Raffles, who was not only the manager of Theatre Workshop but Joan's old man – he of the disobedient hair and deep, merry laugh, eight years her junior – died. He was 51. Immediately after his death, I pulled away from Joan because she was behaving oddly, not like herself at all, or so I thought. This was because I had only known her as a unit with Gerry, so much so that, despite their constant arguing, I hadn't noticed there was a unit in the first place. Joan alone was different. That was something else I had to learn. Some months later, I came together with her again and, ten years later, she set to work on her autobiography. By then she was living in my flat and so was able to draw me in.

At the other side of London, where, in a house all by herself, lived her half-sister Betty, was a small room filled with rows of box files. Joan had put them there but she needed to refresh her memory or perhaps find out what she herself had not known. They contained the daily dealings of Theatre Workshop, the important and the unimportant, that Gerry had carefully saved from just before the Second World War until his death. It was the kind of stuff Joan had not really been involved with because she had been busy with her actors, exactly as Gerry had intended.

Day after day, I went to 29 Stockwell Green where, as I put each letter into chronological order, I could feel the power of a gradually building narrative. Gerry had left a message in a bottle. In it were the knockings on doors, the bills that could not be paid, the arguments with both Arts Council and commercial managements that had been part of the fabric of Theatre Workshop. They gave a context to the hits. Among them were letters from the young Gerry written to Joan in the late Forties and early Fifties when they were apart. They contained clues which I didn't pick up on at once but that, later, would reinforce my understanding of what Gerry wanted for Theatre Workshop. As most of this had happened during my lifetime, I felt as if I had stepped back into a parallel life, one that was all the more fascinating because it was so different from my own.

After I'd summarised the letters and given the result to Joan, she finished the first draft which ended in 1955, before the time of the plays that had made Theatre Workshop world famous. Puzzling over this, I posted it to an expectant publisher. A few days later he rang.

'But there's no *Taste of Honey*, no *Hostage*. I mean, come on, where's *Oh What a Lovely War?* Is Joan mad?'

The conversation ended pretty quickly after that. I put the receiver down and relayed the publisher's question to Joan. Her answer was equally impatient.

'Theatre Workshop was not just about doing plays. It was a design for living.'

Impatience always seized her when someone asked questions about Theatre Workshop. Explanations bored her. At rehearsals, she conveyed ideas through excitement. A to B to C? Forget it. She didn't stop there.

'Harry Corbett and George Cooper leaving the company was the end of Theatre Workshop.'

'So Brendan Behan and Shelagh Delaney and – '

'Writing jobs. I was working night and day to make a script. There was no time for anything else.'

Evidently 'anything else' contained the design for living. What was it, I wondered. However, Joan hadn't finished.

'Tyrone Guthrie was good but he didn't try to change the world. We did.'

Oh, Joan was referring to another director, something she rarely did, at least not politely. When she was young, Tyrone Guthrie was the best director in the UK and, if Gerry was right, the *only* one because he had told me Guthrie and Joan were the only directors this country had produced. So, good as he was, Guthrie hadn't changed the world. That, at least, provided a clue.

A few days later, Howard Goorney, a founder member of Theatre Workshop, rang from Bath to ask if he could drop round for tea after an Equity meeting in London. I repeated Joan's remarks about Harry Corbett and George Cooper, her two leading actors.

'Did she really say that?' asked Howard.

'Yes.'

'I'm glad. That's what I think.'

'Oh,' was all I could think.

My problem was Gerry Raffles. Where did that leave him? Gerry was proud of those shows. Had they not made Theatre Workshop world famous and, from his teens, had that not been his ambition? He especially loved *Oh What a Lovely War*. Almost hugging himself, he used to say: 'It's a little classic and it's going to go on and on.' Joan dismissing that and the other shows was breathtaking. If only I could have heard Gerry's reaction; but he'd been dead seventeen years.

What about this design for living then? It sounded rather grand, and grand can be irritating. It was better not to ask Joan more questions, though. An argument would have followed and, as usual, I would have come off worst. It was not only Muhammad Ali who could float like a butterfly and sting like a bee. Still, I remembered that, if you took the trouble, you could look beyond Joan's grand words and find something practical.

Certainly, if I wanted to understand Joan and Gerry, using what I had learned from them, to find out about the sinews, the stresses and strains, the who-did-what that made Theatre Workshop into the company that broke more ground than any other in Britain during the twentieth century but left Joan wanting more, it looked as if I would have to follow the two aims: Joan's design for living and Gerry's Theatre Workshop.

Joan's odd behaviour following Gerry's death in 1975 meant, to be more precise, that she behaved uncharacteristically. Since that time, I had got to know her alone. I had also got to know her family. I hadn't known them before. So, taking what I learned from watching them and what I had learned from being with Joan and Gerry over the course of ten years and being with Joan for another 23, I could add, as I went along, everything I had found out for myself.

As Joan started out alone, that's where I'll begin.

CHAPTER ONE

A SPARK

Joan was conceived in the spring of 1914. It was a one-night stand and, from that moment on, the father would have no more to do with the flirtatious, dark-haired seventeen-year-old, Kate Littlewood. Fortunately Kate lived at home and had a job as a showroom assistant for a brush manufacturer in south London. The mysterious father had a job in the City and was thought to be rather posh. Apart from that, nobody knew much about him.

When Kate told her father, Robert Francis Littlewood, of the unwanted arrival, he did not climb on to a moral high horse. After all, his daughter brought home her wage each week. He simply went off, found the man in the City, took him through the courts and got him to guarantee six shillings a week towards the child's upkeep. After that, the father was rarely mentioned.

On 6 October 1914, during one of the early blackouts of the First World War, Joan was born, through no fault of her own, as she put it, in Stockwell, at the Clapham Maternity Hospital.

In later years, Joan said that as a small child she was nearly autistic, but then autistic was a word she liked the sound of, with its aura of mystery and isolation. If she had been faced with genuine autism in another person, distress would have sent her off, leaving someone else to cope.

Rather, Joan was a child with imagination but nobody much to talk to, except some chickens in the back yard, because until the age of six she was an only child. When one of the chickens had its neck wrung to provide a meal, it was the loss of a friend. Along with mutton stew, the greasy surface of which turned her stomach, chicken was a dish she refused to eat for a long time.

At Number Eight Stockwell Road, where the family lived, washdays depressed her and, outside, her spirits were not lifted. All she saw were identical streets, dusty privet hedges, lace curtains and geraniums in window boxes. At the top of the road, she was to look up at the long list of recently killed young men on the new cenotaph as it was unveiled by a reverend in a dingy surplice, the crowd moaning their responses.

Kennington Park, to the east, was no better. Joan knew that Bonnie Prince Charlie's men had been brought there for execution in 1746 and had not been executed, but massacred. To the west was the fever hospital, beyond that the road to Clapham, and beyond that the cemetery. For Joan, SW9 was a no-place.

She was aware that there had been talk of sending her to an orphanage. On the one hand this would have made her feel wobbly, uncertain whether she should exist at all, but on the other hand, looking around at what she'd been lumbered with, a rundown neighbourhood and an uneducated family, she could have been inclined to bolshiness. Perhaps her unknown father was handsome, clever, and witty, with a house in a smart neighbourhood. Stuff Kate and stuff Stockwell.

Kate had a temper on her, and with Joan around lacked no opportunity to use it. Once, she chased her daughter around the house with a carving knife because the little girl had tossed her head at her.

Kate called Joan heartless. Joan, when talking of Kate, called her a slut. When writing about her, she avoided the word. However, by portraying her as a flirt and a gambler – even if it was only betting on horses – she implied it.

Still, for all the greyness and bad temper, there were moments of delight in Joan's childhood and she described them with affectionate detail: the receiving, every birthday, of a box filled with beautifully wrapped William pears from her father, winter evenings with Robert Francis and her grandmother Caroline Em, and above all, reading.

Caroline Em had worked in a pub that served food, the Fox and Goose in Threadneedle Street. There, just by watching, she learned how to cook. Joan loved what she served, except for the mutton stews and the chicken, that is, and, from then on, preferred robust English dishes like steak and kidney pudding and bangers and mash. For the rest of her life, whenever she was unsure of what she was eating, she would arrange it on the plate and then arrange it again, a childhood habit that made any cook's heart sink.

In the evening, after the meal at Number Eight, Caroline would sit in the kitchen and take up her sewing. With her tiny nose and her silvery topknot bun, the picture she made was already pretty but then, as she stitched, she gave a little performance. Dishes at the Fox and Goose were conjured up in words, tales of the royal family's private life were recounted, and ditties were sung. Joan loved it. What she did not love were bank holidays when plans to go to exotic Golders Green foundered as Kate lingered in the pub, leaving her daughter outside with a dry biscuit.

Fascinated by Caroline's sewing as Joan was, it was never to become one of her own accomplishments. Darning, she insisted, did. It would be a brave person, though, who would have put her to the test. A demon of destruction lurked inside her ready to jump out when it came to activities and objects that held no interest. Baths overflowed and saucepan bottoms burned. It was the same with gadgets: she admired them but couldn't work them. Merely at the approach of her questing fingers, they would fall apart or explode.

It was different if Joan loved something. Flowers, she adored. She arranged them not only well but originally. The same went for laying the table when guests were coming. That could be left to her and the result would be enchanting. The mysterious wooden box and the tissue paper that the William pears came in probably attracted her more than the actual fruit.

Reading was different. It was not only a love, it was the beginning of escape. Her first school was one of the British and Foreign Society's Practising Schools, this particular one at 21 Stockwell Road. There, she struck lucky. Yes, she was bright and came top in everything but also the teaching was surprisingly good. The schoolmistresses were women who had lost their husbands-to-be in the First World War. They had a vocation which led them out into the world, right across it sometimes, in order to teach. First they had to practise, though, and that's where Joan benefited.

Many children don't like school. For Joan, it was liberation. As soon as she could read, she was lost in books, her first supply arriving by chance. It happened in 1920, when her mother, Kate, married James Morritt, an asphalter. Joan, aged six, was the reluctant bridesmaid. The newly married couple moved to two rented rooms at 33 Stockwell Road, leaving Joan behind with her grandparents. To fill the empty rooms at Number Eight, they took in lodgers and, as these lodgers moved on, so they left books. *The Sorrows of Satan* by Marie Corelli, Macaulay's *Lays of Ancient Rome, She* by Rider Haggard, *Opium Dens of the East End*, and *Under Two Flags* by Ouida: Joan devoured them in no time. Having done that, and having decided what was suitable – blooming for her was a swear word – she read a chapter a night to her grandparents, who themselves couldn't read.

A year later, in 1921, Joan's half-sister Betty Morritt was born and, in 1923, along came plump, smiling Mildred who was always known as Millie. Joan was not best pleased. For a start, they were too young to be company and, worse, she had to make herself useful. It was off to Clapham Common for her, pushing them and her aunt Carrie's baby in a pram. She hated it. She hated making herself useful in principle. One can add brain fever to autism on Joan's list of attractive disorders. She dreamed of having it when asked to fill the coal bucket. 'No, I can't. I've got brain fever,' is what she longed to say. The idea came from an episode she had read in *True Stories* in which the heroine was struck down with it.

When it came to Clapham Common, the best Joan could do was tuck a book in the pram, settle under a tree, leave the babies to their own devices and read the next thrilling chapter. The inevitable happened. When it was time to go home, Millie, a toddler by then, had toddled off. She was nowhere to be seen. After searching the Common, Joan had to go to the police station. There she found Millie gurgling and smiling on a policeman's knee. All Joan could think was: 'He seems to be doing a better job of it than me.'

Kate gave birth to two more Morritt children, Jim, and Jeremy who was known as Jerry. In conversation Joan was always careful to speak of all four – Betty, Millie, Jim and Jerry – as half-sisters and half-brothers. Jim, in contrast, said they always referred to Joan as their sister, not half this or half that, and, what's more, his opinion of Kate was quite different. He thought she was a decent mother and defended her angrily when there was any accusation of slut.

By the age of twelve, Joan had tried to leave home three times. She was edging away, not only from Stockwell but her family too. She recalled Kate at that time saying: 'Stuck up little bitch, too big for her boots.' In later life, there was a word Joan used: 'ethnic'. She didn't use it then but her particular meaning of it, based on what she saw around her, was beginning to evolve. It was not a compliment. 'Ethnic' meant accepting without question what had been handed down to you. If you didn't ask questions you were stupid, so from the beginning Joan's feelings about the working class were mixed. When, as a whole, it came under attack, she stood up for it but, if she thought one member of it was backsliding, that person would be scorned.

Her stepfather was a little different. He was all for the Society of Asphalters attaining Union status and tried his best to stick up for the rights of both himself and his fellow workers, sometimes getting into trouble for his pains. Joan admired that and, from him, began to gain an understanding of wrongs further afield than home, like hungry, jobless men marching from the north east of England down to London.

Two family traits Joan could never escape were hooded eyes – Kate and all her children had them – and truculence. Some people, even actors in her own company, thought that Joan came, not from working-class Stockwell, but landed Warwickshire gentry. The hooded eyes set you right double-quick.

The truculence came from Kate's hot temper and James's orneriness. It was in her half-brother, Jerry, when, as an adult, he took his employers to court, dismissed his counsel and defended himself. 'The freeborn Englishman,' Joan called him. Sometimes she admired that spirit but not if it was only backed by ignorance. Then she despised it and, when it only led to family rows, she hated it. Backchat was great, but flesh-tearing feuds repelled her. Despite her own ability to lash out, she was not thick-skinned.

Actually, Joan had more than the family truculence. Unlike the others, she seemed to have a deep well of anger inside her. It burst out in a boiling torrent that made grown men tremble and women cry. From her diary entries, it is clear that she was aware of this anger and, because it came from her family links, hated it all the more. 'You do that and I'll kill you,' she hissed at Betty during a birthday party for Millie. Betty, without pause, shot back equally vicious words. It looked as if they were going to come to blows. Were they six years old? No, Joan was in her 70s, Betty not much younger.

In Betty you could see Joan's retiring side. Joan may have been tough at work, but away from theatre she found difficult situations hard to face, like birthday parties at which she was the birthday girl. From most of them, she ran away. Betty did that too. She was a mirror image of Joan, only the silvering had worn away in places.

Not all parties drove Joan away. As long as people didn't stand around talking, she could enjoy them as much as anyone else. What she liked was singing and dancing, just as she remembered from a party one Christmas when she was little.

For a few hours, the crackling fire and the colourful decorations created a fairyland that took her away from Stockwell. The pleasurable lead-up to this was the preparation of the pudding, the stirring and the tasting. It took weeks. Closer to the day was the choice of roast, in this case a large piece of beef taken from the rump. It was called an H-bone, the kind of cut Caroline had seen displayed at the Fox and Goose. To look at it was spectacular, and eating it was not bad either, as long as you knew that it had to spend hours in the oven to get the toughness out. On the actual day came the getting in of booze: a crate of stout, a bottle of gin, a bottle of whisky, port and lemon, rum and peppermint. At teatime, neighbours and relatives came to call. James, having laughed a neighbour into silence for singing operetta, took over to play songs on the piano that were easy for anybody to sing along with. That in turn stirred everyone into shifting the furniture so that the carpet could be rolled up for dancing. This was the bit Joan liked best as she had invented her very own dance. When she recounted the events of this day, it was impossible not to think of Mr Fezziwig's party in *A Christmas Carol* and yet she didn't like Dickens.

At the Practising School it was soon noticed that Joan was scholarship material. This was all very well, but she had a horror of exams. The first time she was supposed to take one, she was sick in a drain on her way to school. Back at home, Caroline wrapped her in a soft shawl, put her in Robert's armchair and fed her on sponge cakes accompanied by sips of soda water. With exam day over, Joan felt better.

When the exam day for the scholarship arrived, Joan simply didn't turn up. Only when she thought it would be over did she feel it safe to return. She was met by an unwelcome surprise. Miss Barnes, her teacher, had arranged for her to take the exam on her own. With a deadening weight of responsibility bearing down on her shoulders – no one else in the family had done anything like this – Joan tried to write her essay, *A Day in the Life of a Penny*. Feeling awful, she struggled on, convinced she was making a hash of it but, no, she won the scholarship. It was to La Retraite School in Clapham Park.

At La Retraite, she had to wear a uniform. Jim said how proud she was of it, but behind his words could be heard the widening gap between Joan and him, and the rest of the Morritts. Every night, before going to bed, she arranged her uniform with the care she took over laying the table.

That kind of attention, did not, however go to one particular item of clothing she was given to wear. This one was nothing to do with uniforms and school. It was a brown velvet dress which she had to iron first because it was a hand-me-down. If you add together a garment that had been worn by someone else, her dislike of being useful, in particular her dislike of ironing, plus her aversion to the colour brown, it is not hard to predict what happened next. Attempting to dispel the dullness of her task, she brought a book to her ironing and, during an exciting chapter, let the iron go right through the velvet. Although she often recounted that incident, she always left it unadorned. By not commenting, she was making the accident appear to come out of the blue, she being no more than an absent-minded innocent.

She didn't think the teaching at La Retraite was as good as at the Practising School; it wasn't strict enough. However she enjoyed the airy rooms, the small classes and the atmosphere of learning. As for the Roman Catholic ritual, it didn't frighten her as it does some. She liked it. This started with the girls having to put on soft shoes before entering the school. Perhaps that's what Joan partly had in mind when later she insisted that her actors wear soft shoes at rehearsals. Yes, anyone taking movement seriously wears soft shoes or takes off their shoes altogether, but Joan regarded the stage as sacred. Why else was there a rush of that deep anger whenever she saw a classic play done badly? For her, the perpetrators were blasphemers.

Another memory of convent days that projected forward was that of silence. In the early years of Theatre Workshop, the actors were expected to sit quietly in their dressing rooms for an hour before the performance. 'Our lives were monastic,' said Max Shaw, one of those actors, and he was not merely referring to poverty. La Retraite was called La Retraite for a reason. Joan learned about long periods of silence. People may think this boring or frightening, but this was a silence that could be both comforting and enlightening. Boisterousness may have been a characteristic of Joan's productions, but here we find her quiet, serious side; not a confining seriousness but a releasing one.

The silence of retreat was certainly her only comfort after the death of Carrie, her much-loved aunt, from tuberculosis at the age of 39. Carrie had a caustic wit that amused Joan. Having to watch relatives at the funeral, who hardly knew Carrie, crying or 'blubbering', the word Carrie used to use, merely annoyed her.

She preferred to attend Mass at La Retraite, the first Mass she had ever sat right through. She thought it beautiful and, another day went up for communion but, being neither Catholic nor baptised, was turned away. Mass was far better than listening to the C of E hymns sung around the cenotaph, ones like 'Abide with Me', which she poked fun at all her life.

The Stations of the Cross, she really liked. As with the Mass, there was theatre about it. The influence it had on her came to the surface in the 1960s when she wanted to do a play about the Ronan Point disaster. She saw it being performed like the Stations of the Cross, promenade theatre before promenade theatre.

Mother St Teresa, the headmistress at La Retraite, seeing Joan's thoughtful as well as argumentative side, suggested she become a nun. Joan dismissed the idea because she didn't consider Mother St Teresa clever enough to make a good case, but the idea did attract her.

Besides, other ideas to do with her future were already forming in her head. She had an art teacher, Miss Nicholson, who believed in her and took her to art galleries. Far and away the most important was the one closest to Stockwell, the Tate (now Tate Britain). As soon as Joan discovered it, she knew that she could get there by herself, and did. The number 88 bus came from Clapham to Stockwell station where she jumped on. It then crossed Vauxhall Bridge and arrived at the gallery, the whole journey taking eight minutes. It's a short journey and yet for the rest of Joan's family, it might have been the other side of the world. This was the end of pushing a pram to Clapham Common. Joan had found something much better.

Once in the gallery, she hurried along, twisting her head sideways to avoid seeing the Turners. She had to go past them because her goal was in the gallery beyond, the Constables. She loved those. In the few steps she took to get from the one to the other, you can see the violence of Joan's likes and dislikes. Because he's so modern, Turner fascinates many; not Joan. All she noticed was that he couldn't draw. It is true that his human figures are not great and indeed you don't find them in his most famous paintings but is that a reason to write him off? For Joan it was. On the other hand, one Constable could hold her attention for an hour, an escape and a retreat at the same time. However, despite painting being a passion for her, it was mixed with one even stronger.

CHAPTER TWO

THE SPARK CATCHES FIRE

The spark was struck at the Practising School. One afternoon, Miss Barnes took her class to see *The Merchant of Venice* at the Brixton Theatre. As you would expect of a young person whose life would be taken up with theatre, Joan was spellbound. Yet it was not to the point that she was entirely uncritical. She didn't think much of Antonio or Portia but Shylock, she hung on his every word. Back at school, she looked out the play and learned his speech, 'I am a Jew. Hath not a Jew eyes?' going so far as to put on a big coat, draw a beard on her face using burnt cork, and perform it for her grandparents at evening reading time.

At La Retraite, another school trip took her to a matinee at the Old Vic. The play was to be *Hamlet*. This visit would be the start of a relationship with the Old Vic that takes a bit of understanding. At rehearsals, in later years, Joan did nothing but mock the name. When ticking off her company, it became a shorthand for bad acting, while her imitations had actors doubled up but that is not the whole story.

When, as a child, she told her family that she was going to this matinee, her aunt Fan, whom she insisted wasn't really her aunt, said: 'That blood tub.' It annoyed her. Once upon a time Bill Sykes, it is true, had dragged Nancy by the hair round the stage gauging the number of times he could do it by the amount of booing he was hearing, but those days were over. Emma Cons, a social reformer, had taken it over in 1880 and turned it into the Royal Victoria Coffee Music Hall where no alcohol was drunk and entertainment was decent, if not always interesting. On Tuesday evenings there would be a science lecture. This led to lessons being given to poor would-be students in the dressing rooms and subsequently at the Morley College, an offshoot specially founded by Cons to help working-class people further themselves. It was one of the first adult education colleges in the country. Although this happened before Joan's time, when she reached her Theatre Workshop years, classes were something she too organised. They were for people not necessarily in theatre; the neighbourhood children living near to the Theatre Royal Stratford East, for example. This was part of something bigger she wanted to achieve; but that is yet to come.

In 1898, Cons' niece, Lilian Baylis, joined her aunt to help run the Coffee Music Hall and, when Emma died in 1912, took over the reins entirely. Aware that the Hall's nightly fare was less than thrilling, she cast around to find something that would not only edify but hold the interest. After much prayer, she received her answer: Shakespeare. And though she knew little about the playwright, she instructed the director, Ben Greet, to create a company and set to work, which he did in 1914, the year of Joan's birth. Between then and 1923, all Shakespeare's plays in the First Folio were performed. This had never been attempted before. That is why Joan did not want her ignorant aunt Fan abusing Lilian Baylis's efforts.

At that matinee, the actor she saw playing Hamlet was the Old Vic's first home-grown leading player, the 25-year-old John Gielgud. The cast also included Donald Wolfit, Martita Hunt and Robert Speaight. That was the list she gave when writing about it, one of the rare occasions Joan gave a list of actors we may have heard of. The play had her on the edge of her seat and from then on she went on foot to every new production. Only by queuing up for late door and being prepared to run up to the gallery at the last minute was she able to afford the five pence ticket price. That waiting and longing, sometimes in the rain, was a scene that in 1967 she put into the musical, *The Marie Lloyd Story*. One audience member, Alan Strachan, the director, was so haunted by it, despite it being only a fleeting moment, that 35 years later, he was able to describe it precisely.

Throughout her life, Joan damned most of the theatre actors who were considered our stars. She did not damn John Gielgud or Donald Wolfit. Gielgud she called Edwardian and, like everybody else, imitated him, but there was none of her usual scorn. As for Wolfit, she never said a bad word about him. Maybe this was to do with those two actors being wrapped up in an experience that cast the die for her life.

She went home and once again looked up the play, this time learning 'O what a rogue and peasant slave am I!' Like the Shylock speech, it was spoken by a man. Whether consciously or unconsciously, this marked the beginning of how she meant to carry on: she was always happier with men and was often accused of not liking women, and being particularly tough on actresses. She denied it but said so many things against women, often things she saw in herself and disliked, that one could think there was truth in that accusation. 'Bring back boy actors for the women's parts,' was one, along with: 'The reason why there are fewer funny women than funny men is that women can't be objective.' Another was: 'Women are drawn to directing. They like arranging things and making pretty patterns' – all the while, denying she was ever a director herself.

As for her desire to play men, it would not have seemed peculiar at the time she was acquainting herself with Shakespeare. At the Old Vic, Sibyl Thorndike had played Prince Hal and King Lear's Fool. Admittedly that was more to do with the shortage of actors during the First World War than any idolising of the male sex.

Another production at the Old Vic did not impress her so much but it was the one to inspire her to put on a Shakespeare play at La Retraite. This was *Macbeth*. Gielgud, who was playing him, she described as too decorative but it was that very feeling that she could do better that was her inspiration. A good *Hamlet* would be overwhelming but a not-so-hot *Macbeth*? There's more action and murders in that one, which Joan of course noticed, and it was shorter.

Having decided that she herself would play Macbeth, not to mention Third Murderer and the Old Man at the end of Act Two, she approached her favourite teacher at La Retraite, Mother St Vincent. Not only did Mother St Vincent give her consent, she organised rehearsal space. This left Joan to dragoon the girls she thought would be right into giving up their time to be in the play. She succeeded. As for her, it was no sacrifice. Rehearsals were in the evening and during the holidays. In other words, it was more time away from home and household chores.

'I was the producer and my word was law.' When Joan said that, she was letting slip how things were going to be from then onwards. 'I've never told any actor what to do,' is what she usually said and, while there was truth in it, nothing got on to any stage if she didn't want it to.

Once she had the go-ahead, she had to think about how she was going to do it. At the Old Vic, the productions she saw still had different sets for every scene, and, to cover the big changes, some scenes were played in front of a cloth. Most teenagers wanting to do a play, having been to one in the professional theatre, tend to copy what they have seen. Having done that, they react against themselves and do something else. Joan skipped that stage. She already knew that the Old Vic's productions were heavy and slow. In three years' time, Tyrone Guthrie, would take over as director at the Old Vic and go for a permanent set that would keep the action flowing. It would be the latest thing, in the 1930s anyway. It wasn't, of course, as it was based on the Elizabethan theatre. Many years later, as a seasoned director, Joan wrote that she was comfortable with the Elizabethan layout too. In fact, only a permanent set made her happy. In the Assembly Hall at La Retraite, necessity began to teach her what she would always prefer. There would be no scenery, just the banqueting table.

Of the production, her accounts diverge. When describing it in conversation, she said that she forgot to put stools out, only to realise it worked much better that way. From then onwards, she rarely had chairs on any stage. When writing about it, she said that she made the decision about not having the stools in advance. Instead, she directed the diners to dip down to make it look as if they were sitting. This is a device she used many years later. It worked because, at the end of the scene, you went quickly to the next one. Time was saved because there was no need to clear the chairs. Either way, her desire for speed and flow was already revealing itself.

When it came to her account of the performance, there was no divergence. That was always the same. Before an audience of nuns and schoolfellows, it went like wildfire. Next morning, the headmistress summoned Joan to her study. She thought she was for the high jump but not at all. Mother St Nicholas wanted an extra performance to present to the Mother Superior, who was coming over from France. Joan was thrilled, partly because of the special guest's importance and partly because it gave her the chance to improve the production. This time, the music took most of her attention. At *Hamlet* she had heard 'Fingal's Cave' on a gramophone. It had not been thrilling. For her *Macbeth*, she would have real drums and a real choir. Again, she was beginning as she meant to go on. 'You can't start a play without music,' she would say, 'and it must be live.' This time, parents were allowed to come but only the parents of the performers. Among them were James and Kate. They sat at the back.

When, at the point in the play Banquo was murdered and Joan, as Third Murderer, was stabbing a concealed piece of meat and squirting jets of cochineal, there was a cry from the audience. The Mother Superior from France had fainted. Joan, at first delighted, was soon disappointed. Mother Mary Agnes hurried round during the interval to tell her and the rest of the cast to go easy. Joan's mind began to roam.

After Aunt Carrie's death, insurance money came through. It was to pay for the one and only family holiday Joan was taken on. Ramsgate was the resort. For the occasion, Kate dressed herself in black and walked around with Carrie's little daughter, Marie, saying to anyone that stared: 'She's lost her mother.' Joan, repelled, wandered away along the beach. She found a pierrot show. Because you had to pay to see it, palings surrounded the performing area but even from behind them, she could see enough. The little songs the pierrots sang to introduce themselves and the black and white costumes that seemed to come from no particular period but went right back to *commedia dell'arte* enchanted her. Three performances a day were given. She watched every one. In the evening, coloured fairy lights were turned on and a talent competition was announced. Joan volunteered. 'My Mother's Arms' was the song she sang but all confidence drained away when, to her mind, came the picture of her own mother's arms. The idea of being in them was revolting. Only one person voted for her.

Back at school, Joan tumbled into one of those moods people round her in later years would dread. It was an angry 'I don't know what I'm doing, but, boy, is everybody else going to pay for it,' mood.

She wrote a beautiful letter to the Old Vic offering her services, signing with her father's surname. Kate intercepted the reply. Catching sight of the envelope was all it took to provoke a cold fury.

In central London, Joan joined a march demanding independence for India. Gandhi came out on a balcony at the Dorchester Hotel to watch. Back at school, she organised her own march. It was on behalf of a dead rat. Mother St Teresa warned her that she could be up for expulsion and was risking her chance of going to university. Joan replied that university students were scabs. She had seen students from Oxford and Cambridge driving buses during the National Strike in 1926. She was already aware, because James had told her, that the miners were always stuck out on their own with no one prepared to support them. She was not expelled. She had just won another scholarship. What for or where to, she didn't say.

In the middle of this turmoil Miss Nicholson, her art mistress, showed some of Joan's paintings to the young Barnet Freedman, who was teaching at the Royal College of Art. He would, in 1940, become a war artist. Back in the late 1920s, he foretold a distinguished career for Joan as a painter.

Actually, Miss Nicholson was afraid Joan was taking seriously the idea that she should become a nun. Joan told her not to worry. She was over that. Miss Nicholson, known to Joan as Nick, suggested a little holiday. Joan, caring little either way, accepted. At least she would be away from home. In point of fact, she was not planning on becoming a painter either. She had secretly written for an audition at the Royal Academy of Dramatic Art.

The test pieces arrived. There were two. The first was from *Tamburlaine* by Christopher Marlowe and the second was from *Hindle Wakes* by Stanley Houghton of the Manchester School and, in that, prophetic, given how much that town would feature in her life and work. Both suited Joan. The speech from *Tamburlaine* was Tamburlaine himself speaking, another man, and Marlowe, together with Shakespeare and Ben Jonson, was one of her favourite playwrights. The *Hindle Wakes* speech was the spirited heroine rejecting a proposal of marriage from a dutiful boyfriend who has made her pregnant. He's nice enough but nothing special. She can do better. Joan could easily understand her attitude. All very well, except that the day of the RADA exam was right in the middle of her school exams, known in those days as matriculation.

To be precise, it clashed with a chemistry exam. Unconcerned, Joan set off for Gower Street, where you can still find RADA. One of the judges depressed her by referring to the gap in her teeth, but another judge, by simply saying 'Good luck,' encouraged her. The audition was for a London County Council scholarship, and she won it. Only two were given each year, one to a girl and one to a boy. The boy who won in the same year as her was John Bailey, who went on to a career as a solid, if slightly eerie, stalwart in B-films and television.

Back at the convent, the nuns were not best pleased with Joan's jaunt to RADA. They wanted her to go to university. Miss Nicholson wasn't pleased either. She thought Joan should have taken her chemistry exam and matriculated, which was needed to get into art school. Still, it didn't stop Mother St Teresa from boasting of this scholarship to the Schools Inspector.

Hindsight reveals that this was typical of Joan. On the one hand, fear and wilfulness nearly blew her chances. On the other, talent and determination saw her through. Joan tended to disguise fear with anger, so it could have been nerves about university that made her come up with the scabs accusation, even though some students had indeed been scabs. After all, she knew as little about what would happen at RADA as she did about what would happen at university.

What of the little holiday? Was that off? No, it was still on nor was it anywhere like Ramsgate. It was Paris. Nick, with her maps and guidebooks, knew all the works of art they had to see, but Paris itself made the biggest impression on Joan. It enchanted her.

The trip was tinged with wistfulness, though, because Joan had reached the moment when she had to decide on her future. Once back in London, she would not be returning to school and her father's six shillings a week would stop. That was certain. She had the RADA scholarship and would probably be leaving home. That was up to her. Nobody was forcing her to take up the scholarship, or to leave home. A temptation was to hide in the cloak of comfort Nick offered, and keep painting.

Many years later, when recalling this moment, Joan told of a balcony overlooking Paris where she and Nick sat one evening, Nick pointing out the repetitiveness of long runs in the theatre. This was one of her arguments for keeping Joan at an easel. However, it feels as if Joan was attributing those words to her in the way that a playwright, instead of writing a monologue, bounces thoughts round different characters. To know what a long run feels like requires an old hand at theatre and Nick was not an old hand. Nor, for that matter, was Joan. Long afterwards, she seemed to be dramatising the scene.

Joan continued by responding to this argument with her dream for the future. With Nick cast as the sympathetic listener, she launched into what this time was, not dialogue bounced around, but a monologue:

> Space, light and shelter, a place that would change with the seasons, where all knowledge would be available and new discovery made clear, a place to play and learn and do what you will. I know that work is the only solution to life's problems, creative work with some manual labour thrown in. The inborn hatred, murderous feelings, the hate and aggression that are part of us, even our petty feelings can be transformed by creativity.

[Joan's Book]

This still sounds like Joan, the playwright, at work. The speech divides into two halves. In the first half, just as Ibsen plants two pistols in the first act of *Hedda Gabler*, one of which will kill Hedda in the last, so Joan plants an idea in the 1930s which would mean a lot to her in the 1960s, but would also cause public confusion and private disruption. 'Space light and shelter . . . a place to play and learn,' was an exact description of the Fun Palace which Joan tried to make happen in the 1960s. It's as if she wanted the reader to be aware of it early to show that its roots were deep. If she employed Ibsen's technique, it's because she admired his craftsmanship. After the success of *A Taste of Honey*, she told its author, Shelagh Delaney, to analyse him as a lesson in structure.

In the second half of the monologue, the manual labour bit is slightly funny. To keep afloat, Theatre Workshop did do manual labour but the person who did the least was Joan. She always had an excuse you couldn't argue with: her need to work on the play, whatever that was, and, to be fair, at that she did work phenomenally hard.

'The hate and aggression that are part of us . . . even our petty feelings,' does sound a likely thought, if too well-formed. It would have come from those flesh-rending rows at home and is borne out later on by her dislike of the family unit in plays. Here, rather than in the Fun Palace idea, is where the design for living began, a reaction against everything around her that she hated.

An answer could have been for Nick to adopt her. She offered to, but Kate turned that down and for once Joan was in agreement with her mother. Something told her that, nice as Nick and painting were, this was not the way for her.

'That dyke who took you to Paris,' someone said to Joan of Nick a few years before she died. This did not go down well. It chimed neither with her past innocence, when 'dyke' would have been an unknown word, nor her deep-down primness that was always there.

So, you have Joan giving herself sophisticated thoughts at the age of fifteen that you suspect she had much later, but at the same time not caring to admit to what may have been a simple if crudely put truth: Nick was a lesbian. This would seem to be corroborated by Nick persuading Joan, before they went to Paris, to have her hair cut short, saying that she had a well-shaped head. If you see Nick's painting of Joan at that time, for a split second you are puzzled because you think you are looking at a boy. Only after that do you see the school tunic.

In her indecision – Joan hated making decisions – she needed that click moment that would let her chuck Nick. In Paris, she found it when Nick referred to her illegitimacy. She did it by saying to Joan that a nice boy might not want a girl like her, so she was probably better off with her, Nick. And that was it. Joan was on her way to find her design for living by herself.

CHAPTER THREE

TIME TO GET OUT

S he did not find it at RADA. Still, the weeks before going were fun. Joan made up her mind and did leave home. Or as her half-brother, Jim, seven decades later, put it, 'You fucked off.' 'Yes, I did,' answered Joan, neither adding nor subtracting a word. She crossed the Thames, staying near to the Tate Gallery, and went to lodge with a French woman who would turn out to be quite a figure in her own right.

Brixton, down the road from Stockwell, produced Violette Szabo. Pimlico, near the Tate, produced Yvonne Rudellat. When the Second World War came, both joined Special Operations Executive. Both worked undercover in France and both, for their efforts, lost their lives.

At the time Joan knew her, Yvonne was a dressmaker who took in lodgers. Joan's billet was her big bathroom in which a camp bed was erected. Yvonne herself lived in the basement with her Italian husband and their daughter. Upstairs, the rooms were let out to a Hungarian chef and his wife, and a bookmaker. It was all rather lively, and turned even livelier when Yvonne's French lover came over from Paris. Joan went to collect him from Victoria Station dressed as Yvonne so as to be recognised. Once back at the house, she had the job of hiding him from Yvonne's jealous husband.

RADA wasn't like that. Before Joan set off, Yvonne, using her sewing skills, transformed Joan's school uniform into something that was appropriate for drama school, but as soon as Joan arrived at Gower Street she saw that none of the other female students had to make that effort. Without trying, they had the right clothes and, of course, thought nothing of it, as you do when things are handed to you on a plate. When you don't have something because you can't afford it, you ache. 'It must be awful being poor,' said one of the girls to Joan. And who were these girls? Americans wanting to have an English accent, and debutantes, mostly. It was the days when RADA was thought of as an alternative to finishing school. The idea of grants from local authorities was far in the future, so most of the students were sons and daughters of middle-class parents, like doctors and lawyers, and they could afford the fees. Others came from theatre families. Joan remembered, in particular, a boy called Dance, whom she described as a blob with no talent whatsoever. His father managed a theatre. He had pulled strings. Joan was convinced of it. Other students included Winston Churchill's daughter, Sarah, and Ida Lupino, who, from a dynasty of entertainers, went to Hollywood where she not only acted but became one of the very few female film directors. Joan, knowing her only for her time at RADA, thought her untalented. She soon thought the place was a waste of time and talked little of it thereafter. However, bits came out over the years.

In Joan's first term, Patience Collier, Renée Richter then, had reached her last term. Before leaving, she was in *Epicoene, the Silent Woman,* by Ben Jonson. Joan saw that and, from it, remembered Patience, who would go on to play Charlotta in *The Cherry Orchard* for the Russian director, Theodore Komisarjevsky, alongside John Gielgud and Peggy Ashcroft. She was to come into Joan's life three times later on.

The only subjects for which Joan thought RADA was any use were French, because she wanted to learn it, and movement. French was taught by Alice Gachet, the daughter of Dr Paul Gachet, who had treated Van Gogh in the last months of his life. Van Gogh had lived briefly in Brixton, so there was a link for Joan. The actor Anthony Quayle, during an interview, spoke of being taught by Madame Gachet. He was a year older than Joan and, sure enough, was trained at RADA. Although Joan occasionally mentioned his wife, Dorothy Hyson, whom she always prefaced with the description, 'Very pretty,' she never mentioned Anthony Quayle himself. As for Madame Gachet's classes, Joan could not afford them. They were extra, a guinea a term.

For Annie Fligg, the movement teacher, Joan only needed a pair of tights. Yvonne Rudellat stitched a pair of school stockings to a swimsuit and Joan was in, even if there was an embarrassing twang when she got carried away. She loved those classes, particularly as she had attended ballet classes at the academy and not liked those at all; she never would like classical ballet. 'It's not movement,' she said, 'It's a series of poses.' Nureyev, to her, was a wobbly bottom and crash landings.

The reason why Annie Fligg was of interest to Joan was the system she taught. It was that of Rudolf Laban who was to become one of the most important influences in her life. This system came from observing and analysing every movement a human being can make. It could be applied in many ways, from how to use the body most effectively in factory work, through dance and on, in Joan's case, to drama.

It allowed you to use your imagination too, which obviously would have appealed to Joan. What she also enjoyed was moving out of the limited number of planes most people use in everyday life, such as standing up and facing front.

21

Classical ballet, she thought, took place only in one plane and that's why for her it was not movement.

When it comes to influences, Joan's lack of dogmatism should be made clear. Over the years, many people would influence her but no one ruled her entirely. Theatre professors, who write about her but didn't know her, are inclined to stress one influence as if it totally dominated her. None of them did. Laban was the most important influence, but he didn't stop Joan looking at Renaissance art and the *commedia dell'arte* figures of Callot, which, by the twisting and intertwining of bodies, also suggested the kind of movement that attracted her.

When George Bernard Shaw appeared at RADA, Joan wondered why he should bother with such a place. In fact, she was shocked – but then Joan, when it came to events that challenged her view of things, was rather good at being shocked. For a start, it was well known that Shaw was financing RADA. He gave the academy the rights to his play, *Pygmalion*, which it still has and that includes the musical made from it, *My Fair Lady*.

Shaw didn't teach but he directed a scene from his play, *Heartbreak House*. Joan played Ellie Dunn. Telling her not to copy him, he read the part. Joan was nearly in tears but the next moment was laughing when he read the cockney burglar. She liked his accent. It still wasn't enough to convince her that RADA was a good thing.

Sybil Thorndike gave a talk. Joan thought she was a shocking actress but a good woman and so paid attention when she recommended that actresses should find an occupation other than acting to keep them sane. What that was didn't matter. This did not make Joan take up gardening or petit point, but as she already had so many other interests, like politics and painting, she had, in her own way, already taken Sybil Thorndike's advice.

Joan's scholarship money was eleven shillings a week, five of which had to go to Yvonne Rudellat. That, however, was only for term time. During the holidays there was nothing and, for those periods, Joan took a job at a knitting factory in Tooting. She said that she spent so much time making the other girls laugh that she got the sack. That sounds like she only worked there once but in fact, during her time at RADA, she worked there on more than one occasion.

Extra money was needed in term time too and so she took an early morning job as a cleaner. The story is picked up by Frith Banbury, a fellow student, who went on to be become an archetypal West End figure, directing Terence Rattigan's play, *The Deep Blue Sea* for HM Tennent, the most 'West End' of West End managements. Frith, himself, challenged this establishment image by pointing to the play, *The Pink Room,* which he directed. It was by Rodney Ackland, a playwright who, unlike Rattigan and Noël Coward, did not know on which side his bread was buttered. All three were gay but only he was frank about homosexuality in his writing. The other two, wanting West End success and money, knew that it was best to veil it. Perhaps they had a point. *The Pink Room,* when first produced, was a failure.

So there was the young Frith Banbury noticing that Joan always arrived late for class in the morning. 'When we understood that she had this cleaning job first,' he said, 'we took her under our wing.' Doubtless he and the other students meant well but attention of this kind would still have made her uncomfortable.

Another way to make money was to enter competitions. At first Joan was put off. Her voice teacher told her that her voice was too low, so she went around trilling away until she realised how ridiculous this was. The voice that you have is the voice that you have. You can work on it but you can't swap it. Having realised this, Joan entered competitions vigorously. She had a natural talent for verse speaking and used it. The actress, Rachel Kempson, soon to marry Michael Redgrave and eventually become the mother of Vanessa, Corin and Lynn, recalls in her autobiography tying for first prize in a verse-speaking competition with a small, dark-haired fellow student called Joan Littlewood. Joan, when recalling Rachel Kempson, said: 'She had a face like a scraped bone.'

One of the judges who awarded Joan a verse-speaking prize was the radio director, Archie Harding. He set her to performing Shakespeare on the World Service at three in the morning. She did an excerpt from *Antony and Cleopatra*, playing Cleopatra. The actor who played the clown bringing the asp was Robert Speaight. So there was Joan, still in her teens, acting opposite the actor whom she had seen as Laertes at the Old Vic with John Gielgud only a couple of years earlier. Archie Harding, being to the left politically, was sent into internal exile at BBC Manchester, but not before saying to Joan, 'if you're ever up Manchester way, drop by.'

A teacher of Joan's was established West End actress Marda Vanne. She lived in Gower Street with Gwen Frangçon Davies, the actress who had been John Gielgud's Juliet at the Old Vic. Both were intrigued by Joan, whose low voice would have been most appealing.

'What's a beautiful voice?' Joan used to ask, but then she was thinking of radio actors 'wanking their voices against the microphone.' If it wasn't that, it was the singing of Shakespeare. There's a recording of Peggy Ashcroft as Juliet and Edith Evans as the Nurse in *Romeo and Juliet*. Hearing that, one understands what Joan was reacting against. They coo the words as if to say: 'Don't I sound lovely?' Joan wanted actors to sound as if they were really talking to each other.

For all that, to other people's ears, Joan did have a beautiful voice, and a commanding one too. As early as these RADA days, the actress, Julia Neilson Terry, of the family that produced John Gielgud, said that Joan had a voice full of tragedy. She said it whilst clasping Joan to her scented bosom, which left the teenage girl less pleased than bemused. It all depended on what you were doing with your voice, was Joan's attitude. Still, in later years, her voice, by turns, impressed and charmed people as different as Patience Collier and the man who was to become Ewan MacColl. What's certain is that she liked good, round vowel sounds. In later years, speakers on the radio saying: 'Gerd,' and 'Berk,' instead of 'Good,' and 'Book,' got on her nerves.

Still, whatever it was in Joan that fascinated Marda Vanne and Gwen Frangçon Davies, she wasn't having it. 'I was not going to be drawn into their Sapphic circle.'

Joan fancied men and that was it, and at least at RADA she had a little romance. Gerry Raffles used to tease her about it. 'Your first boyfriend,' he said, 'Stephen Haggard.' This was the actor-writer nephew of the adventure story author, Rider Haggard. During the Second World War, he was posted to the Balkans where he found himself alongside RD (Reggie) Smith, who was to become a radio producer at the BBC but, before that, the character, Guy Pringle, in Olivia Manning's Balkan trilogy, *The Fortunes of War*. Olivia Manning was Reggie's wife.

As part of his job working for the British Council in the Balkans, Reggie Smith used to put Stephen Haggard into productions of the classics and so he too turned up in *The Fortunes of War*. Aidan Sheridan was his character. Haggard, while still posted abroad but already married and a father, fell in love with an Egyptian woman. It was a disaster. Burnt out at 31, he shot himself. Joan didn't talk about this but was later to know both Reggie Smith, a communist, and Olivia Manning, in her opinion, a cold fish.

Joan didn't sleep with Stephen Haggard but, at the age of sixteen, she did have sex with a white Russian who seemed to be merely on hand, not fancied at all. Joan allowed him to do what he wanted as if she were ticking off a to-do list. She referred to the act as the breaking of her hymen, a technical business with no joy in it at all, and not for a long time did she do it again.

At RADA a student could occasionally find him or herself being handed a free ticket to a West End play. Marda Vanne gave Joan a ticket to Somerset Maugham's latest, *For Services Rendered* (1932). Given that the cast included Flora Robson, Cedric Hardwicke and Ralph Richardson, she must have thought that Joan would be impressed. She wasn't. She was appalled. Characters in present-day clothes walked on, poured drinks, sat down, talked and that was it. Was this what she was supposed to be studying for? At least the Old Vic gave you poetry, action and colour.

A year later, Joan saw Flora Robson playing Isabella in *Measure for Measure* opposite Charles Laughton as Angelo. That was at the Old Vic. In her opinion the casting was wrong, but she didn't mind. As it happens, that was also the opinion of its director, Tyrone Guthrie. It gives actors hope to think that if Joan didn't care for Flora Robson in the Somerset Maugham, she could admire her in the Shakespeare. 'I wouldn't pay him in washers,' Joan could say of an actor she'd never seen before, but on seeing him in a different play two weeks later, consider him gifted.

One production did impress her but it wasn't English. La Compagnie des Quinze (The Company of Fifteen) influenced by the work of the director, Jacques Copeau, a lover of beauty and simplicity and a hater of naturalism, came over from France to London. It brought André Obey's play, *The Rape of Lucrece,* and Joan was so struck by its use of two narrators that she was determined to use the idea herself one day. She was also struck by the idea of a company of fifteen that trained to work in a certain style.

Although most of Joan's talk about RADA was dismissive, one remark, made not long before she died, struck home. She said that she felt so apart from the other students that she used to eat her lunchtime sandwiches in the lavatory.

Before the course finished, she began to pull away from it. Up the road was the Slade School of Fine Art and, having an entrée there, probably that extra scholarship she won at the convent, she used to sneak into drawing classes. She made a friend, a Swedish girl called Sonja Mortensen.

At weekends, she attended a literary circle run by a friend of Miss Nicholson's who was known by the one word: Bailey. Joan, by her own admission, was an opportunist. She may have been in the process of dropping Nick but if a colleague of hers did something that was useful to her, then he or she stayed on the list. Actually, there was more to it than opportunism. When Joan said that she wrote Nick off during that evening on the balcony in Paris, it was the 1980s, long after the event. In 1931, while she was at RADA and later at the Slade, she wrote to Nick two of the most affectionate letters she ever wrote to anyone. In the first she has mixed up the days and missed a rendezvous:

> I went to the theatre in the afternoon as the Superintendent of the RADA said we could get a stall at the Phoenix for the matinee. We could have both gone though I should have preferred just to have wandered if I had been with you. It was *Little Catherine* with Marie Tempest, a play about Catherine and Elizabeth of Russia. A perfectly rotten play (I suppose that's why we got the unlimited number of seats). I <u>do</u> wish I could have seen you. Brixton Market looked perfectly lovely and I read *Le Temps* in the library and dried my eyes and thought us back to Paris reading that old newspaper . . . I would give anything I have to be with you now.

She goes on to say that she has been reading Dostoyevsky's 'House of Death' which we would know as *The House of the Dead,* and comes up with some colourful if outlandish theories about it. She finishes:

> I really think old Dosto would have felt an affinity with Jane Austen who was essentially fiercely progressive tho' she progressed in a way that made people think her a gentle soul.

> I expect you are awfully excited (no that's silly) I expect you are looking forward to showing Tonks your stuff. I think the best of it will be that he will give you a good deal of precious encouragement.

Firstly, here's some background information. Marie Tempest was a big stage star of the time. In 1925, she had originated the part of Judith Bliss in Nöel Coward's play, *Hay Fever*. Henry Tonks was Slade Professor of Fine Art, stern and influential. Secondly, here are some details:

1. Joan uses 'perfectly' twice in a way that is unwittingly more RADA than Brixton.

2. She plays with Dostoyevsky's name, something she did to nearly everyone's. Her mother, for example, was Mumski. Often she did this because she didn't like a name and if she didn't like anything, she changed it.

3. In mid-life, Joan dismissed Jane Austen as weak tea, saying that nobody could like both Austen and Smollett, writers who had both set scenes in eighteenth-century Bath. Smollett, much more rumbustious, she loved. However, in her 80s, while working with an actor who was going to play Mr Bennet in *Pride and Prejudice,* she discovered that she admired Jane Austen's talent again.

In the second letter, we learn Joan has been to art class, drawn a head which she didn't think much of, and then got caught in the rain waiting at a bus stop by Waterloo station:

> It would be glorious wouldn't it if I could see you for a little longer on Thursdays you wouldn't believe how I look forward to it, how from the quagmire of awful people I live with I look up to this (what do you have in the middle of a quagmire?) which is you. I've just had some grub isn't eating a waste of time and now I've no time to write anymore which is perhaps rather a good thing.
>
> I am, dear lady, yours while this carcass is
>
> to her Joan Littlewood.
>
> Good night, all my love – Bless you.
>
> Dearest Nick

While directing in later years Joan often said to her actors: 'Take out the full stops. Well, this second letter shows that she certainly practised what she preached – and started early too – though I don't think people thought she meant when writing.

The difference between the tone of these letters and what Joan would write about Nick many years later regarding the dismissing of her in Paris, reveals what Joan would go on to do both in her life and her work: edit and shape to make the clean line she wanted audiences or readers to have. It's rather like rubbing out the hesitant early marks in a drawing to reveal one simple, flowing line.

How come Joan had those letters in her possession? They weren't hers, they were Nick's. Nor were they roughs. The second still has its envelope and stamp on it, three halfpence. It would seem that Nick, for some unknown reason, gave them back.

So, there was Joan in Bailey's literary circle. At these gatherings, members read out their compositions for appraisal. They couldn't have kept much of a flow going. Bailey was an artist, not a writer, and she'd interrupt to make the others hold a pose.

This period of doing a bit here and doing a bit there came to a climax when Sonja, then studying in Paris, suggested that Joan join her and carry on drawing there. Ever since that first trip with Nick, Joan had been bursting to go and, with her savings of nine pounds, set off for Victoria Station and the boat train.

Paris was not the same this time. It was cold and yet the smell of state rottenness hung in the air. Joan had some letters of introduction – Jacques Copeau, with his love of Molière, interested her in particular – but they did no good. One evening, she found herself in the middle of a riot. Stones were thrown. Guns were fired and that night people were killed. It was a popular uprising against an attempted coup by the right wing, and it didn't stop there. Sonja moved on to Italy. Joan thought it was time to make a move too but she didn't want to go back to London.

The little Joan said of her time at RADA and what can be picked up here and there are shards of information that give some context for those who weren't there. Joan was usually strict about the need for context, but not on this occasion. It was a period that she cared little for and what she didn't care for, she, as usual, edited out.

What becomes clear from all those names she was so reluctant to mention is that Joan was not outside establishment mainstream theatre pressing her nose against the window. She was slap bang in the middle of it and could easily have stayed there for the rest of her life, if she had chosen to. To put it another way, inside herself, she was an outsider. Outside herself, she was an insider.

And then there are the names of Archie Harding and Reggie Smith. They give a tiny taste of a time when educated middle-class people turned to communism. The reason was simple: if you were intelligent and kept your eyes open, you had no choice. Conditions in those times were so obviously unfair. What later became of those people who were communists in the 1930s – it frequently involved a turn to the right – would provoke Joan's scorn. 'Thirties communists,' was an insult.

No 'design for living' was found at RADA but maybe Joan was not quite at the stage she wanted people to think she was. Rather than having fully formed ideas about the design for living or a fun palace, it's easier to understand that she hadn't found what she wanted and was beginning to discover that she would have to make it for herself, whatever that was.

At least she was armed. She had a classless accent – no Herry, no Jeck – which, entertainingly, would puzzle people pretty much forever, while the mere fact that she had been at RADA impressed others, if not herself.

After her friend, Sonja, left for Italy, Joan had to ask herself where she could go. Her answer came from her Stockwell childhood. The most famous person in the twentieth century to come from south London before Joan was Charlie Chaplin. Many don't consider him funny today but he was graceful and beautiful, and that appealed to Joan from an early age. Later, while watching television in the 1980s, one of his shorts came on. She fell silent and, when it was over, said: 'Those coffee stalls, those little courtyards, they're not America. They're Stockwell.' At the age of nineteen, Chaplin set sail for America. Joan, also nineteen, decided to do the same.

CHAPTER FOUR

A Breath of Fresh Air

The only way Joan could get to America was to stow away on a ship leaving from Liverpool. She set off on foot. Sensibly she took Archie Harding's BBC Manchester address. Perhaps he would give her a job. It would help her on her way.

Having travelled for a while, she found it best to confront night fears by walking in the darkness, leaving the daylight hours for sleep. When tired but not worried, she could sleep almost anywhere, and soundly too. That was how, one morning, an out-of-work couple in Burton-upon-Trent found a teenage girl lying on the grass, spark out. When they had established that she was not dead, they took her into their house and gave her a cup of tea. The wife, Beattie, went further: she rummaged through Joan's knapsack and found the piece of paper with Archie Harding's name and address on it. She wrote at once.

Over the next few days, Joan, unusual for her, made herself useful. She took a cleaning job as she needed to pay her way. Beattie's letter soon stopped that. At the end of the week, came a reply. It was from Archie Harding himself. He had sent a contract for Joan to write and read a short talk about her journey. It would be broadcast on the *In Manchester Tonight* programme. With the contract, came her train fare.

Sometimes, even as the train pulls into the station, you know you're going to be all right and that is how it felt for Joan arriving in Manchester. Noticing that landmarks were comfortingly closer to each other than they were in London, she made her way to Broadcasting House on Oxford Road.

There the doorman, instead of frightening her, made her feel welcome and in no time she was in front of a microphone with Archie Harding telling her to recite, by way of introduction, a few lines from *Antony and Cleopatra*, as she had done in London. After that, she could give her talk.

It worked. A handful of journalists, lured to the BBC by Archie Harding, most of them from *The Manchester Guardian*, were immediately taken by Joan. This mysterious girl with the classless voice was someone they could lionise, well, at least for a couple of weeks. Useful stories appeared in the papers about 'The Girl Tramp'. However, these stories were also annoying, because they told of her eating turnips and being frightened by cows. This was not true. This was the kind of journalism, with its constant need to spice things up, of which she would remain suspicious.

She was a bit suspicious of Archie Harding and the *Guardian* lot too. They presented themselves as left-leaning and relaxed about sex, but was that really the case? Their conversation was informed, dry, slightly camp – a new sound for Joan – but it didn't take long for her to start wondering. Archie Harding, so Oxford in his conduct, a revolutionary? Was he really going to man the barricades? Journalist, Jack Dillon, married, with a reputation for sleeping around, was that well-earned? 'Tanya's silence is her strength,' she heard one of this lot say of a friend. 'How about Tanya hasn't got anything to say?' she thought.

Joan could live simply enough, if all about her was clean, but the room she had found was frowsty, so when Jack Dillon offered her the run of his house while he and his wife were away, she accepted. It was a kind of heaven, particularly as raspberries grew in the back garden and raspberries were a fruit Joan would love all her life. Idly she fancied being relaxed about sex like her new acquaintances appeared to be, but it was no good. She knew that her prim Stockwell background would get in the way and, just as she was thinking that, what should happen? Beattie's husband from Burton-upon-Trent appeared. He had cycled all the way to make sure Joan was safe. He left convinced she was a kept woman.

However she may have imagined herself, and however fiery she could be, Joan was still caught out by shyness. Invitations to lunches at restaurants came from one or other of the *Guardian*/BBC lot. The menus daunted her. She invariably ordered an omelette.

Just as her BBC fee, roughly two guineas, was running out, and getting to America seemed essential, a message arrived from somebody called Alison Bailey. She had heard the radio programme and wanted to meet up. Joan went along, and Alison, after reminding Joan that they had been at RADA together, told her that she had a job at Manchester Rep. That was interesting. Joan needed a job too. How had Alison managed it? Her father was a director. String pulling again, it was everything Joan hated about RADA.

Even so, it was not long before she was invited to an interview with Carol Sax, an American producer, who was big at the Rep. His lodgings at the time were the Midland Hotel, the poshest in town. As Joan entered his suite, she heard him praising her instinct for publicity – the radio talk and the newspaper article had got around – but this only annoyed her. She did not think of herself as calculating. A straightforward audition was more her style, Lady Macbeth in this case, and, that way, she found herself with a job at the Rep.

It was far from any dream of theatre she had. Lady Macbeth she could act all right, but who was going to offer her the part? Not the Rep. She wasn't the correct type. Maids and comic aunts were her staple and, by means of pebble glasses, jodphurs and riding crops, she attracted plenty of attention. It was a merriment that belied what was going on backstage. Careless rehearsals and showbiz tittle-tattle irritated her and she could not hide her feelings. In the 1980s, she referred to the actor Alfred Marks as, 'One of the lice on the pubic hair of show business.' In the Manchester of 1934, she was already exercising her talent for abuse. 'Dry cankers on the arse of a great art form,' was her description of the actors.

Typically of Joan, that was not the entire story. In 1958, at Stratford East, she cast one of the Rep actresses, Eileen Draycott, as La Celestina, the Spanish procuress, in her adaptation of that novel. However, back at the Rep where the 1935 season was to include Shaw, Priestley, Elmer Rice, Dickens and a Baroness Orczy for Christmas, Joan was not popular. Still, that gave her something to react against, which does speed things up.

One Sunday evening, on the lookout for a fresh stimulus and with America still on the cards, she went with Jack Dillon to a gathering at no 111A Grosvenor Street. Somebody to do with a different kind of theatre was going to be present, and he thought they ought to meet. It was very dark in there. Joan, wondering why she had bothered to come, peered into the gloom. Standing by the fire, wearing a big sweater and short shorts was a teenager her own age, Jimmie Miller. The moment he spoke, she recognised his voice. She'd heard it over the tannoy at the BBC, intoning statistics for a feature about the building of the Mersey tunnel.

Jimmie has a different account of their first meeting. Coming to a rehearsal of *Tunnel* – the title of the feature – he heard, as he approached the studio, a warm, velvety voice that made him ask Archie Harding who it belonged to, i.e. according to his memory, Joan was in *Tunnel* too. Either way, they met and, if Joan had a dream, this was the start of making it happen.

Back in Joan's version, once she had established that the shorts were not an affectation but had been put on for a recent camping expedition, she and Jimmie began to talk. Yes, he told her, he did do the occasional radio programme for Archie Harding who had discovered him busking and, indeed, he was, when required, Archie's voice of the Mancunian working man. However, what really interested him was this company he was part of that used 111A Grosvenor Street as its base. How had he come that far, though?

He was the fourth child of parents who had lost the first three. Consequently, his mother, despite extreme poverty, had done everything she could for him. At fourteen, he had left school but his father had bought him carefully chosen books, and in that way he had continued his education. This he had plenty of time to do, because although he was supposed to be a motor mechanic, most of the time he was unemployed. Once he'd signed on which he had to do every morning, the rest of the day was his and thus it was he had the time to become interested in agitprop.

It worked like this. Little groups of young people, unable to stay silent in the face of unemployment and poverty, rife in the 1930s all around the world, found any platform they could – backs of lorries, say, or steps in front of a big building – and jump on to them and perform short sketches full of information that urgently needed to be heard. You had to be quick because, after a few minutes, the police would be on to you. This was what Jimmie had done with a group called the Red Megaphones.

Their title came from Germany where a group had given itself that name and, what's more, did agitprop extremely well. Jimmie had found this out via a worldwide network along whose threads ran information and material. You didn't have to go anywhere. Stuff came to you, as long as you were interested. In this way he had become familiar with the writings of Bertolt Brecht and the composer, Hanns Eisler, neither of whom would become known widely until after the Second World War.

While talking to Joan, Jimmie described sketches he and the Red Megaphones had performed, like the Meerut one about Indian railworkers wrongly imprisoned. Joan found herself drawn in. It was the way these sketches were performed that did it. Different hats told you what kind of person was talking. A couple of wooden poles gave you prison bars. This style came from a lack of money and the need to get out fast, necessity in other words, but it was what Joan liked anyway. However, this was only the first part of Jimmie' story.

If anything he had been impatient with these efforts. The Megaphones' way of working had been too crude. It was little more than chanting, or plain shouting. He knew that his German counterparts in Berlin were doing better and he'd wanted some of that, sketches that were rounded out and deepened and he'd wanted better acting too; actually, any acting as he didn't think he and his group had been acting at all. The trouble was, he and his group had known nothing about it.

He started a new group, Theatre of Action, which quickly became the theatre of inaction as it wasn't making any headway. Lack of skill at writing and performing meant that lots of energy and effort were going nowhere.

All this had happened before Joan's arrival in Manchester but, hearing about it from Jimmie who, as she often said, sounded as if he could knock a person down with his talk, struck a spark. In turn, for him, her appearance in Manchester was just the ticket. There she was at this difficult transitional moment, and she was a professional on his wavelength. Along the threads of the worldwide network had come a script from America, *Newsboy*. Perhaps she could sort that out and the group as well. It wouldn't be plain sailing because she had to hold down that job at the Rep. Sundays were the only days she had off.

Here's what Jimmie had been trying to tackle and Joan took on. Right from the start of the play, a newsboy cries out headlines and carries on until the end while characters with names like Young Man, Young Lady, 1st Voice, 2nd Voice, and Unemployed, act out tiny scenes illustrating the injustice of life in the 1930s, first at home and then across the world, ending up with: 'TIME TO REVOLT! TIME TO REVOLT!', as did a lot of agitprop.

It was non-naturalistic; you can tell that already: no sofas, no cocktail shakers. What you can't tell is that it had dance and, vital to its success were rhythm and precision, both of movement and of timing: right up Joan's street.

Alf Armitt helped. He was Jimmie's friend. By day, he worked as a lens grinder but, in his spare time, he studied the work of the Swiss set and lighting designer, Adolphe Appia. That way, he'd been able to try out his ideas on some of the Megaphones' sketches, which the Theatre of Action had brought indoors. *Newsboy* required lighting that could switch the audience's attention quickly from one part of the stage to the other. Alf made some lights that could light precisely what he wanted lit and nothing else. They could change colour too. Theatre of Action was at last able to present something new to the public, which it did on the outskirts of Manchester at the Hyde Socialist Church – and it worked. More people wanted to join Theatre of Action.

In London, the central committee of the Workers' Theatre Movement had a problem. It called a meeting. Joan and Jimmie, representing Theatre of Action, went. Both hated London: Joan, because she knew it; Jimmie, because he didn't.

The problem to be tackled was this. Delegates of the Workers' Theatre Movement had been to the Olympiad of Workers' Theatre in Moscow and had come away with an inferiority complex. The Russians, the Germans and the Czechs were better at agitprop, much better. Joan and Jimmie, not realising what was going to happen, thought the answer was simple. Be better yourself. Write better material. Perform it better. It was so clear to them; they gave it no further thought.

What they found in London was a big majority wanting to do something quite different. Its argument was that agitprop, even when rounded out and deepened, was not good enough because nobody liked it in the first place. Not only was it an idiom the English were unfamiliar with but all that haranguing and chanting of facts and figures was alienating. Consequently there was no point in doing it. Joan and Jimmie were shocked and unprepared. They had not worked out a good counter-argument.

The majority wanted 'proper' plays like people were used to. Then and there, an example, 'Curtain Theatre' they called it, was presented to the assembly. Simply hearing the word 'curtain' was enough to put Joan off. As its three acts went on, she and Jimmie sank lower and lower in their seats. There, once more, were the sofa and the cocktail shaker and there again were the exquisitely artificial hesitations that were considered good acting. Joan and Jimmie couldn't get back to Manchester fast enough. They decided – and this gives an idea of their future relationship with the Communist Party – that they would have to go it alone.

Through all this, Joan was still at the Rep, and those goings on in London could not have improved her feelings about it. In fact, she was on the verge of handing in her cards when Dominic Roche, the director – he'd taken over from Carol Sax, whom Joan regarded as mad – announced, as the next production,

Draw the Fires by the German left-wing playwright, Ernst Toller. This was a writer that Joan admired and Toller, by then exiled from Germany and on his uppers, was going to direct it himself. So, she couldn't leave and, what's more, she had a good idea.

The play required men who could pick up a shovel and look as if they meant business. The actors at the Rep, all middle class, couldn't do that. Joan suggested that members of Theatre of Action could, and they did. However, when the production went to the Cambridge Theatre in London for a Sunday-nighter and the management would not make a contribution to Theatre of Action, Theatre of Action would no longer make a contribution to *Draw the Fires*. It walked out. 'Zat young man,' said Toller of Jimmie, 'He sinks he is everybody and he is nobody!'. Joan was caught in the middle and embarrassed, particularly as, by the time they arrived in London, the prompt script of the play had gone missing and Joan was the prompter. To cover for someone else, she patched a script together from memory but it was too much. She'd had enough. She resigned.

With no regular income – odd jobs still cropped up at the BBC – she moved into Jimmie's home, 37 Cobourg Street, Salford, where he lived with his mother, Betsy and his father, Bill. Yes, it was for practicality but putting it flatly like that, as Joan did, was also her way of not talking about her feelings for Jimmie. There was a meeting of minds – that was clear – and they knew that they were special people, but about love she was silent. As for the family, both Jimmie's parents were Scots. Jimmie, himself, had been born in Salford. Bill, because his lungs had been wrecked by his job, steel moulding, spoke hardly at all. Betsy, forced to take any job that came up – she was a cleaner – was filled with a bitterness that spilled out on to anyone who came near her beloved only son. Joan, having not long left the tempestuous Kate, found herself having to face the termagant Betsy.

In love with Jimmie or not, she became pregnant. Decades later, she said: 'I would rather stab my belly than have a child.' It would seem that that thought had already come to her in Cobourg Street because, at once, she set about dealing with the problem, though it wasn't she who solved it. It was Kate who fixed Joan up with a back-street abortion in Stockwell.

To take her mind off her troubles, Joan took with her on the train to London a script that Jimmie had thrown at her. *Hammer* it was called, and it was, of all things, the boring Curtain Theatre play the two of them had seen in London. With war a constant threat and peace being spoken of but never achieved, rich people watch the market go through the roof and buy more shares in products to do with killing. By the time Joan got back to Manchester, she had worked out how to do it. Her ability to push unpleasantness away by means of concentration was both ruthless and enviable. What had been her process?

Alf Armitt was not the only one to read books for his theatre work. It was a Theatre of Action thing and it would be a Theatre Anything thing as long as Joan and Jimmie were involved, and even without Jimmie. They never stopped reading, mostly at the Central Library in Manchester's St Peter's Square.

One of the influences that Joan had discovered there and which would help to focus her thoughts for *Hammer* were the exciting years for art, theatre and film Russia lived through just after the revolution. A movement sprung up called Constructivism. Its inspiration came from factories, machinery, what you could do with metal, everyday street life and the stylisation of posters. You weren't so much a spectator, you were in it and active. The most famous example was Tatlin's tower, an influence on Anish Kapoor's Orbit tower in today's Olympic Park at Stratford. Theatre directors were influenced by this Constructivism like the German, Piscator, with his travelling walkways, and the Russian, Meyerhold, whose characters' psychology was translated straight into movement. Joan was particularly interested in him.

Even so, it is simplest to say that Joan – whether influenced by any of the above, or Chaplin, Laban, Callot, or all of them – was determined to get her actors off those sofas, on to their feet and into action. Her new show which she and Jimmie adapted together, still in the agitprop vein, would not only have a Constructivist set, it would be a kind of ballet.

The thought of this did not go down well with the other members of the company. Jimmie's early Theatre of Action work had been arty enough. Joan's ideas – a banker dressed in rubber rings like the Michelin man, bathing belles in gas masks, a newspanel listing the serious and the trivial and, on top of that, lots of movement – made Curtain Theatre seem surprisingly appealing. Someone asked for a vote. That was a mistake. A Joan put-down was a whiplash and this one was no exception. 'You don't take a vote on art.'

She could back herself up too. If anyone was able to take what they had read in a book and make it work on stage, it was Joan. Thirty years later, the news panel with the serious and the trivial, good for breaking up agitprop facts and figures, went straight into *Oh What a Lovely War*. Back then, the result was *John Bullion* which played at the Round House, Ancoats, Joan's favourite space and where many came to see it. 'The nearest thing to Meyerhold the British theatre has got,' said *The Manchester Guardian*. More people applied to join the company.

Even more people applied after *Waiting for Lefty*, the Clifford Odets play, which came next. It has to be said that *Lefty* is more naturalistic and therefore of an idiom more familiar to audiences, but at the same time, with its public meeting and its use of the auditorium for the actors to roam around in, it has the flavour of agitprop. Its success meant that Theatre of Action had so many members that some of them, new recruits, thought it ought to be better organised. Up until then, it had been merrily chaotic. The people who were pushing for this organisation were middle class and not in sympathy with Jimmie and Joan's ideas. However, they were powerful and, all at once, Jimmie and Joan found themselves branded as prima donnas, and chucked out.

A letter saved their face. It was an invitation for them to become students at the Moscow School of Cinema and Theatre. With it came a covering note from André van Gyseghem, who wrote that all they had to do was pick up a visa from the Soviet Embassy in London and be on their way. Van Gyseghem was an actor whose early career, it should be explained, was more interesting than his later one because, as a young man, he went to Russia and, having studied the work of the director, Nikolai Okhlopkov, wrote a book about it. One of the most vivid scenes he described was that of actors running past spectators, softly brushing them with branches to give the impression of rushing downhill on a sledge. Joan would remember that and Okhlopkov. Van Gyseghem, as did a good handful of actors who were to become absorbed into the mainstream, became a communist, only, like the others, to shun it later. The pushy types who pushed Joan and Jimmie out of Theatre of Action were like that.

Jimmie, before setting off, wanted Joan to marry him. He knew that the Communist Party, not wishing to give hostages to fortune, preferred respectability. Joan, caring neither for the institution of marriage nor for the opinion of the Communist Party, which was beginning to bore her anyway, said no (though probably more vividly). With £12 raised by the Theatre of Action minority that had supported them, the two, not married, set off for London.

CHAPTER FIVE

OUT OF THE ASHES

Obtaining the visa was not going to happen as quickly as André van Gyseghem had told them, so they had to find somewhere to stay. Joan, in a whimsical mood, said that she'd always fancied living in Cheyne Walk, so there they went and, simply by knocking on doors, Joan found shelter. Explaining that she and Jimmie were writers who needed somewhere quiet to work did the trick. An elderly, *bohémienne* said: 'God never made a woman without protection!' and invited them in. She was Mrs Algernon Newton, the mother of Robert Newton, the actor best remembered for playing Long John Silver, as well as for his drinking.

Mrs Newton had a story she wanted turning into a film script, and Joan and Jimmie would be just the people to do it. Neither knew how to write a screenplay, and the story was absurd but, as you would expect, they had read a book, Pudovkin's *Film Technique*. Pudovkin was a director from that exciting post-Russian revolution period. With that and some more books they borrowed from the local library they set to, adapting this story in the morning and going to the Soviet Embassy in the afternoon. That was a painful chore because they always felt they were not smartly dressed enough and feared being moved on by the police. Even when they did get to the door of the Embassy, they never got any further. A hand would come out and take the invitation, which Joan and Jimmie couldn't read because it was in Russian, and later handed back with no guarantee of anything. They just had to return another day. This went on for so long that Joan and Jimmie took up giving lessons in movement and drama which they held in the basement of Mrs Newton's house; this despite her vetoing any guests. By accident, a friend of hers from upstairs found them at it and gave them away. Mrs Newton's bohemianism did not stretch to leaving the young ones be. They were out on their ear.

Over the river, in Battersea, they found a room and started again, only to be joined by Jimmie's mother, Betsy, who was convinced the young couple could not look after itself.

Despite their ejection from Cheyne Walk, they finished the screenplay and presented it. They needed the ten pound fee. Only five pounds were forthcoming. Before the rest could be handed over, there had to be a reading. This was held before twenty people, including the film director, Anthony Asquith, at Algernon's studio in St John's Wood. Algernon was a painter. Absurd though Mrs Newton's story was, Joan and Jimmie acted up their screenplay a storm. It was a great success. Taking the other five pounds, and trying not to laugh, they left, never to hear about the screenplay again.

That still left the problem of the continued silence from the Soviet Embassy. Weeks had gone by and nothing. Another letter arrived, but this time not pie in the sky. Would Joan and Jimmie produce Hans Chlumberg's play *Miracle at Verdun*, the Manchester branch of the Peace Pledge Union wanted to know. They would, so it was not with their tails between their legs that they went home. Like they had always done, they would have to carry on learning by teaching themselves, but the prospect didn't make them gloomy at all.

Miracle at Verdun, in which the dead of the First World War rise up to find out what their sacrifice has achieved, was serious and important, so serious and so important that the Nazis had already murdered the author. It required a large international cast, but Joan and Jimmie got that because the Peace Pledge Union could call on those kinds of resources. University students were drafted in and they became useful contacts for the future.

During rehearsals Jimmie, after a flaming row with Joan – marriage and children not being one of her dreams – persuaded her to marry him all the same. The wedding took place at a registry office in Salford on 2 November 1935. Joan was 21, but only just. Jimmie would be 21 in two months' time.

Although they privately admitted that *Miracle at Verdun* was not their best work (too static), it played at the Lesser Free Trade Hall to packed houses and so improved their mood enough to give themselves a new name: Theatre Union. A meeting was called to discuss what enthusiasts regarded as the crisis in theatre.

The first thing Joan said was that there's always a crisis in theatre: 'It's out of touch with life.' André van Gyseghem, also present, added a softener: 'The English do love theatre but they haven't been theatrically educated. Amateurs do that.' The last bit was true. Amateur companies, such as John Wardle's in Bolton, did better plays than the professionals. They were putting on Ibsen and Chekhov, while the commercial theatre was taken up with froth, and not good froth at that.

'We are watching the decay of an outdated social system. The arts decay with it,' Joan continued. Less solemnly, she quoted from a light comedy, totally forgotten today, that she had seen while at RADA:

Oh just a minute, dear. I must put my hair straight. I had the most sickening hairdresser the other day. Nothing so sickening as a sickening hairdresser, don't you think? Nobody has any idea of the agony I endure through my hair. It won't stay set. You know these beads aren't Chanel really.

Now, at this point, if someone had piped up: 'What about *Love on the Dole*?' as an example of the right sort of thing to be doing, Joan's response would have confused them, but then Joan was good at that. Here was a novel written by Walter Greenwood, a man whose upbringing was identical to Jimmie's. It spoke about unemployment in Manchester. The year before, it had been turned into a play starring Wendy Hiller. 'What was not to like?' we might say nowadays. Plenty, according to Joan. She thought its attitude was like someone saying: 'Oh dear, look at these poor, downtrodden working-class people. Isn't it awful?' That was not for her. She wanted spirit.

'The conflicts of life,' she continued:

> . . . are more tremendous today than they have ever been. We need a new technique, not naturalistic, as in Ibsen, Shaw and Strindberg . . . Destruction of the four walls. The actual floor space, instead of being uselessly flat, is to be broken up into planes on which the actors move and act in different rhythms, expressing the significant complexities of a modern orchestra.

A listener in 1935 might have found that puzzling and theoretical but Joan had already turned it into practice. *John Bullion* had actors working in different rhythms and was played on three different levels and round the audience.

In 1936, two of Joan's actors, Alec Armstrong and Bob Goodman, had already left to join the International Brigade in the Spanish Civil War. Spain needed food. What was Theatre Union going to do to raise money for it? Jimmie could write a topical song – he was good at that – and the actors could take the hat round. It was simple. It was direct. It was not for Joan. Proclaiming that only the best would do for Spain, she said that she and Jimmie were going to mount Lope de Vega's classic play, *Fuenteovejuna*. With its uprising of village folk in the face of an overlord's cruelty, she could point to it being bang-on politically, but you suspect she wanted to do it anyway.

Jimmie made the adaptation – he called it *The Sheepwell* – and arranged the music. The visual side was looked after by three people: Bill Sharples, a young man who felt he could only express himself through his hands, Ern Brooks and Barbara Niven, both artists when they could be. Behind a drinking well upstage, Bill Sharples sculpted a large, towering ram. Behind it, Ern Brooks hung a backcloth of ruffled hessian, painted and dyed in russet, brown and gold. Barbara Niven designed the costumes. After the stillness of the Chlumberg play, action was back and so Joan was returned to her element. With *Fuenteovejuna* Theatre Union reached one of its widest audiences and, out of that, took specially written sketches and poems relating to Spain, some by the Scots poet Hugh MacDiarmid, to perform at public meetings. Chris Grieve, MacDiarmid's real name, became a supporter of the company until he died in 1978.

At this time, Harold Lever who, in 1967, was to become Financial Secretary to the Treasury, became Theatre Union's business manager, bringing with him his friend, the actress Patience Collier, whom Joan had seen at RADA. Patience, mesmerised, like Jimmie, by Joan's voice, became company secretary. Alec Armstrong and Bob Goodman did not return from Spain.

When one puts these ideas, aims, methods of training and productions together and, to them, adds the support of people who would go on to make their names in their own right, it is easy to forget that all of it came from amateurs, people who had to earn their living elsewhere. At a time of great poverty, riches were created, not by money but by youthful energy, inquiring minds, talent, and sticking two fingers up to the rotten.

With subscriptions to Theatre Union being only sixpence – threepence if you were unemployed – Joan and Jimmie still had to find work to keep their heads above water. They found it back at the BBC where odd jobs were turning into more regular employment: Jimmie wrote a history of Chartism, working men's long battle for rights; Joan researched and wrote documentaries that brought men and women from the farms, mills and mines of the north to the microphone, often interviewed by her.

For two reasons, her task was quite a performance. Firstly, all interviews had to be scripted and go past the censor. Secondly, interviews on location required a big sound van and the blocking off, at either end, of the streets where the interviews were to take place. Handy little tape recorders had not yet been invented which, in Joan's case, was just as well. She wouldn't have been able to work one.

The reason why interviews had to be scripted was to keep swearing out. Joan would question her subject, usually in their home, write out both the questions and the answers, get them typed up – Joan didn't type – run the script past the censor and, finally, get the subject, after Joan or someone else had posed the question, to read out the answer either in the studio or at the location.

She wrote her notes in notebooks which she used for everything, radio or Theatre Union, so on one page would be a cast list for a radio play or an interview with a shepherd and, opposite, exercises specially drawn for a member of Theatre Union who needed to extend themselves in the kind of movement she was proposing.

The person who was getting Joan to do most of her radio work was the producer, Olive Shapley. She, like others Joan already knew at the BBC, leant towards communism and, like those others, later changed tack. While in her red (or red-ish) period, Olive, together with Joan, made documentaries on important subjects: *Steel* (1937) and *Cotton* (1938) being two. The highlight was *The Classic Soil* (1939), which has been preserved, so it is still possible to hear it today. Manchester life in 1939 is compared with Manchester life in the 1840s when Friedrich Engels was writing about it. The programme starts with the distant sound of Walton's newly composed 'First Symphony'. It made Joan think of wind rushing across the moors outside Manchester. There follows a mixture of Engels talking – a natural-sounding German was found – and descriptions of daily life given by working people of Manchester. 1939 does not come off well.

During this time, an adaptation of Jaroslav Hašek's novel, *The Good Soldier Schweik*, was sent via the usual international network to Jimmie. The director, Erwin Piscator had written it and then produced it in 1927 at the Volksbühne in Berlin. Not being Czech, he hadn't quite caught the spirit of it, but Jimmie thought it was good enough for him to start work.

When he and Joan advertised for people to come and either be in it or work on it many answered, including – and this shows how in touch with the outside world Theatre Union was – refugees from Central Europe.

Howard Goorney answered too. He was a junior clerk working eight miles away in an accountant's office in Altrincham and he was seventeen. Joan cast him as an old shepherd. It wasn't perverse. Howard's old men, sometimes to his regret, could make audiences cry with laughter and he would carry on playing them for Joan, who laughed the most, until 1967.

The impetus of soldiers moving, through *Schweik*'s many scenes, across Europe during the First World War had to be maintained. Joan achieved this by using a revolve. She had not used one before but she would again. At its every turn, a new cartoon drawn by Ern Brooks in the style of Joseph Lada, the novel's illustrator, would appear. Each was in black and white, as were the costumes. This no-khaki look would re-emerge 25 years later in *Oh What a Lovely War*, as would two scenes from *Schweik*.

Jimmie chose the music. Smetana's *Richard III* tone poem accompanies townsfolk strolling in the park and Prokofiev's *Lieutenant Kijé* was in there somewhere and, for the rest of her life, Joan turned it off when she heard it on the radio, annoying for anyone who liked it; but for Joan, it meant too much. This knowledge of classical music shows a side to Jimmie that people in later years would know nothing of, the side Joan respected and the reason for her sensitivity when she heard those pieces.

Schweik, laughter in the face of war's madness, was the best of Theatre Union. In 1938 it became the most popular show the company had done. Patience Collier, still a member, played Baroness von Botzenheim and then went her way – to Komisarjevsky, Noël Coward and radio drama – until her return in 1960.

In 1938, the Franco-Soviet Pact was broken. Czechoslovakia was on its own. During the run-up to the Second World War, this was the event that most stuck in Joan's craw because, 40 years later, in the 1980s, some of the worst rows she had with a certain French friend, storming out of the room rows, were to do with that pact. In the late 1930s, Theatre Union had to react.

Out came the history books and the newspaper cuttings with each member of the company having to follow a particular story. Rosalie Williams, the perky-faced daughter of a not very thrilled headmaster, joined the company. She was studying English at Manchester University but her extramural interest was movement. In fact, she was one of the people for whom Joan drew those exercises in her notebook. Rosalie's involvement with the company would be greater than she expected.

When read, the script of *Last Edition*, a Living Newspaper, the show that rose out of the books, the press cuttings and the stories brought by sympathetic journalists, is not that exciting. It was back to facts and chanting. However, the show, as performed, became exciting, firstly, because all the material, varying in quality as it did, was so topical – a recent pit disaster, unemployment, the Spanish Civil War, Chamberlain's flight to Munich – and secondly, there was Joan. Always aware that she had to make pure information entertaining, she drew the audience in with narration – she and Jimmie did this as she had seen La Compagnie des Quinze do it in *The Rape of Lucrece* – and with even more performing areas than *John Bullion* had. Then, across the stage for world events, she sent Hitler, Mussolini and Daladier, the French prime minister, not just talking but carrying on as gangsters. That was the way to liven things up. As for Neville Chamberlain, notorious for saying of the Czech debacle, 'A quarrel in a faraway country between people of whom we know nothing,' merely having him appear on stage at all was sensational. Portraying living people on the stage was forbidden, especially Chamberlain, who was Britain's prime minister.

In other words, the show couldn't have been fresher, or appear more daring, particularly as it was being changed from night to night. Certainly, lots of people turned up to see it, so many that further performances were arranged for the town centre. Had anyone in this excitement sent a script to the Lord Chamberlain, the censor? No, they had not. With nightly changes, it didn't seem worthwhile. Two policemen came and asked at the ticket office where the licence was. It should have been on display. No one could give an answer. The show moved to the town centre. The police came again. Some members of the company left. There was, after all, the last scene in which the workers were encouraged not to fight because it was with the wrong enemy:

> Girl: Who is the enemy? The German lads like Bill? The German girls like me? Or the men who make millions out of wars? The men who breed hatred through their press. The men who cut wages and raise the price of food so that whole families live on the fringe of starvation. The men who allowed the Spanish people to be massacred and sent the Gresford miners down to die. I tell you the enemy is at home.

In other words, it's the class struggle. Heartfelt as this opinion was, not everyone held it by any means. It was a minority view.

Joan and Jimmie had started a hare but, as was often the case when trouble was brewing, something happened to Joan which was particularly noticeable given her phenomenal stamina. She fell ill. This time it was a quinsy and, on that night, while she was stuck at home and someone was playing her part, a burly, curly haired lad, 'A giant' as Jimmie described him, joined the company.

CHAPTER SIX

TROUBLE

T he next evening, Joan got herself to the show and, having been cheered by the sight of an undercover policeman laughing at it, waited, curious to see the giant. It wasn't until over three quarters of the way through, when a Czech worker in the streets of Prague was spelling out their country's fate to a group of onlookers, that she noticed something about the group of onlookers. It didn't look the same and that is because in it was not a giant – Jimmie had exaggerated – but a burly schoolboy with a mass of dark, unruly hair: Gerry Raffles.

A member of the company, Graham Banks, had known him at Manchester Grammar School and told him about the show. He'd gone along and Jimmie had put him in it. At the end of the performance he said nothing but, the next night, there he was again and this at a time when company members were dropping out. The police, as well as turning up at the show, had by then visited both Rosalie's and Graham's fathers. Did they know what sort of people their children were consorting with? It would not be long before they visited Gerry's father too but, in that particular case, there was history. Gerry had already been photographed at the head of a May Day march waving a red flag.

As it happened, there had been more trouble but Manny, Gerry's father, would have kept that to himself. Only a few months earlier, he had for a while given over the running of his factory to Gerry to see if he'd be any good at business. The next time he looked, the workers were all for striking; Gerry's idea, and he was only sixteen.

If Joan had known this she would not have been so anxious when she heard of the police visit to Manny, fearing as she did that he would prevent Gerry from having anything to do with Theatre Union. Gerry was already proving himself useful.

Pressure had been mounting on Joan and Jimmie too, so when Alison Bailey bumped into Joan and said, not having spoken to her since she resigned from the Rep, 'I've denounced you to the police,' it was nothing new. MI5 agents had already set up a surveillance operation in Hyde where Joan and Jimmie had their new home. The agents, struggling to find something to report, wrote: 'A number of young men who have the appearance of communist Jews are known to visit Oak Cottage. It is thought they come from Manchester' [*Declassified MI5 documents*]. Never has Manchester sounded so exotic. Its town centre was all of seven miles away. These undercover agents, sometimes not as undercover as they would like to think, would have been spotted by Joan. She was hardly unobservant. Jimmie would have known his position for years. He'd been a marked man since 1932 when the police chief constable of Salford reported him as a Communist Party member of the Ramblers' Section of the British Workers' Sports Federation.

By then, 1940, the heightened sensitivity of the time was only exacerbated by clumsy orders from above. 'Collar the lot,' said Churchill of Italians and German Jews who had lived in the UK for ages. Another order was 'Anyone spreading alarm and despondency is liable for prosecution.' It was enough for the police to close the show. Not only that, Joan and Jimmie were summonsed.

It was then that Joan's on-off relationship with the Establishment – think of her time at RADA – gave her a helping hand. Harold Lever, not yet part of the Establishment but getting there, found a barrister.

Things at the trial didn't look good, at first. The policemen who had been taking notes – not very good ones, according to Joan, she being a stickler for accuracy – attacked the show for its political content. It was inflammatory, they said, and, in those tense wartime days, it was. The barrister, smooth as you'd want him to be, interrupted. Political content, he said, was not the issue. The issue was that this young, artistic company with little experience of the law had, in its excitement, failed to obtain a licence. To prove just how extremely artistic the company was, he produced the elegant programmes for *Fuenteovejuna* and *Schweik*. You couldn't argue. Their spare, angular style made the Manchester Rep ones look tatty.

Joan and Jimmie were fined five pounds each and bound over for twelve months, so they were free, but ten pounds in those days was a big sum.

What happened next shrunk their income even more. Walking into the BBC one morning to work with Olive Shapley, they found the doorman barring their way. No extremists allowed, those were his orders and both were known communists. They might find a way of broadcasting their ideas to the nation. Joan pointed out that this was hardly likely, given that they would be performing a vetted script for *Children's Hour*, but it was no use. Walking away, she wondered if Uncle Mac, presenter of children's progammes, and famous for his signing-off phrase 'Goodnight children, everywhere,' would, as a fascist, be barred too. He wasn't.

Of the days that were to come, Joan said one thing. Of the same period, an MI5 document, declassified in 2006, said another. Joan recalled John Coatman, the north regional director of the BBC, inviting her and Jimmie to a restaurant away from the BBC to tell them that this barring was a lot of nonsense. He would sort the problem out. Nothing happened. They were not reinstated.

The MI5 document, a 1941 BBC memo, has John Coatman expressing fears that Jimmie and Joan could stoke revolutionary fervour among listeners to the north. It was the exact opposite of what he had said in the restaurant. 'Miss Littlewood,' he wrote, 'whose real name is Mrs Miller, and her husband, Mr James Miller, are active communists who have taken a leading part in the organisation of the Communist Party and its activities in this area.'

Firstly, you wonder what would have been the reaction of the Communist Party. Jimmie and Joan were so disobedient, it's almost funny. Then, if you turn your attention to Coatman, you are left to ask if he was straightforwardly two-faced or writing on official BBC notepaper what he thought the BBC wanted to hear in order to protect the north region branch. This is not the end of him in Joan's story. She respected John Coatman and would speak well of him again.

After the excitement of the trial, a quietness was forced on Theatre Union. On the one hand, Joan and Jimmie had to be careful about what they did. On the other, war, tightening its grip on everyday life, was taking the male actors into the services one by one. While thinking about its next production, the company settled down to study. Jimmie drew up a reading list: Greek theatre, Chinese theatre, the Elizabethans, *commedia dell'arte*, Restoration comedy; everything you would expect. The librarian was Gerry. At seventeen, he was at the studying stage. Joan and Jimmie's teacherly qualities impressed him. He wrote an essay on Strindberg's *The Dance of Death*. Anyone who has worked with Joan could guess that it was not unprompted. Her hand was there, a mixture of encouragement and instruction: first, put the play into its context. Then, what is the situation of these characters? How do they earn a living? What is the author really saying? Nowadays this is standard but, in the late 1930s, unusual. It is what Joan called 'reading a play', a command she would, in later years, shout at a radio on hearing a director describing his or her concept.

'The bourgeoisie,' wrote Engels, 'have raised monuments to the classics. If they'd read them, they'd have burned them.' That was a favourite quote of Jimmie's, and a good example was Aristophanes' anti-war comedy, *Lysistrata*, which Theatre Union set about putting on. There would be plenty of fun modelling the old men in the play on real figures in government.

Joan, when not totally absorbed with work, began to notice how Gerry's effortless appeal to girls – his current girlfriend, Clare Ffoulkes, was in the company – contrasted with Jimmie's need to be admired by women and then to dominate them. This he did by using his knowledge to impress girls he'd found at Communist Party meetings. Having done that, he'd bring them into the company, whether they were any good or not. In other words, Joan was going off him. His knock-you-down talk was sounding empty.

Gerry, who loved Jimmie's songs and always would, was still at the admiring stage. Joan, feeling slightly guilty, because she was eight years older than him, was beginning to admire Gerry. Nevertheless, she still had the job of reproving him when, one day, he turned up with his mother's jewels aiming to add some cash to the kitty. Her words worked because those jewels were back in their box before Bertha, his mother, found out. Bertha's hope for Gerry, in the middle of his alarming political-theatrical activities, was that Joan would improve his speech. Words, when they came, tumbled from his mouth in a muddle. Also his Manchester accent was deliberately stronger than his sister's and two brothers'. Theirs had been ironed out and, in conversation, they talked about Mummy and Daddy, not to mention Jebs when speaking of Gerry. Joan did not like that.

His background, then and always, Joan played down. In her diaries, she imagined him, each morning, walking to Manchester Grammar School. In fact, much to his embarrassment, a chauffeur drove him in a posh car and Manchester Grammar School, despite its name, was an independent school. Parents had to pay for their children to go to it. The house he lived in was cheerless, said Joan. Maybe but it was in Higher Crumpsall, an area of the well-to-do. Yes, Manny had started out poor, and yes, he did not lose his accent. In fact his stayed stronger than Gerry's eventually became but, through his raincoat business and a close connection to the Sieff family of Marks and Spencer, Manny got rich and so was able to give Gerry a comfortable middle-class upbringing.

What about Gerry, background or no background? Clear as it is, from the Raffles factory coup, that he was the black sheep of the family, what other things could he be? Shy, sad and mopey some of the time but mostly a boyish, make-things-happen, never-does-as-he's-told young man with a deep, merry laugh. Some fancied the pants off him. Some, faced with his confidence and ability to create comfort, combined with his lack of obedience and knack of getting into scrapes, were annoyed by him.

In that neither of them was like Gerry, Jimmie and Joan were the same. They were not the same when it came to what they thought of him. Jimmie, according to Joan, was jealous. Joan thought Gerry the most beautiful person she had ever seen, a prince who dined only on the most delicious of food. When Rosalie, who was at university with him – he was studying Politics and Economics – mentioned the business of scrapes, Joan was inclined to overlook it, even though she knew that Gerry had accidentally shot his brother Eric in the bottom with an air gun.

Even at this early stage, Joan's admiration for Gerry was already tinged with jealousy. Clare Ffoulkes had golden hair which she wore loose. That's what she said officially. Unofficially, she said that Clare had a miserable, nasal voice. Her description of Gerry breaking off the affair with Clare exudes a sense of relief.

The contrast between Gerry and Jimmie was made most obvious, once, away from *Lysistrata* rehearsals. Jimmie was a keen rambler and proud of the fitness that came from it. Joan, when she wasn't arguing about which route to take, quite liked it too. What Jimmie couldn't do was swim. Gerry could, very well, so there came a day for him to pass on his knowledge to Jimmie.

Standing in the water, wearing his school trunks, the ones with the championship badge on, Gerry put an arm under Jimmie's thighs and a hand under his chin. This made Jimmie look like a baby as Joan, among others standing on the bank, was able to observe. No sooner was the lesson over, and Jimmie was heading for dry land, than he started to give a lecture on how it was all very simple and just a matter of hydrodynamics, which he then went on to explain. It didn't work. The others laughed and behind their laughter was the thought: 'You just couldn't give it to Gerry, could you?'

Civil Defence took over 42 Deansgate where Theatre Union usually rehearsed, so when it came to getting *Lysistrata* on its feet, the company had to look elsewhere. A sympathetic vicar, Etienne Watts, gave them a not very sympathetic space, the crypt underneath his church, All Saints; full of coffins, but it had to do.

During rehearsals, Joan did what she always did at rehearsals and, for that matter, in everyday life. She asked for something difficult. As her demands were mostly difficult-interesting, as opposed to difficult-boring, someone, somewhere would take up the challenge. On this occasion, she asked for the sound of a door opening and closing but not an ordinary one. It had to be specific; if anything, unsettling. Who went off and came back with a wooden ratchet device he'd sawed and nailed together? Gerry. What the effect sounded like Joan didn't say but Gerry's effort touched her. She wouldn't have remembered it otherwise. As for Gerry, it was just the start of him picking up the challenges Joan threw down for him.

Once London had been bombed – that was the Blitz – it was on the cards that Manchester would be hit too. A couple of months later, it was.

Joan, having to find paid work, *Lysistrata* or no, was asked by Bob Reid of the *Manchester Evening News*, to write a report on a family that had been buried alive in Salford. She did, but when she handed in her copy, Bob asked her to build up the tension and the horror. As she thought the facts were strong enough on their own, this only served to reinforce her suspicion of journalism. However, needs must, and the end result was good enough for Bob to give her several more stories. Joan's communism did not bother him.

The threat of bombs falling as soon as darkness came made people leave work as early as possible. Joan was doing just that after a *Lysistrata* rehearsal when a blast from behind threw her and two girls in the company against a wall. No sooner had they counted their fingers and toes than they thought of the crypt. Some of the company were still down there. Back they ran. All Saints had received a direct hit. Fire engines drew up but the firemen didn't dig. They thought the church had been empty and, as for the crypt, they didn't think about it at all. Etienne Watts, who had summoned them, was putting them wise when a figure covered in dust emerged from the vestry, or rather where the vestry used to be. It was Gerry. He turned round to help the others as all of them, thank goodness, staggered out. The church had been very well built.

Lysistrata opened at the Milton Hall on Deansgate in central Manchester and toured various towns round about. Its programme note read: 'As the war intensifies, the work of the theatre becomes more important. This is your theatre.' Brave words when the company was thinking: 'How long can we keep this up?'

They kept it up for a show called *Classic Soil*, which was not Joan's radio feature, though it was like a radio feature. Less specific than *Last Edition*, it was more poetic. The first half was taken from Jimmie's history of Chartism – weavers in cottages forced into factories – the one he had written for the BBC. The second half was a general attack on the waste of war. The Chartism half, though a story that has to be remembered, is dour. The converted would nod away while everyone else would stay away.

To counteract this, Joan did her usual. She beguiled the audience with movement, rhythm and sheer beauty. For one scene, a convention, she drew tiny sketches. They are a lesson in how a talent develops. What jumps from them, firstly, is *The Green Table*, Kurt Jooss's ballet. He created it in 1932 as a reaction to the peace talks of the time, and peace talks in general – the ones that go round and round and only end in death. It used Labanotation, Rudolf Laban's system of writing down choreography.

In the centre of her drawings, as in the Jooss ballet, is a large table almost like a billiard table. Along its sides and at the head, are characters at different angles to it, and, again as in the ballet, all are standing. You can see the main appeal to Joan. No chairs.

Above and below the drawings are minutely detailed stage directions. In later years, Joan, on being handed a new script would, chiming with Shakespeare texts, cross out the stage directions. That way the actors found the action in the words. At 26, Joan was learning. By reading books and looking at paintings, she was putting information into her head which she could try out in rehearsals. The drawings and written instructions, an intermediate stage, acted as memos to herself. With the passage of time, they would be absorbed and so no longer necessary. They would be at her fingertips.

The instructions for the Chartist convention are a kind of choreography. Joan makes energy expended by one character pop up in the reaction of another. 'Graham turns vehemently to Chairman who is perplexed between the two groups – Gerry R catches the movement from Graham and counterpoints it by a downward movement – down in his heels – and hand downthrust in his pockets.' There's one thing about that which stayed the same in all Joan's scripts: the mixing of actors' names and characters.

'As the war intensifies. . .' yes, well it did. *Classic Soil* was Theatre Union's last show before it had to stop altogether. The tin lid, as expected, was call-up.

Before going, Graham Banks, papers in hand, proposed to Rosalie Williams, much to the annoyance of Jimmie, who was having an affair with her. Not annoyed by this, even though she knew of it, was Joan, probably because she was having an affair too, with Philo Hauser, an unsuitable Austrian refugee. It would not last long. About Graham's going, she was very annoyed, Bill Sharples too, except annoyed was not the right word. She was fearful. Graham was going to be air crew and pacifist Bill, the prop-maker, who had gone earlier, had been given non-combatant duties on an oil tanker. Air crew was dangerous. The oil tanker was a sitting duck.

Then Jimmie was called up. He went but two days later, hopped it. The talk that could knock you down masked a spirit that was not so tough. Howard Goorney was next. He joined the infantry. As for Gerry, he was too young to go right away but it was only a matter of time before he had to join up as well. Like Graham, he joined the airforce, where he made himself popular by introducing wine to the mess. Beer, he hated as, by coincidence, did Joan. And Joan herself?

The full BBC instruction, at her barring, was that she could still work on an ad hoc basis in musical and dramatic performances, i.e. she was not totally out of radio. She was freelance which meant that, like any other freelance, she was working but had to scramble for whatever she could get. It started with her being summoned to the BBC in London by a drama and features producer, Marjorie Banks, who sympathised with her politics. Joan was not keen to go because she saw herself heading into the brick wall of the ban. As John Coatman had done before, Marjorie Banks invited her to a restaurant away from the BBC. She had something up her sleeve. As long as Joan's name was not on the script, she could carry on writing and she, Marjorie, had just the job for her, a soap opera called *Front Line Family*. They could write it together. Joan accepted the job, so when, in the early 1950s, she discovered that blacklisted Hollywood writers of the McCarthy era were up to something similar, she would have been able to think: 'Here we go again.'

At the time, she did the job conscientiously, writing the scripts in Manchester and sending them on the overnight train to London, but afterwards she was dismissive. 'The good thing about writing a wartime soap is that when you get bored with a character, you can always drop a bomb on them.' One actress in it went on to a long career, first in films, and then on television: Jean Anderson.

Marjorie Banks couldn't get Joan reinstated, though she tried, but she could put her name about as available for freelance work. As a result, something did crop up. *Tunnel*, the programme which Joan had heard Jimmie's voice on when she first arrived in Manchester, had been written by a poet called DG Bridson. Since then, Geoffrey Bridson, pronounced Bride-son (he came from the Isle of Man, as Joan loved to point out), had become a producer of features. This had brought him into contact with her, but he'd gone a bit quiet after she was barred. With Marjorie's prodding, he thought of something.

When Joan was dropped from the staff, it meant specifically the staff of the Home Service North Region. Today, being dropped from Radio 4 would be the equivalent, except it would be a Radio 4 that had special programmes for the north. What we don't have nowadays but what they did then was Empire Radio, BBC programmes which were broadcast to Canada, South Africa and Australia. Nobody said Joan couldn't work for that as long as it was on a short contract. Bridson sent her one.

Having said 'It doesn't qualify you for a pension,' it went on to offer: '£10 a week, to research, write and produce a series entitled *A Visit To . . .*' Substitute the dots with any town in the UK you care to think of.

To avoid the 'Herry and Jeck' vowels of the usual announcers, Joan found a Canadian, Kent Stevenson, to present the programme, so it would start: 'Each week, Kent Stevenson takes you to one of the famous places in Great Britain where men and women who love peace are living a wartime life.'

Joan's job was to travel to the town in question, find some interesting people, question them, write a script and, a day later, record them reading the script with Kent Stevenson putting the questions, also scripted. As with the radio features before the war, everything had to be on paper first. On the covers of scripts, it said: 'Approved for Policy BBC Department. . . Approved for Security Censorship Unit' with spaces left for ticks. You would then read:

A Visit to Blackpool. Friday 10.7.42. 15 minutes.

After Kent Stevenson had explained to the far-flung listeners that Blackpool was England's Coney Island, this would happen:

FRED FAIRCLOUGH:

> Where are you going wi' that thing, lad? If you don't mind my butting in, like. What is it, a microphone?

KENT: Yeah, it won't bite.

FRED: Why don't you come with us, lad? You'd have a reet good time.

[Joan's script]

Actually, Fred Fairclough was an actor. Joan had known him for quite a while. He was a supporter of hers. These programmes were invariably a mix of the real and the artificial.

In an excerpt from **A Visit to Chichester, England, 17th July 1942**, Kent Stevenson talks to the genuine article:

> KENT: I want you to meet the very pretty owner of the voice you have been hearing during the broadcast. She's standing beside me now – Miss Pearl Turner. Young lady, you cost me my beauty sleep last night. I had to get up at half past four this morning to find you – and where did I find you?

> PEARL: Milking the cows, of course.

Short as this contribution of Pearl Turner's may have been, it's worth mentioning because her singing voice so impressed Joan that she remembered both it and Pearl for better times.

Even before Gerry Raffles' call-up, he and Joan had been falling in love. Sitting together on a bench in Manchester's Piccadilly while Joan waited for her bus to Hyde, he had kissed her and, after that, they'd met for the occasional rendezvous; tea at Woolworth's, coffee at the Kardomah Coffee House and privacy at his cheerless but, at least, empty house in Higher Crumpsall. An especially romantic meeting happened one Sunday while Joan was sitting in bed with a high temperature – ill again – writing the script for *A Visit to Salisbury*. Gerry, in his blue RAF greatcoat, burst in. His presence, both youthful and solid, was just the tonic she needed. She didn't know that it was one of Gerry's scrapes. He was AWOL.

Soon after that, he was kicked out of the RAF. The official explanation was 'Averse to discipline'. 'For reasons of love and politics' is what Gerry himself said. The love was Joan. *Last Edition*'s final speech: 'Who is the enemy? . . . I tell you the enemy is at home,' was the politics. He didn't hold back. He also ordered *The Daily Worker*, the organ of the Communist Party. These boyish passions saved his life. Graham Banks, who had trained to be air crew, was dead, and most of Gerry's RAF contemporaries who had trained with him to be pilots, were killed weeks after he left the service.

Although Joan was impatient with the war – large, boring object standing in her way as it was – she did, while it went along, learn new stuff that would be useful for the time when she could take the dream that was always in her head and do something with it. Recordings, in those days, were not edited. The first programme Kent Stevenson did for Joan was him interviewing non-stop for an hour. He was shattered. Afterwards, he explained to Joan that tape could be cut. You record. You stop. You start again. You then take the tapes back to the BBC and make the programme by editing. Joan liked that. However, Kent Stevenson, after recording several episodes of *A Visit to* . . . found it too tame. His ambition was to broadcast from a plane during a raid. He got his way, eventually, but, in replacing another reporter at the last minute, was killed. The reporter who was supposed to have flown on that mission was Richard Dimbleby.

Joan never stopped writing to the BBC, usually in London. She was either sending adaptations on spec or she was asking for the ban to be lifted. She dreaded having to join the services. At least that's what she put in these letters. Lance Sieveking and Laurence Gilliam, the producers she sent her letters to, are names that remain big in broadcasting today. Their answers were always polite but always guarded. Some of her letters worked. Some didn't. What she didn't put in them was her true situation. The money she was earning had to support, not just herself, but others, one of whom she absolutely could not mention. In all, there were five.

Her grandparents, Robert Francis and Caroline Em, stuck under the Blitz, had troubled her, so she'd asked them to come and live in Hyde. Already at the house but, by then, in need of support, were Joan's mother-in-law, Betsy, and her father-in-law, Bill. Last, but far from least, was the supposedly miles away Jimmie

Miller. That's when he wasn't being hidden by Bill Sharples' pacifist parents who, as Joan had feared, did lose their son. There was one more hiding place he had. It was Rosalie Williams' home. His affair with Rosalie was still on the go, she having turned down Graham Banks not long before he was killed. It was all so exhausting and made worse by Caroline Em and Robert Francis fading away rapidly. They had been happier in their own home under the Blitz. Joan had made a mistake, and she knew it.

She did get more work but the short contracts, the constant travelling, the cold hotel bedrooms, the blackout, the knocking out of scripts overnight and the loneliness were, for her, a grind. For someone who knew that radio was going to be their life, it might not have been so. At least you weren't called up. Joan didn't see it that way. She wanted something else and, much as she liked to see herself as a loner, mysterious and romantic, she knew that two days of that was quite enough. Grub, home cooked (not by her), and a bit of company was what she needed after that.

The job that saw her nearly to the end of the war was a series starring one of the most popular voices of the time, Wilfred Pickles. It was called *Mixed Pickles*. She was brought to it by a North Region producer/presenter, Nan Macdonald. With Nan she got on fine. As well as doing the Pickles series for her, she got to act in her children's plays and give readings at two guineas a time. *The Prince and the Pauper*, one of her adaptations, was commissioned by Nan. It would be the Christmas show at the Theatre Royal Stratford East in 1954, another goody stored up for another day.

Wilfred Pickles she was less keen on. She disliked his taste for double entendres where she could see none, and telling smutty jokes at Rotary clubs. However, he wasn't the one writing the scripts. That was her job, so she could make Wilf, as he was known, sound more intelligent and better informed than he really was. The series is explained by his own introduction:

> WILF: How do folks? The name is Wilfred Pickles and I'll
> be coming to the mike at this time every week. Now
> I'm what you might call a go-between – a kind of link
> between the ordinary man and woman and the great
> body of listeners.

Like the Kent Stevenson programme it was soft propaganda but this time it was more sculpted. Actors recited poetry. Music wove in and out, as in 'Bring up Vi and quartet singing The Oak and the Ash,' Vi being Violet Carson, Ena Sharples in *Coronation Street* years later. Some weeks, instead of the usual visit, it could be a monologue and even when Wilf went to places to talk to people, you began to wonder. For example, in *Come Away to County Durham,* he describes what it was like to be travelling there on a train. 'A girl in khaki was talking politics nineteen to the dozen to a young sailor whose only interest in the world seemed to be swing music.' Joan would certainly have gone to Durham. She had to – there was all that research to do – but did Wilf? He wasn't a reporter. He was an actor. Was it not easier for him to stay by a microphone in the studio and use his skill to lift Joan's script, as radio actors say, off the page?

So however much she despised Wilfred Pickles, Joan could make the programme more hers and even subtly get a point of view across. This was possible, not by expressing an opinion – the censors would have been on to that – but by selecting facts and putting them together to make a certain impression on the listener. Mostly, it was mild. Even so, quoting a colliery's motto: 'United we stand, divided we fall,' before having a miner say: 'Russia is out to smash Hitler and we are out for the same thing . . . You see Russia has lost some of her miners to the Fascists . . . Russia supported us in 1926' *[Joan's script]*, does make one sit up.

The script for Hull, *The Land of the White Rose,* is unusual as it is not uplifting. Joan makes it plain that the women of Hull were hit twice over. If they didn't lose their men from fishing, they lost them from them being in the navy. There's even a reference to the comings and goings of naval ships. That, as you would expect, has a pencil line through it. The earlier truth, which you might think of as bad propaganda, doesn't.

Apart from Sheffield and Hull, most of the programmes have a rural flavour:

SHEPHERD: It's a quiet life but it's a satisfying one.

WILF: How's the hay shaping?

SHEPHERD: Drouthy.

Joan enjoyed dialect but never seemed to take it that seriously. Actors who were proud of doing an accurate, thick, regional accent were mocked by her. What was the point, she thought, if no one knew what they were on about.

Sometimes in her *Mixed Pickles* scripts, she appeared to be having pure fun as in *Canny Cummerlan* she had Wilf say: 'I'd made up my mind to do a bit of climbing so I got myself a good strong pair of boots,' like Wilf was actually going to go climbing. She herself enjoyed talking about trecuni climbing boots because she liked the word 'trecuni'. However, was it real climbing or the show of climbing, the shorts, the cleft stick, the Tyrolean hat that she liked? So often with Joan, it was the latter, the show rather than the real thing.

Altogether, Joan's programmes with Wilfred Pickles were designed to apply a balm to the jagged nerves of those serving far away. This doesn't sound madly exciting, but it taught her lessons. They taught her about Britain. They taught her – in her own words – not to impose and they taught her professionalism which only comes from doing a job over and over again. Gerry Raffles thirty years later, said that Joan could, merely by holding a script in the palm of her hand, tell you how long it would be.

During those radio years, Joan was Theatre Union's only professional who was doing the job they were supposed to be doing and being paid for it. Neither Jimmie nor Gerry could do that.

Jimmie could not appear in public and could not earn. He stayed at home writing plays, hewing out a kind of language that he thought would be right. To sell them, Joan would do anything, like sending them to Bernard Shaw or Donald Wolfit or, if that didn't work, to West End agents and Hugh Beaumont of HM Tennent, people she would normally have nothing to do with. When asked who this young playwright was, she would write that he had travelled widely and served in the army for years. She didn't care what she said. She was just trying to make money. It didn't work. Despite her spirited covering letters, the scripts came back, which led her to reflect that Jimmie's quickly knocked-out sketches written before the war, material that served an immediate purpose, had more life in them than all this careful crafting he was up to. It made quite a contrast to what she was doing, endlessly writing, always to a deadline but, at the same time, always having her words spoken. She did write one thing that came to nothing, a screenplay on a day in the life of a newspaper, but at least she was paid. Curiously, it was based around the *Daily Express'* branch in Ancoats and, in those days, the *Daily Express* was known as 'The Tart's Gazette'. She really would do anything.

Young Gerry was not quite in the same situation as Jimmie. His life's work hadn't started yet. Even so, he must have thought it was going to be something to do with Joan because, after being thrown out of the air force, he didn't make a big career choice. He took jobs that would get him by. He just made sure that they were tough, so that he could align himself with the working class. A friend said he swore a lot at the time, which was not characteristic of him at all. He found work in a fizzy drinks factory, driving a horse-drawn dray whilst resting his feet on the horse's rump, and finally getting work down a mine in Pendleton, where, lying on his back on a bogey, whizzing along, he bashed his knee on the roof of a low tunnel. Together with getting into scrapes, he was accident prone.

It is when Joan, in her diaries, refers to Jimmie as Edith, as in 'Edith went to the hairdressers' when she meant 'Jimmie had a haircut' (in case the police read her diary), that it seems like the two most important men in her life had, for the duration of the war, been turned into eunuchs. They were not, like her, working at drama and being paid, nor were they in the forces, deadly as they were, which everybody else was. Joan's ability to earn from drama, on the one hand and, on the other, plan for the future, like keeping tabs on Pearl Turner, was the only motor that was keeping the show on the road. No wonder she felt lonely.

CHAPTER SEVEN

THEATRE WORKSHOP SETS OFF

J oan, convinced the war was going to end in 1943, was utterly fed up when it didn't. 'Open a second front, now!' was the cry in the streets but that wasn't to happen until 6 June 1944, D-Day. When it did, Joan, ever the optimist, was so excited that, as far as she was concerned, the war was over. In her head, the plan to start a company, one that did nothing but theatre, gathered speed.

While in Kendal writing a BBC script, she wrote to John Trevelyan, Westmoreland's Director of Education. 'I'd like to meet and talk to you about making Kendal a base for local touring.'

Trevelyan was another on-the-way-up Establishment figure of the kind Joan would call on over the years as a potential ally. 1958 would see him become Secretary to the Board of British Film Censors.

On 18 August 1944, he wrote back: 'I like the Kendal idea but there's this Margaret Littlewood who wants to get into radio. Will you and Nan Macdonald see her?' which sounds like: 'You scratch my back, I'll scratch yours.'

It makes one realise that, at this stage, Joan was on her own when it came to writing the obligatory letters to big names like, in her case, Bernard Shaw, Donald Wolfit and JB Priestley. That's because she was the only member of Theatre Union, and of whatever company that was to come, that these people had heard of. Her work at the BBC had done that. So, it was up to her to cope with the problem of Margaret Littlewood. She made a token effort but Margaret Littlewood irritated her. Still, it was enough for Trevelyan eight days later, to write: 'It will be grand if we can make Kendal a real drama centre.'

Not that Joan left it to him alone. When excitement grabbed her, she would talk to anyone. There may have been Trevelyan up in his important post but, on the ground was Fred Wilson. Fred she'd already met.

He'd sung in a choir for a BBC programme and got chatting to her. You can imagine him, an amateur, desperate to get into radio, desperate to get into any kind of drama. How often have professionals been polite to people like that before making their escape? However, this one with his writing paper headed 'Titus Wilson and Son, Printers, Kendal,' had, for obvious reasons, his uses. He knew Kendal inside out and so Joan allowed the correspondence to go on.

'Before the war,' she wrote, 'we were a carefully modelled group like the Compagnie des Quinze,' as if Fred would know what that was, but it sounded imposing. 'I've all sorts of ambitions for our theatre and never want it to be an ordinary little touring repertory company,' which Fred would probably have been perfectly happy with. However, those words of Joan's, drew him into a magic circle. They gave him hope that, with a little fixing from her, he could get his adaptation of *Robert the Devil* on the radio. She sent it, unfixed, straight to Nan Macdonald who rejected it. Did Fred drop away? No. The theatre bug bites deep.

He told Joan to get in touch with John Trevelyan. Thus it becomes unclear whether Joan knew Trevelyan before or whether it was Fred who made the introduction. Next, Fred recommended Howie's Rooms as a base. Joan liked the sound of those but then, in other correspondence of hers, it became Trevelyan who recommended them. It's true he did mention them in other letters but only after Fred had talked them up.

On a piece of paper among this correspondence between Joan and Fred, she wrote 'CONTACT MADE BBC M/C. AWFUL SYCOPHANT SCARED OF OUR POLITICS.' She added, quoting Trevelyan: 'Fred Wilson is a mug and artists should take advantage of businessmen.'

She was ambivalent about Trevelyan too. He had a link with the Council for the Encouragement of Music and the Arts (CEMA), the forerunner of the Arts Council, and that sounded really useful. He could also raise an education grant. Joan, in a letter to Rosalie Williams, wrote, bubbling over with excitement about this, but, in her diary, wrote that she was not a teacher. Instructing the people of Westmoreland in drama was not what she wanted. As actors would testify – and Lionel Bart too – Joan was indeed a teacher, a great one, but it wasn't a job she wanted to commit herself to.

As so often with Joan, this was not all that was going on. Straight after VE Day, 8 May 1945, Nan Macdonald wrote to her suggesting she dig out an old script she'd written, as it would be perfect for the re-establishing of BBC Home Service North Region. Joan was very much back in there.

Without really knowing what was going to happen on the Kendal front, she wrote to Howard Goorney who was still in the forces, serving in Belgium. Get out, she told him, we're starting, and so Howard, by dint of lighting candles and chanting prayers a little too fervently, got out – because there he was in his demob suit.

Also there was Jimmie, only now with a beard and a different name. He wanted people to call him Ewan MacColl. It brought him closer to the Scottishness he so longed for. Being born in Salford had always been a sore point.

Joan's feelings about his desertion were mixed. She knew that if he'd stuck it out in the army he could have been dead but, forever afterwards, she would say: 'He could never look you in the eye.' She once said: 'Maybe it would have been better if he had stuck it out.' Others, from then on, called him Ewan. Joan continued to call him Jimmie and, when his first two children were given Scottish names, she called Hamish, his son, Mishka and said that Kirsty, his daughter, was named after a Swede. This Swede was an actress soon to join the company. Joan called her Kerstin. Everybody else called her Kristin. Nomenclature was important to Joan. She would have people the way she wanted them.

Anyway, that was the company: Jimmie/Ewan, Joan, Gerry, Rosalie and Howard. It wasn't very big. Auditions would have to be held.

Joan could do auditions but she didn't like them. People dropping in to see what was buzzing, joining in and either leaving or staying, was her favourite method of collecting a team.

For this set of auditions, she listened, not very patiently, to the auditioner's set piece and then gave him or her a situation inside which to improvise. Most were horrified but a few, the ones with a quick wit and some imagination, enjoyed it. A small number, even on being told that this was a co-operative, dependent on what came in at the box office, threw their lot in with – with what? A new name was needed for this new company. Some long-remembered words from an American agitprop article came into Joan's head and formed themselves into Theatre Workshop. They joined Theatre Workshop.

The most important person to come through these auditions was David Scase. Joan had wanted him anyway because he was the best sound effects man at BBC Manchester but, when she described him joining the company, she said he came because he fancied Rosalie. He did fancy Rosalie (he and Rosalie eventually got married) but he did also audition. At first, he was inhibited, understandable considering he hadn't set out to be an actor. However, as Joan stretched him with different ideas, the very fact that he wasn't trained freed him to invent. The reason for David being important was that he was an example of a discovery who would stick at it.

That was not always the case. Joan could discover talent all right. Pearl Turner, the Chichester girl, who had sung so sweetly on the Kent Stevenson show, was going to join the company. More immediately, there was Lillian Booth. Joan picked her out of school, encouraged her to improvise and put her into a radio play. She was a natural, but shortly after being asked to join Theatre Workshop she left, as did, sooner rather than later, Pearl Turner. Annoyingly for Joan, there had to be more than talent in her actors. There had to be a deep down desire to do it and keep doing it, a quality that was of little interest to her.

There was plenty of excitement in setting up Theatre Workshop. That was one of Joan's talents – creating excitement – as Fred Wilson was experiencing, but there was uncertainty too. Would Howie's Rooms really be available? The War Office had not let them go yet. Might Theatre Workshop be forced to run a school and, if it refused, how would it survive? At the BBC were wage clerks, typists and organisers like Nan Macdonald. It's easier to be part of that and grumble than go it alone.

For Theatre Workshop, practicality was needed; the ability to explain things to people who were not that bright, all the stuff that bored Joan. Where was that to come from?

Lying in bed with her during one of their snatched moments together – Joan preferring things that way, what with Jimmie still a bit of an embarrassment and she enjoying the roundabout way in any case – Gerry told her that he would devote all his strength to her.

It was not merely love but clear-sightedness that made him see what others in Theatre Union and Theatre Workshop may not have. The talent to watch was Joan's and that's what he was backing. He would do everything to look after that talent, well, as long as she used it rightly. If he thought she was using it wrongly or not at all, then he was not behind her. In 1945 that thought was miles away from his head but it would be there in 1961 when he thought she was not using her talent properly.

Meanwhile, Jimmie was the high priest of Theatre Workshop because he was the one writing the plays or, as Joan put it: 'Once upon a time Jimmie was the genius and I was the handmaiden at his knee.'

Joan had sent a list of plays to John Trevelyan. On it were the two which the company were to open with, *Johnny Noble* and *The Flying Doctor*.

Johnny Noble was based on the research Joan had done for the Wilfred Pickles radio programme on Hull, so it had not gone to waste. In her letter to Trevelyan, she described it, to keep things simple, as a documentary play about the fishing industry in Hull. It wasn't quite that.

Jimmie's script, made up of narration, verse and songs, Joan's conjuring up of places, weather, an air raid and the loading and firing of an anti-aircraft gun, using no scenery and no gun, just movement, dance, lights and sound effects, would best be left to the moment when it was put before an audience.

Johnny Noble only lasts an hour. That's why they neeeded the other show, *The Flying Doctor*. Jimmie's adaptation, from Molière's farce, *Le Médecin Volant*, came from before the war, so little text work was required. For Joan it was like being given a present. *Commedia dell'arte*, her favourite influence, would suffuse it, and Howard Goorney, as Scagnarelle, the servant who pretends to be two people at once, would bring those Callot engravings to life. It's what he did best.

For the play to work, the audience needed to see both the inside and the outside of a house in quick succession. Joan was in the middle of tackling the problem when a character called Bill Davidson appeared. Bill was not a set designer, nor was he, for that matter, an actor. He was an engineer. He knew about the making of aeroplanes. Joan simply threw the problem at him which he was quite happy to solve as long as he could have some wood. Joan got on to her friend, Hilary Barchard, who worked at the BBC and whose father was a timber merchant. In no time, there was the wood. That set the pattern for how Theatre Workshop would survive: the lucky arrival of the right person at the right moment and the good will of those who believed in its aims.

Using high-tension wires to keep it in position, Bill built a wall with a window in it and set it on a little revolve. The result was light, looked good and didn't go wrong. Jimmie was especially proud of that last bit. He may have been fascinated by Piscator but he knew that his lifts and travelling walkways got stuck. Bill remained with the company and became an actor. He was an example of someone dropping in to see what's buzzing and staying.

Jimmie chose the music. It wasn't Lully, Molière's unloved contemporary, but the mock-heroic *Háry János* by the Hungarian composer, Kodály, another piece Joan would turn off when, in later years, she heard it on the radio.

During the rehearsals of both shows which, to begin with, took place in Manchester, Joan received a telephone call. John Coatman wanted to see her. She met him at the restaurant away from the BBC where, four years earlier, he had told her and Jimmie that he would sort out the barring problem.

It was to do with the re-establishing of BBC Home Service North Region, Nan Macdonald had told Joan about, three months earlier. Coatman wanted Joan to head its features department. All that plugging away at the freelance jobs had paid off. She was back in triumph, if she wanted to be.

She didn't want to be, but it meant a lot to her, that offer. Forever afterwards, she could say: 'When I started Theatre Workshop, I wasn't a nobody.' Coatman was disappointed at her turning the job down, even though she was sensible enough to suggest that she and her company could keep up some kind of relationship with the BBC. She didn't know that the man sitting opposite her was the one whose memo had brought about her ejection from it. Nor would she ever.

The next day, news came that Howie's Rooms were off. In fact, they'd never been on. The Ministry of Defence had not once intimated they would let them go. For Joan, the BBC must have looked very tempting. The company went to Kendal anyway and carried on rehearsing in the upstairs rooms of the local Conservative Club.

On 26 July 1945, before the war was completely over and much to the excitement of the company, Labour gained a landslide victory. Kendal was not part of it. Lieutenant Colonel Vane, Conservative, held his seat. His agent, Miss Hilary Overy, interrupted rehearsals to put up a Union Jack outside the window. It was upside down.

The two plays opened at Kendal Girls' High School on 13 August 1945. Joan looked on as various types, Kendal locals, old Theatre Union fans, Fred 'You'd have a reet good time' Fairclough and John Trevelyan, took their seats. *The Flying Doctor* came first. That was the curtain-raiser. The big event was *Johnny Noble*.

Its story turns on exactly the point – women of Hull being hit twice – that Joan had made in her radio programme. Young Mary's mother loses her husband to fishing and forbids her daughter to have anything to do with Johnny, a merchant seaman. Johnny looks for work elsewhere but it's the 1930s and there are no jobs. He joins a Barcelona-bound ship to give aid to the fighters in the Spanish Civil War. He survives, only to find himself still at sea in the Second World War. He survives that too but, when peace comes, he's confronted by The Roaring Boys who want everyone to forget about the war and get back to business, the kind of dodgy, selfish business that was going on when the play started. What will Johnny do?

As the performance progressed, Joan noticed that the audience was not reacting to moments she thought would get them going and, when it came to an issue she felt really strongly about, the black market, it was downright complaisant. What, she asked herself, was going on?

The show was undoubtedly topical but the answer to what Johnny was going to do, i.e. what the audience, in easy going Conservative Kendal was going to do, turned out to be: 'We're not bothered.'

That is not the whole story. The many sound, lighting and music cues, the cinematic cuts and dissolves, the precise miming of complicated actions, would have given the audience something interesting to look at or listen to all the time, while a restrained farewell scene: 'Don't forget your sandwiches, Jim, I've put them at the top of your case. And let me know your address as soon as you get there,' would have worked in any old play.

So, the reception, though not ecstatic, was OK, and Fred Fairclough definitely enjoying himself, along with John Trevelyan, was cheering, but then they were already friends of the company and knowledgeable about theatre. That was an omen.

Two days later, America dropped the atom bomb. Three days after that, the war completely over, Theatre Workshop finished its run in Kendal, with total takings of 55 pounds, 18 shillings and 6 pence, neatly typed on Fred 'the mug' Wilson's paper, and started a tour by moving to Victoria Hall, Grange-over-Sands, ten miles away. The kitty was so empty that only a friend, driving backwards and forwards in his Lagonda, got the company there.

It came back to Kendal in October to rehearse and perform Lorca's *The Love of Don Perlimplin for Belisa in his Garden*: an ugly old man (Howard Goorney) woos a beautiful woman (Kristin Lind, there she was), by pretending to be young. As exquisitely right as it was for Joan, it was exquisitely wrong for Kendal. Audiences, unable to comprehend, scorned it as filth.

The company returned to Kendal only one more time. It was for three performances in May the following year and it never went there again. That was it. There was no school, no more John Trevelyan and no more Fred Wilson. They were the rocket fuel that dropped away.

CHAPTER EIGHT

But How To Keep Going?

J oan's aim was to create a *commedia dell' arte* company, a glowing microcosm
that would travel round, setting an example for the rest of the world. People
would learn how to live by watching the way Theatre Workshop lived.
Inside it, she could be like her heroine, Isabella Andreini, who headed one of
the most famous *commedia* troupes. Not only did Isabella act, she was witty. She
had a brain. Her actors could come from any class. Talent was all they needed. This
commedia structure, however, was not just an aim, it was protection, as Joan had to
have a shield.

One thing the company already knew was who did what. It was simple:
everybody did everything. When David Scase was onstage, Ruth Brandes, whose
main job was making costumes, turned her hand to sound. David himself learned
to become a stage manager. The job of setting up before a show and packing
away afterwards was divided into tasks that could be allotted to each member
of the company. The more he or she performed it, the quicker they became. This
flexibility and lightness would make heavyweight companies look on aghast. It
was hard work but it would be a major part of surviving.

For all that, the outside world still had to be dealt with, the bit that Joan didn't
like. Immediately worrying was the lack of money. Gerry's compensation from
his mining accident, £225, and a loan of £100 from Rosalie Williams' father,
plus some other bits and bobs, had provided £400 but that wasn't going to go
far. The money from Kendal was ridiculous. Grange-over-Sands, which held out
little hope, was surprisingly better but this was haphazard, as was the reaction
to the shows. Wigan was terrific but then Gerry, to achieve all the show's effects,
plugged into the town's electricity supply and blacked out the streets. No more
Wigan.

As quickly as it could, Theatre Workshop had to teach itself business: the
booking of tours, the selling of shows. It was already on the road and, given

that its wares were less accessible than Joan and Jimmie had expected, it was not going to be easy.

Problems of art and problems of business were intertwined. If the company went to a proper theatre with a tradition of theatre-going, it was all right, but these were hard to get into because the nature of the shows puzzled theatre managers. If it went to some hall that hadn't seen a show in a while, it might have little trouble booking it but big trouble filling it.

Johnny Noble and *The Flying Doctor* were easy to understand, once you were sitting there, but they were hard to sell in advance because there was nothing for a potential audience to grab hold of. Good reviews at regional theatres were no use because they didn't appear until it was time to move on. Then, some parts of the country understood *Johnny Noble* better than others. It was usually to do with what kind of war the town in question had been through.

Even before the company arrived, there could be a problem. Staff of some halls were deeply suspicious of Theatre Workshop, considering it to be nothing but a bunch of reds, whatever 'red' meant to them, and so hackles were already raised. When any company arrives at any new place, it must have co-operation. That's where David Scase scored. He had the necessary charm and energy to put life into time-serving old codgers.

Reactions of people outside the company give the spectrum of what was going on. John Trevelyan, Fred Fairclough and others like them across the country, people who were used to theatre could be immediately responsive. A middle-aged woman living in Kendal found herself struggling. While turning down a request for a donation, she wrote: 'I'm not an intellectual. That makes it easier for me to feel the attitude of the ordinary provincial audience. You must reach their hearts before their heads' *[Joan's papers]*. For this woman, *Johnny Noble* was high-brow, and there were Joan and Jimmie simply wanting the people of this country to wake up to what they already owned: their heritage.

Another person who regarded Theatre Workshop as highbrow, surprisingly, was Michael Macowan of CEMA. Joan, knowing that Trevelyan had put in a word with him, sent an invitation to CEMA which, at that moment, was turning into the Arts Council. Michael Macowan, its Drama Director, an actor and director himself, sent another actor, Walter Hudd. He, like André van Gyseghem, was a Thirties communist, well established in mainstream theatre and, according to Joan, mediocre. Having seen *Don Perlimplin*, he went off expressing delight, but it was hard to tell what that really meant.

Some weeks later, Howard, who at the time was business manager, went, together with Joan, to see Macowan in London. That's when he said that Theatre Workshop was highbrow. As he hadn't seen any of the shows, he can only have been using the word as a means of escape, but then he appeared to have no desire to see them anyway.

He looked at the accounts and pointed out that the figures were unrealistic. A company could not operate like that. He wanted to back a venture that was already a going concern. Financially, Theatre Workshop was nothing of the sort. He recommended a change of repertoire and suggested a couple of authors he thought audiences would be more at ease with. Joan pointed out that they were hardly right for Kendal either. Macowan said that a shorter rehearsal period would be more economical. That did not suit Joan. As she had written to Fred Wilson: 'I've all sorts of ambitions for our theatre and never want it to be an ordinary little touring repertory company' *[Joan's correspondence]*.

Even the manager of the People's Theatre, Newcastle, Martin Trower, who was really looking forward to Theatre Workshop's visit, showed how the plays were really perceived. He wrote saying that *Johnny Noble* and *The Flying Doctor* were exempt from tax because they were 'partly educational.' *Don Perlimplin* wasn't, but then nobody had heard of it.

To continue on the theme of education, Joan, despite saying that she didn't want to be a teacher, did teach, but at least it was on the move. Sometimes, part of Theatre Workshop's deal, say when it went to Liverpool, would be to give Saturday drama classes. The trouble was, no extra pay came its way.

On her own, Joan gave a talk at Manchester's International Club. Her scribbled notes give an indication of her interests:

1. What is theatre? Theatre as an art, a social art

2. THEATRE & THE PEOPLE
   The projection of an experience into an illusion – primitive
   people and magic – the magic of words – of an illusion made real
   The dream of a child in a back street
   Where is the outlet for the creativeness of people –

3. Ballads, songs, poetry of the people, of the world
   Dancing

4. Industrial Revolution
   Sheridan – polished comedy/the people in the mines and mills
   Vocal tradition dies in England, dancing dies

5. Outlets for the emotions of people are football matches, pub
   arguments – and at their worst, in the lumpen sections of the
   people, hooliganism.

6. The creativeness of the people not dead – RILKE – or we could
   give up and leave the world to barbarism

7. Laban – the movement choirs of Germany
   Lorca – his poetry in the theatre
   MacDiarmid

8. The theatre as the microcosm of the future
    NO PLACE FOR ART TODAY?
    WITHOUT THE DREAM OF THE BETTER FUTURE THERE
    CAN BE NO FUTURE
    SUCH A THEATRE, ONLY A DREAM AS YET.

9. WHAT ARE THE TASKS OF THIS NEW THEATRE?
    I. THEMES
    II. FORM
    III. LANGUAGE
    ARTISTS WILL ONLY BE CREATED BY THE LIVING
    THEATRE
    ART MUST GET BACK TO THE LIVES OF THE PEOPLE

Joan was shy and thought little of her ability to speak in public but she could, on occasion, become possessed by it. In fact, she was sometimes so mesmerising that listeners, when she came to the end of a speech, said: 'Wow!' whether they had understood her or not. She had a unique way of propelling ideas outwards adding lots of excitement, like she did with Fred Wilson. Practical ways of implementing those ideas, she did not come up with.

This particular speech, the wanting to get back to the lives of the people, to the right kind of singing and dancing and the richness of the English language, would have thrilled those leaning towards her anyway. It was so pure. Whether it would have thrilled the football lovers and the people who enjoyed arguments in pubs, assuming any were International Club members in the first place, is less certain.

It comes down to Joan's ambivalence. On being told, once, by Archie Harding at the BBC that she was working class, she responded: 'I was born among them. I was never of them.' Shame got to her later for saying that but it lurks throughout her life. The trouble was, there were 'The lives of the people' and there were the actual people, the individuals, like the ones who loved football. She hated football.

As Theatre Workshop toured England, Wales and Scotland, this uneasiness was in the background, the good and the unpopular mixed together. As yet unasked was the question of how to discard the unpopular while keeping the good.

Still, this was long-term. More immediate was Jimmie's impatience with the delicacies Joan so loved, *The Flying Doctor* and *Don Perlimplin*. Fine as they were, enough was enough. He wanted to tackle the atom bomb. Theatre Workshop could not ignore that. He had a problem, though, a lack of scientific knowledge, having left school at fourteen. Then again, to hand were Bill Davidson and the company electrician, Alf Smith. Alf had a degree in physics and could explain how the atom was split.

Even before it was written, Joan knew that whatever emerged would lean towards history and lecture rather than drama, but she also knew that it was important and, therefore, worth the hard work to make the science entertaining.

The history established, splitting the atom could become a ballet with dancing protons and neutrons.

Uranium 235 was ready before negotiations with Martin Trower in Newcastle were completed. The company was due there in February 1946. To get a tax exemption right across the board, he had to prove that not only was *Don Perlimplin* 'partly educational' but that *The Bomb Show*, as he'd been calling *Uranium 235*, was also in with a good chance.

The person who discovered that Newcastle and the North East in general was of more use to Theatre Workshop than the North West was Gerry. Knowing that the boss of the People's Theatre, Alf Simpson, was an old friend of the company, he simply went there to fix it. That instinct to go out and get something was not in any other member of Theatre Workshop. It did take on a guy called Mike Thompson but the dates he found weren't much cop. His were the halls nobody went to, whatever show was on. 'Piddling,' one company member called them. Nor could Mike avoid: 'Today, Land's End, tomorrow, John O'Groats.' To explain: when a company books a tour, it tries to make the next town fairly near to where it was before. That's often not possible. The next town can be far away. This problem was exacerbated in Theatre Workshop's case by poverty. Company members couldn't afford the fares and had to become adept at hitchhiking.

Gerry was also the one who actually spotted that the best bets were likely to be the proper theatres such as the People's or the Empire, Dewsbury. He got that as well, a coup in itself. The house was not great but it gave the company the feeling it was doing better.

The People's Theatre actually was better. Although it was amateur – still is – it had an auditorium and, like other amateur groups in the north at the time, had a reputation for choosing better plays than the West End. What's more, audiences went to them.

While keeping going in this chancy way, the company did have strokes of luck or maybe, if you believe luck comes to those who keep trying, they weren't really. Fifteen years after Joan had been introduced to Laban's system, the man himself, as in a Dickens plot, turned up in Manchester. Joan was at the station ready to meet him.

The look of the company, despite Laban's life partner, Lisa Ullmann regarding theatre as risky, appealed to him. It gave him enough confidence to suggest that one of his students, Jean Newlove, join Theatre Workshop. The company that taught itself at last had a trained teacher from outside and Jean became the only person to teach Laban's system in drama. Other Laban teachers choreographed actors. Jean taught actors to use Laban, not only for dance, but for all movement. It was a way to make a character.

At the same time, Joan, constantly on the lookout for useful people, found Nelson Illingworth, a singer and voice teacher. He was brought up in Australia, which would have recommended him to Joan right away. There was less chance of him being in thrall to the south of England middle-class way of speaking. In a letter to Joan, he complained about a badly spoken radio production of *Romeo and Juliet*. Nelson liked good vowel sounds; so did Joan.

In London, he was the artistic director of an evening theatre school, Labour Stage. On the team of teachers were poet and friend of Jimmie, John Pudney, set designer Jocelyn Herbert (who was to make her mark at the Royal Court Theatre), and composer Alan Bush, who was not a 'Thirties communist' because he stayed a communist all his life. It's an indication that after the war there was something in the air, a desire – that was not just Theatre Workshop's – to make art improve people's lives. The question however remained for Labour Stage, as well as Joan and Jimmie: how exactly?

By teaching Theatre Workshop actors to use their bodies and their voices properly, both Jean Newlove and Nelson Illingworth were helping to realise one of Joan's most important dreams: training. When talking of Bertolt Brecht Joan said: 'He uses ready-mades,' actors who come with their box of tricks which Brecht could drop into his productions. Joan wanted to actually *make* her actors, or be the one who released their talent.

At least she knew there had to be talent to start with. Before the 1945 auditions she wrote, in another dig at Jimmie, that she was fed up with Communist Party and left-wing types who'd been in pre-war Theatre Union. She wanted 'TALENT who'd train to make the finest theatre in the world.'

Jimmie was not too keen on Nelson Illingworth, in part because he came from opera, which he regarded as the wrong way to use the voice, but also because Illingworth favoured Gerry. Joan and Gerry happy together was anathema to him, or so Joan thought, and this despite their own relationship long being over. She was particularly annoyed by Jimmie when he said that Laban thought Gerry was best for shifting pianos.

In search of talent, she wrote a letter – another example of her doing the unexpected – to Kenneth Barnes, not only director of RADA in 1945 but director of RADA during the time when she was there, the time she had so hated. Had he any useful students? She was hoping for men. He wrote back, starting 'Dear Joan Littlewood,' as if he had no idea who she was and went on, never referring to her time there, to say that all his young men were busy during the holidays but there was one young woman who was free. She didn't get the job.

This idea of training, Joan's way of training, was one of the first steps in a dance of dysfunction that Theatre Workshop and the Arts Council would keep up for many years. Instead of one dancer drawing a foot back as the other dancer put a foot forward, both dancers would stub each other's toes. One dancer, instead of supporting the other, would let go. That's how it went.

Step one had been Joan writing to Michael Macowan thinking that an innovative new company would be perfect for support. Step two was Macowan not seeing Theatre Workshop's shows but proposing a touring rep quickly rehearsing established plays. Step three was Joan rejecting that.

Step four was Arts Council Manchester Representative, Jo Hodgkinson, going to see a show but finding no one there. Theatre Workshop's performance had been cancelled. Hodgkinson had given no warning of going but the cancellation gave a bad impression.

Step five, and when he finally did see a performance, he was delighted in the presence of the actors but then went away and said something different to Michael Macowan. He said that some of them would have to be replaced, while the rest would have to re-train. Re-train to do what, wondered Joan, stabbed in the back. Her actors were very well trained, she thought.

When Jo Hodgkinson appeared that time, the rest of the company may have been uncertain about him but Joan was quite certain. She didn't like him and walked away. Step six.

You'd have thought, after his betrayal, no one would have spoken to him again, but that applied only to Joan. She could walk away from the unpleasant; the others couldn't. One or more of them still had to sort the problem out. In this case, it was Gerry and Howard. As business managers – they were sharing the job now – they couldn't afford to break off relations with the Arts Council. They didn't have the luxury. They had to keep asking.

There was another visit from the Arts Council but Pearl Turner, the company's best female singer and one of the two narrators in *Johnny Noble* was off sick that night. Joan had to go on instead but couldn't sing. Jimmie Miller never quite forgave Pearl for that.

And so it went on. As late as the 1960s, Theatre Workshop would be uneasily corresponding with Jo Hodgkinson, by then Drama Director and based in London.

But then again, so continued the strokes of luck that, perhaps, were not really strokes of luck. St John's Hall, Middlesbrough, didn't sound promising but no sooner had the company unloaded its gear than coffee appeared, quite an improvement on being yapped at by a little dog. The hot drink, so very much needed, had been made by Mrs Ruth Pennyman. A few weeks earlier, she had seen the company perform *Don Perlimplin* at the People's Theatre in Newcastle and, unlike Kendal, had fallen for it. But, as so often with people who took to Theatre Workshop, she was both inclined their way politically and theatre mad.

Coffee was just the beginning of what she went on to provide for the company. A few miles outside Middlesbrough was her home where she lived with her husband, Colonel Pennyman, and it was there that she invited Joan and her actors to come and eat and sleep. Ormesby Hall was its name, a large house set in its own grounds.

That night, the company sat in the dining room at a long table with Ruth Pennyman at one end and the colonel at the other. Rationing still had another eight years to go, but no peculiar substitutes were served. Dinner was proper soup and proper fish. Joan, who delighted in anything done well, talked happily to Mrs Pennyman about Lorca. Some of the others, while grateful to find themselves in this oasis of hospitality, wondered if they were in the right place for a company that was supposed to be bringing theatre to the people. It felt a bit feudal. Gerry, still aligning himself with the working class, as he had done when swearing a lot among miners, stood up, went over to the fireplace, and scraped his fishbones into the flames. The colonel looked on with equanimity, almost as if he knew what the future held.

CHAPTER NINE

A HOME FOR A WHILE

Theatre Workshop toured as much as it could and the going was intense; a night here, a night there, sometimes. However, gaps were unavoidable and the solution turned out to be Ormesby Hall. Ruth Pennyman, fascinated by the exercises she saw Joan set in Middlesbrough, invited the company to give summer courses. So Jimmie would give lectures on agitprop and the history of drama, while Joan would say to those gathered: 'Go out of the room and come back in, remembering exactly what you did the first time.' It was one of the exercises she used to sharpen observation. She may not have wanted to be a teacher in a formal way; informally, she never stopped.

The important side of Gerry – swearing and scraping, was that really working-class behaviour? – came quickly to the fore. Theatre Workshop, lacking support from conventional sources, had to make friends as it went along and accept what they had to offer. He knew it, and he could see that the protection Ormesby Hall gave was good for Joan. So much so, that when he was worried Colonel Pennyman might turf them out, he persuaded pretty, fair-haired Pearl Turner to go for a walk with the colonel in order to find out if they could stay. Pearl knew what Gerry was up to and did not feel entirely comfortable with it. However, aware that it was for the company's sake, she went for that walk. Nothing bad happened, chiefly because Colonel Pennyman also knew what Gerry was up to and had already decided to say yes.

When Pearl returned with the news, she watched as Gerry turned away from her, picked Joan up and whirled her round. In that moment, she saw, without realising, which way the land would lie for Theatre Workshop.

Rudolf Laban once warned Joan that ambition would take her actors and motherhood would take her actresses. Pearl had a man in her life who wanted her to pay attention to him, not Theatre Workshop. She left soon afterwards. Joan never thought anyone was as good as her at singing the female narrator in *Johnny Noble*.

However, as one talent left, so another arrived. At the start of a summer course, five pounds and five shillings, Joan noticed a new student, a young sailor still in uniform, lying on the floor as part of a relaxation exercise. 'Imagine you're on a sandy beach on a sunny day with the sea lapping at the shore a few feet away.' Joan often used that when it was cold and there was no money to turn the heating on. Would this young man be able to control his large frame, Joan wondered, as Rosalie Williams told him that he could stand up and do some dancing. No not really, but he tried and he didn't chuck the course. First thing each morning, there he was and, for that matter, there he stayed, because he joined Theatre Workshop.

He had to act. Everybody had to, but he wasn't very good at it. Clear speaking and communication were not his strong points. David Scase was better at that. If anything, this young man was quite hard to understand. He wore a beard and through it came a woffle-woffle sound. Nobody could penetrate it except for Gerry. It was something to do with their mutual interest in the lighting board. As this ex-Fleet Air Arm lieutenant had trained as a chemist, he knew nothing about lighting compared to Gerry, but that is where his talent began to emerge.

His name was John Bury. After he mentioned his nickname, 'Camel', that he'd been given at school because there were three Johns, nobody called him John. From thereon in, he was Camel. Why he was called that in the first place, nobody seemed to know. Joan's sister, Betty, said it was because he kept getting the hump which made everyone laugh, except for Joan who was rather annoyed.

Talking with Camel, Gerry, who had a strong voice, would pick up the impenetrable woffle-woffle sound. It was a bond, as they became the firmest of friends. Joan, seeing something she couldn't be part of, would tease Gerry by imitating the two together. It didn't make any difference because, at every mention of Camel's name, Gerry's eyes would go soft. Joan would tease Gerry about that as well.

Alf Smith, the company's first electrician, didn't stay and, in time, Camel took over lighting. He was particularly happy working with *Johnny Noble*'s black background. The pure nothing it provided was perfect for making the company's few lights do exactly what he wanted them to. Design, for which he would become famous, was yet to come.

Ormesby Hall's lack of pressure led to a delirious evening which was Joan's happiest memory of the place. Bill Davidson, having been the duty *plongeur*, which meant that he'd just done the washing up, Joan preferring the Zola-esque French word, returned to the assembled actors pretending to be a film director. With a biscuit tin as a camera, he shouted directions and got everybody to act in his gangster movie. It went all over the house and lasted for hours. Pure invention, no inhibitions, no critics, it was exactly what suited Joan. No critics? Two ladies, total strangers, appeared during this improvisation. Bill, switching from gangster movie to science fiction – the film for the next night – threatened them with his killer ray gun. It was only a torch but the two ladies were not the kind to understand. They ran for it; they were from the Arts Council.

While the company was at Ormesby Hall having a good time but not actually performing, Mike Thompson, he of the 'piddling' dates, achieved one good thing: an invitation to perform *Uranium 235* in Hanwell. It didn't sound much but it was Theatre Workshop's first date down south. Howard saw it as an opportunity to invite Labour MPs, Labour being in goverment at the time. Perhaps they would embarrass the Arts Council into support. Joan, who had no reason to believe that Labour was any more helpful than the Tories, didn't particularly want to go. She was keen not to interrupt rehearsals for Jimmie's new version of *Lysistrata*, *Operation Olive Branch*. It was a valid argument – Joan always had a valid argument – but anyone who knew her, knew that London equalled pressure and judgment which she feared. They went.

Labour MPs turned up all right: Nye Bevan, Tom Driberg, Benn Levy, Ian Mikardo and Alf Robens among them and, as a result, Joan, Gerry and Howard were invited to the House of Commons for lunch. Everyone appeared to be delighted. Howard rang Michael Macowan. They were not delighted, he told Howard, and not a penny was forthcoming.

Only one of the MPs didn't leave things as they were: Tom Driberg. He was fascinated by Theatre Workshop. As he was also a well-known journalist, it was suggested that, before *Operation Olive Branch* went out on the road, he should come up and see it at Ormesby, and he agreed.

The company was back there in the middle of rehearsals when, out of the blue, appeared two quite unfamiliar figures. Where was James Miller? The two figures were plain clothes policemen.

Rumour had it that they were after the wrong James Miller or even that someone had shopped him, but either way, the game was up. Jimmie was arrested for desertion. Fallout made it worse. Though Jimmie and Joan were no longer together, they were still married, while the woman he was with, Jean Newlove, was obviously not his wife. Inside the company, it couldn't have been more ordinary. Looked at from outside, in late Forties England, it was messy.

Even inside the company, there was a problem. Many didn't know about Jimmie's wartime jaunt and Joan, sounding calm and reasonable but not feeling it, had to tell them. She had to tell Colonel Pennyman too. As it happened, his reaction was not at all judgmental. That was a relief.

It wasn't for long, though. *Operation Olive Branch* was about to open and Jimmie was playing the leading part. A young man, not long in the company and not long out of the forces, had to take over. Ben Ellis was his name and just before the first performance, he became psychotic. While serving in the army, he had been left for dead under a pile of bodies and the effect was lingering. At that moment, Tom Driberg appeared.

Two cracking good stories confronted him but he kept quiet, tough for him, the hardened journalist. Instead, for some days, he watched Ben perform in the evening – the first night was thrilling – and check into hospital after the performance. Gradually he got better, if less exciting. At all times, Gerry remained attentive and gentle, which Ben acknowledged when writing to Joan some months later. By then, he was back to normal, complaining, like the others, about Mike Thompson's desperate bookings.

Tom Driberg used to say that what you don't want to get into the newspapers is called news; what you do is called publicity. For *Reynolds News*, known as the voice of the Labour Party, he wrote:

> I have never come across any community, religious or political, or any group of stage people, so free as they are from personal pettiness. They are completely and unselfishly single-minded. In fact, they illustrated for me the meaning of the Gospel text, 'If thine eye be single, thy whole body shall be full of light'. *[Matthew 6.22]*

From that moment onwards, while longing for scandal to write about and sometimes not being able to resist, he remained onside. It helped that he fancied Gerry.

So there, despite everything, was *Operation Olive Branch* up and running, when news came that Freddie Piffard had organised a tour of West Germany. Freddie Piffard was a friend of David Scase – they'd met at the BBC – and now he was on the committee that chose entertainment for the British forces abroad. Such a fan of Theatre Workshop, he was already on its board of directors – yes, it did have one; Hugh MacDiarmid was on it too – and now he had come good. Of course the company would go but it was a wrench because Jimmie was still in prison. Joan, though Mrs Miller only in name, felt that she had to stay.

CHAPTER TEN

GERMANY SHOWS UP THE CRACKS

With Joan and her company separated, communication had to be by letter. Most of them were from Gerry to Joan. His description of the company's behaviour in Germany backs what Tom Driberg wrote. While young British soldiers strutted around, triumphant, Theatre Workshop wanted to learn. Many British people used their cigarette rations for tips and favours. Theatre Workshop gave their cigarettes away. Germans, interested in theatre, thought it was the nicest company they had ever met.

However, behind this united front of good manners, there was unhappiness. Travelling in Germany was informative but the tour was not a success: most of the soldiers were in no mood for *Uranium 235*. Audiences, along the way, dwindled and those that did appear could be tough. Gerry, playing the part of Energy, strong and handsome but with few clothes on, had to suffer cracks about 'poofs'. For David Scase it was:

> David: You can't kill us.
>
> Voice from audience: I could.
>
> David: Can you give me something . . .
>
> Voice from audience: Yes, potassium cyanide.
>
> Big Boss: In a few minutes the audience will leave the theatre.
>
> Voice from audience: We're going now.

It made the actors think. Some decided that, when they got home, they'd leave. Others wanted re-organisation, Gerry, chief among the latter:

> I think that the only possible factor which will stop us being a great popular theatre within the next ten years is Jimmie. I come more and

73

more to the conclusion that his overall influence is directly opposed to the creation of the sort of theatre that you and most of us want. And soon you will have to realise it or another five years of your life will have been wasted.

Even Freddie Piffard, who had set the tour up, wrote, 'Why talk of a popular theatre and play Jimmie?'

From the other side, Joan had Jimmie writing to her saying: 'Rosalie and Kristin are limited' and then of Rosalie, alone – this, after their long affair – 'Replace Rosalie with Billie Whitelaw.' Billie Whitelaw, whom Joan knew from radio, had done a thrilling audition but her mother wasn't having it. Her daughter could earn better money carrying on in radio. Jimmie didn't stop. He was writing a play:

> I want it to be an effective answer to the defeatist poison of the Koestlers and their tribe, the fashionable disillusionment with the Soviet Union. They turned tail and now stand at the very head of the forces of reaction. When things were bad and the poor were downtrodden, it was all right to speak up for them but not now that action has been taken. Now people are frightened of the working class. We see the same in David, Rosalie, Mavis [Clavering], Ruth and the rest of the riff-raff that litter the road to a living theatre art. They are like certain whores who imagine that a disease in themselves can be cured by passing it on.

The tone of this letter suggests that isolation had stoked up bad temper, particularly the attack on members of the company. It's a rant from inside a bubble, with no sense that some of the others were fed up with his work. Facing soldiers barracking his play would have left him little time for those thoughts.

His attitude to Russia and communism and the unmentioned but very present Stalin seems to put him even more out of step with the others but that was not entirely the case. He, Joan and Gerry had signed up, in their minds, to an idea that was established before the war. Joe Stalin was a good thing. None of them, not just Jimmie, would, or even could, bear to hear anyone say anything against him and that would continue long after they were confronted with his atrocities. Knock Stalin and you were defending capitalism. Holding on to the idea of communism and separating it from Stalin didn't seem possible for them, the two together were so ingrained.

Of course, holding strong beliefs is not enough when it comes to writing a play. Joan had already sent one of Jimmie's, *Blitz Song*, to Bernard Shaw, only to have it returned with the comment: 'Powerful but depressing.' It was therefore likely, with Gerry's and Freddie Piffard's opinion of Jimmie's writing on her mind, that she was not looking forward to this new play as enthusiastically as its author was. Nor was it only Gerry's and Freddie's opinion. Somewhere along the line, Michael Macowan had managed to get himself to one of Theatre Workshop's shows and declared it 'Boring.' 'What would he know?' Joan might have argued but once a remark is made, even by someone you despise, it nags. Could there have been some truth in what Macowan had said?

Gerry picked at the company too:

> Let's be small and beautiful instead of, as now, smothered in shifting sand. If you concentrated your efforts on a few people, had David doing nothing but sound, Camel nothing but lights, got rid of everybody who showed no promise, we'd crash the big time much sooner . . . I only hope Scrooge [Jimmie] stays in gaol long enough for you to decide without him. Otherwise we will have a new influx of *demi-vierges* stirred to attempt creativity after a few nights' clumsy love with a red-bearded playwright.

One thing Jimmie and Gerry had in common was that, to sort out problems, they both turned to Joan. You couldn't blame them because at work she was so strong. For the rest, her forthright manner made people think she was strong. Inside, she frequently didn't feel it at all. Right then, she was in a position that was uncomfortable, but it was hers. Letters demanding action were being fired at her from opposing forces, while in England she had to hold immediate auditions to make up for the threatened loss of half the company, while simultaneously rustling up a psychiatrist, preferably with a German accent, to get Jimmie out of gaol. The latter, she achieved, including the German accent, so at least she was genuinely making herself useful. What she wasn't doing was facing that tour. Gerry, aware of Joan's ability to galvanize the company and aware also of his weakness when faced with a pretty girl, begged her repeatedly to join them in Germany but she didn't.

Still, one good thing came out of this tour and it foretold the company's reception over the next few years. Germans who saw the show not only liked it but also said that the English didn't understand it. Gerry, putting it more bluntly, wrote to Joan that the British troops were behaving like Nazis. The point was, Europe, right from the start, took to Theatre Workshop in a way that the UK didn't.

What emerges from the letters is also a prediction that came true. Gerry's demands made Joan chide her young lover for being such a hothead, but most of what he asked for happened. However, it was not Joan who made it happen.

On its return from Germany, the company could put together only a handful of dates. One was back in London, this time at the Rudolf Steiner Theatre near Regent's Park, but the national critics stayed away. One critic who did turn up, admired what he saw and admonished the others for their no-shows. This was Robert Muller, a German Jewish refugee, who would go on to write plays for television, marry Billie Whitelaw and become the theatre critic of the *Daily Mail*.

A few weeks later, the company, almost in desperation, mounted *Professor Mamlock* by Friedrich Wolf, whom they had met in Germany. Desperation because, though it wasn't a bad play, with its clashes between Nazis and communists, fascists and Liberals, Germans and Jews, it didn't suit Theatre Workshop. It required naturalism and heavyweight actors. They couldn't do the one and they didn't have the other. Joan knew it and so did Ossia Trilling, critic and long-time supporter of Theatre

Workshop. He went to see it at the Dolphin Theatre in Brighton. It wasn't Joan's non-naturalistic production – two opposing slopes, no walls – that he objected to. That was the best part, even if not Brighton's cup of tea. It was the lack of talent in the company and plain old inaudibility that was bothering him. This was a reminder of Jo Hodgkinson's reservations and, closer to home, Gerry's, though he was in it. 1947 was winding down and so, it appeared, was Theatre Workshop. It could look forward to absolutely nothing. If ever there was a point when there seemed nothing else for it but to chuck in the towel, this was it.

At that time, the Arts Council was only interested in financing companies that had a base. Nobody at Theatre Workshop has said they were aware of this but was it simply a coincidence that one member of the company announced that if it didn't find a base, and soon, Ormesby Hall being too small, it would die? That member instinctively researching and pushing to find places for the company to go, was Gerry. What he knew for sure, because it was announced at that very time, was that local councils were empowered to levy sixpence on everyone's rates to help in the establishment or the maintenance of theatres. No council was actually doing this but they could have. So, even though the company disbanded, the drive to start up again had some fuel. It helped too that most remained in Manchester, where they found temporary work.

Joan, still the company's one old pro, wrote another *Visit to...* for the BBC. Jimmie, out of gaol and still convinced he was the voice of Theatre Workshop, went to Oak Cottage to carry on writing. Gerry went anywhere that had half a chance of becoming a base. Most places were dispiriting but he had hopes for the David Lewis Centre in Liverpool. In fact he concentrated all his efforts on it.

Having had notepaper printed with Joan's name on it – his faith in her put into practice but also the start of trouble, the company having been anonymous – Gerry set to work. While Jimmie wrote and Joan went for rambles – 'Why did he bother with us?' asked Joan – he drummed up letters of support from famous fans of Theatre Workshop, got anyone who was anyone in Liverpool onside and explained to the Board, very patiently, what a wonderful influence Theatre Workshop would be on Liverpool. Not only would it mount plays but it would teach theatre, and get famous people in the arts world to come and talk.

This makes it sound like the David Lewis Centre was sitting there doing nothing. It wasn't. It was packed with activities, not necessarily interesting ones, but well established. Going to it would mean having to fit in. It would also mean putting down ten thousand pounds in advance.

Although Mike Thompson had left and Gerry had assumed the role of General Manager, Gerry was still regarded as a junior. He had to put his idea first to Jimmie and then to a meeting attended by Howard, Kristin, Camel and his new wife Maggie, Jimmie and Jean Newlove. Jimmie spotted the flaws in Gerry's plan at once. Theatre Workshop had never fitted in and was not going to start. This was in spite of the company not doing anything at all at the time. Where was the ten thousand pounds going to come from? The company already had enough debts. Those mooted activities would weaken the central aim of Theatre Workshop: getting its voice out into the world through plays.

As it happened, Gerry had made a list of plays. It included *The Playboy of the Western World*, *Bartholomew Fair* and *Blood Wedding*; what a national theatre might put on, really. How long would there be to rehearse each one, though? Two weeks, to start with. Things were looking bleaker for Gerry by the moment. Finally, why was there nothing by Jimmie? After all, his new play was nearly finished.

This was really awkward. It was too early for Gerry to express his opinion, even less appropriate to back it up with Freddie Piffard's letter. With Joan, clearly uncertain, he could be putting himself out on a limb, and one he couldn't get back from. A confrontation was just about avoided because the excitement of the others at the thought of a new play brought the meeting to an end.

However the two problems raised at the meeting remained: whether to go to the David Lewis Centre, and the choice of plays. As to the first, that was way up in the air. As to the second, there was, on the one hand, a play that hadn't been read. On the other, there was Gerry's list which, because he was pleasing Joan, sounded borrowed. Were they what he, Gerry, wanted to do, never mind anyone else. Another play on that list was a new *Macbeth* to be commissioned from Hugh MacDiarmid. Joan, provoked by the sight of Michael Redgrave in a plaid at the Aldwych Theatre, had been researching the true story and thought it would be less insular than the Shakespeare. A leaning towards Scotland, headed by Jimmie and MacDiarmid, was always in the company, and Joan was leaning with it. However, it made Gerry's position even more complicated. He'd put the play on the list but did he believe in it? Joan's mind at work was exciting – she wanted to do Strindberg's *The Ghost Sonata* as well – but could you say that either that, or the new *Macbeth*, or the rest of the list jumped out as likely to be popular? Gerry would have to bide his time and learn as he went along.

The first problem was solved almost at once. Nobody had to worry about Theatre Workshop being compromised by the David Lewis Centre because it turned Gerry's proposal down. It didn't need a theatre company. Problem number two was a fight that was just beginning.

Joan may have liked the plays on Gerry's list but she didn't direct one of them. The prospect of doing Jimmie's play, which he soon finished, was exciting the others too much. There was a reading. David Scase and Rosalie Williams, Jimmie's 'riff-raff that littered the way to a living theatre art', as he had previously described them, loved it and so did Jean Newlove. Their reaction was understandable because Jimmie wrote finely. In this case, it was verse and it sounded terrific, so vigorous and rich. But what did it mean, this play? Probing was needed but the one British director Joan had time for, Tyrone Guthrie, to whom she sent it, wrote back that he couldn't be bothered and was content to say he hadn't a clue.

Joan read it. To her, it seemed that Jimmie, ostensibly talking about conflicts in the world, was actually talking about conflicts with his girlfriends. Gerry's reaction was more instinctive. He had a theory that would last him a lifetime. There are popular writers and there are anti-popular writers. Anti-popular doesn't mean you're bad. It means nobody goes to see your plays. Gerry thought Jimmie's plays were anti-popular. OK, there was a touch of the young lion versus the old lion going on. Jimmie still had power over Joan, particularly when it came to music.

For his new play, *The Other Animals*, he wanted to use Mahler's *Symphony No. 2* (Resurrection). In a letter to Joan, he wrote that Mahler was the spirit of Theatre Workshop. It shows, yet again, his interest in all sorts of music, unlike what was to come, his assumption of the high moral ground by means of folksong. Pop, for example, he would dismiss as tainted by commerce.

When it came to direction, Jimmie was sensible. He deferred to Joan. Only she could make his play work, he knew that. At first, Joan wondered why she should bother. Good or bad, there was no money and nowhere to work. Bit by bit, though, she was drawn in.

David Scase and Rosalie Wiliams, by then married, went to dinner one night at Sadhur Bahadur's new place in town. He'd moved there from his old restaurant near the university, where Gerry had eaten as a student. Sadhur loved Theatre Workshop and was happy to offer it his empty house at five pounds and five shillings a week. Given that most of the company were hanging on in dubious dives by the skin of their teeth, it was a relief to have somewhere to go. As its walls were covered with a pattern of green parrots, it became known as the Parrot House and it would bring the company together again. Gerry wished it wouldn't, and he had signed the contract.

In Germany, he'd hoped that discontent would shake out the duds. He'd hoped the same thing while the company was disbanded. Rather, it was the opposite. The duds, having nowhere else to go, came back, and there they were at the Parrot House. In a letter to Joan, he singled out Margaret Greenwood, whom he regarded as conscientious at exercise time but no more. This was awkward as Margaret Greenwood was Camel's new wife, Maggie.

The Parrot House aside, problems remained to be solved, costumes, for a start. There was no money for them. Gerry, back in the spirit of things, went out with Kristin and returned with parcels of beautiful materials, all of them obtained for nothing. How had they pulled that off? Kristin had told the manufacturers, Marshall Fabrics of Minshull Street, that the play would be touring Sweden and that their name would be in the programme. This was sort of true. One of Sweden's top impresarios loved Mahler and was looking forward to putting on a play that used his music. Gerry was still twisting and turning by suggesting other plays, but it looked as if the die was cast. Bill Davidson, who agreed with Gerry, wasn't there and would never come back. Joan was non-commital. David and Rosalie had started learning Jimmie's verse.

News came that the Library Theatre in the heart of Manchester had two weeks available in July. Howard had been pestering the Library for years. There was still no rehearsal space, though. Gerry, realising he wasn't going to win, did the sensible thing. To keep himself away from the play but remain useful, he concentrated on what he was good at. South of the town centre, in the Palatine Road, was a club that

Sephardi Jews went to. It was known as 'The Yackypack' which is what Yiddishers called Sephardis. The man who ran it knew Manny Raffles which embarrassed Gerry, but then the space it could provide, the music room, was what the company needed.

With all this effort being made around her, Joan, though not convinced by the play, was swept along to the point where simply doing some work seemed enticing. *The Other Animals*, if nothing else, offered plenty of challenges. There was the set, for instance. Camel was designing by then but that needs some explaining.

Joan was fascinated by the idea of scientists working in teams, pooling their mental resources to make a breakthrough. 'The composite mind', she called it. Maybe she didn't arrive at those exact words until after James Watson's book about the discovery of DNA, *The Double Helix*, published in 1968, but she used the idea to explain working with Camel, which is odd.

Certainly, Camel's way of working was quite unlike that of other designers and it was integral to what made Theatre Workshop different to other companies. Design was not imposed on the play. It grew around the actors as rehearsals progressed. There were no cute little models – Joan used to say: 'A little thing is not a big thing' – but full-size mock-ups, like a sketch in 3D.

The Other Animals takes place in the hero's head, so there was no argument about the set being non-naturalistic. That was absolutely how it should be. It had a tilted disc up in the air surrounded by silver rods. Even today, you will see photos of it in books about set design. It was that striking. However, throughout the years, Joan repeatedly said that all the ideas for sets were hers and that Camel merely executed them. That doesn't exactly sound like the composite mind, unless it means taking her ideas and realising them very well. About that, there was never an argument.

Gerry did not speak about Camel in the way Joan did. His admiration for Camel was unconditional.

As for *The Other Animals*, a mixture of Mahler, enthusiasm, Joan's work, and sheer relief that Theatre Workshop was back in business, swept the company through to an exciting first night. Tom Driberg brought Nye Bevan and, together, they went to a celebration at the Parrot House where Nye proved himself quite the flirt. Joan in her diary, generous on this occasion, wrote: 'Camel's cage looks very good in Library Theatre', and then: 'Jimmie's a ham. All you can see on his face is self-pity'. Of the play, she wrote that it kidded a lot of people but was cliché with good padding. Between the moment when the company had good reason to think its days were over and this Library first night, seven months had elapsed.

Many years later in the 1990s, Joan went to Australia where she was invited on to the *Margaret Throsby Show*, the equivalent of *Desert Island Discs*. One of her choices was Mahler's Resurrection Symphony. Back in Manchester, in 1948, Gerry had disappeared.

CHAPTER ELEVEN

OUT AND ABOUT IN EUROPE

T
he loss of the David Lewis Centre winded Gerry but it was from that moment on that his beliefs began to strengthen or, if you were not in his camp, harden. The first thing he did was go off and stay with his father. He'd had to get away from the company. The criticisms during that meeting had been humiliating and Joan's uncertainty hadn't helped. For a few days, son and father talked and then Manny gave Gerry money to pay off some of those debts Jimmie had been complaining of, not that Jimmie had offered any solutions.

Conflicting letters arrived. Nelson Illingworth thought Gerry's plans had been vague, pretentious and costly. Gerry, he thought, was too inexperienced at business to be doing what he was attempting. Theatre Workshop should be playing safe but that was what the Arts Council had wanted.

Bill Davidson wrote that putting on a one-off production of Jimmie's unknown play was Theatre Workshop at its maddest, music to Gerry's ears until he read on. Bill was off to Dundee Rep and, by the way, he'd seen a play called *The Gorbals Story* at Glasgow Unity Theatre which he'd thought was excellent. Glasgow Unity may have had links with the Communist Party, but Joan despised it. She thought it was amateurish and that she could do better. Had the Party not been demanding naturalism since the late 1930s but had not Joan and Jimmie rejected it?

Bill then read Jimmie's play and wrote him a letter. Although he, like Guthrie, couldn't work out the meaning, he thought it was good.

It was while these half-baked opinions were whirling around and *The Other Animals* had, to Gerry's annoyance, gone ahead that he disappeared. For a start, his own thinking needed sharpening. The David Lewis plan had indeed been vague. Here, a glance into the future is worthwhile. The David Lewis plan was not dissimilar to Joan's 1961 dream, the Fun Palace. Vagueness didn't help there either. Gerry was learning that lesson, only thirteen years earlier. His immediate aim was to keep Theatre Workshop alive by going off on his own to find it tours and eventually a base. He would be doing something important, far away from *The Other Animals*.

London was his first stop. He went to talk to Tom Driberg. Despite the inevitable price he had to pay, that of fighting off Tom's advances, he did enjoy a talk with him. Apart from Joan, there was no one in the company he liked talking to that much. They spoke about Czechoslovakia. After the war, there had been a coalition government which included the Communist Party but, at the start of 1948, the Communist Party had taken over altogether and, as part of a move to spread art across the country, was inviting artists from elsewhere to come and liven things up; contrast and compare, so to speak. Tom knew about this but was doubtful. Gerry merely saw an opportunity. Visas usually took weeks to obtain. He got one in minutes. Being young, good looking and in love with Joan helped. With 30 quid nicked from the kitty in Manchester, he went to Victoria station and caught the boat train to Paris.

Nobody in the company moved in the kind of circles where you had a contact in Paris, except Gerry. A family friend, David Rothman, put him up while he worked on the next step. He needed a military permit to travel through Germany, another three-week job. He didn't have it at midday but he did have it by the evening, and off he set for Prague.

When he arrived it was at the start of a sunny weekend in July, which was frustrating. Gerry loved holidays – he was trying to teach Joan the importance of them – but there, in Prague, with everyone else on holiday, he wasn't. On the Saturday morning, he went to the Ministry of Information. At least it wasn't shut. However, except for a Madame Hortova, everyone had gone away for the weekend. Her English was not good but it was good enough to say that all the people he needed to talk to had left, not just for the weekend but for the summer. He would have to come back in the autumn. 'Gerry gets into scrapes,' Rosalie Williams had said. For a moment his trip across Europe must have seemed like folly but then Madame Hortova went on: perhaps it would be worth Gerry coming back on Monday to see the Minister himself.

The rest of Saturday and the whole of Sunday spread out before Gerry with nothing to do. Instead of kicking his heels, he went to the Poets, Essayists, Novelists Centre (PEN) and there he found an ally in Jirina Lumovà, PEN's secretary. She introduced him to theatre people, took him round Prague and told him to write an article about Theatre Workshop that she would translate and circulate. He wrote it overnight, so that the next morning he and Jirina could carry on sightseeing. He found Prague even more beautiful than he expected. That evening Jirina made the translation and had it delivered to the newspapers.

On Monday morning the Minister of Information, Loewenbach, told Gerry that an autumn tour was out of the question. Disagreeable though he was, he took Gerry to lunch. Sitting at the next table was a leading theatre critic. It was only after an hour that Loewenbach introduced Gerry to him. In spite of the language problem, Gerry's description of Theatre Workshop excited him. Alec Clunes, in a production from the Arts Theatre in London, had not. Theatre Workshop had to be better. What's more, four important theatre directors were returning to Prague the next day. It was worth Gerry staying on, and, indeed it was. By Tuesday night, a whole tour was booked and somehow, during that day, he had obtained a visa to travel through Poland. He needed that because he had to get to Stockholm.

Poland would fascinate Gerry in a few months' time but, on that Wednesday, all he saw from the train window was devastation. By Thursday, he was on a boat heading for the southernmost point of Sweden, Trelleborg.

Sweden was not quite such a shot in the dark as Czechoslovakia. Straight after the tour of West Germany, Kristin Lind had returned home and prepared the ground. Definite interest was there and even the money for the fares. The country itself was a shock. As Sweden had been neutral during the war, not only was there was no devastation, there was no shortage of food in the shops. Gerry took an immediate dislike to it. Food there may have been but it was cripplingly expensive, as was the accommodation, while the people, so unlike those of Czechoslovakia, were discourteous. On top of that, it was the weekend again. In a letter to Joan, he begged her not to mention any of this to the company. The trouble was, he'd mentioned it to Joan and, when an opinion came from someone she liked, she was impressionable.

Despite Gerry, more organised this time, having informed the tour organiser, Emwall, of his arrival, Emwall was not there. He was there the next day but it still annoyed Gerry, who thought he was being treated like a tourist. It was only after four more days of heat, frustration and having to wash up in a restaurant that he was able to get away to England. The tour was confirmed, though.

When it came to the tour itself, Czechoslovakia and Sweden, one straight after the other, Gerry's short experience of those countries, proved, over the weeks, to be the same for the company.

Joan was nervous at first. In her head was prime minister Neville Chamberlain talking in 1938 about: 'a quarrel in a faraway country between people of whom we know nothing.' With those words, he had betrayed Czechoslovakia and it could have been a bitter memory. She need not have worried. The welcome was immediate and generous and, as the company moved around the different parts of Czechoslovakia, that is the way it stayed. If anything the huge number of dumpling-laden meals, despite rationing, plus the meetings and the greetings, were too much. The company wanted more time to itself to make sure the shows were in good shape each night.

Jimmie became the old Jimmie and made up songs to sing on the bus, much to Joan's delight. The two female interpreters took a fancy to Gerry, and then an old colleague of Joan's from pre-war radio days appeared, Vladimir Tosek. When Vladimir had failed to deliver a script about Christmas in Prague, Joan, never having been there, had written it instead, shown it to the BBC censors and got Vladimir to read it at the last minute. Gerry was convinced that Joan and Vladimir were having an affair or pretended he was convinced: 'What a bitch you are to make me so mad with jealousy.' Similarly Joan was convinced that Gerry was having flings with the two interpreters: 'You don't expect me to believe that you didn't taste Miss Bedworthy's charms,' and again that could have been pretence too. A sort of fun sulking was going on.

It wasn't fun, though, when Gerry discovered that Joan had brought *The Other Animals*. He was hoping it would be left behind. In the meantime, his own work was having good effect. His translated article had not only been printed in newspapers, it had aroused the interest of readers. How does Theatre Workshop go about things, they wanted to know.

When Joan set out for the first theatre, she was full of idealism. It was a dream of hers that communists took art seriously. The running of the building would be tip-top and the productions exciting. What she found backstage were several stagehands, wearing Communist Party badges, loafing around doing nothing but clogging up the wings. Snobbishly, if anything, they watched as the company members did everything themselves. Communists were as capable of slacking as anyone else, Joan was to discover. One evening, when the company was not performing, it was taken to see a show. What it saw was long, slow, boring, heavy and, as it turned out, unrecognisable. It was *Twelfth Night* but then it was to counteract this stodginess that the Czech government had invited in companies from other countries. After years under Nazism, it was time to look outwards.

The Other Animals opened and Gerry was vindicated. Jimmie thinking about his girlfriends but talking about concentration camps, interwoven with Mahler, annoyed the critics. The same thing happened in England when Noël Coward wrote *Post Mortem*, a play set in the First World War. What did either of these authors know about their subjects? They weren't there. In Jimmie's case, the Czechs knew about concentration camps only too well. Joan wondered if she'd made a bad mistake. The next night, the double bill, *Johnny Noble* and *The Flying Doctor*, put things into a brighter light. The appeal of the songs and the action was immediate and the company went on to a tour, happy if perhaps overburdened by functions, that lasted over five weeks, playing sometimes in big theatres and to large houses. If it wasn't for all Czech currency having to be spent or left in Czechoslovakia, it would have made good money. Joan fell for the Czechs and promised herself that when she got home she would do a new *Schweik* using her first-hand experience.

Six days ahead of the company's departure, Gerry, revelling as he was in the attention of the interpreters, tore himself away. He had to double-check Stockholm. This time, though, he did not have to hurry through Poland. He stopped off, went to the theatre and liked what he saw. It stayed in his mind. This was an odd time for him. He was uncomfortable, short of money, so lonely he wished he could be back in *Johnny Noble*, and yet he was doing what he wanted although, once again, he was away from the company. His energy and determination, as always, came from Joan, and a little bit from Benzedrine. Many years later Joan found a prescription that he had kept. She thought it was the start of him losing his health for Theatre Workshop's sake and as Theatre Workshop, in his eyes, was Joan, she thought he had done it for her.

When he arrived in Sweden, Kristin Lind was already there. With her knowledge, she was going to act as the hostess for that part of the tour. As Gerry was not in any of the shows and didn't know Sweden, his function there lasted only a few days. If he was going to keep making himself useful – there were no dates for the company's return – he had to get back to England as soon as possible. If he had budgeted correctly he could have stayed for a couple of days more and so overlapped with

Joan. It wasn't to be. His figures had come from Kristin and she had forgotten the last leg of the journey. 'She certainly is a cretin,' he wrote. In years to come, Joan would talk only of Kristin's beauty and resourcefulness. She had put a golden glow round her. It was not there during this tour in 1948.

It was hardly likely to be. Although Sweden was to give Theatre Workshop and Joan in particular some of the best reviews of their lives, Joan, either picking up on Gerry's letter or all by herself, took violently against the country, the people and the tour. 'I have never seen such terrible architecture, such ugly people, such bad taste in clothes.'

The hospitality was not nearly so generous as it had been in Czechoslovakia. There were plenty of the usual unwanted functions – that was the one similarity between the two countries – but there were gaps in between when the few kronor David Scase, the treasurer, doled out did not go far, certainly not as far as afters. That was Joan's word for dessert or pudding, which she needed to take away the taste of the main course. Once, at a station café, she ordered 'the cheapest dish, boiled mutton which everyone took with milk. I ate the revolting food but all afternoon I was as sick as a dog. I cannot bear the sight of milk and only drink black coffee now.' Given that Joan never liked mutton stew or milk, no matter where she was, she really was in the wrong country. The others, who regarded milk at the very least as nourishing, did not complain.

Joan did not stop complaining. When she wasn't eating food she didn't like, she was fainting with hunger, and when she went to a restaurant alone to think things through, she was turned away. Restaurants did not approve of women on their own. The best place for her was a fisherman's caff where she ate what appeared on the menu as 'bifsteak'. She felt better after that.

Milk and her dislike of it did not go away. She had to travel overnight on a train with bunks:

> In the dim light, I saw three huge female arses, no faces or arms attached to them apparently . . . The air burnt me so I took off nearly all my clothes to try to sleep but the arse near me quivered. It was huge in front of my eyes, looming up bigger than the biggest hill I've seen in Sweden and, as it quivered, a long drawn-out, wet, fluttering fart was emitted, redolent of years of milk and grease.

Sometimes the company played to good houses in big theatres. Sometimes it was well received, but again there were gaps. Performances were cancelled. Money was lost. 'The places we have played have been fantastically bad. We wouldn't have looked at them in England. This tour could have paid and brought us in money.' Joan was going off Kristin: 'Kristin is hopeless, works hard but is quite unable to comprehend a simple objective first. It's a form of neurosis and peculiar egotism.' A particular niggle was the translation of the reviews. Gerry needed them badly for publicity in England but Kristin somehow couldn't get around to it and when she did, according to Joan, she mistranslated them. Providing somebody with exactly what they want does mean suppressing your own ego, not that Joan was very good at that either, but she was the one with the talent.

Sweden sent Joan into a fugue. Twice, either through oversleeping or just sitting in a café for too long, she missed trains that were to take the company to its next destination. It was as if, for a while, she stepped out of life and vanished. Actually, it wasn't just in Sweden. At any time in her life, you could arrange to meet her at a certain spot but you couldn't see her because, though she was under your nose, she was not looking out for you. She was somewhere else, usually lost in a book. For the company, this was exasperating. It didn't know about fugues. It just thought Joan didn't care. At least she was aware enough of that to feel guilty. It wouldn't have been any good if they'd had a go at her, though. She would have thought they were being utterly unreasonable.

Towards the end of the tour, Joan, becoming a little more generous in her opinion of Kristin, allowed herself the thought that she had pulled off quite a coup but added that she probably didn't do so well because she didn't look like a professional tour organiser.

Howard Goorney, on the other hand, thought that Kristin had done a superb job and, knowing Gerry shared Joan's opinion of her, was preparing to fall out with him when he got home. It didn't happen. When the tour finished, Kristin stayed in Sweden, annoying for Joan who'd had no notice, but Kristin was to have her uses in years to come. Poland, where Gerry wanted to settle with Joan, would not happen and, more sadly, neither would Czechoslovakia. Joan and Gerry were keen to go back there, so much so that Joan was already writing to Ota Ornest, head of Art for the People, while she was in Sweden, but her only answer was silence. At first she blamed herself. *The Other Animals* must have done it. 'I curse the day I decided to make do on settling for that play.' Later, news came through that the parting of the clouds in 1948 which allowed Theatre Workshop to bask in Czech sunshine was only brief. The clouds came back together again.

Joan may have written of Sweden: 'I have never known a country where there are so many artists and so little art', and, shortly before she left, 'I still hate Sweden!!! Christ, another four hours to Göteborg and the bloody show tonight and I have a head like a cinder track with ball bearings on it.' But it would be Sweden the company returned to.

During this cursing of Sweden's ungracious, stingy people and the ups and downs of the tour, which the rest of the company was not nearly so troubled by, Joan did one thing that was nothing to do with the company and everything to do with her as a human being. It went back to those limbo days after RADA and even to her childhood. She set off in search of Sonja Mortensen.

Sonja was the girl alongside whom Joan had drawn and painted and with whom she'd gone to Paris the second time. She had been encouraging and Joan hadn't forgotten. A six-hour train journey northwards took her to Ljusdal where she found Sonja living in a farmhouse. It didn't belong to her. The farmer tolerated her, or rather he was given money to keep an eye on her. She actually came from a rich family who thought she was mad and that this was the best they could do for her. Joan was appalled. It was freezing there and Sonja was so thin and had so little, and didn't seem mad at all. If only she could have some paints and brushes, but by then it was too late for Joan to buy them for her. The farm was out in the middle of nowhere. 'This is the final symbol of the Swedish bourgeois attitude,' she wrote to Gerry, 'cruelty and grossness.' Sonja herself didn't seem that bothered. Smilingly, she accepted the life she had been given. It moved Joan even more when, back in the village, people twigged who she was simply because Sonja never stopped talking about her.

The Mortensen family was annoyed by Joan's description of this scene which she put on paper in the 1990s. Sonja was perfectly well looked after, they insisted. She lacked for nothing. Joan did not retract. Whatever the accuracy of the depiction, in Sonja, she saw, as she saw in her half-sister, Betty, that withdrawn child who found so much of life too painful to bear, the child she thought she too could have been when describing herself as autistic. The difference was Joan had resilience. Sometimes she wrote letters to friends warning them of what appeared to be her imminent suicide. These friends, barely able to speak with fear, would ring her, only to discover that she was sitting in the front of the television happily eating bangers and mash. All her misery had gone into the letter.

Joan's attitude to Sweden so dominated her thoughts while she was there that the company and the performances took second place. If it wasn't that, it was what Gerry was up to in England.

CHAPTER TWELVE

Keeping the Home Fires Burning

Gerry started to write Joan letters even before he reached Sweden. Knowing that she would be setting sail for Trelleborg from Odraport on the Polish-German border, he left a note at the buffet there. It was stuck in the mirror behind the bar and, a few days later, one of the actors saw it and gave it to her.

By then, Gerry, his task in Sweden over, brimming with frustration at not seeing Joan, was sailing third class from Gothenberg to Tilbury. Sitting in first class, the only place with a flat surface, he wrote again, using M/S Saga paper, Saga being the name of the ship. While he was travelling, he wrote, he was in a limbo, whereas his destination held nothing good for him. 'Everything is grey.' He wanted an England of 'belief and revolution.'

Joan, he continued to insist, had definitely been having an affair with Vladimir Tosek and so he, Gerry, evidently, was de trop. When he wasn't acting the wronged lover, a performance Joan, later, took great pleasure in mocking, he made sensible suggestions about what she should do when she, in turn, sailed on the M/S Saga in a month's time, that is, where to put her luggage, where to sit, where to go to in order to disembark the first. At the same time, he fretted about her getting enough to eat and keeping warm. This he did throughout his life and, though it was a constant subject for teasing, it was absolutely what she wanted, as were the practical tips, 'Cheapest cigarettes Robin Hood, also Blue Master.'

Gerry had a point. Joan was hopeless at looking after herself and was often cold and hungry. You can add chesty coughs, toothache, back ache and period pains to her troubles. She seemed to suffer from one or the other all the time. Underneath, though, she was a survivor and that was the difference between her and Gerry. He was strong, but that's not the same thing.

Affairs were different. When Joan had the few she had, Gerry would be cross and sulky. When Gerry had them, chiefly as a holiday from Joan – she being, as she well knew, extremely demanding – then she would be devastated.

What was happening in Gerry's letters and the ones he would receive from Joan during the Swedish tour, what with Czech Beatrice fancying him, and Swedish Torsten madly in love with her, was something else. Given that it amused both of them to invent torrid affairs for members of the company, it might be safe to assume the same thing was going on here, i.e. not much, if anything at all. It was a way of stirring up long-distance desire.

What made their agony more exquisite was the gap between letters. Each thought, or at least wrote, that the other no longer loved them because they had heard nothing for ages. The truth was not so dramatic. Letters simply took five days to arrive, which, in Europe, was rather a long time. Still, the separation, both spiritually and physically, did make them, occasionally, lose heart for real.

All the letters were long, as sometimes the writing of them was just for writing's sake. While the pen moved across the paper, there was a connection. Lifting the pen broke the connection, and that was unbearable. Their positions were different, though. During the four weeks of the tour, Joan was doing a pre-arranged job that she only fitfully enjoyed. Gerry was improvising.

Having nowhere else to live, he was basing himself at his father's house in Higher Crumpsall, an immediate example of things really not being great for him. His brother Ralph was there, and they had little in common. If they weren't arguing about politics, Ralph would fall into a sullen silence. For Gerry, it was like being with Jimmie and when he wrote about this to Joan he hoped, in turn, that she didn't have to spend too much time in the company of Jimmie and his Jean. Joan begged him not to hate Jimmie and to get on with him as a comrade.

There was more from Joan along the lines of setting personal feelings aside for the sake of the cause. As there was no person less capable of setting personal feelings aside, these passages are good for a laugh, if only a rueful one.

Breaking off from his usual Manchester work, of trying to find a base for the company and a flat for Joan and himself, Gerry cadged a lift from his other brother, Eric, and came to London. He had high hopes of the People's Entertainments Society which he thought might be the equivalent of Czechoslovakia's Art for the People, if it could be stirred up. Eric installed himself at the Dorchester. Gerry, having nowhere to stay, sat in Lyon's Corner House where he wrote to Joan for as long as he could. She was not pleased. It looked like his lack of a bed for the night was her fault because he was doing this on her behalf.

Breakfast for Gerry was at the Dorchester with his brother, price six shillings and sixpence, but it was bad. He didn't think much of Eric's room either, which cost two pounds and fifteen shillings a night. Czechoslovakia had better for less.

Mr Hoskins of the People's Entertainments Society, after all that, was not available, but Gerry, despite having to go back to Manchester, didn't stop trying. He'd try anyone, even commercial managements like Howard and Wyndhams, or Jack Hylton who usually produced The Crazy Gang. To be fair, the play Bill Davidson had written about, *The Gorbals Story*, had also been put on by Jack Hylton. It went to the West End and was made into a film, so it's understandable that he was worth a shot.

Howard Goorney and Jean Newlove, on hearing of this, thought Gerry was ignoring old contacts, like Laban, and that his churlishness would lose allies. The impression Gerry gave, not by what he said but by what he did, was that he was slightly bored with these allies and wanted to find people who really had money and could really make things happen, even if they were less sympathetic.

Simultaneously, on went his dance with the Arts Council. Drama Director at the time was a character actor known for playing judges, Llewellyn Rees. Given that Gerry got the same old reaction, it could have been anybody. Either Llewellyn Rees, like Mr Hoskins, was unavailable, or Theatre Workshop had no show on for him to see.

As in the letters during the German tour, the 'Who shall we get rid of?' game carried on. Jimmie, because he'd gone off a woman in the company, chipped in by asking for her to go. Joan made a note to keep her on. In fact, during those early days what actually happened was less to do with actors being sacked than actors simply leaving. It's not that they were going for a more exciting life, merely to make a little money or start a family, a reminder of Shaw writing, in his preface to *Heartbreak House*, that theatre is a young person's game. These departing actors, even when Joan thought little of them, were usually damned as traitors, mad or mother-fixated.

Because living 'en masse' at the Parrot House had depressed Gerry, he was working extra hard to find that home for him and Joan. She needed to live in comfort and privacy, away from the company. Anything else threatened to lower the standard of work. That was his thinking, though the desire to have Joan to himself would have come into it as well. However, he was hampered in his efforts by not knowing where the base was to be. He wanted this home to be near it.

Encouragement came when he found out that All Saints, the church where he had nearly been entombed during the Blitz, was available for a change of purpose. What with Manchester Council saying that it had a plan to encourage the arts, the signs looked good. Impatient to get a reaction – without one he could do nothing – he asked for an immediate decision from the company, enclosing the cost of converting the church to a theatre. It wasn't low. Jean Newlove became worried that the need to put on plays quickly one after the other to make money would eat into choreographing time.

There was another worry. It wouldn't have been a worry for any other group but it was for Theatre Workshop. Grosvenor Square, Manchester, in the middle of which sat All Saints, was comfortably middle class. To be more precise, it was near the town centre, off Oxford Road where the BBC was, and just before you got to the university. Perfect, if you weren't trying to align yourself with the working class. Gerry would have preferred to be near a factory, but no space near a factory was forthcoming. All Saints would have to do, assuming of course he got it.

Such was the fervour of Gerry's dream, and it must have been of Joan's too, because she never commented, that both were blind to All Saints' look. Its position, surrounded by its own land, may have been excellent but the actual building, a nineteenth-century structure with a disproportionately tall and consequently daunting tower, was ugly. Still, it was early days and Joan wasn't back from Sweden yet.

Although Gerry's work while Joan was away could not have been more urgent – there was nowhere to live and nowhere to work – it was his writing about the company's aims which turned out to be more important. He had heard Aneurin Bevan patting himself on the back by saying that his suggestion of touring Greek tragedy had, contrary to expectation, worked well: 'How can anyone,' wrote Gerry, 'possibly say that English workers want tragedy in the theatre or comedy, for that matter? No one knows. A football match, yes, a circus with wild animals, yes, and singing in the pub, yes. That has to be in a popular theatre to attract a working-class audience. It could be comedy or tragedy.'

Much as he liked Czechoslovakia, that one day in Poland seemed to make an even greater impression:

> The acting I saw in Warsaw, which impressed me so much, gained its effect through the immense sparkle and life of each character. They were 100% alive, nothing of their action came from "outside" despite the stylisation [he doesn't say what this is]. Although, offstage the actors seemed fairly ordinary, onstage they had tremendous personality. There was no holding back at all, and so, in the audience, you couldn't help going along with them.

> We don't want naturalistic acting but there is no excuse for indulging in bad 19th-century ham. Phoney emotion, vocal pyrotechnics could be admired – by anyone given that way – but can never have an audience. Like all forms of "cleverness" it precludes the audience from joining in and taking part emotionally: and that is what the job of acting is – to create an intense participation between all factors of a production – this includes the audience. That is why you are so right when you say we must have "humanity" in our work. Cleverness is sufficient for an audience of blasé socialites and would-be-blasé and petty [sic] bourgeois types, but they are the only audience it will attract.

> The job of a theatre is to play to an audience, and unless the audience can feel the warmth and love of life underlying each production, we will never have an audience that I, for one, want to play to.

> Unless you are prepared to exercise as critical an appreciation of the script as you apply to every other aspect of a production, I feel your own great creative gifts will always go awry.

So there was Gerry's dream, and it's not a bad description of what Theatre Workshop was to become.

At the end of the Swedish tour, disappointment at not being able to stay a few days longer revealed the gap between the company and Joan. The company had been happy. Joan had been miserable. The thought of England brought them together. What did it hold for them when they got back? It was a worry.

The first and obvious thing to do was bang the drum, have the Lady Mayoress of Manchester hold a big reception with all the press there. It didn't happen. For a start, the Lady Mayoress ignored Gerry's request, so no reception, and then what press did turn up for the conference he organised couldn't make that vital all at once splash. It was as if the company hadn't been away. There was one good thing. Joan had a place to live. Gerry had found a flat.

The All Saints project was a big one requiring architects' drawings which Gerry went ahead and commissioned. In the meantime, the company began a tour of schools around Manchester with *Twelfth Night*. It was the same as today: do a Shakespeare that's on the syllabus; that way, you keep going.

Tom Driberg tried to help the company's fortunes by writing to backbench Labour peer and former cabinet minister, William Wedgewood Benn, Tony's father. 'I'm sure he's a poet,' he answered, writing of Jimmie's play that he'd just read, 'and I think he's a dramatist,' but there were:

> ... lapses from both poetry and drama – the latter more frequent and prolonged. The Arts Council should give a hand but this is where the violent divergence of opinion begins. Three and possibly four from the Arts Council have seen performances and unanimously found them terrible! Respectable outside opinion, however, such as your own, is enthusiastic and that is why we decided to send emissaries from the Drama Panel itself the next time Theatre Workshop is performing within call.
>
> It hasn't happened yet because the company hasn't performed in England since it went to Prague. As soon as word comes . . . some of us will duly attend.

There, in black and white, was what Joan and Gerry, and probably Jimmie too, had long been suspecting. What was to be made of it? One has to bear in mind that this judgment was made by people who were used to actors enunciating without moving their lips, leading ladies pouring half cups of tea, drama students being taught how to talk on the telephone and the way Laurence Olivier delivered 'Once more unto the breach,' which nowadays sounds embarrassingly artificial. On the other hand, Joan, Gerry and Jimmie, though sticking up for themselves in the face of a hostile Establishment, were always complaining of a lack of talent.

While the company kept going either at the Library, Manchester, or on the Edinburgh Fringe before it was the Fringe, performing plays it had been doing for a long time, Gerry received a letter from Henry Elder, the architect who had been sending him the drawings for converting All Saints into a theatre. It contained a quote from the Ministry of Works. 'I regret to inform you that a building license for the construction of a new theatre in Grosvenor Square, Manchester cannot be granted at the present time in view of other high-priority work which must be fitted into the Building Programme.'

The company may have had its reservations about All Saints but Gerry, nagged by the thought that nothing would be right, until a base hove into view, had single-mindedly been working on this project for a year.

With this lack of good news, a way to cheer up the company, after several revivals, was to do something brand new. Joan wanted to do *Cock-a-Doodle Dandy* and wrote to its author, Sean O'Casey. He, having seen none of Theare Workshop's productions, decided that he didn't trust her and turned her down. This was a shame, because in 1954, she would do what she regarded as one of her best pieces of work, *Red Roses for Me*, an earlier play of his. O'Casey needed an ally in British theatre and throwing in his lot with Bernard Miles at the Mermaid, which he later did, was not the right decision. It lacked an extraordinary talent.

Joan had to make do with Irwin Shaw's *The Gentle People*, a good production but hardly Theatre Workshop, or so the company thought, as it was not experimental enough. While it was on, one of her actors, Peter Varley, a discovery of Tyrone Guthrie's, a link like GBS that she never gave up, walked out. It was most inconvenient, until she remembered a fellow who had asked to join the company not long before but had been turned away because there was no room. He'd seemed a likely lad, and so he was summoned.

This was George Cooper, a 24-year-old Yorkshireman, not long out of the army and, at that time, a draughtsman for a firm that made concrete. As soon as he arrived, Joan sent him on in a part that had no lines – *Uranium 235* was that evening's show – and then took him through Peter Varley's part in *The Gentle People*, and that was it. He was in; and throwing himself merrily into whatever chore needed doing helped too. It marked him out as the right kind of actor for Theatre Workshop. As, on Equity's books, there was another George Cooper, he became George A. Cooper.

His arrival was significant. Joan and Gerry had been complaining of a lack of talent in their different ways; it was George who began the change. For Gerry, he brought strength. For Joan, he brought invention. His only problem was that yesterday's invention would be today's, 'I can't remember.' Joan, usually keen to chuck stuff out, had to remind him of some delightful thing he'd done, yesterday, just before lunch.

It was nearly Christmas and the idea came to the company to be hard-headedly commercial and put on a Christmas show. Money would roll in, they were sure of it, but what show would do the trick? *Alice in Wonderland*. Joan adapted. John Bury, using a gauze, something he had never done before, designed, while a character called José Christopherson came up with some surprisingly elaborate costumes. Best of all, in true Theatre Workshop style, Jack Evans, a school friend of Jimmie's who'd spent the previous seventeen years in Russia, re-appeared just when he was needed. He could write music and so, he did.

They opened in Barnsley. It seems almost cruel to go on, but pennies were thrown. It was a disaster. Taking the show off, though, was not possible. A tour was already booked. One of the dates – and this slightly spoils the story of Theatre Workshop going to Stratford East for the first time in 1953 – was the Theatre Royal, Stratford. The 'East' was added later to distinguish it from Stratford-upon-Avon. Gabriel Toyne, an ex-actor Joan remembered from her Manchester Rep days, ran it. He tried to get his hands on the company's tax exemption money. As at the People's Newcastle, this was still proving a help. Gerry put him firmly in his place but it was the last good thing about that date. The backstage crew took no care over the lighting and the audience could hardly see a thing. If it had been some tawdry drag revue, it would have been all right, thought Joan, who was a good deal less vulgar than she made out.

The seventeen years Jack Evans had been in Russia had been spent studying music and earning his living by interpreting. What he told Joan and Gerry over dinner one night was the start of an education. Thinking he had gone too far, he wrote to them the next day:

> As you know I had a very good position in Moscow which took me about ten years to build up. I had my own little flat there and I thought I could settle there for many years . . . Somebody seems to have turned the Russians against me although I worked for the Russian government for many years as a translator and I have never written anti-Soviet stuff, nor do I intend to. The Russians did not refuse to give me a return visa. They just left it hanging in the air.
>
> So to this day, I feel 'up-rooted' and sometimes it gets me down.

The gist of his letter was that he utterly believed in the aims of Soviet Russia and could see that, surrounded by powerful and hostile neighbours like Germany and Japan during the war, it was not surprising that the authorities had been tightening the screws. However, fearful as Russia was of attack from America or its satellites after the war, this tightening had continued, and it was not pleasant. Distinguished Russians, known to all, would be held up while a junior soldier would scrutinise their passes for minutes on end, knowing perfectly well who the holder was.

> From all this, you can imagine that the atmosphere for stage people and musicians and other intellectuals is not very healthy. People like Shostakovich and Prokofiev don't matter two hoots. Meyerhold was picked up by the NKVD one night. The next day bandits (and there are still bandits in Moscow) broke into his house and slaughtered his wife and servant.
>
> My memory of Moscow is full of horrible stories and sometimes those horrible stories make me depressed. That is why I behave so strangely and rottenly sometimes . . . The theatre today is so bad in Moscow that I think you would die of a stroke if you saw any of these filthy rotten plays written by tired and scared little men.

It later seemed that it was Russia's fear that had made Jack a victim, and that is why he had not been allowed back. It was a case of 'rather a million thrown out than one spy left in.' Even before he had left, though, he had written to Joan saying that Russia was snobbish. 'They only want people who are a bourgeois success.' He then listed people like Bernard Shaw, HG Wells and André Gide.

Joan and Gerry's friend, Hugh MacDiarmid/Chris Grieve, had only recently flown to Russia, cheered on by them. These first-hand accounts were disappointing. Joan, Jimmie and Chris, all, as it happened, thrown out of the Communist Party for not doing as they were told, were idealists, as was Gerry. Each one of them so wanted Russia to succeed. In 1957, Joan would find out herself about that snob thing but, even so, like Gerry, she still hated to hear any chipping away, whether true or not.

Nevertheless, Jack's story chimed with Czechoslovakia and Poland going quiet when either Joan or Gerry wrote to them. Gerry, using the tours in Europe as leverage, was by then trying for Berlin and Tel-Aviv. Encouraging answers came from them but there was always a catch, like they couldn't provide the money for the fare or the person writing the letter didn't have the authority to say yes. Another target was Paris. Gerry went once without telling Joan. Another time, he did take her. Joan, having watched Sartre's new play, *Le Diable et le Bon Dieu*, at the Théâtre Antoine, spotted the author in a café talking to Jean Genet. Of the play, she wrote: 'No real conflict'; of the author, 'He should have married Genet for a while instead of playing the French genius and boring himself and the poor Beauvoir with their famous intellectual affair . . . the French take the cake for hypocrisy. Gide never had the courage to admit who he was.' About Camus she felt differently. She admired him. Her only regret was that, though he wrote plays, the company he worked with was not distinguished. If he had worked with her, things could have been different.

Paris didn't happen, not then at least, and it looked as if Gerry was failing left, right and centre. In fact he resigned from the job of manager and Howard Goorney took over. Muscle flexing is a better way of seeing Gerry's efforts at that time. He wanted Theatre Workshop to be the best company in the world and to be that you needed to get out there and you weren't going to get out there if you didn't try. He'd been trying.

While he looked outwards towards other countries of Europe, so Jimmie looked more and more towards Scotland. Much as Joan loved its songs and poetry, she didn't care for nationalism, and that is what she saw in Jimmie. Hugh MacDiarmid used to say that one Scot was worth two Englishmen. It was that kind of talk Joan found unhelpful and when Jean Newlove taught the company the Highland fling, she, Jean, having previously sniffed at it, Joan was disappointed. It was a dead end and, anyway, there was a risk of Jean forgetting her Laban. Saying that it was an accident when she told Hugh MacDiarmid that Jimmie was born in Salford, thus reducing Jimmie to tears of rage, is not easy to believe of Joan. If she thought someone was out of line, her instinct was to slap them back in again so that it stung. You can tell how much it hurt if you consider that, in Jimmie's 1990 autobiography, packed with well-remembered names, the name Jimmie Miller appears not once.

There was time for this reflectiveness about Europe, Sartre and Scotland, because in 1950 there was another big gap. Just before it, the company had given some performances in London including a Sunday night at the Adelphi Theatre. Perhaps the British Council would come and then finance a tour abroad? No, the British Council, along with the Arts Council, stayed away. John Moody of the Arts Council did slip in one evening but, while enjoying the physicality of *The Flying Doctor*, thought that the actors were still not up to much and that Theatre Workshop should, therefore, re-apply in two or three years' time. How on earth did he expect it to survive with no help for three years?

He didn't bank on Theatre Workshop's phenomenal optimism. For fifteen pounds, Gerry bought a second-hand lorry, painted the names of the countries that the company had visited on its sides and, after twice failing his driving test, obtained a licence. Sets, costumes, props and the company would all go in this lorry and, to raise money, the company went out into the country, picked tomatoes and sold them at a profit in town. Accompanied by Joan, Gerry then set out with all their contacts and quickly booked a series of one-night stands across South Wales. Until the end of 1950, the company performed a zingier *Uranium 235* – Joan never left anything alone – while in early 1951 it was Jimmie's new play, *Landscape with Chimneys*, a story of squatters and their eviction. It needed a song to cover a scene change. He wrote 'Dirty Old Town'.

The tour ran through a freezing cold winter. The lorry broke down. Fog sometimes stopped them altogether. Performances had to be cancelled. Digs included a pub where the other guests had, in merry mood, gathered for a hanging. Why did the company bother? Perhaps the answer to this question was that, despite periods of no money, no food, no heat, nowhere to live, rehearse or perform and lots of debts, life was lived at a higher level of excitement than it would have been in any other job. Gerry's inside info from visits to commercial managements would have helped. There was not much other acting work about anyway.

When the going was at its toughest, Gerry, on spotting a gap, would, very occasionally, whisk Joan off to the Strand Palace Hotel near Piccadilly Circus, where they would spend a couple of nights. Joan was more capable than most of sleeping on a floor, but she revelled in comfort too, and Gerry seeing to that made it even better.

After that, it was back to the one-night stands and, with still no base in view, the company was, yet again, wondering what would happen next.

CHAPTER THIRTEEN

COMING IN TO LAND

Kristin Lind, on the tour of Sweden, may have given Joan the pip but it didn't stop Joan writing affectionate letters to her that gave no indication of how irritated she'd been. They worked because, straight after the one-night stands in South Wales, the company found itself on a ship in the North Sea again. Theatre Workshop was off on a tour of Scandinavia, first stop Norway, where Joan was able to discover that – putting it in simple terms – Norway is not Sweden. The landscape was not the same and consequently neither were the people. It made a difference, for the better.

When the company did eventually fetch up in Sweden, the critic Sven Stahl wrote: 'Joan Littlewood is worth the entire Old Vic. Her name should be written in letters of fire until the blinkers are burned off the eyes of the English theatre public.' Later on, this helped Joan put round Sweden the same sort of golden glow that she put round Kristin Lind.

On the company's return, there were more one-night stands but this time they were in the North East of England, familiar and happier stamping grounds. It was spring too.

If there was one person for whom things were not that great, it was Gerry. Still uncertain about his role as manager – the return to Sweden was more to do with Joan – and goaded by Jimmie's put-downs of his acting, he got fed up and started an affair. It was only a fling, but that's when Joan was devastated. Setting aside her personal feelings for the cause not one jot and, in fact, out of plain jealousy, she sacked the girl, using the excuse of lateness. The girl, a vivid personality who is very much around today, and friends with everyone, didn't actually go but hovered in the shadows.

Joan stopped eating, lived on black coffee and attempted suicide. What she saw as the falseness of Jimmie's marriage to Jean and of David Scase's to Rosalie – the husband playing the field, the wife shutting up – was not for her. In any relationship she had, there would be two and that was all. Gerry did not take this attempt seriously. If anything, their roles were reversed. Usually it was Joan ticking off the wayward son. This time, it was Gerry reproving the tempestuous daughter. Recalling the event, and back on form, Joan said that the room she tried to gas herself in was so large, to fill it would have taken a month.

It was while the company was once more at the People's Theatre in Newcastle that Alan Lomax appeared. He was the son of John Lomax, the discoverer of Lead Belly, the black American folk and blues musician who had come up with the song 'Goodnight Irene'. Both father and son collected folk songs. Alan was looking for Jimmie, but Jimmie was off giving a talk up the road in Berwick-upon-Tweed.

Alan stayed to see the show and, afterwards, beguiled the company with songs. It was slightly different with Joan. He both teased and annoyed her. He said that there was no carelessness in her production. This suggests that she was still in her Kurt Jooss, 'Gerry catches the movement from Graham and counterpoints it by a downward movement', period. This, in turn, accounts for those hard-to-understand – 'brilliant production, shame about the actors' – reviews the company had been receiving.

There was just enough in Alan Lomax's teasing for her to let him have sex with her, though other thoughts were going through her mind as well. She remembered those *Guardian* types from before the war, like Jack Dillon. They were in open marriages, and even at that time she wondered whether that was the cool thing to do. Here was an opportunity to find out, and there was also a touch of revenge in it for what Gerry had just done. Annoy Joan at any time in her life and, a day or two later, something unpleasant would happen to you.

She didn't enjoy the experience. For a start, Gerry was much better at sex than Alan. It made her conclude that 'cool' was not for her. Back from this jaunt, she was confronted by Gerry who pulled her into his lap and had sex with her crossly; not romantic, no, but the relationship was back on.

On the artistic side, Gerry wrote a play, *The Long Shift*. It was based on his experience of working down the Pendleton mine during the war. It's not a bad play, and the set, a narrow tunnel seen from the side, was as claustrophobic as you could want it to be. And there the company was, in the north-east, with all its mining towns. It seemed perfect. It wasn't. The last thing miners wanted in the evening was to watch a play about what they had been doing all day. It was, however, an important lesson which Joan remembered for the future. If you are faced with a tough subject, don't go at it head on. Come from an angle and don't forget to entertain.

'Are you Reds?' asked a figure in a shabby, camel-hair coat who was hanging round one day. This young man, an actor from Chorlton-cum-Hardy Rep, south of Manchester town centre, joined the company. His name was Harry Corbett but, because of Sooty, the glove puppet on TV whose operator was also called Harry Corbett, he became Harry H. Corbett.

His question has some bearing because, in pretty quick succession, he was joined by his girlfriend, Avis Bunnage, who had been at the same rep. Neither shared Joan and Gerry's politics. However, they brought conventional but useful theatre experience. Far more than that, though, they brought talent. What with the arrival of George Cooper, a gradual change was occurring. Gerry was beginning to get what he wanted. Avis, as well as Harry, was to become important to Theatre Workshop and Gerry never stopped admiring her because he always valued people who could do their job. To put her in her place politically, though, he and Joan always referred to her as 'petty' bourgeois but that was in private.

In turn, Harry and, in particular, Avis, would stay on because Joan would give them good work, a kind of work they would not have been given elsewhere because, elsewhere, they would have been typecast: when they were not with Theatre Workshop, that is what happened. Avis, for example, always played someone's mum, despite never being a mother herself.

Harry used to say that she was better than he was. Certainly, there aren't stories of Joan torturing Avis in rehearsal. There is one of Joan torturing Harry. All his early performances were imitations of film stars. Joan had to break that. She did it during one of those school tours of *Twelfth Night*. Harry was playing Sir Andrew Aguecheek. The easy way to play him is to adopt a funny walk and put on a funny voice and, indeed, for some audiences, that sort of performance can work.

Joan went through her usual process. Who is Sir Andrew? He has a title, so he doesn't work, but he has no fortune. Olivia's family tolerate him but it doesn't want him. Even Olivia's uncle, Sir Toby, who brought him in, only has him there to patronise. He is a sad fellow. Just before Harry was about to face a crowd of rough schoolchildren, Joan pressed this idea on to him. He was furious but he took it. He kept Sir Andrew utterly lost and it worked. The children found him even funnier.

This donnish side to Joan had another purpose. It was to do with building up, not breaking down. Talented actors came to her with little in the way of education and, because of that, had an inferiority complex. She too knew – her RADA days had done it – what it was like to feel small and so she wanted her actors to feel big. Reading the history behind and around the play, then analysing the lines to see what they really meant, began to arm them against the Establishment artifice of the Old Vic and Stratford-upon-Avon.

The tour of the north-east was fine enough and Joan had collected three durable actors. However, the company had been touring for six years and still there was no sign of a base. She became so convinced that it was time to throw in the towel that when Jimmie told her there was a date in Scotland coming up, and that *Uranium 235* would be the show, she wasn't interested. Jimmie could do that by himself. This was something she often did, push work that bored her on to someone else, even when that person was unsuitable.

Jimmie wrote her a letter:

> You will accuse me of selfishness if I say I could no more produce *Uranium* than I could conduct a symphony and St Andrew's will present tremendous problems. I can drill crowd scenes, but when it comes to revealing the organic rhythms of the play, I'm lost. *Uranium* needs a producer of genius if it is to be anything more than a cabaret.

Joan thought Jimmie was being chicken and reneging on his duty. That was another thing she did, mistaking someone's intention so that she could turn them into an enemy. Another person reading that letter could interpret it quite differently, particularly if they had read all of it. Jimmie bows before Joan's talent as deeply as Gerry did, only, being a writer, more gracefully.

A few days before setting off for Glasgow the company was about to go for a run-through when Gerry told Joan that he'd invited Sam Wanamaker along. It was 1952 and Sam had recently arrived from Broadway to direct and appear in Clifford Odets' play *The Country Wife*, known in the UK as *The Winter Journey*. In America, where he was well established, he had been subpoenaed to appear before the House Un-American Committee, and he wasn't going back. Others in the same boat, like the film directors Joseph Losey and Cy Endfield, also headed for Theatre Workshop. Their politics were sympathetic.

For all that, Joan was unhappy about this intrusion. Anything like that made her angry. Eventually she would admit to what others had long suspected. Underneath the anger was fear.

Gerry bringing Sam along is an example of what he would do repeatedly to Joan. Yes, he was an organiser, and like no other in the company, but the way he did it could be roughshod. For a start, he didn't consult. Whatever he planned would be a *fait accompli* once it was presented. Of course, if he had told Joan there would have been time for her to say no or walk away. He wasn't chancing it. No sooner had he told Joan about Sam than Sam walked in.

This particular incident is an early illustration of Gerry's willingness to talk to people Theatre Workshop was wary of because, a moment later, in walked Sam's co-star, Michael Redgrave. Years before, Redgrave, unlike any other Establishment theatre star, had moved towards Theatre Workshop but had backed away from it because of its politics. His association with the company was not good for his career. However, here he was, back again, so Joan was even less pleased. From her RADA days (Joan Kempson) until her death (Vanessa Redgrave) she would reserve her harshest judgment for the Redgrave family: 'How do these untalented people make it?'

Pulling back from all this, and to be absolutely fair to Joan, inviting guests to watch an early run-through is dangerous, however sympathetic those guests may be. Actors who should be feeling their way through the play start to perform and, if it's a comedy, strain for laughs. It's irresistible but it's wrong.

Still, there they were, Sam and Michael, and throwing them out had become too difficult. They stayed. The run-through went ahead and both admired it immensely.

The company went off to Glasgow and, just as things had been when it started out in 1945, friends made things go with a swing. The friends, this time, were Norman Buchan, not yet a Labour MP, and his wife Janey Buchan, not yet a Labour MEP and a champion of gay rights.

It was all very jolly until Joan remembered that the company lorry had been driven up not by Gerry, but by Harry Greene, a recruit from Wales and the only other person who knew how to drive it. Fine, but where was Gerry? A telegram arrived. He was down south in hospital with a torn bowel. As always, when Gerry got ill, so unlike Joan, he really got ill.

For Gerry to get better, the two went to Cassis in the south of France. Gerry loved the sun and would love it even more when worse was to come in later years. Joan, who didn't like the sun, was happy to stay in the shade cooled by a sea breeze.

A telegram arrived. It was from Sam Wanamaker. He and Michael Redgrave wanted to present *Uranium 235* at the Embassy Theatre in London in two weeks' time.

Nowadays, the Embassy, which is near Swiss Cottage underground station, belongs to the Royal Central School of Speech and Drama. Back in 1952 it was run by Oscar Lewenstein who had come from Glasgow Unity, the company Joan thought was amateurish. Sam Wanamaker was a friend of Oscar's and that is how Oscar had become involved. It was the start of a relationship with Joan and Gerry that would manage to be both fractious and long-lasting. Only after Joan gave up theatre did it become harmonious. She never lost her love of books and, at his home in Hove, Oscar had a library. It became a refuge and, when Joan was not there, she could always amuse herself by imitating his hoarse, squeaky voice.

Uranium 235 was admired by the few, which got it a run at the Comedy Theatre, but remained unseen by the many, which meant that the run was short. The critic Kenneth Tynan saw it and wrote that Joan kept her actors in chains, which echoes Alan Lomax teasing her about the lack of carelessness. Both Jimmie and Joan had always been suspicious of London and its theatre critics. This visit only confirmed their suspicion. Gerry was different. Like it or not, he suspected, those critics would have to be faced. If you want to be the greatest company in the world, people have to know you're there. For the rest of their working lives, this opinion would cause conflict between him and Joan.

As for Oscar, he remained in London, working first with the writer, Wolf Mankowitz, and later at the Royal Court, producing plays both in subsidised and West End theatre. He had a relationship with Jack Hylton, the producer in the commercial world, whose interest Gerry had tried to engage. Oscar's politics were to the left and he put on many plays which broadly reflected that. However, he worked with directors and actors whose methods were both conventional and accepted, so for him life was easier than it was for Joan. She rejected those methods.

Broke again, the company pitched tents that summer in the grounds of Tom Driberg's home, Bradwell Lodge in Essex, a part-Tudor, part-Adam house, where he lived on and off with his new wife, Ena. What with his interest in sturdy young men of the kind Gerry was, Tom had had some close shaves with the law. The marriage had been arranged by John Freeman, who seven years later would become the interviewer on *Face to Face*, the popular BBC TV programme.

The company earned money by stooking wheat and when it wasn't busy doing that, Joan rehearsed a political thriller of Jimmie's called *The Travellers*. It was booked for Edinburgh that August. There was just about enough money for the fares, but there wasn't for the set. With only a bag of nails, Harry Greene set off with another company member and, right across the Oddfellows Hall in Edinburgh, spread a series of train seats, the essentials of which, wood and metal, he had managed to scrounge. That was the set. It was not for nothing that he became king of DIY on television in the 1970s and 1980s.

The travellers who made the journey in the play were symbolic. They represented the countries of Europe rushing towards war. 'Propaganda thinly disguised as experimental drama,' wrote the critic of the *Spectator*. He admired the production, though. Joan considered it one of the most exciting pieces of staging (with the audience being almost on the train too) she had ever done.

Scotland seemed to be turning into the company's base, which would have suited Jimmie fine, because soon there was Glasgow again, this time doing Joan's new version of Molière's *Le Malade Imaginaire* called *The Imaginary Invalid*. As it happens, the person who found the place for the company to live was Gerry. It was a big house in Belmont Street owned by an eccentric millionaire who allowed them to have it for a peppercorn rent which Gerry paid in farthings.

Would have suited Jimmie, if he had been there. By then he was increasingly away on singing dates. Meanwhile, Joan got on with her Molière production. She commissioned a translation especially for the occasion by the Scottish teacher, and writer of political songs, Morris Blythman. Joan found it heavy-going and made her own. Morris didn't know about this until he saw the first performance. He was not pleased. The hall being almost empty didn't help. There were no laughs. He left saying, more prophetically than either he or the company realised, that it would be better off in London.

Here was an example of something Joan would do more than once. Maybe that translation was heavy-handed, but her utter conviction that she was right and that her version was better, considered from another angle, was riding roughshod over Morris Blythman.

The houses picked up, and with them came the laughs. Howard Goorney, George Cooper, Harry Corbett, that girl Gerry fancied, and Avis Bunnage, in particular, as Toinette, the mocking, down-to-earth maid, came together to make a proper company, at last. The *Glasgow Herald* critic was able to praise not only the production but the actors. Of the translation, he wrote: 'The dialogue . . . had the great merit of propelling the theme fluently, wittily and with dramatic bite.' That's exactly what Joan could do: propel fluently. She *was* right but it's difficult not to feel sorry for Morris Blythman and the others whom she brushed aside as time went by.

The translator's name on the programme was Thurso Berwick, which Joan would imply, in conversation, was a name she had invented for herself to get out of a tricky situation. It was easy to believe, too, as she often used funny pseudonyms, like Eleanor Griswold and Jeanne Petitbois. However, it was not the case. Thurso Berwick was the name Morris Blythman adopted when he was writing poetry.

It was in the middle of winter with nothing much on the cards when Gerry told the company that the Theatre Royal Stratford had fallen empty. They could go there, not for the usual night or week, but for a season and, when he said empty, he meant empty. Gabriel Toyne and a useless backstage crew were no longer a problem because they weren't there. The company would run the place themselves. A meeting was called.

CHAPTER FOURTEEN

A BASE AT LAST

They were only talking about a season of six weeks but the company took it seriously. Joan said that Jimmie didn't attend. Whether he did or not, his feelings were already clear. As for the others, what could they anticipate even before leaving Glasgow?

The pros were: at last some kind of base, one that was in a working-class area too, a real theatre, not an all-purpose hall that audiences didn't go to; an end to one-night stands; an end to the lorry breaking down; and the possibility of living in the same place from night to night.

The cons were: leaving the north where all that had been good for Theatre Workshop had happened; going down south to the hated London where nothing good had happened; a possible dependence on the critics of the national papers; and having to pay overheads, rent, gas, electricity and telephone.

Jimmie was suspicious of London because he didn't know it. Joan was suspicious of London because she did. In Lancashire, she loved the brusqueness that hid warmth. In London, she hated the sentimental and meaningless 'Aaah' that cockneys came out with when they were told of something sad. She was torn, though, because at the back of her mind she knew, like Gerry, that right then, principles or no principles, there was not much else in the offing. They almost had to go and so the decision was made.

Jimmie's decision was to leave Theatre Workshop. Joan talked about this, employing a tone that seemed to say it was a pity, as if he could have stayed. George Cooper, remembering the rows between Jimmie and Gerry and the tension that they had created in the company, said that there was a feeling of relief. There had been factions. Company members were either pro-Jimmie or pro-Gerry. Howard Goorney, David Scase, Rosalie Williams and Jean Newlove, had been pro-Jimmie. George had been pro-Gerry. By then, David and Rosalie had left the company to have children, so Jimmie was feeling that there was less reason for him to stay. His own view was that he was frozen out.

Joan, when not being officially regretful, sounded quite different. Jimmie, as might be expected, given his many absences to sing folk songs, went off to do hootenannies, informal gatherings by folk singers. Joan, drawing on the silly and childish sound of the word, had the same sort of fun playing with it as Edith Evans had with 'A handbag?' She also poked fun at folk singers' bleating tones and the hand over the ear, which was supposed to be so genuine but which she regarded as an affectation. What she really regretted was Jimmie setting aside his enormous knowledge of classical music which, along with his own songs, had so helped the company.

There were a couple more remarks she made. First, let us remember, 'Once upon a time, Jimmie was the genius, while I was the handmaiden at his knee.' She finished it with: 'Turned out the other way round really, didn't it?' Then there was: 'Jimmie wanted to be the Great Writer instead of just writing.' The tougher remarks may sound cruel but they sound more genuine than those in which she claimed he didn't have to go.

About Gerry there was no ambiguity. From all those letters that he wrote to Joan, it is clear that he thought that Theatre Workshop would get nowhere as long as Jimmie was the company's writer. In his eyes, Jimmie/Ewan MacColl, was anti-popular.

Howard Goorney would stay on but not lose touch with Jimmie, whose writing he continued to believe in.

It was a Sunday night when, having either hitchhiked or crammed into Gerry's car – he had an old Alvis by then – the company arrived at the theatre. Apart from it being on a corner, it didn't have a special position like All Saints in Manchester. It was simply tucked in among houses. However, along one side, not the entrance side, was Angel Lane, which had little shops in it and a market. The theatre itself was Victorian and the auditorium was decorated with gilded cherubs and curlicues, or rather gilded is what they should have been, as the place was in a bad way. It stank of drains, unwashed clothes, stale make-up, cat's piss and scented disinfectant. The previous show had been *Jane of the Daily Mirror*, a striptease revue based on a cartoon character devised for the same reason as page three in the *Sun*, everything that Joan hated.

That night there was nothing else for the company to do – there being no food – but to make homes for themselves in dressing rooms and go to sleep.

The next day, they spent the morning cleaning the place to make it bearable and printing posters using their own printing machine. Had it been any other company, it's difficult to see that their efforts would have been successful enough to allow for a performance that evening, but then Theatre Workshop was used to it. It even had a name for the cleaning team: The Black Squad.

Not many people came to that performance – it was *Twelfth Night* – and George Cooper, who was playing Malvolio, remembered, during the run, pennies being thrown at him, and being called Big Head because of his tall Elizabethan hat. A local critic thought the show was rather good but a bit highbrow for Stratford.

Instantly it was clear that the usual Theatre Workshop way of going about things, i.e. long rehearsal periods and a small number of shows, would have to change drastically and quickly. A new play would have to be put on every two weeks. This wasn't so bad because the present company had been together for a while and was, in Joan's words, 'tuned up'. It could work fast without standards dropping. In any case, the next two plays were *The Imaginary Invalid*, and *Landscape with Chimneys*, which had a new name, *Paradise Street*. Those had already been done. Wasn't that last one a play of Jimmie's? It was, and Jimmie, while carping at Theatre Workshop's activities, came back to give Sunday evening concerts. Three months later, Joan mounted his adaptation of *Lysistrata* and eight months later, *The Travellers*. The end of the road for Jimmie at Theatre Workshop it wasn't, not entirely. Jean Newlove popped back too to give movement classes and to choreograph.

Immediate problems, once the company had arrived, were accommodation, the state of the theatre, and the lack of money.

The dressing rooms would remain the company's home until such time as it could afford to move out. Considering that the takings, which they shared out among each other, were minute, that day would not be speedy in coming. Living in the theatre was strictly illegal too.

Whenever the fire inspector paid a visit, a code name 'Walter Plinge' would be sent out and Gerry had to describe any mattress not pushed into a cupboard, as a day bed for relaxation purposes. Any gadget that indicated someone was living there, like a gas ring, had to be stowed away pronto.

For meals, ingredients were bought in the market costing pennies and, after a better week at the box office, there might just be enough to eat at the Café L'Ange in Angel Lane, where Bert and May Scagnelli cured their own hams and made their own apple pie. At first, the stall owners were a bit suspicious of the actors: 'Why don't you get a proper job?' but Bert and May took the company to their hearts and became part of Theatre Workshop history.

As well as rehearsing, the company had to mend seats, unblock drains, put out buckets to catch raindrops, and fix the boiler that kept going out. Even so, heating could only be switched on just before the audience arrived and the auditorium was often freezing, as the regulars – there were some – were to find out. It was best to come well wrapped-up.

Camel, realising that he could no longer fall back on black material and lighting, beautiful as the latter may have been, knew that there had to be sets for every production and minimal as they were (his style anyway), they still had to be built.

The working day was eighteen hours long. If the stall holders and Equity had realised how much hard work was going on, they would have been respectively impressed and horrified, except that Equity didn't have much to do with Theatre Workshop in those days because none of the actors were receiving a minimum wage. As it happened, Joan and Gerry's relationship with trade unions (Equity and later on, ACTT, the film technicians' union), was never comfortable. Theatre Workshop had its own way of doing things and this way did not coincide with fixed hours and demarcation. If it had paid attention to those, nothing would ever have been achieved. Howard Goorney did believe in Equity and remained a prominent member for as long as he was able to.

Referring to the hard work as well as those periods of silence, Max Shaw, who joined the company at Stratford, said: 'Our lives were monastic but it didn't matter because we didn't have any money to go out anyway. There was nothing else to do but get on with work.'

The Theatre Royal had an office and Gerry settled into it, there to have, if you go by his correspondence, a gruelling time. Not only the future had to be coped with, but the past too. He was dealing with a firm called Theatres and Music Halls [South] Ltd., run by one Rowland Sales, and he wanted to sort out the dirt and dilapidation Mr Sales had allowed, not to mention an unpaid telephone bill. Mr Sales aggressively tried to push everything on to Gerry and, while he was at it, insisted that advertisements be projected on to the safety curtain at each performance, as agreed. Gerry projected them just before the audience arrived, until he was found out.

Behind all these orders was bluster. You could tell because Mr Sales wanted his cheques made out, not to Music Halls [South] Ltd. but to himself. It was 1953, Coronation year. Everyone was buying a television set. Variety was dying. Rowland Sales was desperate to get out, and Gerry, awkward as he was to deal with, could provide him with an exit. He asked if Gerry wanted to stay on. He did, and signed for another few months. It was the start of Gerry gradually taking control of the whole building, a job that would take years because different parts of the theatre belonged to different people. However, because of his belief in a base, he kept at it.

While trying to cope with Rowland Sales, he was writing to Newham, the borough where the theatre was situated, and all the surrounding boroughs asking for that sixpence from the rates he had learned about when trying for the David Lewis Centre five years earlier. Things hadn't changed. They all thought it was a cheek. So, when Gerry wrote to those same old names at the Arts Council, John Moody and Jo Hodgkinson, and the answer was if he could raise £1,000 locally they'd match it, the situation was still a 'no go.'

Before that, Gerry tried to get a grant for a new play, *The Colour Guard* by George Styles. Such grants did exist. Gerry had done his homework but plays had to be read by a committee and that took time. Gerry didn't have time. It was opening next month.

The first ever grant from the Arts Council didn't come until the following year. It was £150 to help pay for audiences to travel home at night if it was difficult for them. No sooner had Gerry received it than he was asked to account for it. That was a constant bugbear, accounts. The Arts Council never stopped asking for them but, as we know today, accounts don't come cheap and Gerry couldn't always afford them. In any case, given his buccaneering spirit, it wouldn't be surprising if that £150 went on whatever debt needed paying most. If ever there was a time when he needed to believe in what he was doing, it was then.

Down on the stage, that satisfyingly deep stage, things were quite different. Joan was having a whale of a time. For the next three years, it was a national theatre. In fact, Joan was sometimes heard to say: 'We were the National Theatre.' It was as if the list of plays Gerry had drawn up for his humiliating David Lewis Centre meeting, had been lengthened and then performed. At the Theatre Royal, there was plenty to complain about, like hunger, poverty and the cold, but no one complained about the plays.

The only problem was that not many people were coming to see them. Joan sat in the gallery delighted by her actors, but she could often find herself alone. Actually, there was one actress who annoyed her: 'The silly born bitch, she's missed her entrance. Oh, it's me.' This was a sign of Joan wanting to pull away from acting.

Even today people like to scoff. Theatre for the working class? They were never interested. If Theatre Workshop had an audience, it came from elsewhere. It didn't know what sort of play it should be putting on. Things weren't that simple. One play, *Van Call*, written by a local author, kept audiences away. *The Good Soldier Schweik*, the production Joan had promised herself in Czechoslovakia, though not obviously relevant, was discussed enthusiastically on the bus home. That last comment came from one of the Soundy sisters. Doris and Peggy Soundy, after seeing *Paradise Street*, formed a supporters club all by themselves. Nobody told them to. They had two thousand members at one point.

In her diary, Joan offered some of her own views on what she liked and didn't like. It happened during the rehearsals of *The Troublemakers*, a play by an American writer which was brought to her by an agent, Leslie Linder. The company performed it after the summer break in 1953. In the entry is a comment from an actress called Jean Shepherd, who, recommended by Nelson Illingworth, the voice man, had joined the company. She didn't last long as it was all too intense. The comment wouldn't have done her much good either. Joan wrote:

> Leslie Linder comes to look and help. There's a violence scene that has to be physically "real". So I let him take over. Don't like it. Prefer stylisation like the Chinese – much more effective – anyway Jean Shepherd looks at me and says: "Isn't it nice to have a man take over?" It was such a surprising thing to hear her say.
>
> This play was dealing with a contemporary theme but really it's not worth it. People can get their news in the papers. Theatre must give them much more. I don't mind direct agitation – agitprop – but when it comes to all this real-life "political" American drama – Miller + school – one is really bored. Drama sustains like poetry and reflects society profoundly when it is poetry (Jonson). Do these plays do this? They are better done in the cinema anyway and even then one comes out yawning – head aching, if one sat it out.

It would seem that George Bellak took notice because he spent the rest of his long career in television.

At Christmas time, despite thinking RL Stevenson's position vis-à-vis the English was on the cringing side, Joan directed *Treasure Island*. George Cooper was Long John Silver and the production packed the place out with school children. Here Joan relishes her idea of violence:

> Marvellous changes of set. Have made adaptation like a film in one shot – we have a fight in the rigging on just ropes – a bit of sail – and Harry Greene prepared to break his neck – Harry rigs this work of art and contrives a fall that takes your breath away – ACROBATICS necessary in any company that wants exciting theatre.

When Joan was young, she wasn't used to holidays. Work was all she wanted. It was Gerry who taught her the importance of stepping away from it. By 1953 she was so used to holidays that she thought everyone else ought to have one as well, so she invited Harry Corbett and Avis Bunnage to go with her and Gerry in his car to France. Joan was exhaustingly full of bright ideas. As for Gerry, he believed strongly in people going abroad, so that was OK. It was to be a camping holiday and Avis, who had never left the UK in her life, was a little nervous. Harry had served abroad but not in Europe.

The holiday wasn't totally bad but there was an echo of Joan insisting that her grandparents come up to Hyde during the Blitz. She thought she knew what was best for people, but people didn't always react the way she wanted them to. The principle of the holiday was excellent and being with Joan and Gerry could be exhilarating. It could also be disorientating. You were entering their world, the one in which Gerry charged about taking risks and Joan would enthuse everyone with an idea and then go off it. You could land with a thump.

It rained all the way to the south of France and Gerry, always a fast driver, drove even faster to get through it. Harry thought Gerry had been drinking and was frightened by this crazy speed. 'Gerry, you shouldn't,' Joan would say, though tickled that he did. In any case, Harry and Avis's demand for English cups of tea was getting on her nerves. The blue of the Mediterranean, when they got there, was great, but the lack of money for café stops on the way home made Harry irritable. Joan thought he was ungrateful. Had not Gerry spent all his money on their transport?

Anyone tempted to look down on Harry and Avis, as Joan and Gerry did, should have first tasted Life with Joan and Gerry. They would then feel sympathy for them too. Once home, Joan immediately caught a cold.

These early years at Stratford were an explosion of Joan's taste and it was then that she was able to explore her very favourites, the Elizabethans. In 1953 she tackled, for the first time, her absolute favourite, Ben Jonson. The play was *The Alchemist*. Howard Goorney was Subtle, Harry Corbett played Face, and Avis Bunnage was Dol Common. George Cooper as Sir Epicure Mammon, pushed on in a wheelchair, was nearly killed when the iron curtain hurtled down all by itself. Only Harry Greene pulling him backwards in the nick of time saved his life. That was another mark against Rowland Sales. The theatre was a death-trap. Aside from that, Joan thought it was one of her best productions and loved her actors for their performances. It was socially she was less keen on them, as the trip to France showed.

From time to time, she would say: 'I'm rich', and you'd wonder why because you could see no evidence of money in large amounts. On this occasion, it was because of Ben Jonson. It was his words that made her rich. Woe betide anyone else having a go at him, though. If she had met them, she would have killed them.

Shakespeare she wasn't quite so keen on. For her, he was too politically middle-of-the-road but, like many people, she loved the poetry of *Richard II* and, in 1954, that is what she started with. Poetry still meant finding the sense and the right energy, though. 'We are getting so much physical excitement from just playing what is written.'

When acting herself, Joan was said by Theatre Workshop members to have been a bit of a ham, not Theatre Workshop at all, but she was good at verse speaking. It sounded so natural. Using this talent, she spent night after night working with Howard Goorney on John of Gaunt's dying speech, most of which is one long sentence. In those days, it was common to make it elegiac so that the actor could show off his voice. Joan heard something else: anger.

In any case, whatever the speech, she wasn't interested in 'voice wanking' and what a perfect opportunity arose, in those weeks, to contrast that with her way. *Richard II* was also being done by the Old Vic. John Neville, tipped to be Gielgud's successor, was playing the king. Joan sent along a new recruit, Canadian George Luscombe, to see it. He came back mightily cheered and spent the rest of the day sending up the sound of the Old Vic actors. There, quite specifically, was an example of Joan setting out to cure an actor of an inferiority complex.

Her Richard was Harry Corbett, who found the right energy for 'I wasted time, and now doth time waste me', by having one ankle tethered to a stake, so that he could only walk in a circle. Joan was very proud of his performance.

Van Call came next, the play that despite a local author, Anthony Nicholson, did not attract an audience. Gerry commissioned it. No longer was he commenting on what he thought was wrong, he was actively trying to make what he thought was right. This is the first occasion he can be seen doing that.

The play was set in a market and in her staging Joan brought the outside market inside. You can hardly think of a better way to involve the community and yet the play failed. Peggy Soundy of the Supporters' Club said: 'In *Van Call*, you were trying to put across a line and you could feel it. If it doesn't come from someone's gut, in a real sort of way, it shows, and I think the locals saw this.' Gerry still had a way to go, but it wouldn't be long now. The wheels were turning.

Joan carried on with her Elizabethans. The author of *Arden of Faversham* may not be known but the play was published when Shakespeare was 28. It doesn't have his poetry, but being based on a true murder story of the time, it has a documentary excitement.

As feared by Joan and Jimmie, but wanted by Gerry, the national critics were beginning to come and Ken Tynan, writing in the *Observer* was taking a tentative interest in Theatre Workshop. 'The climax,' he wrote, 'with Arden stabbed and dragged out into the fields tingles with grimness.' He was disappointed that there wasn't a set for the last act and that cuts had to be made to accommodate this, but then: 'the rampant Bovarysme of Barbara Brown's Alice [in real life Barbara was mouse-like] could hardly be bettered and Harry Corbett plays Mosbie with a dark, cringing bravura which recalls the Olivier of *Richard III*.' The Harry/Olivier comparison would not have gone down well with Joan, had she read it, because she'd seen that performance at a matinee and thought Olivier was not trying. In her eyes, that damned him forever.

As for reading the critics in general, Joan said she never did, which no one believed. When, towards the end of her life, she gave the reason, you could think otherwise. 'I never read the critics because, if I had, I might have given up.' Gerry read all of them: 'It's my job.' Whether this new attention was what Joan wanted or not, you can sense the outside world, the one that, so far, had taken no notice, edging towards Theatre Workshop.

Towards the end of its run, Gerry shot off to Paris again, taking a load of photos with him. A few days later, he returned. The very next year, Theatre Workshop was to be the official British entry for the Paris Festival of International Drama. At last, he'd done it.

This festival had only started the previous year but it was already important. The Berliner Ensemble had brought *Mother Courage*. Great Britain had brought TS Eliot's *The Confidential Clerk*, which in comparison had seemed thin gruel.

Running the festival, which in 1956 would be known as the Théâtre des Nations, was Monsieur Julien, boss of the Théâtre Sarah Bernhardt (now the Théâtre de La Ville) and he'd been worrying about what the British would be able to send the next time. So too had Ken Tynan. After grumbling, in one of his articles, that *Mother Courage* had been 'acclaimed everywhere in Europe save in London' he went on to pose the question: 'Where, in the absence of a national playhouse, is our best to be sought?' Hardly had he asked this than fans of the Old Vic were appalled to discover that it was at Theatre Workshop. That's what France thought, anyway.

The man Gerry had actually spoken to was Julien's assistant, Claude Planson. Gerry's romantic enthusiasm had charmed him. 'You must love her very much,' he said of Joan. It was the start of a long relationship between him, Gerry and Joan. Soon, he would take over from Julien and, as the director of the Théâtre des Nations, he would ask them back many times, even when they didn't have anything to bring.

The show to go was *Arden of Faversham* plus something else. '*Volpone*,' said Joan, fired up. She couldn't resist another Ben Jonson. It didn't happen at once, though. On a roll, she did her new Czech-flavoured *Schweik*. The tunes she'd picked up there were what made the difference. As Peggy Soundy said, the locals loved it. This made someone think that the middle European residents of Swiss Cottage would love it too. Off the show went to the Embassy Theatre. They didn't love it. Even more annoying, Joan was without a company. She had to put together a scratch one in order to do Dickens' *The Chimes*. This she adapted herself as she had done Balzac's

Père Goriot the previous month, and would Mark Twain's *The Prince and the Pauper* the next month. Again, Joan was simply writing, rather than being the Great Writer. In the cast of *The Chimes* were Thelma Barlow who, six years later, would play Mavis Wilton in *Coronation Street*, and the young Michael Caine.

Joan said that Caine couldn't use his arms. They hung limply by his sides, like Michael Redgrave's. If you look at a long shot of Redgrave in the *The Quiet American* (1958), you notice that Joan's observation is right. After *The Chimes*, Joan said to Caine: 'You can't act, so you might as well fuck off up to the West End or get a job in films.' 'Best bit of advice I ever had,' said Caine once he was a star. By coincidence, in the remake of *The Quiet American* (2002), he played the same part as Michael Redgrave.

'Probably the best show we ever did,' said Joan of *Volpone*, 'and without changing the name we got them in.' Nobody in the UK wanted to pay the fare for the production to go to Paris, though, except for one commercial theatre producer. 'We haven't worked all these years for him to put his name at the top,' was the company's attitude and so they put on their costumes, picked up the set, trees for *Arden*, pillars for *Volpone*, and at Calais, called them personal luggage. They didn't go to the Sarah Bernhardt – that would come later – but to the Hébertot, a smaller theatre, nearer to the size of the Theatre Royal, in the north of Paris. Camus had worked there.

> The company from the Theatre Royal, Stratford, representing England at the festival, opened their double programme with the anonymous Elizabethan play, *Arden of Faversham*. The effect upon both the public and the press was one of immense and unqualified success. The critiques, spread frequently over two or three columns, were unanimous in acclaiming the company as a revelation. Even M. Jean-Jacques Gautier (the critic of *Figaro* who cultivates a flourishing reputation for severity) enveloped the whole cast with one broad flourish: "All the actors are excellent," and went on to eulogise several members in particular. Paul Gordeaux, writing in *France-Soir*, said, with reference to criticisms published in England concerning the choice of Theatre Workshop, that "the English theatre could not have been better represented." *Arts et Spectacles*, frequently given to uncontrolled outbursts of enthusiasm, stated with wild abandon that Theatre Workshop was the best acting troupe in England.

That came from the *Spectator* in 1955. Even so, Claude Planson still had to find the fare for the company to go home and there was no time or money to have fun while they were there. During the day, the company was too busy thinking of what came next. What actually came next, at this climactic point with Gerry triumphant, was, in more ways than one, the end of Theatre Workshop. Firstly, a woman called Mavis Clavering who had joined the company many years before, given it £100, trained, left and wanted her £100 back, was making Theatre Workshop bankrupt. Secondly, Harry Corbett and George Cooper resigned.

The bankruptcy problem was solved by Theatre Workshop Ltd., starting up again as Pioneer Theatres Ltd. The Harry/George problem, the way Joan saw it, was never solved. It was not, however, the end of the story of Joan and Gerry. For Gerry, it was a new beginning.

CHAPTER FIFTEEN

END OF/BEGINNING OF AN ERA?

Wh

hat led to Harry and George announcing their resignation? Something must have been going on. It seems their reasons were not entirely the same. Both wanted to earn more, or rather *something*. However George, under pressure from his new wife, Shirley, who'd been working in wardrobe, wanted a quieter life, while Harry wanted to spread his wings.

George, who never liked the idea of long runs – he only did one, *Billy Liar* – continued acting mainly in television, so that he could be at home in the evenings. Strongly featuring in his post-Joan career were Lindsay Anderson and Ken Loach. They were the only two other directors he respected.

Harry's outlook was not so straightforward. He had been noticing changes in Theatre Workshop for a long time. At first, it was a co-operative with everyone having a say, and it was also anonymous. No one had billing on posters. Gerry was not that interested in either of those principles. At company meetings, he puffed on his pipe, listened, first to Joan saying, 'No meeting should last longer than an hour,' before going on to talk for ages, and then to the actors complaining. After that, he went away and did what he wanted to do.

One of things he wanted to do was to promote Joan, hanging the whole of Theatre Workshop on her name alone. Consequently, it started to appear on posters, growing bigger and bigger, while the actors' names didn't appear at all. To be fair, neither did Gerry's, not for quite a while anyway.

Joan was not totally at ease with this but when Harry pointed it out to her, said that she hadn't really noticed. What Gerry was doing was single-minded or, if you prefer, ruthless, but you could argue that he was right. Joan had the greatest talent, and his plan worked. Democracy is slow. Gerry and Joan were, by nature, benevolent despots. That's fine in theatre: if you don't like it, you can go. Harry went. The tin lid, Joan thought, was Paris; all that success but not a penny coming in, and no time for fun, only work.

Neither Harry nor George left at once. Something important had come up and they were needed.

Ken Tynan complained about *Mother Courage* not being acclaimed in the UK. Gerry had been doing something about it. During 1954, he was in contact with Eric Bentley, Brecht's best-known translator into English. Bentley, an American, first wanted to get rid of some Americanisms in the text and then he wanted to come over to co-direct with Joan. Gerry, while pointing out that Theatre Workshop had a special way of working, didn't actually say no. Being the first British company to do *Mother Courage* would be quite a coup and Gerry was not unaware of the publicity value. Staying open to any suggestion, or appearing to, he agreed to consider casting actresses like Marie Löhr and Peggy Ashcroft who were nothing to do with Theatre Workshop. Thinking he had the rights – he did, from Eric Bentley – he told Oscar Lewenstein, who suggested that he, himself, and Wolf Mankowitz should present it, together with *Richard II*, at the Taw and Torridge Festival in Devon the following year.

A problem arose. Gerry didn't have the rights from Brecht. Oscar, who knew Brecht, went to Berlin to sort something out and succeeded. The result was a contract, in which it said that Harry Corbett and George Cooper would be in the production and that Joan would direct and play Mother Courage. Brecht had seen photos of her in a play called *Haben* (*The Midwife*) by Julius Hay. She was playing the eponymous midwife, a woman who provided poison to wives who wanted to get rid of tiresome husbands, and according to Brecht, she looked just right for his lead. Gerry, optimistically, was happy to go along with this.

A little thought would have told him that it wasn't a very good idea. Mother Courage is a huge part, and whoever plays her shouldn't have to worry about directing. Brecht suggested he send a young assistant, Karl Weber, to help out. Gerry and Joan accepted this, but then rehearsals hadn't started yet.

On the first day, Joan told Karl not to hold back but to say anything, absolutely anything. By the end of the week, he was out. It appeared he was trying to impose a carbon copy of Brecht's production on her. There are letters from Karl and Brecht about this time. Neither was angry, more regretful. Joan was difficult but they recognised that she was talented. The letter from Brecht was typed by Elizabeth Hauptmann who, these days, is credited with writing more of *The Threepenny Opera* than Brecht cared to admit.

What made everyone, including Oscar, put their foot down was what Joan was up to with the part of Mother Courage. She wasn't playing it. She'd put Katherine Parr, an actress whom she probably remembered from her rep days, into the part. This would not do. Oscar reminded her of the contract, and Joan had to learn her lines on the train to Devon.

The first night was a disaster. Harry Corbett and George Cooper were fine, as was Barbara Brown, but Joan, under-rehearsed and unable to sing Paul Dessau's songs, was firmly reminded of this by Ken Tynan in his review. She had another problem, one which the audience was not aware of. Mother Courage plucks a chicken and the chicken that night, was off. Joan was trying not to be sick. Exactly the same thing happened to Diana Rigg at the National Theatre in 1995.

This is when Harry and George left. The next year, George played Tiger Brown in Brecht's *Threepenny Opera,* produced by Oscar Lewenstein. In it too was Jimmie Miller/Ewan MacColl. Harry, introduced to Peter Brook by Ken Tynan, played First Gravedigger in *Hamlet* with Paul Scofield at the Phoenix Theatre later that same year, in December 1955. He complained to Joan that, when he asked about doing the usual text analysis he'd done with her, Peter Brook said that he expected him to do that alone at home.

This production went to Russia. After it, Harry invited Joan and Gerry to lunch at the White Tower, a Greek restaurant off Charlotte Street. Avis came too. She was ill at ease. Of *Hamlet* going to Russia, Harry said:

'It should have been us.'

'But Harry, there is no us now,' said Joan.

She was utterly downcast and so was Howard Goorney. Plays still had to be put on at top speed. New actors had to be brought in and, of course, they hadn't had all those years of training. That is what they, Joan and Howard, meant by the end of Theatre Workshop.

'Not at all,' said Gerry. 'It's merely the end of an era.'

'Some hope of conquering England now,' said Joan.

'We will,' said Gerry.

Nevertheless, he was fretful too, but for a different reason. He was worried about the number of classics and revivals Theatre Workshop was doing. They made Joan happy and they were good but something – that explosion, whatever it might be – wasn't happening. As usual, there was no money either. He wrote to Kristin Lind. She could at least help with another tour of Scandinavia to keep the company afloat. She did. *Arden of Faversham* could go early in 1956. No later, said Gerry, or Theatre Workshop would go bust.

Before going, Joan did *Big Rock Candy Mountain*, a show for children using the songs of Woody Guthrie. Alan Lomax co-wrote it, and came over from America. Afterwards, he sent a letter to her, once more having a dig at the exquisiteness of her production. Joan could have taken it as a compliment but she didn't. She was rather annoyed.

She wasn't particularly thrilled about Scandinavia either. Her new *Arden* company, she thought, was not nearly as good as the old one. Scandinavia didn't notice.

Theatre Workshop's tours of Europe, in retrospect, were feathers in its cap. At the time, they were survival. On this occasion, Gerry's efforts were not rewarded but punished. There he was, still plugging away trying to get bits and bobs out of the Arts Council, when all Jo Hodgkinson could ask was: how can the Arts Council finance Theatre Workshop if it isn't there? At least the bankruptcy was discharged. Joan treated herself to *Edward II*. She'd been promising herself that since her first go at *Richard II*. No worries about middle-of-the-road politics with Marlowe. Simply being himself was subversive.

During rehearsals of *Edward*, a play that made Joan happy, came something that would, at last, make Gerry happy and, in so doing, change the course of Theatre Workshop's history. It came via an odd route, the Scottish folk scene that Jimmie favoured. While the company was performing in Edinburgh, and hanging around with Scots poets, a songwriter from Ireland had introduced himself. His name was Dominic Behan. Joan, smelling phoney, had taken an instant dislike to him, a dislike that would remain for the rest of her life. Nevertheless, a link had been formed because, when the Abbey Theatre turned down *The Quare Fellow*, a play written by Dominic's brother, Brendan, Brendan, having also read about *Schweik* in *The Worker*, sent it to Jimmie, and Jimmie sent it to Joan.

Her description of its messy manuscript is cheerily colourful. What she didn't convey, because she didn't need to, was what the Abbey Theatre would have found: a full-length play in three acts. This should be made clear because there's a Theatre Workshop legend that Joan invariably made hits out of a few pages.

On reading a couple of scenes, though, the reader at the Abbey would have felt their heart sinking. There was no shortage of funny stories and funny lines, but nothing happened. A bunch of prisoners and a bunch of warders in a jail either stood or sat there talking. It wasn't a play. If left as it was, it would have become boring. This disappointment for the Abbey Theatre and, as it happened, Howard Goorney, was, for Joan, a challenge. It is what separates her from the others. Howard's disappointment was not quite the same as the Abbey's because he knew Joan; maybe she could make something of it, he thought, but it would be hard work and, at that moment, he couldn't face it. He got a job in a rep company where all he had to do was learn the lines.

The rehearsals of *The Quare Fellow* took place during the run of *Edward II*. That gave Joan and the company four weeks. Even to do a play not requiring script work, four weeks is hardly long, though theatre managers would disagree. Joan used to complain of herself that she was lazy and could only work in bursts. They were some bursts. That furious concentration she'd developed when reading books as a child was part of it. Sometimes she would go to bed as late as three and get up at six to work on a script. Gerry would then drive her to the theatre where she would give her rewrites to a secretary for them to be typed up by the time the actors arrived at ten.

Brendan Behan wasn't there to start with, so Joan worked on, making changes by herself, wishing he'd hurry up and come. Gerry attempted twice to get Brendan over by sending the price of the fare. Brendan spent it, maybe on drink, though not necessarily; the dangerous drinking had not yet started. He didn't have the money for it. The third attempt worked: Gerry had sent a ticket. Brendan arrived, stuttering with shyness, as he hadn't been in England since his three-year stint in Borstal as a teenager for bringing over explosives from Dublin.

In his script, he gave almost no indication of what his characters were up to while they were talking, so Joan set her actors to creating an ordinary day in a prison. That meant slopping out, cleaning cells and walking round in a circle during association, which was the prisoners' free time and exercise. As the actors didn't know what was going to happen next, they were driven crazy walking round and round on the theatre's roof, a place strictly out of bounds when Rowland Sales was in charge.

Once they settled down to work on the actual play, all was revealed. The work they had been doing gave the play little gear changes and punctuation. The dialogue could then be floated in over the top.

When not with the actors, Joan looked at the different stories and flows of thought, which some today call units, and, seeing that a unit on this page would have more impact on that page, moved it. For example, inside Act One, Brendan had put a suicide. Joan moved it to the end of Act One. Some units gave away too much or repeated what had already been said. The former could be moved. The latter could be cut. Two characters could be made one, while a chunk of dialogue given to one person could be shared out among other characters who had nothing to do. Individual lines could be sharpened by being shortened. Individual funny lines could be moved to where they would be funnier. Discussions about the pros and cons of hanging were brought right down. It was better for the audience to work those out for itself as the play went along.

What did happen in Brendan's script – and here he was providing one big dramatic muscle – was a hanging at the end. Given that capital punishment had not yet been abolished, it made the play not only new but topical and relevant, and that is what would have made Gerry happy. Joan had to carry on working. In the play, it soon becomes clear that, firstly, the audience is not going to see the quare fellow, and secondly, that he is guilty – there's no doubt he's committed murder, what's more a brutal one – and that therefore no reprieve is possible, so no tension can be built up that way.

Without adding any plot at all but by continuing to tweak in order to keep the dialogue rippling along and the changes of thought or mood coming just at the right moment, Joan was eventually able to hold the audience's attention, while not allowing it to forget what was going to happen. The tension was not the usual. The characters didn't feel it. The audience did. By this jigging around of existing material and not adding lots of new dialogue, Joan was also being faithful to Brendan's intention. On other plays where the plot was OK but the dialogue not so hot, Joan took other measures.

Songs, carefully placed, as Shakespeare knew, were useful too. Brendan had provided one, the 'Old Triangle', and was usually a great source of song, but he wasn't there. Joan, in her own script, wrote the name Ewan, thinking she would have to be in touch with Jimmie. Her faith in his songs hadn't wavered.

In the end, the result could not have looked simpler but to come up with that kind of simplicity requires quite a gift.

Brendan said that he knew of no convict who was hanged who didn't thoroughly deserve it. What he was getting at was the effect it had on all those people around the execution. The audience, while laughing at the many funny lines in the play, becomes one of those people, which is why Ken Tynan wrote: 'I left the theatre feeling overwhelmed and thanking all the powers that be for Sydney Silverman.' Silverman was the MP campaigning at the time for the abolition of capital punishment.

This was the moment when Tynan unequivocally took to Theatre Workshop and in particular Joan; Gerry's work coming to fruition, one might say. His review finished: 'The Quare Fellow will belong, not only in such transient records as this, but in theatrical history.' Another well-known critic of the time, Bernard Levin wrote: 'Brendan Behan has, at one bound, achieved immortality.' In 1965, Silverman succeeded.

The Quare Fellow opened sixteen days after Look Back in Anger and, were you only to have read the reviews, it seemed much more important, but it's John Osborne's play that is regarded as the big gear change in British drama. Maybe it's because Brendan was Irish, while Look Back in Anger was giving younger English audiences, for the first time, the sound of their own voices, their own tune. Of John Osborne, Brendan said: 'Angry Young Man? He's about as angry as Mrs Dale's Diary.' Mrs D was a radio soap opera of the time.

So there was Gerry, the closest he'd ever been to his ambition, the greatest company in the world, and there was Joan at the beginning of a period which she dismissed as not being Theatre Workshop but just writing jobs. Howard Goorney who came back and took over a role in The Quare Fellow, thought the same.

Brendan, arriving on time for the first run-through said: 'Christ, I'm a bloody genius', and, on the first night, standing on the stage: 'Miss Littlewood's company has performed a better play than I wrote.'

Joan regarded The Quare Fellow as Brendan's one proper play and his greatest. What a relief the Abbey turned it down.

Until that autumn The Quare Fellow and Schweik took on their own lives. Both went to the West End, while The Quare Fellow also went on tour. Claude Planson, by then Director-General of the Théâtre des Nations, invited Schweik to Paris, this time not to the Hébertot, but to the bigger, more central Théâtre Sarah Bernhardt, a building Joan was happy to be in. Actually, the actor playing Schweik was wrong. Max Shaw, taking over from George Cooper, was too lean, too obviously clever. It's an indication of how Theatre Workshop, still with no grant, was under constant pressure. Problems had to be solved overnight and that led to compromises. Max as Schweik was not the worst, because he found his way through it.

When autumn came, Gerry, thinking it was time for a holiday, put Joan in the Alvis with some sleeping bags and set off for Italy. Seeing Eduardo de Filippo's company in Naples was all Joan hoped it would be. That's unusual. Often she would imagine something wonderful in a far-off place, only to be disappointed when she actually saw it. De Filippo had a theatre in the poor quarter of Naples, where he wrote and put on plays that were about the people who lived round about.

On the way home – in Florence, to be specific – Joan noticed Gerry stopping to drink at every drinking fountain. They headed on north – Gerry was keen to make it to Ljubljana in Slovenia, then part of Yugoslavia – but the rain came down so heavily they had to forgo camping and find a hotel. It was there that Joan saw Gerry

SENIOR LECTURE HALL STOCKWELL TRAINING COLLEGE, S.W.

Above: Joan's first school and in her words, the best.
Left: The portrait 'Nick' painted of Joan.

Above: For the Spanish Civil War; Below: Joan in her radio days.

Right: Kristin Lind as Lysistrata.

Right: John Bury (Camel) pointing.

Above: The Travellers. Ewan MacColl (Jimmie Miller) in the background wearing glasses, Harry H Corbett clutching a briefcase, Avis Bunnage, eying a soldier; *Below: Uranium 235.* Gerry as Energy.

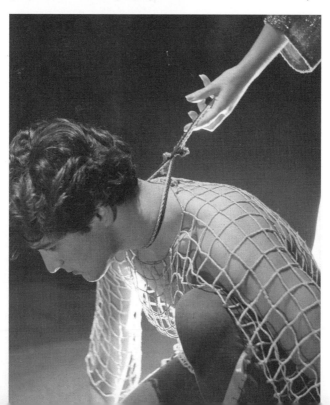

Above: Theatre Workshop in Czechoslovakia; *Below: Twelfth Night.* John Blanshard, Avis Bunnage, Harry H Corbett (Theatre Royal Stratford East).

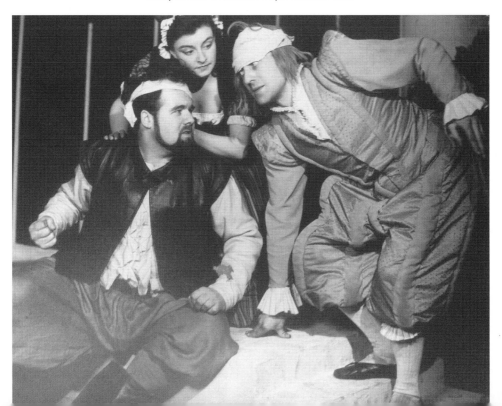

Above: The Alchemist (Theatre Royal Stratford East); *Right: The Dutch Courtesan.* Howard Goorney with slashed sleeves (Theatre Royal Stratford East).

Above: Amphitryon 38 (Theatre Royal Stratford East)*; Below: Red Roses for Me*. Avis Bunnage on the left, Margaret Greenwood with the basket (Theatre Royal Stratford East).

Above: Arden of Faversham. Israel Price, Barbara Brown, Howard Goorney (Theatre Royal Stratford East);
Below: The Good Soldier Schweik. Harry H Corbett, George A Cooper, Barry Clayton (Theatre Royal Stratford East).

Above: Arden of Faversham. George A Cooper kneeling, Barbara Brown, Maxwell Shaw, Harry H Corbett (Theatre Royal Stratford East); *Below: The Good Soldier Schweik.* Maxwell Shaw in bed furthest left, Howard Goorney next to him, George A Cooper, fourth bed in, Gerard Dynevor next to him and John Blanshard next to Gerard (Theatre Royal Stratford East).

Above: The Prince and the Pauper (Theatre Royal Stratford East); *Below: Volpone*. Barry Clayton,
George A Cooper, Maxwell Shaw (Theatre Royal Stratford East).

Above: Volpone (Theatre Royal Stratford East);
Below: The Midwife (Haben) Avis Bunnage, kneeling (Theatre Royal Stratford East).

Above: Mother Courage with Joan as Mother Courage, Barbara Brown, in cart
(Taw and Torridge Festival, Devon); *Below:* Joan and Gerry, Paris Festival of International Drama.

Above: The Sheepwell. Howard Goorney in the middle (Theatre Royal Stratford East);
Below: Edward II. Peter Smallwood in the centre (Theatre Royal Stratford East).

Right: Edward II. Peter Smallwood, Maxwell Shaw (Theatre Royal Stratford East); *Below: The Quare Fellow*. Glynn Edwards, second from left, Brian Murphy, fourth from left (Theatre Royal Stratford East).

Above: You Won't Always be on Top. Stephen Lewis, Dudley Sutton, Brian Murphy, Murray Melvin,
Richard Harris holding can, George Eugeniou (Theatre Royal Stratford East);
Below: Unternehmung Ölzweig (*Operation Olive Branch*) (Maxim Gorki Theatre, East Berlin).

Above: The Maxim Gorki Theatre welcomes Joan and Camel at Berlin's Tempelhof airport; *Below: The Hostage.* Glynn Edwards, Murray Melvin, Margaret Greenwood standing on stair, Eileen Kennally, Robin Chapman, James Booth, Celia Salkeld (Theatre Royal Stratford East).

in the shower. He had lost a lot of weight. Joan, when she first told this story, said that she was shocked but later the word 'shocked' was omitted. People would be asking, 'Hadn't you noticed before?'

In the same way that Joan could step out of life and disappear, she could, sometimes, not see what others could. It was an instinct that kept her away from what would upset her. Throughout her life, when something bad happened, she was often not there. The news would have to be brought to her. It linked up with her retiring side that could also be seen in her sister, Betty. Very serious problems had to be dealt with by someone else, usually Gerry. This time the problem was Gerry.

The worst part of the journey still faced them, driving through the Dolomites – there was snow by then – but the old Alvis just made it. Once in England, Joan and Gerry went straight to Manchester to see a doctor Gerry trusted. The diagnosis was diabetes. Joan, knowing nothing about the condition, asked when Gerry would be better. The doctor took the easy way out and said that it would take two years. He couldn't bring himself to tell Joan that it would last the rest of his life, and rule it too, in the sense that Gerry was not the best patient. Apart from pushing himself too much, he loved wine, and sugary things, and would suffer for it. Someone more disciplined might have fared better, but then they wouldn't have been Gerry.

On top of that, Joan was not the best nurse. She would flutter around in a surprisingly un-Joan-like way, constantly suggesting one thing after another, thus bringing herself very close to being told to shut up. She did at least learn to recognise hypoglycaemia which is an excellent mimic of drunkenness. The speech is slurred. The sufferer becomes quickly and heavily drowsy. She had to learn because when Gerry became depressed, he could start drinking brandy and get drunk for real.

No longer was it only Joan who needed protection: Gerry did too. Driving across Blackheath, he saw a sign, Flat To Let. He took the flat. It was the whole of the upper floor of a large white house which was surrounded by trees and a garden wall. Inside, at one end, was a spacious living room that looked out on to the heath. The front room, Joan called it, as if the flat was a two-up, two-down. At the other end was a big kitchen from which steps led down to the garden. The whole place was called Mill House and when you approached it across the heath, it had a way of disappearing like Aladdin's palace, which suited Joan and Gerry fine. They didn't particularly want to be found. Two years later, Gerry's father bought the lease.

Perhaps it can be imagined that this flat did not have a good effect on certain members of the company, particularly as Joan – like she did with Gerry's comfortable childhood – would play it down. That only made it worse. If you were born with not much, joined a company that was a co-operative and then saw the flat, it's understandable that you might feel a bit narked. If you were born into a comfortable household and hadn't had to worry much about money, you couldn't have cared less. Still, the money Gerry had access to from his father did rankle through the years. On the other hand, if Manny hadn't coughed up when the company was in serious trouble, it could have folded. What this emphasised, though, was the fact that there was Joan and Gerry, and then there was the company, the fulfilling of a wish that was clear in Gerry's letters when Joan was touring Sweden.

He made it into a lively place, though, with a tickertape, a short wave radio, duvets before everyone had them – clouds Joan called them – a pool with koi carp in it, a shower with jets that hit you from several angles, the scent of Roger et Gallet carnation soap, an Aga, a fruit juice squeezer and a huge coffee grinder. Joan, fine for adding the finishing touches, could not have created that kind of comfort and, while complaining non-stop, secretly enjoyed it. Play readings took place in the front room and many people stayed at Mill House, including Brendan Behan and Wole Soyinka, and actors who couldn't get home after dinner. The latter would be roused in the morning by Gerry striding through the flat in a white towelling dressing gown crying out: 'Awake and see your father hanged!' Tom Driberg would like to have moved in. He was a lonely cove and being at Mill House gave him some family feeling.

Downstairs, the neighbours suffered dreadfully, not from noise but from water – the washing machine, to be precise. Torrential leaks flooded their flat. Joan never saw the problem herself: 'It's only water,' and she did have a baby-like love of the stuff.

Bucharest, Warsaw, Leipzig: you can imagine the signs, as in a film, rushing by but, despite Gerry's continuing efforts to get to them, these were not the towns Theatre Workshop made it to. Warsaw was particularly sad, given Gerry's one-day love affair with it. On the other hand, an invitation came from Moscow, first stop Zürich.

CHAPTER SIXTEEN

TO RUSSIA, TO BERLIN, TO COURT

J oan wanted to take a new play. The company would, after all, be appearing
under the banner of the World Youth Festival. Jimmie was writing something
that sounded as if it might have some appeal, *So Long at the Fair* (not to be
mistaken for the Dirk Bogarde film of the same name). Perhaps that would do.

In the as yet unfurnished flat at Blackheath, Joan held a reading. The first scene
was a monologue. A demobbed soldier, on the down escalator at an underground
station, reacts to the advertisements. In the second scene, he joins his friends and
goes round a fair. It was more than promising, but there was no more. Could Jimmie
have it finished on time? No, he couldn't. Another play would have to be thought of.
Joan's habit, when in a jam, was to turn to the classics. They could do *Macbeth* and
Jimmie could play the title role. Jimmie was furious. He had never shared Joan's love
of the classics, so that was that. Not only was his play out, he was too.

Joan, who tended to think that any project she left never happened, thought that
So Long at the Fair began and ended there. It didn't. Jimmie carried on and, years
later, the Maxim Gorki Theatre in East Berlin, which Joan would soon be going to,
put it on under the title, *Rummelplatz*. When Joan was told this, she wouldn't believe
it. Fixed in her head was the conviction that fairs looked dramatic from a distance
but lost their drama on closer inspection. She had to be shown the brochure of the
Maxim Gorki's season.

With Jimmie gone, Joan was minus a Macbeth. New to the company was Richard
Harris, but he really was a raw recruit. It would mean her sitting up with him night
after night, as she had done with Howard Goorney when he was playing John of
Gaunt in *Richard II*. She couldn't face it, and cast Glynn Edwards instead. Glynn we
know nowadays as an amiable stalwart from films like *Zulu* and *The Ipcress File*. Most
famous of all, is Glynn saying to George Cole: 'Evening, Arfur,' as the barman, Dave,
at the Winchester club in the TV series *Minder*. He wasn't a Macbeth. So, not the
right play and not the right actor. Here was a more damaging example of pressure

121

leading to compromise at Theatre Workshop. Glynn was slow, so slow that students in Zürich barracked him. Joan wished she'd made the effort with Richard Harris.

At the Moscow Art Theatre, the company, instead of rejoicing at having made it there, hit up against the unexpected hierarchy Jack Evans had warned Joan of many years before. 'Who is your leading lady?' asked an official, wanting to put her in the star dressing room. It might as well have been the West End.

Going even further back than Jack, Joan remembered André van Gyseghem's pre-war book about the innovative director, Okhlopkov. He had a show on: *Hamlet*. Joan went. Forget actors rushing past you with branches to make you think you were tobogganing downhill. This was dead conventional. Up on a proscenium arch stage was heavy scenery, a different set for every scene, actors who were too old for their parts and it was painfully slow.

Back in London, things were ever-so-slightly perking up on the Arts Council front. A new man was at the top, Sir William Emrys Wiliams, and he was interested in Theatre Workshop. Even so, he was still asking for matching – we give you a £1,000, your local councils give you £1,000 – but, for years, Gerry had been saying this wasn't going to happen. It happens everywhere else in Great Britain, said Sir William. Yes, but it doesn't happen in Stratford, said Gerry. Sir William couldn't believe it. He asked for a meeting with representatives of all the local councils to be present. They didn't want to come: they didn't see the point. Sir William announced that he was going to come in person. The local councils changed their minds. At the meeting, Sir William made a shaming speech about how valuable Theatre Workshop was to the East End and that, if no money was forthcoming, it would have to close. The local councils gave in and contributed a few hundred pounds each year until 1964. The Arts Council gave £1,000 a year which, by 1964, had become £3,000 a year. At that point, the English Stage Company based at the Royal Court – Oscar Lewenstein and his artistic director, George Devine – were receiving £20,000 a year.

Gerry, continuing to explore every avenue, discovered that the Arts Council occasionally gave grants to writers. Very occasionally, as it happened, because there was a belief that writers should suffer until they were accepted and then, when they were accepted, they didn't need help from the Arts Council. Gerry sent them *You Won't Always be on Top*, a play set on a building site by a man who knew about building sites, Henry Chapman. A member of the Drama Panel wrote a report:

> I am sorry but I am unable to make head nor tail of this play. It seems
> to me to consist of a series of disjointed and more or less meaningless
> conversations between a set of peculiarly uninteresting workmen on a
> building site. It also has the disadvantage of being so abominably typed
> that it is almost unreadable.

Theatre Workshop did it anyway. Another heart-sinking hour for a reader was another challenge for Joan and, though she described it as hard work, she thought it one of her best productions. John Bury, using, as he often did, the back wall of the theatre with its three arches in the brickwork, came up with a set that filled the entire stage. Because it was a building site, he was also able to give a part to his favourite toy, a cement mixer. Many of his sets benefited from that mixer because it was used to provide texture, texture being Camel's watchword. Stephen Lewis's first acting job was in this play. Later, he would become a writer as well. Today, he is known for pulling faces and talking in a funny voice for the television comedies, *On The Buses* and *Last of the Summer Wine*. That is not the whole story.

Joan had actors who could do Theatre Workshop but didn't really understand it. Some, on going away to direct, went straight back to weekly rep – learn the lines, learn the moves – and she was disappointed. One of her dreams was unrealised. Stephen had a thoughtful, schoolmasterly side to him and came nearer than most to understanding her. Even more unusual – because he had put on a show himself – he understood Gerry. Most actors, by this time, thought Gerry was just the boss who did the hiring and the firing and was always trying to save money and pay actors as little as possible. You complained to him or you complained about him. As it happened, much of the firing was done because Joan asked for it, not that actors knew. Gerry wanted her to appear to have nothing to do with that side of things. If he thought differently to her but fired the actor to please her, it was especially unpleasant for him. That is what Stephen understood.

The critics disagreed with the Arts Council and gave *You Won't Always be on Top* not bad reviews. When Gerry then sent the Arts Council a play that was properly written, had been done before but wasn't actually much good, the result was almost predictable. *And the Wind Blew* by Edgard da Rocha Miranda got a grant. £100 was the sum. Its run, five weeks, allowed Joan to go to the Maxim Gorki Theatre in East Berlin to direct Jimmie's version of *Lysistrata*, *Operation Olive Branch*. In German it was known as *Unternehmung Ölzweig*. Gerry put a time limit on Joan being away – he didn't want the Arts Council hounding him about Theatre Workshop not doing anything again – and negotiated a decent fee, part of which was able go into the kitty. How did he do deals for Joan's services, someone was curious to know: 'I ask for the first big figure that comes into my head,' he answered. 'It usually works.'

While she was away, a Yugoslav director, France Jamnik, the reason why Gerry was so keen to get to Ljubljana on that holiday, came over to direct Pirandello's *Man, Beast and Virtue*. When Joan directed herself, she preferred the casting to emerge during rehearsals but, because it wasn't going to be her directing, she cast this play in advance, and carefully, giving Richard Harris the lead. On the list that she drew up, she wrote: 'Mickser [that was his nickname] has more talent and presence than anyone else in the company.' Unusual circumstances had made her put on paper the kind of statement she rarely made.

Joan always said she was very happy in East Berlin. Anything a director could want would be laid on. Wherever they rehearsed, the set would be put up, for example. The letter she wrote to Gerry at the time was more nervy. She started by saying she was worried about his problems at the theatre, to which she had contributed, she was sure, but then this was a ritual self-flagellation that she would be performing until long after his death. Second on the list was driving. 'I wish you would promise me – and <u>keep to it</u> – that you will take care of yourself and <u>please</u> please don't take such risks while driving. I don't feel so bad while I am with you because I feel I can watch for both of us? Many bad things happened to Gerry during his lifetime but, as with other fast drivers, it wasn't while driving.

Joan smoked a lot. When directing, it had a particular use. The few seconds needed to take the cigarette out of the pack, strike the match and take the first puff gave her vital thinking time. At the Maxim Gorki, it wasn't allowed: 'I've found a way of smuggling 2 a morning but that's my lot. I'm even getting used to it. I suppose it's just as well for I was smoking far too many in London.'

Having set the scene, she talked about work:

> Today I completed the first rough rehearsals to the end of the play. What hell this play is in <u>any</u> language. Also I've managed to make the cast accept cuts which in Germany is a major feat. They squeal like stuck pigs if you try to take <u>one</u> word from them and of course they all had Ewan's inordinately long original script. Most of the week, we've been working in cuts, rewrites and rearrangements as well as rehearsals which is why I haven't had much time.

Being in East Berlin and the theatre world as well, the inevitable happened:

> They brought me straight to this hotel for lunch from the Tempelhof [airport] – and of course who should be sitting at the next table but Karl Weber [Brecht's assistant she'd thrown out of *Mother Courage* rehearsals] – I pretended he didn't exist but he had seen me first and was very embarrassed. I was with Vallentin [boss of the Maxim Gorki] and a dramaturg from our theatre. Later Camel [Joan took John Bury] came in with a little queer who does decor and, of course, Karl leapt up and greeted Camel and was very effusive to me, though as arrogant and impossible as ever, I thought. He invited me to the Schiff [Theater am Schiffbauerdamm, home of the Berliner Ensemble] but I asked Camel to fix it through our theatre, not through W. I hoped we should not see him again but we did yesterday in the local May's [Bert and May's in Angel Lane] called the Trichter where we eat and drink now. Camel actually mentioned me to W in conversation and I was very cross and asked Camel not to mention me to Weber. I intend to have a good row with him when I have time and perhaps start a war of the theatres here. It's just what they need, everyone is trying so hard not to offend anybody. The Brecht theatre will be dead in 2 or 3 years, that is the general verdict. None of the "young men" are individually capable [Brecht had died the year before] – and Weigel [Helene, actress and Brecht's wife] isn't a producer. They are doing a year's "homage to Brecht" and fishing out everything he ever wrote including *The Private Life of the Master Race (Fear and Misery of the Third Reich)* which I think is terrible and Weigel is all set to devote the rest of her life to "Homage à Brecht."
>
> I must say that I am very happy here. It's fascinating trying to do this job [Joan didn't speak German]. I'm working much harder than I do at home at rehearsals, jumping about all over the clean stage in my new slippers. They're wonderful to work in. They wanted to get

through the play quickly. They're dead scared about time. They usually have 15 weeks – and we go on on December 22nd. [*And the Wind Blew* opened on November the 12th]

I'm afraid I have to show them far too much because it saves time on interpretation. Camel says I go too fast and try to say too much. I will be able to slow down – but not much. The soldiers scenes have been the most successful scenes so far – I've managed to do two decent adaptations on those. Only really good rehearsals I've done.

The actors over 30 are brilliantly efficient, if they had the right incentive they would be great – the younger ones are hopeless – hopeless, untrained, egotistical, they cannot move nor speak – of course they are much more confident and efficient than ours at home. But the older ones! How wonderful they are with the text and I can make the older ones act. I think I will be able to. Something old in them is re-awakening, something that goes back to Laban. Camel says he definitely saw one with a Theatre Workshop expression on his face working his notes in the rehearsal over coffee. Of course, as the dramaturg, Klaus, says, they think only of "the text" not the mime but he says it's because no producers ask for movement at all. And the women!!! Ours are angels compared with them. They fight and sulk and throw temperaments if you cut a word. They fight for more words not for peace. One has been to the president of the republic merely because she doesn't know whether or not she is to use dialect or not. Another refused to rehearse because I'd cut her lines. Lysistrata is perturbed because I don't give her enough attention. They can't work for more than an hour without drooping. Jesus! The dialect one is a real Carmen! [Blanck-Sichel, a German actress who was in Joan's production of *The Dutch Courtesan.*] Anyway, I'll break them in – next week.

The decor man is an irritating little queen – but I've got him squashed – he tried to make "arrangements" of the actors to suit his fiddling little decor the 1st and 2nd day so I put a stop to that. There's a hell of a lot of subjective feeling but it's mainly because the bastards haven't enough *real* problems to face . . . I would like to come back and do a real play with these actors, knowing German.

When Joan got home, she was so fed up with the Theatre Royal and the lack of all that she had been given in East Berlin that she sacked Avis Bunnage on the spot. It happened at the start of rehearsals for *La Celestina,* an adaptation Joan had made, while in Germany, of Fernando da Rojas' novel. This was the play for which she dug out Eileen Draycott, the actress who had been at Manchester Rep with her before the war. Avis turned up a little late in a playful mood. Joan didn't see the funny side, lost her temper and out Avis went. It could have been a delayed reaction. In Joan's mind, it could have been one of the actresses in East Berlin that she was firing.

As to her losing her temper, this was often manufactured. 'Denouncing,' she called it, calculated to humiliate the actor in front of the others and send out a warning.

The actor's ego, only there, in her opinion, to serve the actor's interest, no one else's, was to be crushed. However, on this occasion, she simply lost it.

Avis, 'Bunn' had been with the company for over five years and, after her man, Harry Corbett, had left, had stayed on. Murray Melvin, who had not long joined, found her sitting on the long bench in the foyer in a state of shock. So was he when she told him what had happened – as was Gerry. Avis was too valuable to the company. This time, unable to go along with Joan, Gerry became the go-between. Shock wasn't the only thing, though. When Joan turned against someone she had known for years, it was as if she hadn't known them at all. It was frightening. Three months later, Avis was back.

During a *Celestina* rehearsal – a struggle to find the style – 'Eileen Draycott, hammy; the young ones, nowhere near it' wrote Joan – two plain clothes policemen appeared and took her to one side. They spoke about *You Won't Always be on Top* which puzzled her as she'd already forgotten it. Notes they'd taken at performances showed the dialogue to have been no longer what the Lord Chamberlain had approved. As the run had gone on, changes had been made, on top of which actors had ad-libbed.

Given that the play's only strengths were honesty and immediacy, the continuing work Joan and the actors had done seems to us now to have been essential. In those days, it was breaking the law. One particular moment had got to the policemen. It was when Richard Harris had peed into a hole in the ground while impersonating Winston Churchill. Joan, Gerry, Richard and the author, Henry Chapman, were summonsed. A heavy fine, if imposed, would close the theatre.

Déja vu springs to mind. Had not the same thing happened before the war during the run of *Last Edition*, even down to the note taking, which, when the case came to court, proved to be equally incompetent? More than that, Harold Lever, who had helped all those years before, became involved again. He brought in Gerald Gardiner as barrister, later to be Harold Wilson's Lord High Chancellor. Both took the case for free. Also offering support was Wayland Young, the journalist who campaigned to bring an end to theatre censorship. Two years later, he became Lord Kennet. It was a further example of enlightened Establishment figures and Joan coming together.

The case itself, with the policemen trying very correctly to read out building site slang and getting it hopelessly wrong, had the magistrate contorting himself trying not to laugh. All the accused got off scot-free, so, this time, no fine at all.

A photo appeared in the papers of Joan, Gerry and Richard, smiling and waving. They look a jolly lot, thought the nineteen-year-old Shelagh Delaney in Salford; I'll send my play to them.

CHAPTER SEVENTEEN

SHELAGH

nly a few weeks prior to the photo in the paper, a friend of Shelagh's, a young man, had taken her into Manchester to see Margaret Leighton in a pre-West End performance of Terence Rattigan's play, *Variations on a Theme*. Fascinated as she was by Margaret Leighton's height – Shelagh was tall too – she did not allow it to cloud her judgement of the play, which turned out to be the same as the national critics' when it arrived in the West End. It was no good. Actually, Shelagh's immediate reaction was that she could do better than that.

She sent the play to the theatre with a covering letter addressed to Joan. The envelope was opened by Gerry. Like reading the critics, which Joan didn't do, script reading was one of the jobs he had taken on. It's an important one, but most of the time it's not much fun. Many people, working in theatre and film, try to get out of it. Gerry didn't.

In the letter, Shelagh tells Joan how the young man, who was trying to improve her mind, took her to the Opera House in Manchester and that she came away after the performance realising that, after nineteen years of life, she had discovered something that meant more to her than her life.

The next day, she'd bought a packet of paper, borrowed a typewriter and 'produced this little epic'. It took her two weeks. 'I should be extremely grateful for your criticism – though I hate criticism of any kind'. She tells Joan about knowing nothing of the theatre but the script, 67 foolscap pages – another arrow in the five pages legend – is divided into acts and scenes and is not that badly typed. 'The End. Thank God!' it finishes. Almost as a postscript to the letter Shelagh writes: 'I don't really know who you are or what you do – I just caught sight of your name in the West Ham magistrates' proceedings'. Earlier she had written: 'No matter what sort of atrocity it might be, it isn't valueless so far as I'm concerned'.

Gerry did not return it. He sent a telegram to Shelagh asking her to come at once. He then sent her the fare. 'Dear Mr Raffles', she answered, 'I'm catching the

12 o'clock train from London Road station on Saturday afternoon ... Would it be possible to meet me – or somebody else – at the London station? I daresay I could find my way to Stratford alone – but that might involve my utilising the entire resources of the London constabulary.'

Joan and Gerry were supposed to be putting on Bernard Kops' play *The Hamlet of Stepney Green* – the best thing about it was the title, wrote Joan – but it was swept aside and so was the author, whom Gerry requested leave the building. *A Taste of Honey* was on the stage of the Theatre Royal the very next month, which would have pleased the director, Ken Campbell, who used to complain of 'brochure theatre.' It was posted in April and put on in May.

Nearly everything that happens in the play that Shelagh sent happens in the published version, but not necessarily in that order. That is one of a few general observations that can be made. Jo, the girl, Helen, the mother, Jimmie, the black sailor who gets Jo pregnant, Peter, Helen's boyfriend with the missing eye who is to become her husband, Geof, the gay art student; they're all there and talking pretty much as they always would. If there was a problem, it was the ending. In the original, Jo is taken to hospital by two ambulance men, while Helen and Geof are left in the flat talking in a desultory way about the baby which is soon to be born. Joan, in a version that she wrote, had Helen, sometimes using words that had been cut from Peter and Jo, throw Geof out. Then, on hearing that the baby was going to be black, she too had gone, and for good. Jo was left alone.

This was performed briefly and some in the audience were immensely affected by it. Others were puzzled and so that version was re-written, thus annoying the people who had seen Joan's first version when they came back to see it again. The published version has Jo, alone but with the possibility of her mother coming back, singing a nursery rhyme which Shelagh had included earlier. It came as a sort of reprise with a hint of uplift.

Before that, Helen returns to Jo because Peter has kicked her out. That was not in the original. Shelagh has Helen simply turn up.

About halfway through the original, Helen and Peter, having talked outside the flat, drop in on Jo and Geof and talk some more. During this scene, Peter takes Geof for a ride in his new Lagonda. Joan had Helen and Peter burst into the flat – no chat outside – Peter drunk, aggressive and unpleasant to Geof. It's a quartet that builds to an angry climax. Even so, Helen and Peter leave Jo and Geof alone at the end of it.

In an earlier scene, Shelagh had Jo go off to bed leaving Geof standing alone. In the published version, Geof too gets ready for bed and lies down on the couch, always talking, which means that he can call to Jo in that particular voice people use when they're in bed in different rooms; no new plot, just a gear change.

Before leaving the general observations, you can see that Joan, herself an awkward character with a mother she rowed with, could, with her experience of fast writing in radio, write dialogue for Helen and Jo until the cows came home, though not quite as quirky as Shelagh's. Avis Bunnage, a Manchester girl, with an extraordinary flair for ad-libbing tart remarks that kept inside the play as well the character, added little stings all the way through, like: 'Can you cut the bread on it?' when talking of the baby inside Jo. Avis, back after the sacking, played Helen. 'Thank God', to quote Shelagh, who was not only talented but lucky.

As to Shelagh's dialogue, she wrote sentences which had a tendency, in terms of rhythm, to go on a few syllables too long. Sometimes that was funny. Sometimes it was clumsy, and Joan cut those ones to make the dialogue bounce more. A line that was completely cut was: 'You couldn't chain yourself to that impersonation of a man forever more till kingdom come.'

When Geof first appears in the original, he states that he has been thrown out of his flat and thinks he'll be sleeping under the arches. To add muscle, Joan turned those statements into questions asked by Jo. 'Has your landlady thrown you out?' 'You didn't fancy sleeping under the arches, did you?'

In the original, Geof tells Jo some drawings she's done are good. In the published version, he taunts her with them. 'There's no design, rhythm or purpose.'

In the published version Geof, worried that Helen will not be on hand for the birth of the baby, asks Jo if she has her mother's address. He doesn't in the original.

Helen, in the original, is Irish. Avis was from Lancashire and, on stage, turned outwards to speak to the audience as if she was in variety. She loved variety.

When it came to production, Camel designed a set that gave the essentials leaving plenty of air. It was not a box set. To lift the play out of kitchen-sink realism which didn't interest her – poetry did – Joan had John Wallbank, who was working backstage, go up into the stage-right box and play jazz with a small combo. It covered passages of time, marked the end of one scene and the beginning of another and set the tempo for that scene. 'I think it's going to be all right,' said Shelagh after a run-through.

Joan was under the impression, when the play opened, that the critics didn't like it, but Ken Tynan, still at the *Observer*, did:

> Miss Delaney brings real people on to her stage, joking and flaring and scuffling, and eventually, out of the zest for life she gives them, surviving . . . There is plenty of time for her to worry over words like "form" which mean something, and concepts like "vulgarity" which don't. She is nineteen years old and a portent.

Graham Greene bought her a typewriter.

Between Shelagh, Joan, and Gerry there evolved a parent-daughter relationship, Joan growing ever crosser with her disobedient child.

Once the play was a hit and running in the West End, Shelagh rang Gerry, who was holding the purse strings, to tell him that she wanted to buy a sports car, despite not being able to drive. His answer provoked a letter from Shelagh to Joan:

> I had a very interesting telephone conversation with Gerry the other week but as he started to speak to me in a language, that was arrogant, pompous, witless and hamfisted I soon cut the cackle short on that one and tried to contact you . . . I have never liked being told what to do and I've no intention of starting to like it now.

As well as having a go at Gerry, Shelagh was having a go at Joan for not liking her new play, *The Lion in Love*. 'I didn't expect a word like ARTY . . . I thought you were above that sort of thing.' Anyway, was Joan going to do it or not? 'Lots of love, Shelagh.'

Joan replied:

> I cannot imagine what you expect from me with inferior backyard abuse aimed at someone else . . . Your sense of grievance and self-pity is very disturbing, so is the fact that you still seem to think that plays can be written and sent to theatres to put on. Whether it was Aristophanes, Molière, Shakespeare and his colleagues or Chekhov or Strindberg or any other dramatist worth their salt, half of their work was done alone. The rest must be done actively, in co-operation with the group of artists who are to bring that play to physical life. The rubbish I hear secondhand through Una [Collins, Joan's costume designer and friend of Shelagh's] about "Joan writing your work" appals me. Your work, like anybody else's, had to stand the test of production. In fact, you should know yourself, you have not written "a play", you have produced a good deal of raw material from which you, and, or a group of actors may or may not produce a good play. If you want any sort of talk from me which is any use at all, you'll have to work with me.

This letter was written in 1960 which explains Joan's reference to *The Hostage* in the next part:

> You must know that to work on somebody's play as I did on "Honey" or "Hostage" you must love the authors very much. You must love and understand their work more than you love yourself. It is a tremendously hard task to "form" a play. Without feeling very near to the author you cannot do it.

The letter went on. Joan was not letting Shelagh get away with any of the points she had made. The next section was on Shelagh's inability to get through to Joan, and it's true: in those days, when Joan was at the height of her fame, seeing her was like seeing a rare bird. You counted yourself lucky. Joan, nevertheless, answered:

> Some little while ago, when I wanted very much to talk to you during a couple of days' rest from theatre in Manchester, I missed you. You are equally fatuous in turning up and expecting to grab me at Wyndham's when I had just managed to snatch a few hours there to to make up for lost time on *Hostage* problems. The truth is that neither of us are good at planned encounters. I hate them.

Joan returned to the plays which means there was something other than *The Lion in Love*.

> The first one you sent me which I'm extremely sorry I returned to you – was vivid. It had good writing. I loved a lot of it as I had "Honey" but it was too full of incidents. It hadn't enough development and needed a tremendous amount of technical work done on it. This would have

been done. You took it back, lost it and, eventually sent me another. Now I'm not a reader of plays but at the first attempt I found it very difficult. Any honest person of average intelligence would tell you the work is "arty". If you haven't a slang dictionary, read "schematic" . . . I have lived a long time in theatre and I have seen too many people go that way not to be very upset about it. My first husband [Joan was not married to Gerry], another brilliant Salford writer, went wrong like that. To me, it's a tragedy when this happens. So what was I to say to you. What on earth can I do.

You haven't bothered to send me the rest of the first play. You never felt it was worth your while to work with me at Stratford while this job of forming plays was going on. You must learn yourself. No one can teach you anything. If you want to work at Stratford, let me know.

It was at this time that Joan told Shelagh to study Ibsen in order to learn about structure, as Ken Tynan had mentioned in his review. 'There is plenty of time for her to worry over words like "form"'. Bright, lazy and wayward, Shelagh never really did. What she did do was carry on making laconic remarks – to chic French film director, Roger Vadim: 'How long does it take you to tousle your hair like that in the morning?' – and writing quirky dialogue that was always her own. Anyway, Joan's good instructions were really a roundabout way of turning *A Lion in Love* down. While hating to say 'No' outright, she had no intention of putting it on. Wolf Mankowitz did, though. He put it on at the Belgrade Theatre in Coventry from where it transferred to the Royal Court, Oscar Lewenstein back on the scene again. Clive Barker, one of Joan's actors, directed it and Una Collins designed it. However, the run was short and Shelagh was badly hurt. It was exactly what Joan and Gerry, in their autocratic way, perhaps, were trying to protect her from.

There's something else in that letter of Joan's, the tiniest hint of her sense of humour evaporating as it did with her exasperating half-sister, Betty.

As the years went by, Shelagh could often be seen at Mill House, so at least the friendship carried on, and Joan would not have said: 'Shelagh can drag you down to a point where you think you will never come up again,' if she hadn't been very fond of her.

CHAPTER EIGHTEEN

SUCCESS, FOR WHAT IT'S WORTH

O ne morning at Blackheath, not long after *A Taste of Honey* had opened (May 1958), Joan and Gerry were breakfasting on bacon, eggs and mugs of tea, not because they wanted to but because Beatrice Behan, Brendan's wife, had made it for them. She and Brendan were staying at Mill House and, having been brought up in Ireland, she would have presented the dish as 'Rashers and eggs'. The tea, unless it had been taken from Gerry's selection of exotic teas, would have been even less popular, as both Joan and Gerry preferred coffee.

The scene set, they turned to the morning papers: 'British soldier found dead in Nicosia,' was the headline and, when they read on, they saw that he was only eighteen years old and had been taken hostage. Was there a play in that? It rang a bell in Brendan's mind. He had once taken a hostage out on a pub crawl round Dublin.

This was the story that Joan always told when asked about the origins of Brendan's play, *The Hostage*. Until the late 1990s, that is, when a *Guardian* journalist, wanting to speak to her, rang up and told a different story. It annoyed her no end. Only a few months before *The Hostage* opened at the Theatre Royal Stratford in May 1958, Brendan's *An Giall*, a one-act play written in Irish, had been put on in Dublin, and its plot was the taking of a hostage.

After the breakfast at Blackheath, Brendan went abroad, wrote to Joan and Gerry that he was sober and busy, but came back to Blackheath with nothing. Joan knew because she looked in his room while he was down the road in the pub. The next morning, Gerry, on seeing Brendan and realising that he had not been home all night, jumped out of the shower and, naked, chased him across Blackheath. Joan began to wonder what other play she could do. The trouble was it needed to be something new because, by then, Theatre Workshop was famous for the new. Even Joan, with her love of the classics, was admitting that.

Brendan appeared with a sheaf of papers saying how well the character, Monsewer, sounded in English, which suggests that all he had done was translate

An Giall, particularly as that sheaf came to one act. From then on, it was bits of paper and postcards sent from different places, songs sung over the telephone and Gerry theatening Brendan with his service revolver. Beatrice said that Gerry never understood Brendan, adding: 'Yer man has to have his drink,' which is hard to understand given that 'yer man' died at 41. Or 39, if you were listening to Joan, who took years off people she liked and added them on to people she didn't.

Perhaps, if Brendan had been inarticulate, things might have been different but, with a drink inside him, he could entertain people very well by simply talking, and so the discipline of sitting down with a piece of paper faded.

Three acts or no three acts, it was time to start rehearsals. Joan assembled the company. Brendan came. A crate of Guinness was brought and, for one afternoon, he told story after story, Joan and the actors memorising them. In Joan, this was a well-developed muscle. During her time in radio she had been listening to people's stories for years. As rehearsals continued, Brendan rang in with more funny lines and snatches of song. These allowed Joan and the company to reach the end of Act Two. Her specific task had been, ever so casually, to keep the audience laughing at the stories and yet thinking about the hostage at the same time. In *The Quare Fellow*, the audience knows what's going to happen. In *The Hostage*, it doesn't.

It was the Saturday before the show opened and there was no Act Three. The idea came to create an instant climax with a mad raid. 'I'm a secret policeman and I don't care who knows it!' During it, the hostage, the eighteen-year-old British soldier, is accidentally shot and killed. However, he's not down for long because, a moment later, he's on his feet singing 'The Bells of Hell go Ting-a-Ling-a-Ling', with which the rest of the company joins in. What really makes this scene work, though, and here we're back to rhythm, is the scene that comes before it. At night, an otherworldly dreaminess takes over the characters as if they were not quite the people we knew, then 'Bang!' we're off again.

The Hostage was much more successful than *The Quare Fellow* but Joan did not regard it as Brendan's best work. That would always be *The Quare Fellow*, and for her *The Hostage* was just another of her 'writing jobs'. It went to Paris and New York where Brendan was good value on chat shows, talking again, not writing. A woman called Rae Jeffs, for whom Joan had no time, recorded Brendan and made a book from the tapes. It was not the same as Brendan writing. Nevertheless, when Joan was desperate to extract another play from him, *Richard's Cork Leg*, she too tried recording, but neither she nor Brendan could work the machine. They ended up in a tangle and stopped.

Eight years later, a director, Alan Simpson, having finished the text which Brendan had started, mounted a production in Dublin. As with *So Long at the Fair*, Joan insisted that this couldn't have been possible. There was not enough there. More quietly, she said that she didn't like it anyway because it showed a dark side of Brendan which repelled her.

When Joan remembered Brendan at his best, she described him as an alchemist because he took a horrifying subject, hanging, and turned it into gold. She also said that he taught her tolerance. Her actors were grateful to him for another reason. It was his influence that eased the monastic atmosphere backstage before each show. Joan used to insist on one hour's silence in the dressing rooms. Brendan going round, during that period and chatting to the actors, broke this silence but did no harm. Max Shaw, the one who remembered this, added that he once saw Brendan standing behind an usherette who was leaning over a freezer to take out some ice creams. Said he: 'What's it to be? Fucked or frozen?'

The Hostage was the next play to open at the Theatre Royal after *A Taste of Honey*. Only four months separated them. Four months later, came *Fings Ain't Wot They Used T'Be*, which means that three of the five shows Theatre Workshop was most famous for were first performed inside ten months.

Frank Norman, who wrote the play which became *Fings Ain't Wot They Used T'Be*, was the writer who suffered most from the breezy 'only five pages,' assertion. In fact, he typed 48 foolscap pages, which were divided into three acts with scenes inside the acts. What had led up to it?

It started with the 27-year-old Frank, after an early release from a three-year stretch at Camp Hill prison on the Isle of Wight, writing his account of prison life, *Bang to Rights*. Not only did it find a publisher, but Raymond Chandler wrote the foreword. It got Frank known.

The poet, Stephen Spender, having accepted an article on slang from him for the magazine, *Encounter*, of which he was the editor, suggested he write a play. Frank, barely knowing what a play was, tapped out those 48 pages on his 1904 Olympia typewriter, then put them away. Only when Penelope Gilliatt, features editor at *Vogue*, also suggested he write a play, did those pages see the light of day again. They were based on Frank's time as a teenager laying about at No 86, a café in Soho, or 'kayf' as he would have written it, where he started his stealing and burgling career. He gave the pages to Penelope Gilliatt.

The next thing he knew, a letter arrived from Gerry. He and Joan were keen on this play and wanted him to come down to Stratford for a talk. The tune Joan had heard in the dialogue had got to her.

In the pages of *Fings Ain't Like They Used T'Be*, the play Joan had read, razor king Fred Cochran in his Soho spieler mourned past glories. Lily, his old woman, though not his wife, complained of having to do all the chores with no reward. Redhot, the burglar, in his heavy coat, having just left jail, dropped in and sold Fred a posh stolen jacket. Tosher, the cowardly pimp, urged the prostitutes, Rosey and Betty, to get out on the streets, which they didn't want to do because a new law has made soliciting almost impossible. Fred had a win on the horses and summoned a decorator to have the spieler done up ready for a grand re-opening that night. Rival villain, Meatface, heard about it and came round to carve up Fred but not before the Honourable Percy Fortescue and his girl, Myrtle, had appeared to add the touch of class Fred wanted, and also to recognise his jacket. Sergeant Collins, the bent copper, dropped in for his dropsy. All that was also in the hit show that packed the Theatre Royal Stratford for fourteen weeks and, what's more, packed it with locals, and then went to the Garrick Theatre in the West End where it ran for two years. That needs saying before looking at how this success was achieved.

What went from Frank's original were Effel, Fred's off-stage wife, and the moment when Lily, at the end, ran out into the street waving a gun to fend off any villains who wanted to harm her man Fred. It was melodramatic and inconclusive. What came into the revised script was logical.

Sergeant Collins was an ever-present threat, so he was made ever-present. He didn't just come on at the end. Instead of the prostitutes merely talking about what they did, they were seen at the beginning of the show, out in the street, trying to solicit for custom, with Sergeant Collins doing nothing about it. He was going to collect his backhander later. The decorating scene in Frank's version went for little. Making the decorator decisive and flamboyantly camp, injected energy. A prostitute who worked upstairs was only mentioned in the original. In the performed show, she appeared but hardly spoke. Fred and Lily weren't married, so as a climax they got married on stage. Fizz was added, as the play went along, by telephone conversations held between Tosher, played by James Booth, and a character James had invented called Wozzo Newman.

Some people believe that most of the play was casually ad libbed by the actors during rehearsals. That is not the case. Across Frank's 48 pages, Joan scribbled, in pencil, notes like 'needs extending' and 'needs developing' and *that* is what the actors did. Although you could not have put Frank's play on the stage as it was, those improvisations and ad libs, guided by Joan, were driving towards one thing, which was to make what Frank had written work. Even James Booth's telephone conversations were contained units like *lazzi* in *commedia dell'arte*.

It went further. When Joan and Gerry, with their belief in the power of song, brought in Lionel Bart, whose contribution was probably what made the show the hit it was, the process still carried on. Lionel reacted to what he saw at rehearsals. Fred Cochran was always going on about the good old days, so it was logical and concise to turn his complaining into a song, 'Fings Ain't Wot They Used T'Be'. Nobody could be bothered to get up and do any work; it was just a mood, but it became 'Layin' Abaht'. Redhot was always cold, so his dream – it was Lionel's too – was to go 'Where it's Hot'. One single word in Frank's script, 'contemporary', became a production number, 'Contempery'. With only minor changes in plot, Frank's original play was utterly transformed, but it was transformed from the inside. Joan's letter to Shelagh about having to love the author comes to mind.

However, Joan's faithfulness to Frank's intent meant that *Fings* remained slight, or 'froth', as she called it, and keeping froth frothy is tough. It was symptomatic of what was going on all around Joan at that time. Between May 1958 and May 1960, she was almost completely taken up with not only creating *Honey*, *The Hostage* and *Fings*, but looking after them as well. She managed to do revivals of her *Christmas Carol* and Marston's *Dutch Courtesan* but, though she liked them well enough, she didn't think they were as good as her original productions. Her actors in those earlier ones had benefited from years of in-depth Theatre Workshop training.

Looking after shows included taking them off at Stratford, putting them on there again to be ready for either another visit to Paris, or a transfer to the West End or Broadway, shifting her actors, like Avis Bunnage and Murray Melvin, from one show to another, re-casting with actors she hadn't worked with before and refreshing the parts of shows where once joyous ad libs had become fixed and tired. 'The audience reacts to the moment of invention, not the actual ad lib,' she used to say. It was work that was making her, in this country, phenomenally successful – four shows in the West End at once, taxi drivers recognising her – and internationally famous. None of that kind of work, did she like. She was spinning plates and yet she wasn't actually doing anything, which is one of the reasons why she accepted an unusual job, directing the musical, *Make Me An Offer*. A fast buck was another.

Unusual, because it was a ready-made. Oscar Lewenstein and Wolf Mankowitz brought it to her. Wolf had adapted a novel he'd written about selling Wedgewood and Spode in the Portobello Road. Monty Norman, who would compose the James Bond theme, and David Heneker, later of *Half a Sixpence* fame, had written the songs. The designer, Voytek, had been chosen. The principal casting had been done. It was all ready to go. Joan just had to rehearse it at Stratford and send it to the New Theatre (now the Noël Coward) in St Martin's Lane.

Wolf, whose real name was Cyril but had turned himself into Wolf because it sounded more imposing, was not a great writer. He was, however, a professional, so the nuts and bolts were already in working order. That kind of writer, though, tends not to like changes that haven't been written by them. Consequently he was not pleased when he overheard Joan telling the actor Wally Patch to alter a line to suit himself, if he found it hard to say.

Joan, in turn, was not pleased at having Wolf sitting next to her at rehearsals making judgmental remarks about the actors. Having suggested, in her thunderous denouncing voice, that he try getting up on the stage and doing it himself, she put her arm round his shoulders and walked him out into the foyer. She was throwing him out of the rehearsals of his own show. Unlike her sacking of Avis Bunnage, this was Joan doing her usual – erupting, but not really. Moments later, she was back rehearsing and laughing. You can't do that if you've genuinely lost your temper. Anyway, the show arrived safely at the New Theatre and won the *Evening Standard* Award for Best Musical of 1959.

With all this fast work going on and no time for training, Joan, when searching for new actors, discovered a shorthand: cabaret performers. These were people who sang, danced and played comedy, sometimes to tough audiences, and who could bring an energy and a directness to the stage that a drama-school trained actor couldn't. It accounted for Barbara Windsor and Toni Palmer, who played Rosey and Betty in the West End production of *Fings*, and Victor Spinetti who was in *Make Me An Offer*, though not playing the part Joan wanted him to,

Charlie, the lead. Wolf had already booked Daniel Massey, whom she regarded as a dud. Sheila Hancock, who was also in *Make Me An Offer,* was a special case. She had been to drama school but, like other actors arriving at that time, had felt, as had Joan all those years before, that they didn't fit in because they didn't have the right look, the right shape, the right voice, but also felt there had to be something out there for them somewhere. That something turned out to be Theatre Workshop.

Victor, who in the space of eighteen months went from *Make Me An Offer* to Jonson's *Every Man in His Humour* at Stratford East, to *The Hostage* on Broadway and to *Fings* at the Garrick, never mind being twice miscast, enjoyed working with Joan because, as he said, she set him free. Barbara and Toni tended to disapprove. They had only auditioned because they knew they were coming to the West End, and their training, mainly in dance, had taught them to learn their lines and do exactly as they were told. However, their antipathy so amused Joan that they became her teacher's pets. After all, they could deliver the goods. Barbara, Toni and Victor were all working in cabaret with Danny La Rue.

Gerry, who was spending much of his time ferrying Joan round in his pale blue Buick with soft suspension, protecting her from importuning journalists and stardom-seeking actors, while supervising contracts and changing the telephone number at Blackheath, had sort of got what he wanted, recognition for Joan. Of that he could have hardly got more, but things weren't really right. The Arts Council was still proving difficult, this time in a different way. Jo Hodgkinson was extremely interested in all this money that was coming, or supposedly coming in. Where was the Arts Council's cut? Gerry, after fifteen years of the Arts Council not being interested in Theatre Workshop, and still not providing the kind of grant that would put an end to Joan having to spin plates, was in turn not very interested in Theatre Workshop being helpful to the Arts Council. He wanted the money for new plays, and so the dance of dysfunction went on. Still, his belief in Joan's talent and in the Theatre Royal as a base for new and relevant work was solid. Joan did not feel like that.

For her, the Theatre Royal was old-fashioned and limiting, while scrambling for hits and losing actors was giving her the pip. Her aims and Gerry's aims were taking the two of them in different directions.

CHAPTER NINETEEN

An Old Dream Revived,
or Just Buggering About?

It would be wrong to have the idea that Joan's aims were as clear as Gerry's. It's safer to say that she was entering another 'I don't know what I'm doing but, boy, is everybody else going to pay for it' period like she had in her teens. And people did pay because the energy she could bring to not knowing what she was doing was dangerous. The build-up to this period had begun ages before but, by 1960, it was accelerating.

Claude Planson asked her to bring an English classic to the Théâtre des Nations, but quickly. Not too confident, she mounted a production of Ben Jonson's *Every Man in his Humour*, the one that had Victor Spinetti in it, in London, that is. He couldn't make it to Paris. The money he was earning in cabaret with Danny La Rue was vital to him and his boss there, Bruce Brace, would not let him off, not even for four nights. Instead, Murray Melvin, free of Geof in *A Taste of Honey*, had to take over Brainworm, Victor's character. Bob Grant was also in the play and he won the Théâtre des Nations' Best Performance award playing the merchant, Kitely. It was gratifying but Joan did like to get things right for Paris and the feeling persisted that she hadn't.

John Bury's set for *Every Man*, covered in real bricks, became the set for *Sparrers Can't Sing*, which was Joan's next production. Stephen Lewis's play was another example of her taking work that would never have been accepted by anyone else and making something of it. What Steve wrote was almost entirely a monologue spoken by Gran, an amusingly loquacious character based on his own gran. There was almost nothing there and yet a feeling came off the page that was golden. Joan broke up the monologue and, by means of lots of comings and goings, managed to pull the wool over the audience's eyes, while preserving the golden feeling. It ran for ten weeks at Stratford and the following year, 1961, was revived in order to go to the Wyndham's Theatre. Looked at on its own, there would seem to have been nothing wrong. It was teaching Gerry that, as with *Fings*, characters who talked like people who lived near the Theatre Royal but didn't lecture them, would draw a local audience. As far as Joan was concerned, though, it was a play that had to be taken off, put back on and then transferred.

Hal Prince came over from America with a new play by James Goldman, *They Might be Giants,* that he wanted to try out at Stratford East. It was about a mad man who thought he was Sherlock Holmes. Joan's actors liked the play. Joan liked the play. James Goldman liked Joan. Joan liked James Goldman. Hal teased Joan because he saw her being driven round London in a Rolls-Royce. Harry Corbett came back to play the mad Sherlock Holmes character. The mood was not bad. There was more money than usual for the set and Camel and Joan were pleased with their idea for *periaktoi,* quick scene changes. These are prisms, usually three-sided, with a different scene drawn or painted on each side. You line them up, so that they create a flat surface but when you turn a handle that connects them all, the prisms revolve to give you another picture. Although the word *periaktoi* is Greek, they came into their own during Renaissance times. They don't always work. 'When they all turn together it is magical but that is seldom,' Joan wrote. 'Better still when all the bloody screens are gone for that last mad "theatre scene" and the whole stage is open. Really and fundamentally dislike "set changes", prefer the Elizabethan and Greek permanent.'

They Might be Giants, clever as it was, did not catch on here, nor back in America, and neither did the film with George C. Scott playing the Sherlock Holmes part. The day after the play closed in London, a month after it had opened, something in Joan snapped. She was with Gerry and Tom Driberg at the time and it was nothing more than a casual remark, a bit snide perhaps, that did it. She walked out into the night, away from Theatre Workshop, which she had long thought dead anyway, away from the Theatre Royal, and away from Gerry. For anyone who had put a lot of themselves into Joan, watching helplessly as she walked away, would have been terrifying. They'd be watching their own life walk away with her. In letters as a young man to Joan, Gerry said that all his energy came from her. If he knew that she was at hand, he could do anything. The opposite was happening now and, only two weeks after the papers were signed making him owner of the Theatre Royal.

If there were moments when Joan came near to her idea of autism – cutting oneself off from the outside world – this was one of them. Otherwise, the cruelty of it is hard to understand. As with her going off people, it was as if she had never known the person at all. Over the years, she continuously chastised herself for her actions but she didn't stop doing them.

She went to the block of service flats where Jim Goldman had been staying and moved into his empty room. Tom Driberg found her, told Sidney Bernstein, boss of Granada TV, and suddenly Malcolm Muggeridge, the journalist and TV personality, had cut short his holiday in order to interview Joan on television. It indicates how extraordinarily famous she was by then. Her departure from Theatre Workshop had already been an item on the television evening news. Other theatre directors did not receive that kind of attention. On the Muggeridge show, she clowned around as if nothing was really wrong, sticking her bottom out towards the camera as she turned to retrieve her lost woolly hat.

She received a hundred pounds for the interview and that was how she was able to buy an air ticket to Nigeria. She had plans to film Wole Soyinka's play, *The Lion and the Jewel*.

Because of her fame, many film producers wanted her to direct for them, Harry Saltzman being one. He was co-founder of Woodfall, the Royal Court's film arm, and the producer of *Look Back in Anger*. He thought *The Lion and the Jewel* would be great.

She went to say goodbye to Gerry. He cried. She couldn't wait to be off. A few days later – a visa was needed – she went to look at a grand old house that had been opened to the public for a day. Tom took her. A young man with long dark hair falling over a stiff white collar walked round with them. He didn't go away. This was the 26-year-old architect, Cedric Price.

In one evening, he became the symbol of what would immediately happen to Joan, a rackety way of living, and of a dream that would run through the rest of her life. It would fly in the face of all Gerry's aims.

They started an affair at once. Joan was so taken aback that she cautiously referred to Cedric in her diaries as Z. For the rest of that month, the two pinballed around London, then Paris, Turin, and Rome. She was so unused to paying for anything herself that she took to writing out all her expenses, right down to a cup of coffee. Next to these lists would be: 'Feel terribly lonely – alone and depressed'; 'JL VERY depressed'; and 'VERY MISERABLE.'

Nigeria didn't suit her at all. Although she found the people she met entertaining – 'black Irish,' she called them – the heat dragged her down and her hair started to fall out. Even in the middle of nowhere, she only had to say the word 'film' and eyes lit up at the thought of Hollywood and dollars, two words in everyone's vocabulary. She was supposed to be meeting Wole but he, as much of a butterfly as Joan, had made himself scarce. He was In Venice, wondering where Joan was.

Dreading her upcoming birthday – she would be 47 – she wrote: 'IF ONLY I'D NOT SPLIT, IF ONLY I'D NOT MET SOMEONE ELSE AND SUCH A ONE! WE COULD HAVE LEFT STRATFORD TOGETHER, MADE FILMS together – ANYTHING TOGETHER.' Well, possibly, but she didn't, and the film idea was a bit optimistic anyway. She had no experience of making them and Gerry didn't like the people who did. After a month of Nigeria getting her nowhere – Wole did turn up but only at the end – she came home, where she immediately complained of the cold, got toothache and learned that Gerry had been in a serious accident.

It was Harry Saltzman who told her, but only in passing. Here was another case of bad news being brought to her. Harry was actually in the middle of trying to push the *The Lion and the Jewel* along, though with Joan and Wole it wouldn't have been easy.

Gerry, Joan discovered, had just returned from travelling the waterways of France on a motor boat he'd bought, when, berthed near Beaulieu, he had lit a match in the galley and nearly sent himself to kingdom come. Cookers on boats are often fuelled by Calor gas, and Calor gas has no smell.

Joan went to Salisbury where Gerry was lying, badly burned, in hospital. Sitting by his bed, she did what she usually did in awkward circumstances. She rattled on about everything that was of no interest to the person she was talking to at all. Weeks later, when Gerry was well enough to go home, she installed him at Blackheath with a housekeeper, sat with him for a while, which made him happy, and then went off to see Cedric, which made Gerry unhappy. Cedric was ill too, very ill, but he got better. In the weeks to come, the mere word 'architecture' would infuriate Gerry, while Cedric said to Joan: 'If you leave me, I'll kill you.'

The pinballing carried on. Avis Bunnage referred to it as, 'That time when Joan was drinking brandy.' Normally Joan hated spirits. Her diary took on a different tone. Crammed together, suggesting a certain buzz but little more were lots of names: Shirley Bassey, Bernard Levin, Lionel Bart, Victor Spinetti, Sidney Bernstein, Dan Farson, Henri Cartier Bresson, Peter Brook, Peter Hall, Alun Owen, Peter Shaffer, Peter O'Toole and Orson Welles. Along with these were restaurants, Scott's, Leoni's, The White Elephant and many others, plus entries like 'Drinks at the Ritz with Ken Tynan,' or 'Muriel's horrid club.' This was the Colony Room in Soho where members would go for a drink in the afternoon. If there was one thing Cedric had in common with Gerry, it was a knowledge of restaurants and booze. Outside one pub, Joan sat on the kerb and thought: 'I have gone mad.'

She kept saying to herself that she had to drop Cedric. It wasn't as if he was thoughtful or attentive like Gerry. If anything, he was rather unpleasant. Sitting in the front of a car, knowing that he was snogging Shelagh Delaney in the back, hurt her in a way that she was quite unused to. This pain, however, made no difference. She was amazed at the number of times she went back to him but then, he listened to her dream, and that would last long after the affair was over.

The dream went right back to her hatred of family squabbles as a child and the scabbing Oxbridge students of the National Strike in 1926. 'A place where all knowledge would be available . . . a place to play and learn . . . The hate and aggression that are part of us, even our petty feelings can be transformed by creativity.' Those thoughts that Joan imparted to her art mistress, Nick, when they were in Paris together, the ones that came across in her book as an Ibsen-like plant, they were what she imparted to Cedric.

Without telling Joan, Cedric went away, set to work and came up with that kit of parts known as the Fun Palace, which would influence, among others, the architects, Piano and Rogers, when they settled down to design the Beaubourg Centre in Paris.

Cedric, however, was young and unmindful of practicalities like money. Joan, just by talking, could create the Palace before your eyes but soon she would be talking to people who would go away thinking: 'What was that all about?'; and those were the people who would be giving planning permission and providing money. What Joan was actually on about was more akin to a university, one that anyone could go to. Unfortunately, Jennie Lee, arts minister of the time, said: 'What people want now is fun.' It inspired Joan to come up with the name Fun Palace, but it caused confusion.

This is reminiscent of Gerry and the David Lewis Centre in Liverpool shortly after the war. It was no good being vague, he had learned. Maybe, with the experience he had gained since that time, her could have helped Joan out. He didn't. The idea of the Fun Palace was anathema to him. As far as he was concerned, it was a whim, a waste of Joan's time and talent. In public he said nothing but, occasionally, he would let slip the odd giveaway remark. 'Off with your pooves and punks?' he said to Joan, watching her prepare for one of her disappearing acts. Even that was a coverall. Joan had lots of pooves and punks as friends.

Designing the Fun Palace, finding patrons, finding a place to put it and meetings with authorities happened over a period of years, so it had to come in between Joan doing other work.

She read the script of *Blitz*, Lionel Bart's new musical, and even said that she would direct it, knowing full well that she wouldn't. Peter Hall asked her to direct *Henry IV, Parts One and Two*. This went as far as auditions. Joan told a story about sabotaging them by sending the actors to the pub opposite, while Peter Hall and Peter Brook sat waiting in the dress circle. It ended with her sailing off into the street with Zero Mostel, her Falstaff, whom the two Peters had attempted to audition. This story is slightly spoiled by Joan later excusing herself graciously in a letter to Peter Brook, explaining that she didn't just do shows. Everything she did had to have an *arrière-pensée*. Peter then put Zero into a short comedy film he directed about an opera singer coming to London as a last-minute replacement. He had to rehearse in the car travelling from the airport. Joan didn't know about that.

In 1962, Peter Hall tried again, this time with John Gay's *The Beggars' Opera*, to be performed at the Aldwych Theatre. The letter he wrote was casual and jolly, but it casually and jollily included the casting; with Derek Godfrey, Doris Hare and Patience Collier among the names. Patience and Joan went back to RADA days but the others suggested that Peter Hall was insuring himself with the thought of solid performances, whatever Joan got up to. In the end, those actors did appear in it but with Peter Wood directing. Sean Kenny designed it. Sean had been discovered by Joan for *The Hostage*. In the case of the John Gay, he was the only one the critics admired unreservedly. The *Two Henrys* were supposed to have been designed by John Bury and, though that particular project foundered, he became Peter Hall's designer at Stratford-upon-Avon, the Aldwych and Glyndebourne, ending up head of design at the National Theatre when it moved in 1976 to its current home on the South Bank. This didn't please Joan one bit.

The Lion and the Jewel slid informally to the back burner. Casting actors in another country, setting up the right team for filming in a difficult terrain and Joan's inexperience at everything to do with film was nagging at her, not that she let on just yet. When Joan didn't know what she was doing, the front she put up was so convincing that no one spotted a problem. If anyone could, it was Gerry, and Harry Saltzman suggested that he be some kind of producer, but another project took over.

Together with Stephen Lewis, Joan wrote a screenplay entitled *Sparrers Can't Sing*. It wasn't really Steve's stage play. It was the story of a character who, in the play, was only talked about. This was a film that would be much easier to make and Harry Saltzman was still interested. He didn't do it, though, and Joan found herself working with a producer called Donald Taylor based at Elstree Studios, home of the Cliff Richard musicals and some tired old triffids lying around on the back lot.

She had the cast she wanted, all Theatre Workshop actors, including its stars, James Booth and Barbara Windsor, and it was all going to be great fun. Joan's mood was light-hearted. 'I always thought of film as peripheral,' she said, her idols being Chaplin and the Marx Brothers, whom she saw at a time when people went to the flicks and, as like as not, sloped in halfway through. However, the fun soon ended.

Before the war, with unemployment all around, film technicians had to put up with working all hours. After the war, they didn't. Hours became strict. Tea breaks were on the dot. Overtime was costly. Demarcation was precise: Hair had nothing to do with Make-up and neither had anything to do with Wardrobe. The camera had four people working on it. Sound had four too, even when little Nagra tape recorders came in. Imagine Joan coming in on this set-up. With those sorts of rules and regs, Theatre Workshop would not have lasted a day.

Even before filming, things were not going well. Donald Taylor sent Joan out with the cameraman, David Watkin, to shoot tests. Joan, with Chaplin in mind, asked him to shoot no close-ups. Donald Taylor used this as an excuse to sack David who went on to light *The Knack*, *Help!*, *Charge of the Light Brigade*, *Catch-22* and *Out of Africa*. Happily, he did get to work with Joan but not on this film. The cameraman Joan had to cope with was Max Greene, known to his colleagues as Mutzi Grünbaum. If you wanted a creamy close-up of Anna Neagle with sparkling earrings, there was no one better, though it took him ages to achieve it. For Joan he was hopeless. Along with most of the crew, he had no interest in her way of working, which was assembling the entire cast each morning, instead of scheduling them, rehearsing for quite some time, not choosing angles, and only then shooting. It cost a fortune.

Bringing in John Bury and Una Collins as consultants only elicited angry letters from the ACTT union, while Equity, the actors' union, got het up because Joan wanted to use May Scagnelli of Bert and May's to play a stallholder.

It's painful to read this list of misfortunes, because there were technicians around who would have been sympathetic to Joan's way of working. All she needed was the right producer to assemble them, but she was out on her own and that was never a good thing.

This experience, which Joan relayed to Penelope Gilliatt in a huge *Observer* interview, put the tin lid on *The Lion and the Jewel,* as Joan explained in a letter to Harry Saltzman when turning it down. He, however, was on his way to the airport and the filming of *Doctor No.*

Gerry, to whom Joan had returned, and who used to say, 'You think everything stops when you go away,' had been busy.

CHAPTER TWENTY

OH WHAT A LOVELY WAR

Gerry was desolate at Joan's departure but he didn't let go of the Theatre Royal; after all, he did own the bricks and mortar. The flames in the galley explosion left his face intact, so he looked pretty much the same and wore pretty much the same too: chunky sweaters in the winter, open-necked shirts in the summer and trousers that were always falling off. He was big but his hips were straight. Next to his skin, though, from then on, had to be silk: it was all he could stand.

While Joan was making *Sparrers Can't Sing* which led him to use the expression, 'The dead hand of the British film industry,' he listened one afternoon to a radio programme, *The Long, Long Trail*. It was a feature, the sort of programme Joan had made before and during the war at the BBC. The subject was the First World War and it had come about as a result of something that had happened to its producer, Charles Chilton.

While holidaying in France, he had gone looking for the grave of his father who'd been killed there in the war. He'd wanted to take a photograph but couldn't. There was no grave. What he found was a wall with his father's name on it, along with those of 35,942 other soldiers who fell in the battle of Arras and who had no known graves.

How had so many been killed in such a small area and in such a way that they could not be buried? This question led Charles to produce *The Long, Long Trail*. By means of First World War songs and a commentary, it told the story, not of the officers, but of the men. That was the hook that caught Gerry. A hunch came to him that a show could be made about the First World War, so, knowing he wanted to use those songs in this show, he contacted Charles Chilton. After that, he commissioned Gwyn Thomas to write the actual play. Thomas did, but it didn't fit the bill. Gracefully, he bowed out. Gerry tried again. He commissioned the Canadian writer Ted Allen, and that, amazingly, brought him to the beginning of 1963. Amazingly, because what happened before the next three months were out, most people would have thought could only have happened over a much longer period.

As the year started, Joan and Gerry were on what, even for them, was a remarkably rotten holiday. They were in North Africa. 'Colours of Morocco, all repulsive,' wrote Joan who had a bad cold, while Gerry was looking ill. His face was pale and there were shadows under his eyes. Excursions, with Gerry driving at top speed up mountains, only had Joan 'stiff with fright,' while one excursion with local hitchhikers on board nearly got both their throats cut.

What started out as a pleasant walk through a market inspired Joan to suggest that Gerry adopt an Arab boy. This, at its best, was puzzling and, at its worst, cruel. Gerry knew Joan didn't want children: 'I'd rather stab my belly.'

Next, floods forced a huge detour which so tired Gerry that he ended up sprawled across the dinner table with his nose in the coffee and, that night, in their bedroom, Joan was either feverishly hot or freezing cold.

The flight home was delayed and, at Blackheath, there was thick snow. The next morning, Joan complained of a bad ankle and toothache. Having returned home after seeing the dentist, she wondered vaguely what she was going to do next and, once more, picked up *The Lion and the Jewel* but then wrote: 'Wole, I have overrated. He overwrites.'

Ted Allen and his wife, Kate, came for lunch. Joan found Ted intelligent and the next day agreed to do 'Ted's war play.' Gerry went off to book Avis Bunnage and Ann Beach. Ann had been with the company for some years. Joan wrote in her diary, 'I am safe in theatre – yes, because Gerry protects me – and the work.'

Three days later, she actually read Ted Allen's script and put this in her diary. 'HE HAS NOT PULLED IT OFF!' For the rest of that day she didn't say anything. Gerry cooked Dover sole with a good dressing.

The next day, made filthy tempered by the play and with toothache again, Joan went on the attack, but it wasn't Ted Allen she went for. It was Gerry of whom she had just written, 'Gerry protects me.'

'You and Ted don't know what you're saying,' she said.

That evening Gerry had a bad attack of hypoglycaemia. He was crying and confused. Joan sent for the doctor. Sugar was needed, not food. Balance was restored, but Gerry was very cold in bed that night. Once more, Joan chastised herself. It was her fault.

The next day Ted Allen came for lunch. Joan didn't have a go at him, because there was no bust-up. In the afternoon, Raymond Fletcher, the military adviser, dropped round. He suggested that Gerry contact Basil Liddell Hart for help (Liddell Hart was an admired military historian). More immediately, Gerry spoke to John Bury, who was by then working at the Royal Shakespeare Company. Joan wasn't pleased. She resented his attitude to Gerry. 'Trying to act superior to his rejected father figure. So now his new dad is Peter Hall.'

That was the weekend over. On Monday, Joan couldn't face 'Ted's awful play.' 'Why go on?' she thought, 'Why shouldn't Gerry just be happy? He enjoys this house! He says he loves it. He says he hasn't long to live! I reject that! It needn't be.'

'Bloody film again,' was Joan's next entry in her diary. She was ringing Harold Lever to see if she could have her name taken off *Sparrers*. It didn't happen. In the evening, she went to see the play, *Semi-Detached* by David Turner: 'Author wants me! IT'S AWFUL,' she wrote, while, at the stage door, she bumped into the play's star, Laurence Olivier.

The following evening, for half an hour, she looked at Ted Allen's play before John Bury came round for a meeting. At the meeting, she said her piece. 'It's anti-German. Haig must be presented as a hero. It's pro-gun, pro-bomb.' Haig was Field Marshal Douglas Haig, commander-in-chief on the Western Front during the First World War. His tactics brought about huge losses on the British side.

The next day was the beginning of another weekend and, with it, came another ailment. Joan had a bad chest. Those of her actors, who are still alive, will remember that this happened almost invariably during the last few days of rehearsals, and Gerry always did the same thing: he brought mugs of hot milk down to the stage. Joan, as she had made plain in Sweden, hated milk and hid the mugs behind the proscenium arch.

There were no mugs of milk when she and Gerry, that Saturday, had another think about the dilemma they were in. Joan suggested using press cuttings of the period, material from Shaw's play *O'Flaherty VC*, and dances of the time. Shaw is often criticised for arguing so well on behalf of both sides, that no one knows where he stands. *O'Flaherty VC* is a short play that is not like that. It is Shaw at his most outspoken. It was also Joan looking to the classics again when in a jam. That afternoon, she went to the Tate Gallery, the one place she could be sure, when she was a little girl, of being happy.

'Sunday 3rd Feb,' wrote Joan:

> THE DAY. YES! GERRY bullied me to work on WAR PLAY. So to front room and dictated idea to Gerry till 3 p.m. Took white wine, nuts and olives. Felt great, ENERGETIC AT LAST! Made lunch, finished script idea. Then wrote analysis of *Semi-Detached*. Gerry to T.R. [Theatre Royal] to show Camel my idea. Camel likes it. When Gerry back, tell him I'm sad.

But why she was sad she didn't say. What she had been dictating was the skeleton, which, with its flesh on, would become *Oh What a Lovely War*.

During the week she had to go back to cutting *Sparrers Can't Sing*. Work went very slowly. Charles Chilton, whose name Joan kept spelling wrongly – Chiltern, she always wrote – came to Blackheath with his arranger, Alfie Ralston. 'Boring cronies,' Joan wrote, which was all very well, given they were going to be with the show for quite some time; Alfie especially.

Monday, 11 February: the first day of rehearsals for the war play. Assembled were Victor Spinetti, Ann Beach, Brian Murphy, Murray Melvin, Griffith Davies, Fanny Carby, Myvanwy Jenn, Stephen Lewis, Larry Dann, Bob Stevenson who was going to choreograph and some BBC singers off Charles Chilton's radio show. Avis Bunnage would not be involved until much later.

Gerry played Charles's programme on a tape recorder. Joan was revolted by the sentimentality of the singing. Victor, with childhood memories of Remembrance Sunday in Wales, was revolted by the songs themselves. The company read *O'Flaherty VC*, had a look at Ted Allen's script and talked about the research they were all going to have to do. Stephen Lewis, having said that he could do better himself, walked out, as did most of the BBC singers. The opinions of the others, assuming they had any, did not impress Joan.

The next day, Joan went back to working on *Sparrers*, leaving the company to get by on its own. Some afternoons, that week, Joan popped in to rehearse. Saturday was the first day she could settle down again to the script. Gerry brought her a bunch of flowers.

On Sunday, Joan had the idea of the pierrots, 'girls swathed in tulle.' It was, in other words, more thinking about an approach to this big subject. It wouldn't be head-on but oblique, through stylisation. At one stroke, the pierrots would take away khaki – Joan hated brown on stage – blood, realistic deaths and real guns. The idea came, of course, from the pierrots she'd seen on that one holiday she'd had as a child in Ramsgate. She was pleased with herself.

Back and forth Joan went between the cutting rooms in Soho and the stage of the Theatre Royal until she reached the end of the week, which allowed her to do some more work on the script. It wasn't Shaw that went into it, but *Schweik*. The walk in the park and the beer stall scene at the beginning were a straight lift. Joan grabbed anything when she was in a hurry.

The next day, the company read what she'd written. Gerry had the problem of dealing with the screaming Ted Allen. It was the discarding of Morris Blythman all over again. Joan had to have the spur of something that didn't work in order to make something that did. Ted Allen's play was a hectic fantasy that didn't allow an audience in to understand what was going on. He'd used some of the songs but only because Gerry had told him to. He did mention profiteering and he did ask for a gadget that gave the casualty figures but, there, all resemblance to the show known as *Oh What a Lovely War* ended. As to the gadget, Joan had used information on placards before the war in her agitprop days. From this bad play, she saw that telling the story in simple scenes, allowing the songs full prominence to further the action, was her way forward. Even so, she did begin to wonder if she could pull it off but, a day later, felt that she was at last getting down to some real work.

Two days after that, she got up early to read Barbara Tuchman's book, *The Guns of August*, which influenced her greatly, and Alan Clark's *The Donkeys*, which, she said, didn't. Alan Clark later sued, claiming the unauthorised use of his material and, when the film rights were sold, got a piece of the action. That evening Joan went with Tom Driberg to the Kentucky Club, a haunt of the Kray twins. Both Tom and his friend, Bob Boothby, the politician and TV personality, were involved with the Krays. Joan knew them because they had helped with traffic organisation on the film. Gerry, when he heard about this visit, was furious. Joan was complaisant. Her sympathies lay with the working class who loathed the police and preferred to deal with the mafia.

That Sunday the title of the song, 'Oh it's a Lovely War', became the title of the show except 'it's' was changed to 'what'. Ted Allen claimed that this was his idea and, to this day, he is credited with it.

On Monday, Joan spent the day with the company 'learning to sing the songs as if they were making them up, as if they were in those <u>circumstances</u> not just BLOODY SINGING!'

'GERRY GETTING A NEWSPANEL FOR ME! ! !' This, in Joan's diary, stands all on its own, not on any particular day. It was very important. Joan had seen one going round the side of the Friedrichstrasse station when she was working in East Berlin and had fancied having one ever since. This would relay both trivia and the number of battle casualties. Way back on *Last Edition*, Joan had been doing something similar but then, altogether, the experience she had gained in agitprop days and on radio features were a huge influence on the show that was to come.

The actors may have been rehearsing all day on Tuesday 26 February but that evening they piled off to the première of *Sparrers Can't Sing* at the ABC cinema in Stepney. After all, Victor Spinetti, George Sewell, Griffith Davies, Murray Melvin, Brian Murphy and Fanny Carby, all in the *Lovely War* company, were all in the film too. Joan rang the Krays to ask what they were doing. 'We're blowing up balloons.' It was irresistible. Gerry drove Joan past the Kentucky Club. The balloons said 'Welcome to Princess Margaret from the KENTUCKY'.

Princess Margaret didn't show, but the evening went well and the reviews the following day were not that bad. Slight as it was, this, for Joan, was a relief.

Gerry, who could not have been more behind Joan on *Lovely War*, sent for an army sergeant to teach the boys in the company rifle drill. When he arrived, he immediately ordered the women off the stage. Joan and some of the others hid in the gallery. There were no rifles to rehearse with, which annoyed the sergeant, but the walking sticks and umbrellas that the actors picked up were not far off what really happened at the start of the First World War. There weren't rifles available then, either. 'It is so obscene, it's funny,' wrote Joan. Murray Melvin, who, contrary to what the others thought, had done his national service, got the giggles, which only made the sergeant crosser. Joan kept that bit in.

Because of the sergeant's obscene language, which would have been impossible on a stage in 1963, with the Lord Chamberlain still active, Victor Spinetti, who was playing the drill sergeant, came up with a gibberish version. It was simply something he could do. French, Welsh, neither of which he knew, and the sound of famous actors, he could do them all and as Joan wrote: 'It's screamingly funny.' That same night, she also wrote: 'This show will be the making of Victor Spinetti.'

Of course, the next day, the run-through was flat. Joan told Victor to drop out and watch George Sewell play his part in the first half. According to Joan, Victor immediately spotted the flat bits and knew what to do. Victor, himself, couldn't remember this happening at all.

Either way, the company entered that period when you've been at it a while and the whole thing feels as if it's going to be a catastrophe. This was particularly true of Joan's shows because there was always so much on-the-spot invention and writing going on. Ann Beach burst into tears because she couldn't see where they were going. Joan said: 'Yes, it's hell when you're working properly.' And off she went to give hell to Colin Kemball, one of the BBC singers who had stayed. His tenor voice would soon be praised by the critics for his singing of 'Silent Night' and 'When this Lousy War is Over'. The hell was over his way of walking. It was more of a waddle. By the next Saturday, 'Everybody up to their neck in the suffering,' wrote Joan.

Sunday 10 March. 'Work all the difficult bits. Vic great V.G.!'

Monday 11 March. 'I love the company and the work we are doing. Charles Chiltern doesn't go for it. Where's the tragedy!' When, in the months and years to come there were arguments about billing and who did what, Joan held this against Charles.

Wednesday 13 March. Surprise, surprise: 'We were to open but Gerry has agreed to postpone. HE HATES DOING THIS. Always thinks I will stretch it more and more – HE IS RIGHT.' The fact is, there was hardly a single show of Joan's, the opening night of which, she did not try to postpone because there was always more work she wanted to do, which, in turn, would keep the critics away.

During those days of grace, Gerry was 'working like a demon on photos, nightly sessions, painstaking detail, writing the announcements for the newspanel.' What Joan didn't say was that she would change her mind about those announcements and, for those who had to re-do them by pricking holes in strips of paper, it was a laborious task.

Saturday 16 March. 'Camel too wants blood + death in slides. NO, no dead bodies. NO! Only live soldiers. THIS IS ABOUT LIFE – I will use some stylisation – in gas attack etc.'

Sunday 17 March. 'Work all day. Bribe Co. with booze, anything.' 'Booze, anything' was champagne and smoked salmon sandwiches which Victor Spinetti later remembered, during a break, when filming with Richard Burton and Elizabeth Taylor. Richard Burton was quite surprised.

Tuesday 19 March. '3 p.m. Dry run with band and I knew it would be all right.'

Opening night of O.W.A.L.W. GERRY'S BELOVED SHOW

Perhaps, my darling Gerry, I can, with this, pay you back for some of the hurt and distress I cause you "beloved one". We go to Boulestin with Tom and his friend. I am too rushed and tired to change – and escaping too [on first nights, Gerry always drove Joan to a restaurant where they would dine without any of the company but often Tom] so, still wearing striped cutting jacket.

Joan's striped jackets and blue and white checked trousers came from the chef's outfitters, Denny's, in Soho.

In all, conceiving, researching, writing, and rehearsing *Oh What a Lovely War*, if you include Joan's Sunday for the skeleton, took 38 days, but you could add a lifetime.

That Sunday, in the *Observer*, Ken Tynan wrote: 'Littlewood returns in triumph,' and went on: 'Miss Littlewood's passion has invaded one's bloodstream, and after the final scene, in which a line of reluctant heroes advances on the audience, bleating like sheep in a slaughterhouse, one is ready to storm Buckingham Palace and burn down Knightsbridge barracks.'

Monday 25 March. 'Gerry has had fourteen West End offers.' One of them was from Hugh (Binkie) Beaumont, the epitome of West End but also Bertolt Brecht's choice of producer for *Mother Courage*, if, all those years before, Brecht had had his way. Gerry stuck with Donald Albery who had already (sometimes with Oscar Lewenstein) brought *A Taste of Honey*, *The Hostage*, *Fings Ain't Wot They Used T'Be* and *Make Me an Offer*, to town. Gerry didn't like Albery but his attitude was one of 'Better the devil you know.' Then again, Albery was not himself crazy about Theatre Workshop. Brian Murphy was convinced that Albery breathed a sigh of relief whenever a Theatre Workshop show closed at one of his theatres.

A week after *Oh What a Lovely War* opened, Joan was back looking for Cedric and back on the Fun Palace trail. 'Am I mad? It's impractical. It's an intellectual game,' but she didn't stop. She made a short film to advertise it. Some of her actors were in it and Walter Lassally, who had lit *The Loneliness of the Long Distance Runner*, was her director of photography. Not only that, Jeremy Isaacs of *The World at War* gave her studio space and Ken Adam, the James Bond set designer, helped out. Here was an example of film people she could get on with, but they came too late for *Sparrers*.

The rest of that year, which should have been happy but wasn't, Joan went back to rackety living, 'drinking too much brandy.' Work consisted of getting *Lovely War* ready for the West End, which meant dropping one actress, Bettina Dickson, and replacing her with Avis Bunnage, who was by then available. Later, Joan was approached by an angry Bettina in a restaurant. Joan couldn't understand what was the matter with her.

Gerry, who was describing the Fun Palace as a 'flirting, time-wasting killer' was taken up with trying to quash an injunction brought by Ted Allen threatening to close the show if he couldn't get recognition. Gerry succeeded but Ted simmered on, which is how he eventually obtained that credit.

That year, Gerry and Cedric had something else in common. They both proposed to Joan. In the case of Cedric, Joan did not think he was being very serious. Actually, she thought he was queer, like all other men who had been to Cambridge.

In June *Lovely War* went to Paris and shared the top award with Peter Brook's production of *King Lear*. That did make Gerry happy. Doing well in Paris was always important to him.

The Earl of Harewood, who was running the Edinburgh Festival, invited Joan to bring a production up for 1964. *Arrière-pensée* or no, Joan said yes and chose the *Two Henrys*. The Festival she already knew well and she wouldn't have Peter Hall checking to see if the verse was being spoken the way he liked it. He and Joan had argued about that.

Before Christmas, Joan thought the *Lovely War* company needed some exercise and put on a show for children, *The Merry Roosters' Panto*. It would be performed in the afternoon. Barry Humphries joined the cast as a fairy godfather riding on a sparkling ultra-fashionable Moulton folding bike. Victor Spinetti and Brian Murphy were the ugly sisters, Eartha and Dumpy, and Peter Shaffer, an old friend of Victor's, wrote the script. You might have thought that Peter, so apparently West End, and Joan would not have got on, but they did. Peter's way of working wasn't that different from Joan's. He watched rehearsals and came back the following morning with re-writes.

Although the show, once set before an audience was great fun, Joan got fed up before the end of rehearsals and went to Brussels, leaving Gerry behind, in the show, playing the spoilsport theatre manager, Red Socks.

On 31 December, she wrote:

> What a HELL OF A HELL, JAY YEAR. And I thought she had given
> Gerry something this year – O W A L W but at what a price.

CHAPTER TWENTY-ONE

AN INVITATION TO EDINBURGH

It wasn't actually *Henry IV, 1 and 2* that Joan took to Edinburgh. It was *Henry the Fourth*. Nothing to do with Pirandello, it was an adaptation Joan had made using both parts of Shakespeare's *Henrys*. Easily her favourite was *Part One*. She liked its full-bloodedness, fired by the passion of the character Hotspur. Part Two, with the death of the old King, and the rejection of Falstaff, is more melancholy, dealing as it does with old age. However, it has Mistress Quickly's farewell to Falstaff as he goes away to war, and a cynical recruiting scene. Those two were what Joan added to her *Henry the Fourth*, which ended, as *Part One* does, with the death of Hotspur.

The timing of the production was handy. That autumn *Oh What a Lovely War* was going to Broadway. The simple thing to do was take it off in the West End before it had faded away, rehearse and perform *Henry* with much the same company during the summer, and then set off for America. Barbara Windsor was going with them, so she could be in it. Richard Harris had started out with Joan, so he could be in it too.

Joan had long before stopped doing drawings and minute stage directions. All that was inside her head by now, so this is an opportunity to see how she was working in later days.

As there was no play being performed at the Theatre Royal, the first part of rehearsals began on its deep stage, a black floor that slanted up to a brick wall at the back. On it were two benches and some chairs, facing not the auditorium, but the other side of the stage. Joan and the actors were simply in a space. The proscenium arch was being ignored.

Like schoolchildren, the actors sat on the benches, while Joan was perched on a stool in front of them, smoking a Gauloise and sipping cold, black coffee from a shallow glass cup. Things didn't stay that way for long. Joan got up, rubbed her woolly hat backwards and forwards on her head, took a puff from her cigarette and began pacing up and down.

The moment she started talking, anyone who had done English Literature at school knew that they were going to have to leave 'Lit. Crit.' in the classroom. A professor can speak knowledgeably to actors and the actors can nod wisely. They can also get up and carry on acting badly. Joan, in her own words, was a 'shit shifter'. Having described *Henry IV* as not so much red as white hot, and told the company that there would be no 'daffodils up arses,' she quickly got the actors to their feet.

The script was neither a Penguin nor an Arden edition. It had been specially typed out with lots of cuts – Joan making sure it was going to be white hot – and with the verse printed as prose – Joan making sure about the daffodils, or lack of them, rather.

She didn't start at the beginning. She jumped into a tavern scene. The actors didn't read it or shuffle about with their noses in their scripts. Joan thought of a situation in the present day with a parallel to what was going on in the scene. 1964 was the time of Mods and Rockers: Mods, cool, chic and 'today'; Rockers, hot-blooded, unfashionable and 'yesterday'. Suddenly Victor Spinetti and Murray Melvin were improvising two bored Mods on a street corner. However, as soon as the point was made, Joan stopped them which is what happened with all other games. She didn't let them trail on. In addition, the reason for these games was always clear to the actors.

When Joan did get around to some reading, the wrong actors read. Barbara Windsor was Falstaff, Brian Murphy was Doll Tearsheet. Joan wanted to maintain an atmosphere of shared discovery to avoid actors thinking, 'This is my bit,' and then pre-planning what they were going to do.

Getting the right stylised rhythm for a battle cry became a problem. Joan insisted on something like a football chant. Standing in the middle of the actors, she asked each one in turn, without thinking, to say the words and suddenly an actor got it.

This intelligent mucking about went on for a few days and you might have thought, with everyone having a go at lots of characters, that the play hadn't been cast and that Joan had simply assembled a bunch of nice actors with no idea about what they were going to do. That may have been the case for some but, after a while, it became clear that George Cooper, back after a long time away, was going to be Falstaff, Avis Bunnage was to be Mistress Quickly and Julian Glover, a newcomer from Stratford-upon-Avon, was going to be Hotspur. That was pretty straight-forward. Other casting wasn't.

The newspapers had indeed announced that Richard Harris was going to be in it. He wasn't. Jeremy Spenser, a famous child actor in the Fifties and a recent Marchbanks to Dulcie Gray's Candida, might have been expected to be playing Hal. He didn't; he wound up as Francis, the potboy. Joan gave Hal to Frank Coda, a cockney Italian, who'd been in the play *Sparrers Can't Sing*. Barbara Windsor was going to be Doll Tearsheet which is what anyone would expect. She left at the end of the week. 'Personal problems,' Joan said, but, years later, Barbara said it was Joan getting her to be Falstaff that put her off.

Yes, Barbara had worked with Joan before in *Fings Ain't Wot They Used T'Be* and the film version of *Sparrers*. However, she came into *Fings* after it had been rehearsed and put on at Stratford East. Having worked in the West End as a child and then in nightclubs, she had not been interested in experiment. She had just wanted to be in a West End hit.

As it happened, Barbara was intelligent and gifted and, at her audition, had ad libbed the dialogue of a prostitute very well. Other games made her impatient and now Falstaff was the last straw. Perhaps, she realised, decades later, that the company was going through a freewheeling, exploring stage. It intrigued Joan to hear Barbara speak the words because what came out was absolutely fresh. Doll would not have been a problem. For a start, she speaks in prose.

Each time Joan started a new scene, she didn't tell the actors what to do. She gave them jobs, or even told them to think of a job, and it was up to them to get on with it. As she didn't like people sitting and watching, 'No judges, no critics,' she made anyone sitting there join in. One such person found himself as a regular at the Boar's Head tavern. Thinking it was acting and yet also a way of being invisible, he came on bent double. Joan stopped the rehearsal. 'Think of Elizabethan portraits, how four square the people stand and yet, at any moment, those very same people could be stabbed in the back or have their heads chopped off. All this hunching up and turning in on yourself is post-Freudian.'

One evening, Joan was working on the scene in which Hotspur reads the message that propels him to go off to war. She wanted to show what a wrench it would be for him to leave hearth and home. She made two people, not in the show, sit at his feet. One became a child, the other a huge hound. Myvanwy Jenn, who was playing Lady Percy, Hotspur's wife, could then exploit them in her desperate fight to keep Hotspur away from a battle, the outcome of which was already looking dodgy. Thus, Julian Glover as Hotspur had physical things to react to, rather than having to produce something by thinking about it. What Howard Goorney, as the stable lad who has to fetch the horse, was getting up to at the back of the deep stage, was another matter. He was tugging at the imaginary reins of an imaginary horse in a vain attempt to get the nag out of the stable. During those days, work was a mixture of invention and flights of imaginative clowning.

Occasionally, when a proper actor went to the lavatory, Joan would ask a non-actor to stand in. The response would be swift. 'No, drop out. That's acting.' Joan was attacking a particular sound bad actors make. 'Acting in the past tense,' she called it. This means it's evident the actor has had time to read the speech and decide on how he's going to say it, colouring words as he goes along. It's unspontaneous and the result is that any fool watching is bound to think: 'I know he's acting.'

Once, two actors brushed past each other and ignored the accident. 'Stop,' said Joan, 'You're both dead.' Instantly, she restaged that moment with herself and Brian Murphy. At the moment they touched, they stepped lightly apart, doffed imaginary hats, made apologetic movements and went their separate ways. It was a tiny everyday incident, but it was alive, and something good had come out of something unpleasant. 'You must acknowledge each other,' continued Joan, 'or you're dead.'

In the recruiting scene from Part Two, where Falstaff recruits the most hapless bunch of men you're ever likely to see, Murray Melvin was playing the thin, pathetic Shadow. Joan, to convey an idea to him, did something she strictly forbade, as a rule. Falstaff tries some drill and you're expecting Shadow to ass around and get it wrong. At the back of your mind, you're also expecting it to be not very funny. Joan wanted the opposite. She had seen a piece of film of a concentration camp prisoner coming out to greet liberating soldiers, trying desperately to look and walk as if nothing were the matter. So she took a rifle and demonstrated. That's what directors are not supposed to do. She tried very, very hard to do the drill correctly but failed because she had no strength. The rifle, being so heavy, took over. It was a devasting piece of clowning as it was both sad and funny.

An exercise that may sound funny but was serious, proved to be useful when a certain problem blew up. The scene was Act Five, Scene One, where the Earl of Worcester goes to the King's camp to express Hotspur's purpose. It's the last chance to put off the battle and starts with the King saying:

> How bloodily the sun begins to peer
>
> Above yon bosky hill!

Worcester enters. The King chides him. Worcester puts his point of view. The King dismisses it. Hal offers to take on Hotspur in single combat. The King sends Worcester off to get an answer. The actors had got bogged down in detail. The central thrust wasn't there. Joan asked Howard Goorney, who was playing the King, and Brian Murphy, who was playing Worcester, to do the scene in gibberish. This is quite a feat in itself. It forces you to listen very hard, but Howard and Brian were old hands, and there immediately was the urgent rhythm of argument and counter-argument.

On the last day of rehearsals in London, Joan assembled the actors to give a little summing up talk. 'The critics are going to think it looks like something put together on a drunken afternoon and then thrown on the stage missing it. Well, we've sweated blood to achieve that effect but don't expect approval.'

During those Theatre Royal days, Murray Melvin would tell anyone interested in the set to look in dressing room number seven. There, they would find John Bury's model. Camel, though working with Peter Hall by then, was still Joan's designer – just. It was a long catwalk made of wood. If anyone said that it was an impressive set, Murray would respond: 'But it's not a set. It's a nothing.' That was kind of true, but set or nothing, few people had the faintest idea of where it was going or how it would work. Nor, because of the way Joan worked, did they find out during the Stratford weeks. She wasn't bothered. Nobody was told where to go. The actors simply acted the scene and it could be at any angle on the stage.

You realised how things were going to work on that first Monday morning in Edinburgh. You walked past John Knox's disapproving bust into the Assembly

Hall. The space was square with a balcony that ran right round it. John Bury's catwalk leapt from one side to the other with entrances at either end. If you were sitting down in the main area, this stage was just above eye level with sets of steps at certain points that went from the auditorium floor up to it. The court scenes were played at one end and the Eastcheap scenes at the other. In any scene, there was never more than one chair and perhaps a stool. The exception was the meeting with Owen Glendower. He had huge cushions which, of course, put his guests at a disadvantage. And that was it. The recruiting scene took place in the middle, and the battle used the whole stage. Joan's 'white hot' theory was being put into practice. One scene could easily overlap with the next. No need for pauses.

'Tyrone Guthrie had a thrust but I've gone further,' said Joan. Sixteen years earlier, Guthrie had directed Sir David Lindsay's play, *The Three Estates* in the Assembly Hall. For it, his designer, Molly McEwen, had built a thrust stage that projected halfway across the hall. At the time this was innovative, but Camel's stage went right across.

Joan carried on rehearsing as she had done at Stratford. She didn't place anyone and yet everyone was in the right place. John Bury simultaneously walked quietly round the stage in between the actors, pressing on the floor to find any creaks that needed fixing. He may have done the lighting too but you would have had trouble noticing. There were no lighting sessions. It was the Theatre Workshop way of working.

A few sweet middle-aged Edinburgh women were employed to swell the scene. They would make their main contribution in the battle. Right from the start, Joan had said she didn't fancy doing a big battle scene with lots of carefully rehearsed fights. She'd had another idea: refugees. Clutching their belongings, and led by Fanny Carby who was in the company, these women were to run the full length of the catwalk. It was dead simple but it told the story.

At their first rehearsal, these ladies couldn't resist casting panic-stricken glances behind them and wailing. Joan cut the acting at once. She told them to concentrate on not losing their bags and getting from A to B. If you're under that much pressure, you don't have have any excess energy for pulling faces and making noises.

Actors started to appear in costumes. These were a mixture of made and borrowed, absolutely not to look designed, despite Una Collins, who had done the *Oh What a Lovely War* costumes, being on hand. Hal and Poins, Frank Coda and Victor Spinetti had tight, slinky petrol-green trousers made of cotton with a slight sheen to it. This picked up on the Mod idea from that first Stratford afternoon. Murray Melvin got himself a pair of these too, but he was playing the Earl of March. What he really wanted was a cloak. On their feet were soft suede boots with rubbered soles. Joan was adamant about that. She hated the sound of footsteps and always wanted shoes that allowed actors to stay in control of their feet. In the same way, she didn't want Falstaff to have a lot of padding. She had once seen a Falstaff costume that stood up all by itself and thought it utterly wrong because the actor didn't have control. George Cooper had one breastplate of padding under his jerkin and that was it.

Doll Tearsheet, now being played by Myvanwy Jenn, wore a dress made of ribbons and sweet papers as if she had picked up glittering bits of trash she'd found in the street and threaded them together. Sir Walter Blunt played by George Sewell, had Tom Fleming's cloak from Peter Brook's production of *King Lear*. Texture was all the rage in those days – to be fair it was John Bury who had started it – so it was interesting to see what had been applied to the leather, tiny bits of latex, dyed brown to look like mud.

Make-up was not allowed. 'That went out with gaslight,' said Joan. The girls, however, were allowed to wear street make-up.

Joan got fed up with the parchment scroll Julian Glover had for the letter that provokes Hotspur to join battle. 'Spies are everywhere. They'd have got hold of a bloody great thing like that,' and so a gofer nipped out to a seller of antiques in the Grassmarket and bought a little leather-bound book. The message was contained in that.

Even if you've only been in a school play, you know that tension mounts during the last days of rehearsal. You might even know that it's the most trivial detail, often to do with a costume, that can trigger an explosion.

One afternoon, Joan was onstage with some of her actors going quickly through notes to be in time for an imminent run-through. This was not Joan just sitting reading. Sometimes she would leap to her feet and act the note or get the actors in question to do it, right there and then. Into this semi-charged atmosphere flounced Victor Spinetti wearing his Owen Glendower costume, a heavy blue djellaba thing. He wasn't happy. 'I look like a G-Plan sofa!' Funny but badly timed. Joan, furious at being interrupted and aware of how overworked Una Collins was, let rip. Most people's voices go up when they lose their tempers. Joan's went down. She thundered at Victor for his selfishness. He swept off to the dressing rooms.

Joan losing her temper was frightening but this was probably one of her artifical eruptions, that one crack of the whip you sometimes need to pull the actors together. You could also speculate on what was really in her mind at this point. A director knows by then which actors are not going to be any good but it's too late to do anything about it, so feelings have to be bottled up. Victor, as it happens, was going to be very funny as Owen Glendower and glitteringly suave as Poins, but he was the one who got it in the neck.

Before the show opened there were previews. Large audiences came and enjoyed it. Peter Shaffer came to a matinee and took Victor out for tea. Apart from him, that's Victor, and also Avis Bunnage, Peter had been unable to hear any of the cast. Victor, never able to keep anything to himself, came back and told the other actors. Peter may have been right. The catwalk had about it a tremendous energy, but with audience on either side life was not made easy when it came to being heard. Nevertheless, saying something like this to actors, rather than the director, before the show opens, can be very damaging.

The opening night came. There were no hitches, but then there shouldn't have been. It was, technically, a very simple production, utterly reliant on the actors. Mistress Quickly's farewell to Falstaff was heart-stopping. As Avis Bunnage watched and waved the old knight stomp off to war, using the full length of the stage, it was a tough job not to cry.

The next morning, all the notices were stinkers. Frothing at the mouth the critics were, so angry that they made mistakes about Shakespeare, never mind the production. What was the big deal? Well, it would seem that even in swinging 1964, the critics wanted the actors playing posh parts to talk posh, or rather their idea of posh. George Cooper's slight Yorkshire accent and Frank Coda's cockney twang were, for them, unbearable. Alone among the actors, Julian Glover, who had been at Stratford-upon-Avon, was exempt.

When critics in the 1960s pontificated about verse speaking, they were often remembering what they had heard as children and were assuming it was correct. However, it is that very singing sound, which ignores sense, coupled with a slight vibrato, that puts off people not brought up on Shakespeare. For them, the more they hear sense, the better. Joan had offended the critics' *idea* of Shakespeare, not Shakespeare. Her prediction had proved right. If only the critics had come to the rehearsals.

Fortunately, and it was typical of what happened to Joan, the press was so intrigued by the critics' rage that it demanded an immediate conference. Joan, Vic and Avis went and, to demonstate what Joan didn't want, impersonated famous actors doing Shakespeare. Joan did Vanessa Redgrave in *As You Like It* and brought the house down. The press conference, at least, was a smash. A comfort to the actors over the ensuing days was the sight of full houses which lasted for the rest of the three weeks.

When the show was up and running, an old Scottish friend of Theatre Workshop's, Bill McLennan, asked Joan to some kind of launch at his office where his latest venture was publishing the *Urdu Times* on different coloured paper for each day of the week. Bill had pale blue eyes with a faraway look, and invariably wore a kilt. Also invariably, he had some new project on the go and would pin you into a corner with those eyes and tell you about it. In other words, he belonged to that small band of longstanding, loyal Theatre Workshop supporters that Joan would do anything, hide under a table even, to avoid. This time she couldn't get out of it. However, people at the launch, were unexpectedly handed a piece of folded card. When they opened it out, they saw that it was the design for the Fun Palace by Cedric Price, the architect.

Joan had talked about the Fun Palace, not long before, when she had been interviewed by Huw Wheldon on television. She described it as a place where you could be show-offy or shy, learn, or be entertained, all at the same time. So, this drinks do was 'Edinburgh gets a foretaste', courtesy of Bill McLennan. It turned into another press conference. Joan, caught on the hop, but not showing it, spoke about the future, how marvellous it was going to be with all the advances in science that would improve everyone's lives. Gerry Raffles, who usually went everywhere with Joan, was not there.

CHAPTER TWENTY-TWO

TUNIS AND TWANG

Tunisia's president, Habib Bourguiba, keen to impress the outside world, took the advice of his adviser, Lebanese-born, Manchester-raised, Cecil Hourani, and let him start an international drama course in Hammamet. After *Oh What a Lovely War's* run at the Broadhurst Theatre on Broadway, that's where Joan and Gerry went. It was the summer of 1965. Before going, Gerry went on a crash Berlitz course in Arabic. When he arrived in Tunisia, he was delighted. In the summer sun, his diabetes was less vicious, his body needing to make less effort to heat itself. Joan was able to overcome her dislike of heat by working in the early morning and in the evening, which was how things were done in Tunisia anyway.

Peter Brook was there too. Joan warned him off her students. She thought his seriousness might bring them down when she was trying to build them up. 'Peter's an intellectual,' she said, 'I'm not. Before he starts anything, he has to find a new influence.' She then went on to list them: Jan Kott, Antonin Artaud, Jerzy Grotowsky, Chinese theatre. 'He got one over me, though,' said Joan, 'he could eat a sheep's eye.'

'Build them up', meant Joan using her long experience of making her Theatre Workshop actors feel good about themselves. She wanted them to be strong in the face of that daunting but bogus edifice constructed of directors from Oxbridge and actors who, at drama school, she remembered, had learned a posh accent but little else. In Tunisia, it was a question of drawing French-influenced Arab students away from the Comédie-Française and encouraging them to rediscover their own way of telling a story.

Una Collins, who worked with Joan in Hammamet, said that Peter Brook was not only respectful of Joan but intrigued by the way she worked. Another of his influences, in later years, was Berber storytelling and, as Joan would try to do, he assembled in Paris a group of actors from different countries.

Because Joan considered lectures a waste of time, 'In one ear, out the other,' she spent that summer getting the students on to their feet to make them use their heads and their bodies. All round, it was a dream come true because Gerry loved it as well. Given what happened that autumn, it was a dream Joan and Gerry were only too happy to return to, the following year.

Back in London (still in 1965), Lionel Bart, riding high on the success of four musicals in a row, announced his latest show, *Twang*. James Booth and Barbara Windsor were to star. Oliver Messel was to design and Joan was to direct.

Late that summer, Joan, back from Hammamet, could be seen in Shaftesbury Avenue, her skin lightly tanned, her hair a sophisticated red, wearing round her neck a black velvet ribbon tied in a bow. If you had a sensitive nose, you might also have noticed a waft of Balmain's scent, Jolie Madame. Typical of where she was, the West End, it was here that she bumped into Noël Coward who actually said: 'At last we meet.'

For those few moments, these two who seemed to come from such different worlds, amused each other no end, but then they didn't come from different worlds. Both were born in south London. Both hated it and both escaped by catching the number 88 bus: Coward to stage school, Joan to the Tate Gallery.

Shaftesbury Avenue, Noël Coward, Jolie Madame, it was all so not Joan; and then there was Oliver Messel. Here, working with her, was this designer who, before the Second World War, had made his name creating masks for Diaghilev and an all-white bedroom for CB Cochran's English-language version of *La Belle Hélène*. Nothing could have been further from John Bury and his cement mixer or, for that matter, Sean Kenny, the designer you'd expect for *Twang* – he being Lionel's soul mate, and whose set for Joan's production of *The Hostage* had launched his career. Oliver Messel did painted backcloths and gauzes, pretty-pretty stuff. Joan, when questioned about him, answered: 'He's the one I get on with best. I've always had a soft spot for nymphs and gazebos. Sean Kenny's cantilevered gantries aren't right.'

Rehearsals started at the Four Feathers Boys' Club off the Edgware Road. The front hall was lined with photos of Oliver Messel's model and the various scene changes. They did not have the 'Oh yes!' effect of John Bury's clean and daring catwalk for 1964's Edinburgh *Henry IV*. They looked muddly.

Joan and her actors were already shut up in their room when a large, long car drew up and out jumped Lionel Bart wearing a chalk-striped suit and a trilby hat. As he walked into the rehearsal room, Joan was merrily listing all the people who go into making an American musical: someone to come up with the story, someone to write the dialogue, someone to write the lyrics, someone to write the tunes, someone to arrange the dance music and someone to arrange the song music. 'Which am I?' she wondered as Paddy Stone, the choreographer, taught the dancers the title number in the room above. Thump! Thump! Thump! 'Ter-wang!'

The script, which nobody seemed to be looking at, was bound like a screenplay and, inside, the lyrics were typed in capitals, all very professional. It was never seen again. Most of the people in that room were more fascinated by the razzmatazz of getting on a big new musical.

The idea of *Twang* was to take a sexy, irreverent look at the Robin Hood legend. There was going to be a naughty song about chastity belts and a naughty bubble bath scene. The influences were American musicals like *Roman Scandals* and *Dubarry was a Lady*, which had characters going into the past but talking in present-day slang, usually with breathtaking filthiness. *Twang*'s characters, though, were already in the past. Parisian nightclubs like the Lido and the Casino de Paris did something similar. However, those nightspots had only one spectacular scene that needed no plot, which is significant, given what was to follow.

The writer was an American, Harvey Orkin. He'd been a resident wit on the TV satire programme, *Not so Much a Programme, More a Way of Life,* the kind of person who didn't need a script because he could be funny spontaneously. As Joan talked, he seemed to be relaxed and amused by what was going on around him. No pens emerged from his pockets. No paper appeared to be about his person. He was not seen opening a script and, after a while, he was not seen at all.

Most of the actors had worked with Joan before. There, again, was George Cooper and Howard Goorney. George was Friar Tuck. Howard, Sir Guy of Gisborne. Frank Coda, no doubt there for his bel canto voice, was doing bits and bobs. Prince John was Maxwell Shaw and the Sheriff of Nottingham was Bob Grant. Bob's carrying corncrake voice made him seem quite the old-fashioned actor but he was also the actor who had won Best Performance in Paris as Kitely in *Everyman in his Humour* five years earlier.

Kent Baker who was playing Mutch the Miller's Son, Elric Hooper who was going to be Alan-a-Dale and Philip Newman, who was going to be an invented character, Roger the Ugly, had been on the European tour of *Oh What a Lovely War*. So, Joan had got much of her own way. Even Ronnie Corbett who was a newcomer, had, like Barbara Windsor, worked in cabaret with Danny La Rue.

The only complete newcomers were big Bernard Bresslaw who was going to be Little John and Toni Eden who was going to be Maid Marian.

Bernard Bresslaw brought something of a name too. He'd got it from a popular TV sitcom called *The Army Game* which had given him a catchphrase: 'I only arsked.' When young, he had been with Unity Theatre where the teenaged Lionel had started out.

Toni Eden was there for her voice. The fun female character was Maid Marian's gurgly, bubbly, best friend, Delphina, another invented character, and that was Barbara. What with being in *Fings* and the *Sparrers* film, she had fortunately made a name for herself, as had James Booth. He too had been in *Fings* and *Sparrers* and an amusing couple they made, he tall and rangy, she, small and luscious. The fact that they had both started out with Joan, become stars and had worked together before couldn't have been more encouraging. There, painlessly, was the draw you had to have for a commercial show. One way and another, the cast seemed both up to the job and Joan-friendly.

The dancers were different. They had been chosen by Paddy Stone and were there to do exactly as he told them. What tough choreographers got up to with their dancers was something Joan knew little about. Theatre Workshop meant 15 to 20 actors and that was it. No one went off into other rooms, there to have no contact with her.

Most days, these dancers were seen trooping upstairs to be tortured by Paddy who could be heard yelling at them savagely. It didn't help that some accident or palsy had left his mouth in a permanent sneer. He was there because he was regarded as the top British – he was actually Canadian – choreographer of the time. Ken Tynan, the theatre critic, had written that his dances for Lionel's *Maggie May* were the next best thing to Jerome Robbins' choreography for *West Side Story*. In England, in the mid-Sixties, that was some compliment.

Paddy's dancers were divided into tall girls, showgirls, and little dancers, chorines. The showgirls could dance a bit but were mostly there to look stately. The chorines were there to be jazzy and brilliant. At all times these dancers seemed self-contained in a world of their own. While they worked, there was never anything on their faces, neither happiness nor misery. The dazzling all-purpose smile of the professional dancer would only be switched on when it was needed.

Why was Joan directing *Twang* and allowing herself to get into this unusual situation? The answer is simple. It was the Fun Palace again. She wanted money for it and, anyway, Lionel was an old friend, going back to the days of *Fings Ain't Wot They Used T'Be*. As it has a bearing on what was to happen on *Twang* it's worth remembering how things had been in those days.

Not only was Lionel brought in on *Fings*, he was brought in on a unique working style. He just had to watch, get an idea, nip up to the green room and, not long afterwards, come down again with a song. It might not have been quite the one Joan was expecting but in no time she'd find a place for it.

This sounds delightfully casual but perhaps it wasn't. Perhaps it was simply a very good way of working that had been evolved by Joan over a long period of time. Lionel was lucky. It suited him perfectly. He didn't have to be alone in a room facing a blank piece of paper. He just had to react. 'I get ideas like a flashbulb going off,' he used to say, and that was true. His was not a long-haul brain. Somebody else had to do that kind of thinking. Not for many years was Lionel to work in that happy way again.

After *Fings* had come *Oliver!* which Joan had not wanted to direct. 'All those children running round the theatre.' If you look at the show, you'll notice that the structure follows the David Lean film. The filleting, in other words, had already been done. Chances are, Lionel never read the Dickens. He didn't have the patience.

Oliver!, as we know, was a huge success and it projected Lionel into a class of his own. It also led him to enter what he described as: 'My flash git period.' Everything was what he wanted and everything was what he got.

Blitz, based on his childhood memories of the Second World War, had some good tunes but a soapy plot. Joan had turned it down. The critics didn't think much of it either but were impressed by Sean Kenny's sets. Its run was respectable and so, to a lesser extent, was that of his next show, *Maggie May* – Jesus Christ and Mary Magdalene relocated to Liverpool – written by the highly professional Alun Owen. That's where Paddy Stone came in.

Since Lionel's Stratford East days, six years had passed and he was a changed man. His undoubted talent for song, combined with his immense success made him think that he could, and should, be on top of and in control of everything. That is a hard person to work with, and the one with whom Joan now had to work.

Still, there, starting out was a jolly Theatre Workshop bunch of actors, with plenty of rehearsal time, some good tunes and Joan who had the reputation for being able to make something out of nothing.

What was in that professional-looking script, though? *Fings* may have been slight but there was something in it that was good and true. *Twang* was another matter. If you were to have turned the pages, you would have found a childishness that took your breath away.

As the dancers carried on thumping in other rooms, Joan, often without Lionel, worked quietly and patiently with her actors. For example, she might hit on a scene with a gap in it. There would be an A and an E but no B, C, and D. Quickly Joan listed a series of subjects to which she gave concise and memorable titles, then chucked them at Little John and Will Scarlett. Bernard Bresslaw and Ronnie Corbett, who was playing Will, stored the titles in their heads and then ad libbed their way through, carrying it off with remarkable élan. After all, neither was accustomed to working with Joan but what they said made sense, stuck to the point and was even entertaining. All they had to do was run through it a couple of times and it was fixed in their heads. Hey presto, a nice little scene.

If anything, Joan was introducing a sweetness to the show, not sticky but fresh. Most sweet of all was a tiny chance encounter between Delphina and Alan-a-Dale. Suddenly, as the two talked, they realised they fancied each other and became shy teenagers who could speak only haltingly. A laughter of joyful recognition bubbled up. Joan was weaving a golden tissue of gossamer lightness while, thump, thump, 'Who's the beautiful baby?' or rather:

WHO'S THE BEAUTIFUL BABY?

WHOSE ARE THE TWO EYES OF BLUE?

. . . came yowling from somewhere else. One song did chime with what Joan was doing, 'You Can't Catch Me'. You think Robin's going to be defiant in the face of the Sheriff, but no. It's a wistful song that reveals a will-o'-the-wisp side to Robin when it comes to romance. This was a good example of Lionel not doing the obvious. James Booth didn't go away to sing it. He did it right there in front of Joan and it worked.

Rehearsals for the actors soon left the Boys' Club so, one dark afternoon, you could climb the stairs to a library in Gower Street hearing, as you went, a raised voice. 'I fink,' Lionel was flashbulbing, 'I fink Robin should come on on a fork lift truck.' There followed a tiny pause of irritation among the actors. It sounded like this was just one in a long list of unhelpful suggestions. 'That's a marvellous idea, Li,' said Joan. 'Unfortunately my brain's slower than yours. It's going to take me a while to get there.' Lionel turned and left. Toni Eden flicked two fingers at his departing back.

Joan shrugged and carried on trying to get Robin on in a way that was at least human but it was hard to concentrate and soon she let the actors go. As they went their way, she opened a black attaché case, her 'James Bond', took out a piece of paper and, using the case as a desk, started to scribble. 'I've got to explain to Lionel. I've got to explain why I'm right.' This was the first sign among the company that there was a problem. Even so, a few minutes later, when an assistant asked her what she would be doing the next day, Joan gaily answered: '*King Lear* with Marlene Dietrich and John Gielgud. Marlene will be Lear, Gielgud will be Goneril.'

The note Joan sent to Lionel was not the last. There were others, not written in her charming handwriting. They were typed by a secretary and didn't pull punches. The most important was the one in which she told Lionel that, talented as he was, he could not do structure and had to leave that to others. Throughout her life, Joan wrote many notes. Most were a form of entertainment but some denoted the chilling of a relationship, a distancing. They acted both as a weapon and a shield. Joan could attack without the pain of facing the attacked.

The Shaftesbury Theatre, formerly the Prince's, where *Twang*, after try-outs in Manchester and Birmingham, was going to have its West End run, became dark, so Joan was able to rehearse in the right space. However, it was not a perfect theatre. The auditorium was big but the stage, disproportionately shallow.

On to it came Oliver Messel's sets. He had been inspired by jewel-like miniatures in a very old Bible: big people, little castles, that sort of thing; amusing but less so in three dimensions with real human beings. If anything, it was ever-so-slightly clodhopping. Getting from one scene to another did not delight. Changes had to be hidden by frontcloths, an old-fashioned device. And who, in the 1960s, had got rid of this clumsiness? Why, John Bury and Sean Kenny.

Oliver Messel, himself, only appeared once and it was not in the auditorium. Joan was in a corridor backstage, looking for a lavatory, when, all of a sudden, a dazzling white raincoat, made of a fabric both expensive and mysterious, bustled towards her. Above the coat, lustrous dark eyes made themselves very round. White teeth shone against a Caribbean tan. Deep brown hair gleamed. He wasn't young but, by God, he was well preserved. Joan and he exchanged conspiratorial smiles and, as suddenly as he came, he was gone, but it was as if a sea breeze had blown a cloud away.

Alone, Joan and her actors wove delicately for days and days. When she was at this kind of work, it seemed like it could happily go on forever. In Hammamet, it did but in England, an audience soon had to be faced.

There was a costume parade. This is when the actors put on their costumes and come onstage under some lighting for the director to look at and make comments. Joan enjoyed it. She'd take a hat from one character and give it to another, turn a cloak inside out and declare it a vast improvement. In this way, she broke up hard-edged perfection and made the costumes look as if they belonged to the actor.

At one side of the stage, Barbara Windsor fussed over a silver chatelaine that hung down over her flouncy aquamarine dress and then looked slyly out front. 'I love it really.' Meanwhile James Booth bounded about in a pair of Lincoln green tights and not much else. It would have been more to the point if he'd had his tunic, but James was the kind of actor who never seemed to have the whole of his costume when it was needed. Costumes, make-up and props don't interest such an actor, only comfort. A 'little boy lost' look at a pretty wardrobe assistant was the best he could manage. Joan stared at the tights and said: 'Go and put on your codpiece. What I can see is far too interesting.'

The showgirls came gliding on to the stage in floor-length medieval gowns with the waist just under the breasts. These dresses were made of silk and each one was a different soft colour. Body was given to them by several layers of underskirts, each of them lined and each of them in a different colour. Careful handling was needed to show them off. The same went for the men's cloaks. Fold after fold fell gracefully to the floor.

Into this courtly picture bounced a couple of tumblers, wearing special tunics that looked like giant string vests but knobbly. 'Handwoven by Miki Sekers himself,' murmured Bob Grant. Handwoven may have been an exaggeration but Miki Sekers was indeed famous for making sumptuous materials at sumptuous prices.

During rehearsals, the actors had frequently been obliged to go off, causing a scheduling problem Joan didn't normally have to face. This is what they and Bermans', the costumiers, and Oliver Messel had been up to and very beautiful it was too.

The afternoon was a bitty one, so Lionel who hadn't been around for ages, took the showgirls through the words of a song. Their Ts were indistinct, so he told them to sound deliberately common by adding an S after the final T. Thus, if you take 'Indistinct' as your example, you would sing: 'Indistinc-tser.' Lionel liked attending to this kind of detail, something small he could fix there and then. It took his mind off something big that was much harder to fix.

Next day, the curtain was down and the band was in the pit. The musicians were learning the arrangements. That means a first performance is very close. They didn't half sound brassy, those arrangements. Glissandos and wah-wahings may have been right for all that thumping the dancers had been doing. They certainly weren't for what Joan had been doing. There had been no boo-boom gags in her rehearsals.

Nevertheless, eveything that had happened so far had been private, as it should have been. Sensational fallings out in front of the company had not occurred. It was just another show, if a rather expensive one.

Days later, all that changed. Simply by reading the papers, everyone in the country could find out what was happening. *Twang* opened in Manchester to terrible reviews. Joan walked out. Burt Shevelove, American director and co-writer of *A Funny Thing Happened on the Way to the Forum*, took over. Birmingham was cancelled. Articles appeared in the newspapers. Penelope Gilliatt wrote a sympathetic piece listing all the good things that should have made the show a hit, chief among them, Joan, whom she described as the linchpin.

The revised show opened at the Shaftesbury Theatre just before Christmas. As you would expect, a starry first night audience rolled up but it was not long before the performance turned into every nightmare an actor could have, only there was no waking up. All that had so far not gone wrong, went wrong: the sets, the lighting, the sound, the lot and, in the auditorium, someone opened a door to the street and let in a mob of boo-ers.

The next day, Jak's daily cartoon in the *Evening Standard* was captioned: '*Twang* goes Thud,' Toni Palmer, the actress, was invited on to *Late Night Line-Up*, a TV arts programme, to give her opinion. Despite having been in *Fings* and therefore a friend of nearly the entire company, she couldn't hold back. It was no good.

As the twenty-first century is well into its stride, it can safely be said that *Twang* was one of the most notorious flops of the twentieth century, rivalled only by Peter O'Toole's *Macbeth*.

What would you see if you booked a seat at the Shaftesbury? For a start, against Joan's usual instruction, the men were plastered in make-up, bright orange. Then there were Max Shaw's desperate eyes darting about the house. Was he counting? The song 'Twang' or 'Ter-wang' was out of the show, and so was George Cooper. A smaller actor in a smaller part jigged about in his place. The dancing girls had no underskirts. Their legs protruded jazzily where a panel of material had been cut away altogether. Unfunny gags were sold out front. Roger the Ugly was a Gonk, a novelty doll of the time: thick fringe, big nose, nothing else. Amusing for a moment but what was Phil Newman expected to do afterwards? Any gossamer, any charm was long gone, blown away by the brass.

Very little time went by before the show closed. Shockwaves rippled outwards, rocking Lionel violently. In the meantime, bits of information about Manchester started to filter through. It began with Kent Baker, who had played Mutch, giving his account of the show, which he had rechristened *Twinge*.

Bernard Delfont who was behind the show, very far behind, as nobody had seen him, had asked Joan to make changes. As they were not the kind she wished to make, 'I'm not here as an Assistant Stage Manager,' she said that someone else would have to. Burt Shevelove, play doctor, had come in with sheaves of new material, announcing in a wheezy, husky voice Kent imitated with glee, 'These are the gags, kids.' Each day, more gags appeared, so many that the cast had been forced to pin them to the backs of the trees in Sherwood Forest, having had no time to learn them.

The heavy make-up had been demanded in order to sell the characters. It's like, when writing, we sometimes underline words for emphasis. Yes, we're not supposed to do that either. Paddy Stone, who hadn't been on hand for the costume parade, had glanced once at the showgirls and said: 'My gurrls kee-ant dee-ance in those.' He'd then given instructions for the front panels to be removed along with the underskirts. George Cooper had seen his part shrink to less than his contract specified and, for that reason, had gone.

£70,000 the show had cost; so much money but no co-ordination. That's why there was that shocking contrast between Joan's work and the musical arrangements. And Paddy Stone can't have seen Oliver Messel's designs for the showgirls. If he had, he'd have spoken up earlier. How ironic that Joan had made fun of the different departments on an American musical. *Twang* had been neither fish nor fowl, neither Theatre Workshop nor Broadway.

More bits came out over the years. Joan recalled reporters milling about the lobby of the Midland Hotel in Manchester. She wasn't angry. 'After all, it beat trudging across the moors looking for more bodies.' This was the time of Brady and Hindley and the Moors Murders. 'At least the Midland lobby was warm.'

Bernard Delfont, funnily enough, she had liked. He had said his piece and there was no rancour. Paddy Stone, master of zip and pzazz, was another matter. Joan had never been happy with what he was doing. One day she had found George Cooper rehearsing a routine laid out on the floor with a chorus girl's foot on his neck. 'You don't treat a friar like that,' she said and then went on to encourage the dancers to rebel and think for themselves. Barbara Windsor referred to this in a TV interview. 'She told the dancers to do their own thing. Well, of course, they didn't know what she was on about.' Barbara knew from experience that dancers in hardnosed commercial musicals have been disciplined from childhood to do exactly as they are told. They know nothing else.

Bob Grant, who had been got up to look like Edith Sitwell, remembered Oliver Messel going round the dressing-rooms with make-up charts, things he had never seen before. 'I've still got mine,' he said, 'It's lovely.' Had he actually used it? 'Good heavens, no.'

Twang was the last West End show Oliver Messel designed. In fact, it was the last show he ever designed. Chronic arthritis sent him back to his home in the Carribean where he found a new lease of life designing the interiors of rich people's houses. 'Messelina,' Joan called him affectionately.

When talking about Lionel, Joan said that he had been impossible. The essential teamwork had not been there. Lionel, on the other hand, said he thought that his fault was being too co-operative. 'I never wrote more songs than I did for *Twang*.'

What he also did for *Twang*, it emerged, was attempt to save it by selling his rights to *Oliver!* only to watch the show and all his money – by then the show had cost £100,000 – go down the Swanee.

After *Twang* closed, the press went back to the usual Lionel-type stories; stories about his exciting future projects. First, there was going to be a stage musical of Fellini's film, *La Strada*, then there was going to be a spectacular production of *The Hunchback of Notre Dame* for Broadway, both shows one might expect of Lionel. There was no sign that there was anything wrong, except that neither show happened. In the first half of the Sixties, four of Lionel's musicals had bounced into the West End, one after the other. From then on, not one.

'Joan laid a curse on me,' Lionel sighed. 'She's a witch. She said that *Twang* would be my end.' That, however, was not the end of Joan and Lionel but seven years had to pass and Lionel had to be bankrupted before they came back together again.

CHAPTER TWENTY-THREE

TUNIS PART TWO,
INDIA PART ONE

The following year, 1966, Joan, much less harmed than Lionel Bart, returned, with Gerry, to Hammamet where she, together with the students from the year before, took the previous summer's games and made them into a play, *Who is Pepito?* It was a picaresque adventure satire about a young Arab boy travelling to Paris in the hope of a better life, but finding only a bidonville. A bidonville was a kind of shanty town that could be found on the outskirts of Paris. A bidon, itself, is a jerrycan and that's what these shanty towns were made of.

For this international drama course in Hammamet, a theatre had been built specially; René Allio, set designer for the director, Roger Planchon, had been the architect. Planchon was the nearest France had to Joan, both in politics and style. He had a theatre in a factory-dominated suburb of Lyons and had done a *Henry IV* rather similar to hers. However, as Joan was trying to steer her students away from the influence of French culture, she would have nothing to do with this theatre. She said it was ugly. Her show would be performed all over the place, she so wanted her Arab children to reawaken their own culture, a subversive, long-hidden one of storytelling.

One of the moments she liked best was a Lebanese student, Sarah Salem, playing Madame Pillule, giving a patronising lecture about the pill to a crowd of women who hadn't a clue what she was on about.

Ronald Bryden, the *Observer* theatre critic, having got wind of some fun on the go, wanted to come. Joan did not want him to come. He did and when he arrived was treated by Joan with deep suspicion. Not that you would have known from his article. Firstly, it was huge and, secondly, he was having a whale of a time simply taking in the whole scene. One of Joan's students, another Lebanese, Nidal Achkar, who had been to RADA and learned to be terribly British, merrily told him how Joan had shifted all that. As for the show itself, Bryden said it was one of the best pieces of work Joan had ever done, possibly the best. But what a pyrrhic victory, he went on, because nobody would see it.

There was the rub, so like those early Stratford East years: Joan, happy up in the gallery watching her shows, shows that were playing to nearly empty houses. Perhaps Ronald Bryden, though barely knowing Joan, spotted this reclusive side when he described her as very shy. She loved her work but dreaded the judge's pointing finger. A judge can kill not only a show but a spirit. There, in Hammamet, Joan could work with no finger pointing at either her or her children who, if they were not to end up carbon copies of the Comédie-Française, needed all the encouragement they could get. It was, for her, ideal, if not for others.

However, it couldn't and didn't last. She and Gerry had to return to England to pick up their still diverging threads: Joan to chase up the Fun Palace, Gerry to concern himself with the Theatre Royal. For Gerry, leaving Tunis must have been a particularly wistful moment. It had been an oasis of sunshine and swimming, so good for his health, and the food had been good too. Unlike Joan, who loved only the names of exotic food, Gerry was adventurous when it came to grub. The pretty young female students fussing over him – 'Gerry, Gerry, je t'adore,' they sang – would have been welcome too.

Before leaving, Joan told the students to keep up the good work. They tried but things quickly fell apart, and that's something else to do with Joan. Often she was disappointed that no one seized the torch and carried on but her natural dominance had a way of putting a stop to anything that wasn't her.

Back in the UK, she found herself invited by an Indian arts organisation, to a theatre seminar. She went and was proudly presented with a production of Peter Weiss's *Marat/Sade*, made famous by Peter Brook in London two years earlier. Energetically biting the hand that fed her, Joan denounced it. Why were they putting on to their stage this calcified turd?

As usual, she still made friends. She always did. It was Hammamet all over again, this steering of ex-colonies away from their ex-bosses and urging them to revive their own culture. A denunciation from Joan was more invigorating than praise from a lesser artist. Writing home, on Air India paper, she said that India was revolting but she was going back any minute to make a film.

It didn't take long before it appeared to be off.

Home again, Joan did not manage to pick up her Fun Palace thread. Dare to say that, however, and you could be sure of a rocket. If only she could have been boring because that's what the authorities wanted, the boring details, like where do young mothers, wanting to study, put their babies, but Joan found that hard to tackle. You could also ask how things would have turned out if, behind the project, had been Gerry.

Gerry did succeed in picking up his thread. Early the next year, 1967, he put an announcement in the paper. Theatre Workshop was to start up again. This was something of an event, as there had been no Theatre Workshop productions since 1964. However, during those four years, Gerry had not let the theatre go. He'd rented it out. His guiding rule was shove anything in, absolutely anything, but don't let the theatre go dark and that is what he had done. It was fortuitous that the company he'd handed the theatre to, had, after four years, gone bust.

CHAPTER TWENTY-FOUR

THE FUN PALACE
COMES TO STRATFORD EAST

The play Gerry decided to open with had recently caused a sensation in New York. This and its topicality is what interested him. It was Barbara Garson's *Macbird*, a blackly comic verse drama using the plot of *Macbeth* to satirise President Lyndon Johnson and the assassination of Jack Kennedy.

For it, Brian Murphy, Howard Goorney, Myvanwy Jenn, Bob Grant, Fanny Carby, Frank Coda and Toni Palmer, the actress who had slated *Twang*, returned to the fold. Joining them were Nidal Achkar, the student from Hammamet, and Sarah Salem, Nidal's best friend.

When Barbara Garson gave permission for Theatre Workshop to put on her play, she could have had little idea what would hit her. The first thing Joan objected to was the iambic pentameters, and most of the play had been written in those. They may have been fine for university students in America but they would not do for her. Their clumsiness offended her ear for verse. In fact, as far as she was concerned, the whole thing was shrill, ugly and amateurish. So, during rehearsals, she built up dialogue written by herself at night based on the actors' improvisations during the day, plus the reading of history books. To this, she added snatches of genuine Shakespeare and, in between, the occasional song like: WAY SOUTH IN TENNESSEE / THAT'S WHERE I LONG TO BE / DOWN WHERE A MAN'S A MAN / HOME OF THE KU KLUX KLAN which was not by Barbara Garson but Tom Lehrer. Whenever Barbara Garson objected, and in New York her script had known nothing but success, Joan said that the show, as written, would not work for Stratford East.

A charismatic director can turn actors against a writer and that's what Joan was doing. The company trusted her, not Barbara Garson who soon came to be known as Barbara Ghastly. Granted, Garson was charmless but once Joan took against a person, he or she would, before your eyes, become talentless too, whether they were or not. When that happened it was best if the victim left as soon as possible. Soon after her arrival, Barbara Garson left. Perhaps she would have been happier at the Royal Court.

For anybody unaccustomed to working with Joan, all this may seem difficult to understand. If she didn't like the play, why was she doing it? Well, it was that topicality Gerry needed and she knew it. As the Vietnam war was still on, the subject was hot, so hot that the theatre had to become a club for the show to go ahead. In turn, Gerry would have trusted Joan, with her experience of political satire, to simply take the idea and turn it into a show, which she did in a way.

What she ended up with exuded warmth and flowed along entertainingly. It was not what the critics were expecting and they didn't like it. Among them was Ken Tynan who had seen the New York production and objected to Joan turning this scabrous satire into a jolly vaudeville. Joan merely said: 'What else could I do?' One critic enjoyed it, Tariq Ali who, at the time, was theatre critic for a fashionable magazine called *Town*. But then, he was perceptive enough to spot something Joan was up to, which nobody else had noticed.

The Fun Palace, though not built, was still in her head. Her aim was to bring ideas from it to Stratford East. To that purpose, she had approached the Arts Council with a plan to transform the theatre into a Fun Palace. Nothing had come of that because it did not regard the realising of her ideas as part of its function. Wanting to take the seats out of the stalls to make way for tables and chairs, she had asked Gerry. Nothing came of that either. He said it was impractical. You had to have so many seats in a theatre or you had no chance of making money. Tables would have lessened that number.

What Joan did achieve, very much a Fun Palace idea, was rolling entertainment.

If you turned up at the theatre early and wandered into the auditorium, you found the actor/writer Stephen Lewis onstage, holding *Dr Lewis's Surgery*. If you asked him a question about your health, he would give you a funny answer. At eight o'clock, came *Macbird*, the main event, in which he also appeared. After that, when you'd had a drink, you could come back and watch a tiny French farce. Joan found beginnings and endings hard to do. Rolling entertainment solved her problem: there weren't any. Tariq Ali was the only critic who saw all three events and, by experiencing the total effect, found his evening enjoyable.

Other details helped. During the interval, if an actor needed to set a prop the other side of the stage, he or she was encouraged by Joan to cross over the stage – there was no curtain – rather than go underneath. This sounds simple enough but there was a catch. As she or he crossed, the actor had to turn to anyone still in the auditorium, smile and wave. It had to be done sincerely and that is not as easy as it sounds. Joan, therefore, left things up to the actor. She didn't say that everyone had to cross over the stage, only those who felt like it. This is where she differs from other directors. Other directors occasionally dragoon their actors to go out front. Some years later, it happened at *Nicholas Nickleby* when the RSC performed it in 1980. Before the show started, the actors mingled with members of the audience for a chat. The stiffness of their conversation told you how they longed for their dressing rooms. Joan knew that talking to an audience as yourself – even walking across the stage as yourself – is hard. That's why she didn't force it.

The actor playing the sheriff of Dallas, Pat Tull, was a bustling extrovert by nature, so when the interval was over, his job was to go into the bar and round up the audience. Because the summons was made by a human being who was actually present, this was friendlier than the sharp bell which we still have 46 years later, or even the voice of the stage manager which was introduced in the mid-1970s.

It has to be said, *Dr Lewis's Surgery* and the little French farce weren't easy either. For the surgery to work, plenty of questions had to be thrown at Steve. However, as audiences were tiny and as those few sitting in the auditorium were shy, not many questions were coming at him. So he had to plant actors out front with questions he'd written; not ideal. Today, with audiences keener to join in than sit quietly, *Dr Lewis's Surgery* would be quite in tune with the times.

As for the farce, it was fine as long as Bob Grant, Howard Goorney and Brian Murphy were performing it. Firstly, there was the pleasure of seeing Bob, who had been Lyndon Johnson in *Macbird*, now playing a stuffy department head in a French ministry. Secondly there was the combined accomplishment of all three actors. They were expert farceurs. The next French farce which accompanied the next main show, performed by less expert farceurs, taught you that rolling entertainment made heavy demands.

Occasionally, for this late spot, Joan invited The People Show to perform. 'Amateurs! They shouldn't be allowed,' said some of the company as it looked down from the gallery. The titles for the The People Show's events were simply numbers. At Stratford East they were in single figures. Today, they're at *126*, which suggests it was worth taking the risk.

Theatre Workshop, right from the beginning, had been proud of its lighting. West End lighting had made Joan say 'Pastel-coloured air,' and John Bury, with a few lamps, had evolved a style that moulded but didn't decorate. In 1967, Joan was bored with all that. 'Light the audience,' she instructed, 'Make *them* look good.' It didn't happen right away but one can see that this too was a Fun Palace idea. She wanted its visitors to feel good about themselves.

The set for *Macbird* couldn't have been simpler. It was a silver rail that continued the curve of the dress circle right round the stage to meet up with the other side of the dress circle. Suspended above the stage, was a chandelier that mirrored the chandelier hanging above the stalls. In other words, it wasn't a set but a device for making the audience feel included. Inside the semi-circle, the stage was grey. Beyond, it was black. There were no wing pieces – that's curtains or flats at the side – and no borders, bits of material to hide the lights, nothing. As there was a good chance you could be seen when you weren't officially on, this required even more sensitivity from the actors than usual. The older ones longed for wings, or masking as they called it.

There was a designer, a recommendation of John Bury's. Gerry, who adored John, had brought him down from Nottingham. This chap had wanted to do something with rags but Joan had scotched that. The no-set set was her idea and the silver rail was the idea of a young student who didn't work in theatre, Martin O'Shea. He dreamed of the rail lighting up, which would have been good fun, but it didn't. Neither the will nor the money was there to help him. Theatre professionals would have been resentful.

Joan may have been bored with lighting but she loved gadgets. At the Fun Palace there would have been lots. Even in *Oh What a Lovely War* you had the newspanel with its travelling lights. So, having frozen out the designer – he could never get the hang of Joan anyway, who wanted everything feather light – she asked Martin O'Shea, whose speciality was gadget making, to take over. He built a three-sided computer on wheels, each face with differently arranged flashing lights. Turning it between scenes to denote scene changes was not easy for the turners because they had to dance a jig at the same time. One of them was Kent Baker from *Twang*. He had joined the company well into rehearsals, something that often happened with actors at Stratford East. Despite the computer's tendency to wander where it wasn't wanted, it was the first example of lights flashing in time with music. This has been a disco commonplace ever since but it was yet another example of Stratford East audiences seeing something for the first time.

Joan didn't want a conventional programme, so she asked Anna Lovell, an artist friend she knew from the Fun Palace side of things, to come up with an idea. This was one sheet of card with all the necessary information on it, plus dotted lines. You could fold it into a dart and throw it, which is what the audience did. Each morning, the cleaners had even more to sweep up in the stalls than usual. Gerry did not regard those programmes as a success.

During rehearsals it emerged that that neither Nidal Achkar nor Sarah Salem were allowed to speak on a British stage as they weren't Equity members. This may seem a small detail but Joan's drive to make things international, mix things up, meant so much to her. Years later, actors from all over the world became an important feature of Peter Brook's work in Paris. Nidal left but Sarah stayed. In June her anxiety for her family during the Six-Day War was clear to everyone. At least, here was a theatre that was in touch with what was going on in other countries.

CHAPTER TWENTY-FIVE

THE SUMMER OF '67

Shortly after *Macbird* opened, the company was invited to the green room for a reading of *Mrs Wilson's Diary*, a play with songs made from the popular column that was appearing every fortnight in the satirical magazine, *Private Eye*. John Wells and Richard Ingrams were the authors (Richard at the time, was the *Eye*'s editor). The boys' inspiration had been *The Diary of a Nobody* in which, Mr Pooter, a Victorian city clerk makes his entries, failing to see what the reader can see. John and Richard's diarist was Mary, the wife of the then prime minister, Harold Wilson.

Joan rarely allowed ordinary readings, the kind at which the actors read the parts they're going to play. At her readings, you could find a single actor reading everything for a while and then handing over to someone else. It kept things fluid, Joan, as she sometimes did, not casting until rehearsals were well under way. In the case of *Mrs W*, John and Richard took turns in reading the whole play themselves, laughing at their own jokes while failing to notice Stephen Lewis handing round toffees from a noisy paper bag.

The trouble was, what the company was hearing from John and Richard sounded literary: wodges of cleverness that simply sat there. Actors use the phrase 'The dialogue comes off the page.' At this reading, it stayed on it. A bedtime bossa nova for Harold and Mary, *Cocoa Time*, had charm but, after the reading, nobody said much and when Joan muttered: 'That took them all of an afternoon to write,' nobody said anything.

'Vanbrugh,' replied Joan to Tony Shaffer's question, 'What's next?' as the two of them sat in the empty theatre after a performance of *Macbird*. Tony, later the author of *Sleuth*, knew Joan because his production company, Hardy Shaffer, had made some egg commercials with her four years earlier. That's when she had been reunited with the cameraman, David Watkin. 'Silk and silver,' Joan went on, instantly conjuring up a world of lightness and elegance. 'There's nothing like a classic for separating the sheep from the goats,' she added and so set about adapting Vanbrugh's *The Provok'd Wife*, which she placed mainly by the Thames because she loved rivers, and which she called *Intrigues and Amours*. Adapting, in this case, meant cutting dialogue from some scenes while adding a card playing scene from *Journey to London*, another of Vanbrugh's plays. Being full of double entendres, this scene provided Lady Brute, the female lead and her lover, Constant, a sexy tête-à-tête after a rowdy moment involving lots of characters.

Peter Snow, the artist, appeared at the theatre. In 1959 he had designed *The Dutch Courtesan* for Joan but was best known for the set of *Waiting for Godot* when it was first performed in the UK at the Arts Theatre in 1955. He brought a model of what he proposed to build. Despite Joan disliking those, preferring the gradual but noiseless appearance of the set round the actors during rehearsals, she didn't complain. She merely simplified what Peter had done and, together, they came up with a shape with which she was always happy.

This was Restoration doorways at either side of the stage, balconies above them, and, beyond those, the full depth of the stage where, at the furthest point ascending as far as the eye could see, was an enormous blow-up of an engraving that depicted Greenwich Hill. To one side and halfway back, was a gazebo with room in it for a little band of harpsichord, cello and flute. When the time came, at the end of rehearsals, all sorts of people turned up one Sunday morning to paint fine black lines, hatchings, to create squares over both the steps, which led down into the auditorium, and the stage itself, now pale grey. The steps, as was the entire production, were a present to Joan from Gerry. They covered the pit and their effect was to spread the play out into the auditorium and provide new entrances and exits. That was all fine.

Costumes were more of a problem. Joan didn't want full period but a kind of lightweight version as you might find at the Folies Bergère. The costume designer, Cuthbert Jackson, had a go but couldn't make it work. Joan wrote to Jean-Louis Barrault to see if he had anything spare. Marie-Hélène Dasté, one of his most senior actresses, responded with a selection of cloaks and tricornes and, most graceful of all, a dress of the palest pearl grey that, under certain lights, turned pink. Lady Brute wore it. To be honest, it was of the wrong period as it came from a Marivaux play – think of Watteau – but no questions were asked. The rest of the costumes came from all over the place, including a very 1960s shop called I was Lord Kitchener's Valet. There, you could buy bright red military tunics with gold epaulettes, a fashion started by the Beatles in their Sergeant Pepper phase. Although this sounds muddled, by the time Joan had edited the colours, it looked, under the lighting designed by Gerry himself, beautiful.

When talking about colour in general, Joan said: 'If you have no money, stick to black and white with splashes of red.' There was quite a lot of that in this show. The silver she had first mentioned, was, in the end, confined to the colour of Lady Brute's hair.

'Light the audience,' Joan had said weeks before. Well, Restoration comedy was precisely the right time to do it. During the show, the lights were only half dimmed, which gave the same look as in Restoration times.

Through all this, Joan was still dreaming of the Fun Palace that she also wanted to place by the Thames. You could see the overlaps. Part of the play is set in Spring Gardens, pleasure gardens where people used to go in order to become what they secretly desired to be. This is also what Joan wanted for the Fun Palace. Vanbrugh's main job in life was architect. Joan was still very much in contact with Cedric Price. In fact, she took the company to his office so that he could give it a slide lecture on Vanbrugh and his buildings; Castle Howard, Blenheim Palace and Seaton Delaval.

'Usually I make plays out of nothing. Now you'll see me take a classic and make it look like nothing,' said Joan before rehearsals started. 'Nothing,' meaning it would seem not heavy and produced but light and spontaneous. There was still, however, the question of the sheep and the goats. She was right on that point, only too right. A couple of actors caught the style. The rest could not and the play didn't run. At matinees, the actors were sometimes performing to two rows. During rehearsals, Joan made her actresses – untypically, it was the women who were weakest – go over and over their dialogue, smoothing out the bumps to achieve the merry, rippling flow that was Vanbrugh's.

That merriment was vital to Joan. She reminded her actors that the lives of the characters in the play were short, requiring them to pack in as much fun as they could, while they could. So, when Lady Brute's niece, Bellinda, enters saying: 'Drown husbands! for yours is a provoking fellow,' her voice had to be filled with joy. Half a morning was spent making these entrances, with the actresses playing Lady Brute, Bellinda and Lady Fancyfull coming on individually, saying 'Good morning' and improvising to the audience what they had been up to the night before, good or bad as it may have been but always with that underlying merriment. Over and over they had to do it until it seemed almost cruel. It would only be when you saw other actresses in other productions that you would understand what that effort had been for. All the bumps would be back. All lines would be said as if the characters meant them, and there would be no merriment. The play would seem heavy and slow.

At this stage in her life, Joan never directly referred, during rehearsals, to any of her early influences. These simply came out in the games of imagination she invented as and when they were needed. However, when she said that the dialogue was a stream into which you could throw sticks but which you must never stem, you could see that she was stretching the gliding and sliding efforts from Laban into the way characters spoke. It was the same when she talked of characters moving on bubbles. Laban wasn't mentioned, but he was there. It took a classic to do it, though. Good education as these rehearsals were, they were, sadly, nothing to do with what was going on at the box office.

Gerry assembled the company in the green room, told it that he had run out of money, and was taking the play off. 'And when we open again, it'll be with something contemporary and relevant.' Evidently he wished the play had never been put on. The Fun Palace subtext and talk of architects, bearing in mind Joan's relationship with Cedric Price, could not have helped. Nearly four years later, what Gerry had implied was confirmed. He looked over the shoulder of the person who was writing out Joan's CV for some programme notes and crossed out *Intrigues and Amours*. He also crossed out *Macbird*; so he hadn't liked Joan's adaptation either.

When he finished his green room announcement, Joan said that she was staying put and anyone wishing to do the same was welcome. A handful, Stephen Lewis, Myvanwy Jenn, Johnny Lyons, Pat Tull, Kent Baker, Sandra Caron and Sarah Salem, did. They sang songs and performed sketches, sometimes in the theatre bar, sometimes in the upstairs room of The Red Lion pub over the road. They were The Buskers.

To advertise this show, a girl who worked at the post office, dipped a tiger's foot cut out of sponge into a pot of paint and dabbed the sponge all along Angel Lane right up to the bar door. She got into trouble but it was the kind of initiative Joan admired and so Christine Jackson, nicknamed by Joan, 'The Tigress', left the post office and started a new career.

Strictly speaking, as far as the theatre was concerned, what with no proper show on, things were at a low point but when you had Joan's restless mind and energy there, it didn't feel like it.

The Buskers was not all Joan got up to. Plans for the redevelopment of Stratford had been drawn up after the war but since then nothing had happened. Joan was convinced that children were finding things worse in 1967 than at any time she could remember. At the far end of the road in which the theatre stood was an unofficial rubbish dump. She decided to clear it and make it a playground. She may not have had her Fun Palace but she could try out some more Fun Palace ideas.

On a Sunday in July, she and a team of helpers, including Christine Jackson, cleared that rubbish dump. Gerry helped too. He could see that there was no harm in strengthening the theatre's relationship with the surrounding area and, after Joan going off in 1961, he probably thought it better to indulge rather than lose her.

There wasn't actually much on the playground. It gave Christine Jackson another opportunity to show her talent. She rang up local firms and asked for donations. 'Conning,' Joan called it. Christine talked different surfacing firms into providing samples of their wares and that is how the playground was covered, with a patchwork.

Some of the locals, most of them old, did not take to Joan's efforts. 'This was a nice area,' they said, a remark that took one's breath away as anyone could see that the truth was the exact opposite. It had been a filthy area and shamefully so. Nevertheless, from a story in the local paper, 'Joan gives Stratford the blues' (a pun on the colour of the playground's wall), the *Daily Express* heard of these objections. Down came a reporter who wrote an anti-Joan story. This explains why, some time later, on spotting the journalist, Sandy Fawkes, Joan chased her down the length of the foyer shouting: 'Bugger off! It's not my fault you work for a bloody awful rag like the *Express*!' It was 'my theatre' not 'dump' when she was under attack.

One afternoon, a middle-aged man, all fired up, came over to complain about the children's language. He started off with: 'I'm only a common docker,' which had Joan and the children falling about for weeks – well, in Joan's case, for years. Still, the common docker, who it turned out was unemployed, dock work being hard to find in 1967, ended up working in the bar of the theatre, thus fulfilling one of Joan's ideas, the figure of eight: the theatre pushes energy out into the world and energy from the world comes back into the theatre, and round and round it goes.

Like the Fun Palace, the playground was not just for fun. A teacher, Michael Holt, provided some coloured blocks of different shapes. Shifting them around and making patterns seemed like a game. In fact, it was maths.

One afternoon, it was possible to hear something going on in the theatre and, if you were a ghost, you could put your head round the gallery door and look down. The auditorium was dark but the stage was lit. Teenagers were doing some kind of play. 'When did they rehearse this?' you might wonder; 'How did they learn all those lines?' Out of the darkness walked Joan. She asked the teenagers a question and, from that, you would have found out what was going on. Too old for the playground, but wanting something for themselves, they had been invited by Joan to improvise on the stage. Their subject matter was their own lives: rows at home, getting into cinemas through lavatory doors, starting dead-end jobs, crossing the police. This was much better than Joan's real actors.

As the summer wore on, The Buskers drifted away. They'd had fun of sorts – Wole Soyinka had been along to recite some of his poems – but they needed properly paid work. The children on the playground stayed and so did the teenagers. Their improvisations took place every evening on the stage. It was quickly discovered that it was no use having the girls and the boys at the same time. When mixed, they just fooled around to the point where one of the girls said, 'We're boring ourselves.' But then concentration was always a problem. At school it had not been learned and that is the most damaging part of a poor education because, very soon, as early as seventeen, the ability to concentrate and absorb, if you've had no practice, starts to fade. So far, most of these teenagers' ingenuity had gone into pranks, like locking the chemistry master in the stinks cupboard. You can see more and more why Joan wanted that Fun Palace.

Anyway, one night, it would be the girls' turn and another night it would be the boys'. It sounds stereotypical but the girls were good at over the garden wall stuff, the slummocky neighbour who is always calling round for a cup of sugar and the gossipy one who is known as 'A proper little Stratford Express.' The boys, who soon came to be known as The Nutters, were good at breaking and entering and the subsequent clashes with the law. Sometimes this would end up in a Bundle, a silly fight in which everyone joined but in which nobody got hurt. Sometimes things would end up with a court scene. The jury and the sentence would always be much tougher than they would have been in real life.

Less funny was a first day at work. Suddenly a sixteen-year-old boy would realise he was condemned to a noisy, repetitive job that would put calluses on his hands. Quarrels with the boss often ensued and instant sacking. Joan, who was there the night a boy had been sacked, got him to play the boss. One of the most intelligent of the girls, Liz Langan, pointed out that it was those dull jobs that tempted the brighter boys to crime. And what's more, the reason she was attracted to such boys. Joan, more down to earth, said: 'Cockneys. Thieving goes in with the mother's milk.'

Friday night was Posh Night when The Nutters, using the theatre's costumes, stored underneath the stage, indulged their fantasies. Doug Quant, a compact, powerful presence, a good actor if ever there was, wanted to stay in bed and have Jayne Mansfield come round. His girlfriend arrives but he turns her away. Jayne Mansfield comes with her agent but turns Doug down. He orders fried rice. His mother appears and reprimands him for staying in bed and removes all his literature.

Roy Haywood, gentler than Doug but one of the most inventive, ordered grapes that had to be dropped into his mouth by a nubile girl. At the same time, another luscious beauty gave him a manicure. This soon bores him and he goes out in his gold Rolls-Royce to the Hilton Hotel where he tries to procure a girl but she is engaged elsewhere. He orders lobster and a bottle of wine but sends the wine back because it's the wrong vintage. Cross, he sacks the head waiter and buys the hotel. He goes home. The girls in these improvisations were always played by boys. It worked best that way. Without the girls there, the boys were free to be feminine.

It also meant they were uninhibited when it came to sex. One evening's improvisation went like this. Doug Quant and his mate, Sam Shepherd, go to Canvey Island for the day. They see two birds standing by a slot machine. Doug goes up to it. 'How does this machine work?' he asks, looking down at the machine but not really. 'Do you give?' he said suddenly and the girls tell him their house is empty, which is good. The boys like to have it away with birds they don't know, so they won't shout about it. They go to the house, Sam downstairs, Doug upstairs. For a while, things go silent but then Mum comes home and shoos the boys out. Doug finds another bird:

'Where do you come from?'
'Grimsby.'
'In a chalet?'
'Yeah.'
'Alone?'
'Dunno, yeah.'
'How much?'
'Ten quid.'
'You're only 15.'
'Fully experienced.'
'Do you have to wear a johnny?'

'No.'

'In the raw?'

'Yeah.'

'For ten quid, I want it in the mouth. I'll pay you when I enter the house.'

'No, now.'

'When I enter the house.'

'No, now.'

'Halfway through?'

'No, now.'

That would have been impossible with real girls.

On some nights, attempting these improvisations could be quite disheartening. Either not enough Nutters turned up or the improvisation disintegrated into silliness. Still, Joan, with her vast experience of theatre and life, did not realise, before that first invitation to the stage, what she had opened up.

During the daytime, when both the children and the teenagers were in school, or supposed to be, Gerry was in the theatre holding auditions. What for, nobody knew. 'You might as well go out into the street and pick the first ten people you meet.' Joan was looking down from the gallery at Gerry sitting in the dark at the front of the dress circle. He had just been listening to a young woman sing, 'I'm jist a gurrrl who cain't say no,' out of tune.

To anyone wondering if Joan had a point, Gerry explained: 'Yes, you could do what Joan said and what she'd get from those people on the street would be wonderful but that's not the point. Acting is a sickness. You have to want to do it night after night. People from the street would only do it once.'

CHAPTER TWENTY-SIX

A THROWAWAY BECOMES A HIT

Autumn came. *The Times* announced that Joan Littlewood was to direct *Mrs Wilson's Diary* with a cast including Stephen Lewis, Myvanwy Jenn, Sandra Caron and Johnny Lyons, all of whom had been buskers. So that's what Gerry had been auditioning for, but then he always played his cards close to his chest. 'I wanted it to be a ten-minute strip cartoon to start the evening,' said Joan. 'We could have changed it every night but the boys wouldn't have it. They insisted on a full-length show.'

John Wells sent down Brian Eatwell, a set designer. His enthusiasm did not impress Joan. She took against him and, using the excuse that he failed to measure the stage, dismissed any thought of him designing the show. This taking against someone was an editing out of a person who could block her imagination. Sometimes you'd wonder whether that would have actually been the case. When it happened with someone she knew well, it was alarming. In Brian Eatwell's case, Joan caught the gleam in his eye that told her he wanted to do a proper set-type set, 3D and lovingly detailed. A cosy reproduction of Ten Downing Street, however, was absolutely what she did not want. She wanted that strip cartoon idea. So, Brian Eatwell went off and was next heard of as the designer of a camp horror film called *The Abominable Dr Phibes* starring Vincent Price. His notices, Brian's that is, were excellent.

Joan, instead, turned to Hazel Albarn, the wife of the artist Keith Albarn, whom she already knew. Hazel, herself, was a teacher which was to come in handy. For the idly curious, she and Keith are the parents of Damon Albarn, not that he was born then.

Rehearsals started with the two Restoration doorways at either side of the stage, left over from the Vanbrugh. The rest: a table, two chairs, a chaise longue and the *Oh What a Lovely War* screen, arrived gradually during rehearsals, the typical Theatre Workshop way of going about design. Those pieces of furniture were not real. They were jigsawed out of plywood by Guy Hodgkinson, the young propmaker. This was partly to do with style – their two-dimensional quality added to the strip cartoon look – and partly to do with Joan's age-old hatred of comfy chairs on stage. Not wanting her actors to sit for long, if at all, she made sure all furniture was uncomfortable.

It was a small, sceptical group of actors that assembled for the first day's rehearsal, only eight, unusual for Joan. Sensing the mood, she did not start with a reading. She played a game of imagination, an appropriate one. 'Where would you all rather be?' The point was, it had the actors thinking and moving right away, even if it was only laying out an imaginary towel on an imaginary beach to sunbathe under an imaginary sun. Reading a scene didn't seem so bad after that, though Joan did tell Bill Wallis, new to the company and playing Harold Wilson, not to attempt the Wilson voice yet. It's easy to get bogged down in mimicry.

In no time, they were doing an improvisation on Inspector Maigret, Simenon's pipe-smoking French detective. It was a parallel to something Joan had spotted in the script. Again, the actors were on their feet using their heads and enjoying themselves. As with *Henry IV*, they were not shuffling about the stage with scripts in their hands. This led them into the opening breakfast scene and 'Shazam!' Bill Wallis, having found himself a cloak, was on as Harold, convinced he was Superman.

That was all good fun but when he sat down at the table and started a long speech about why there was no newspaper, you could have been up in the green room again with the authors reading. Joan loved her friends to recount old, familiar stories but when they did, she always interrupted; telling them that they'd missed a bit or got a bit wrong. Anyone who had dinner with her family realised where this came from. They all carried on like that. For the person trying to tell the story, it was hell but, for the listener, it was funny. Joan did that with Harold's speech. Neither Gladys (Harold's nickname for Mary) nor Inspector Trimfittering, his bodyguard, wanted him to find the paper and so they kept interrupting with distractions. The scene took on an energy that was not there before. The dialogue came off the page.

At break time, Gerry came down from his office to tell everyone that they had three weeks' rehearsal and that they had better not forget it. 'Why so long, Gerry?' asked Joan, 'When we were tuned up, we could put on a classic in eleven days.' Gerry's announcement had, of course, been purely for her. Usually he gave Joan five to seven weeks' rehearsal, a long time by any other theatre's standards and, even then, Joan, with the first night approaching, would always say: 'We open Thursday? But you never told me.'

Gerry's announcement worked, though. Within a very few days, the actors were able to run a surprisingly large chunk of the play. Richard Ingrams came to watch. He roared with laughter, unaware of what Joan had done, which was to put sedentary dialogue on its feet and make it dance. The effect on him was productive. He went away and had other ideas. The Maharishi Mahesh Yogi was in the news and he decided that Wilson should have his own guru.

The next Monday, Joan asked an assistant to sit cross-legged on the stage and say some lines to Harold, which Richard had brought along. It was as if she was drawing a pencil sketch to see if the idea was worth pursuing. It worked because, suddenly, there was Howard Goorney, back with the company, playing the guru.

The play had no structure to speak of. There was merely a threat. Because Harold Wilson had spoken out against the Vietnam War, Lyndon Johnson, the American president, was going to bomb London at midnight. That was it. At the same time, in that morning's newspaper, Wilson's popularity had dropped off. That's why Gladys and Trimfitting didn't want him to find the paper. They knew what effect it would have, and it did. Ignoring everything else, Harold spent the day trying to think of ways to restore his popularity. It was only near midnight that he realised he had to act fast to stop the bombing. Mrs Wilson, during this day, as well as coping with her husband, had to deal with her neighbour, Audrey Callaghan from number eleven, the delivery of a lewd statue, and Gerald Kaufman's moods. At the time, Gerald Kaufman was one of the kitchen cabinet. The whole play was just a series of interruptions and when the actors tried them out for the first time, they were very funny. By the end of the second week, they weren't funny at all and Myvanwy Jenn wasn't getting Mrs Wilson either. John Wells, now free to attend rehearsals, was suicidal. 'Rather less than orgasmic,' he murmured.

At the same time, other things were going on. Digby Morton, Mrs Wilson's real-life clothes designer, rather treacherously, you might think, offered to design the clothes for the fictional Mrs Wilson. Joan, however, was sticking to her cartoon idea. Gladys wore a plain cream dress decorated with felt flowers backed with Velcro so that during the show she could move them around.

Underneath the stage, Hazel Albarn had the children from the playground painting slides to back project on to the *Oh What a Lovely War* screen. These pictures either acted as a counterpoint to the action on the stage or told you what was happening off it. For example, President Johnson sends the bombers, and that's what the children painted. Joan's push outwards on to the playground had found her artists and now their energy was coming back into the theatre: the figure of eight. Hazel, being a teacher, had the experience to supervise their work.

On stage she took pieces of string and drew them tight across the floor, the furniture and the Restoration doorways. Regardless of logic, but using the strings to create a hard line, she painted everything in bright, shiny, contrasting colours. It was simple. It was cheap, and Joan had her cartoony look.

Two nights before it opened, the actors thought as little of the show as they did at the first reading but then a preview audience came, quite a big one. They liked it and Myvanwy Jenn, after being told by Joan that she had it in her to be a great light comedienne, found Gladys. She had a comic sweetness that, when something went badly wrong, turned to only the mildest of dismay. It happened in the nick of time.

On the first night, the actors were still uncertain. As they stood in the wings waiting, Stephen Lewis said to Bob Grant, who was playing George Brown,

'Wouldn't it be funny if, years from now, we're being wheeled on in this.' They weren't saying it but they badly needed a hit.

As it happens, they got it. You could tell at the interval. After a riotous first half, Joan came through the pass door from the gallery where she had been taking notes. 'We were better off busking,' she muttered grimly. At that moment you knew everything was going to be all right. It was because Joan was so gloriously perverse.

The next morning, the critics praised the show and, for the next few weeks, the theatre was packed. The run lasted only a few weeks because Donald Albery, the West End theatre manager, wanted the show immediately at the Criterion. The producer, Tony Palmer, then at EMI, even made an LP and, because of the small cast, the show made a profit; the first ever. Gerry said that *Fings Ain't Wot They Used T'Be* had packed the theatre for fourteen weeks without making a penny. If there was a problem, it was at the box office. It couldn't cope or, as Bob Grant put it, 'The Theatre Royal box office is only geared for failure.'

What was little known then was what Gerry had been going through with the Lord Chamberlain. In April of that year, 1967, he had sent him the script and, while Joan had been either out on the playground or inside improvising with the teenagers, quite a battle had taken place. In principle, the Lord Chamberlain hadn't wanted the show to go on at all. The portrayal on a stage of living public figures, in particular cabinet ministers and members of the royal family, as Joan had found out before the war, was still frowned upon, even if it was no longer illegal.

In the end, it came down to individual lines. Here are three examples:

> **One.** *1-11 You have agreed to omit from:*
> *'Was meant to be dining'... to and inclusive of '......*
> *Notting Hill'.*

The full line was 'He (Lord Goodman) was meant to be dining with some old friends who happen to live in one of the more colourful areas of Notting Hill.'

> **Two.** *1-16 You have agreed to omit from:*
> *It's his poll you see......' to and inclusive of '.......last*
> *few months'.*

The full lines were:

Gladys: It's his poll, you see.

Audrey: Oh Gladys, it hasn't shown a marked falling off again.

Gladys: It has. It came as a nasty shock I can tell you, especially as he's been getting his 56% more than satisfied over the last few months.

> **Three.** *111- You have agreed to omit 'I shall never forget the time Audrey Callaghan had that embarrassing moment in the Cumberland Gap.'*

If there is anything shocking about those lines, it's their mildness. After all, the three BBC satire shows, *That Was The Week That Was*, *Not so Much a Programme, More a Way of Life* and *BBC 3* had all been and gone. In those, you had send-ups of not one but two prime ministers and a sketch in which religions were compared as if they were products being tested by the consumer's guide, *Which?*

Once the show opened, Colonel Johnston from the Lord Chamberlain's office came down. Gerry, to put him in a good mood, fed him well. Here's what arrived a couple of days later:

> *Dear Mr Raffles,*
> *Thank you very much indeed for inviting*
> *me to the opening performance of 'Mrs*
> *Wilson's Diary' and for the kind way in*
> *which you and your staff looked after me.*
> *I enjoyed the play very much.*
> *I did notice a few deviations from the*
> *licensed manuscript due, no doubt, to re-*
> *quirements which had become apparent during*
> *final rehearsals. No doubt your running*
> *order and routines will have settled down in*
> *the next few days and, if necessary, you will*
> *be sending me any additional material; after*
> *which I am sure you will take care to see*
> *that the licensed version is adhered to.*
> *Yours sincerely,*
> *A. Johnston*

The curious thing is that the show never stopped being altered and that meant right through its run at Stratford and afterwards at the Criterion, the biggest change being the resignation of George Brown. It was included that very night and, not long afterwards, Nigel Hawthorne, who had been in another of Joan's shows, was drafted in to play Roy Jenkins. While Harold was out, he called round to see Gladys, saying as he left: 'You must drop round to have a look at my Jackson Pollocks.' To which Gladys replied: 'And you must pop up and have a peep at my Holman Hunt.' It all seemed to happen so easily, that is from the censorship point of view. It wasn't quite so easy for Joan if one reads the following memo, written when she knew the show was going to transfer.

'J.L. to MONSIGNOR WELLS & LORD INGRAMS
for attention of IMPRESARIO RAFFLÉS

SUBJECT The Mrs. W. Story.

PLOTLESS

NON-PLAY   Fun-Mobile

NON-PRODUCTION

About to be calcified in some West End A*** Hole.

AFTER B'Heath P. Mortem chat, intention apparently to take Playwrite job seriously. Why not then do a new one says Jay Hell [Producer's consultant] since none of this epic would stand up to Kunst analysis. Small wind machines have to be put under such bubbles as this constantly if they are to be kept afloat. This happens at pre-show sessions each night and will have to continue during Mausoleum stay. New jokes and songs are better than firm structure. Also this team "for better or worse" shared the peculiar and unique experience of getting this epic on to a stage.

To dislodge, re-cast, improve or cast to type will create an entirely different attitude to work. A hierarchy is formed, good "Performers" step into dead men's clothes, it's disaster. I know because I've made this mistake before.

This contradicts J.L. yes-chat at B'Heath Meet but HELL so opposed in first place to old world mounting of this show that it didn't seem to matter anymore what happened as she was on dreary transfer waggon again.

Also suggest that Prologue and Entr'acte clownerie should go in:-

"COMMERCIALS", "LECTURES" with slides. GNOME EDITORIAL, O'BOOZE REPORTS and Theatre should have P. EYE DECOR MOTIF.

Various points in this memo need picking up. To start with, one can see at first hand some of Joan's reasons for her leaving theatre six years earlier. Two specific examples she often talked about come to mind.

When *A Taste of Honey* was first produced, the part of Peter, Helen's fancy man, was played by John Bay, a witty American who, during rehearsals, had contributed greatly. Unfortunately, he drank and Donald Albery, the show's West End producer, regarded him as unreliable. Nigel Davenport, who had never worked for Joan before and never would again, was brought in to replace him. He provided the solidity and safety that producers, looking forward to a long run, required, or 'Eight performances a week,' as they put it. For Joan who prized, above all, invention and quick wits, he was the good 'Performer' stepping into a dead man's clothes.

The second example happened during the run of *Fings Ain't Wot They Used T'Be*. James Booth, who had created the role of Tosher – and that meant really created, because he had turned Frank Norman's old man into a young, Ben Jonson fixer with funny telephone conversations he had made up himself – was leaving. An actor who looked like he could play the part, Maurice Kaufman, was cast. Again, he had not worked for Joan before, and never would again. She was so depressed by his performance that she summoned Victor Spinetti all the way back from Chicago where he was having a perfectly nice time appearing in *The Hostage*. Victor, Welsh and no cockney spiv, was completely wrong for the part but he had a bounce and presence that Joan badly needed. Maurice Kaufman was typecasting.

Another point in the memo is the part that goes: 'This contradicts JL yes-chat at B'Heath Meet'. Like turning against people, Joan changing her mind was something that happened often. Picture John Wells, Richard Ingrams and Joan sitting round the kitchen table at Blackheath, eating lamb that had been slowly roasted by Gerry in his Aga, and drinking Fleurie wine. You would imagine everything was going fine: Joan, John and Richard talking enthusiastically about the transfer as Gerry produced more dishes. For the two boys, a transfer was, after all, a new experience. The next day, they were confronted with that memo. It would have felt like cold water dashed in their faces.

Gerry, of course, was familiar with the cold water treatment and knew only too well Joan's attitude to the West End, so his feelings were likely to have been mixed. *Mrs Wilson's Diary* was the first hit since the Theatre Royal re-opened in March of that year, so, as its manager, he was bound to have been pleased, while the move to the Criterion was the icing on the cake.

A West End transfer may have been tedious for Joan but, for many others, it still commanded respect. However, it would have been better, altogether, if Theatre Workshop had been given a proper grant so that it didn't need to transfer shows. Gerry, by then, knew that but, after all these years, it had still not happened. Referring to the knack for raising money possessed by the actor who ran the Mermaid Theatre in Puddle Dock, he sighed and said: 'Bernard Miles is better than I am.'

Finally, there were Joan's ideas for what ought to be going on around the show at the Criterion. Lord Gnome, it should be explained, was the fictional owner of *Private Eye* and a send-up of Lord Beaverbrook, the ultimate interfering newspaper owner. Richard wrote that. Lunchtime O'Booze was the *Eye*'s fictional political columnist. Those ideas were some of Joan's small wind machines and very much in keeping with her desire for rolling entertainment. But, in the West End, where you didn't own the bricks and mortar and had to deal with the theatre's own management, those little wind machines were much harder to switch on, if at all. In the end, there were some Willie Rushton cartoons lining the walls as you descended to the auditorium.

When it came to the show's poster, Gerry summoned his regular designer, George Mayhew (posters along with photos and logos being Gerry's self-imposed responsibility). Understanding that a company had to sell itself, he regarded them as important. In particular, he admired the simple logos adopted by the Berliner Ensemble and the Théâtre National Populaire in Paris. Joan, holding different opinions on the subject of photos and George Mayhew, left Gerry to it. Photos she did not like at all, and posters by George Mayhew she disliked too. Mayhew provided a widely accepted good taste that gave the company a certain respectability. Joan, hot on design herself but, after Gerry's disapproval of the *Macbird* dart, offering no alternative, railed at whatever he came up with. In the case of *Mrs Wilson's Diary*, it was a rose-tinted vignette of Number Ten Downing

Street with the title in copperplate lettering. Cartoony it wasn't. If anything, the ghost of Brian Eatwell hung about it, but that was typical of the constant tension between Joan and Gerry.

Another facet of their relationship could be observed three months into the following year, when the cast at the Criterion was told that *Mrs Wilson's Diary* was coming off. 'Oh Gerry, can't you keep it on?' pleaded one of the actors. 'Yes, Gerry, can't you?' chimed Joan adding, the moment that actor's back was turned, 'What a bore for you, Gerry. It's quite obvious the show's dead on its feet.'

Nicholas de Jongh, the theatre critic, in his history of British theatre censorship, was amazed at the gentleness of *Mrs Wilson's Diary* when he read it. Alistair Beaton's 2001 play, *Feelgood*, at the Hampstead Theatre would have seemed to him much harder-hitting. What he couldn't know, because he hadn't been there, was how it felt to be in the auditorium at Stratford East in 1967. When Joan was on form, a breathless, warm, what you are seeing is happening now, sensation lifted the audience to the point that it felt impelled to jump on to the stage and join the actors. It's what kept the show alive and what Joan dreaded having to keep going throughout the run at the Criterion. That kind of lightness and freshness makes great demands. At the Hampstead Theatre, you had a properly made play, no songs and a realistic set. You watched it but you did not think of joining in.

'Wouldn't it be funny if, in years to come, we were being wheeled on in this.' There was a follow-on to that remark of Stephen Lewis's. As a result of him and Bob Grant appearing in *Mrs Wilson's Diary*, they were cast in the TV sitcom, *On the Buses*, which ran for years. Joan hating it, referred to Bob and Steve, from then on, as The Trusses.

CHAPTER TWENTY-SEVEN

JOAN LOOKS BACK

The show Joan plucked Nigel Hawthorne from was *The Marie Lloyd Story*. That spring, a script had been lying about in the green room. It was only too easy for anyone to pick it up and have a read. Three people were responsible. The book and lyrics were by Dan Farson and Harry Moore and the music was by Norman Kay. Dan was a journalist and a friend of Joan's. Harry Moore was not known in theatre but Norman Kay was familiar from his TV themes. The dialogue, which most people respond to first when reading scripts, was cardboard. Why would Joan do that? If you stick around in theatre and film, particularly film, you will find that a script can have poor dialogue but a good plot, and that something can be done about it so, enter Joan.

At first, she and Gerry were unsure. For them the problem wasn't so much the dialogue as the songs. They were angular and, if anything, Kurt Weill-ish. Their answer was to give them to Avis Bunnage to record. If she could make them work, then maybe there was a chance for the show. Avis recorded them and made them work. At that point, she was asked to play Marie. In later years Joan always said: 'We did *Marie Lloyd* as a present for Avis,' which was a distancing device. If Avis had not been able to make anything of the songs, the show would not have been done.

The reason why Joan accepted the script was because Dan had chosen the most interesting part of Marie Lloyd's life, the last part. Ned Sherrin and Caryl Brahms had also written a Marie Lloyd musical, *Sing A Rude Song*, and had also sent it to Joan. This one told of Marie's rise to fame, not so interesting because there was little conflict. Her rise happened very quickly at the age of nineteen and she stayed at the top for many years. That's not a story. Stories happen when things go wrong, like taking a violent young lover, clashing with moral guardians, finding yourself in competition with films and dying onstage of mercury poisoning (mercury being used to treat venereal disease). Those were Marie's last years.

Joan, though loathing the hypocrisy of the Edwardian era and not liking Marie much either, could make something of this. Scene One was a Monday morning band call in Sheffield. Instead of asking her actors to read the scene, the dialogue being all feeble wisecracks, Joan appointed two or three people to be stage hands and get on with bringing in skips and calling up to the flies to get battens, which were to hold cloths, at the right height and angle. The rest of the company were sent off into the theatre's scene dock which in the Theatre Royal's case led to the street and, there, the actors had to form themselves into the various acts, one with a newborn baby, and imagine themselves arriving, either from the station, or their digs on a cold morning. Once on the stage, each act's task was to get the musical director, in this case the real musical director, Alfie Ralston in the pit, to run through their music. The sooner you had that out of the way the better. Anyone not involved with music went to sort out his or her dressing room. This they did by climbing the stone steps at the other side of the stage to where the real dressing rooms were. If they didn't like them they could come down and complain. Nobody said anything funny. They just got on with what they had to do.

Halfway through the morning, Dan Farson walked in and was appalled. Not one word of his dialogue could he hear being spoken. And for the rest of the rehearsals he remained appalled, getting drunk in the bar and attacking the actors for not saying what he had written. Joan often gave the instruction, 'Don't be clever. Have the courage to be ordinary.' This scene was a good example of that and the more perceptive of the critics were impressed by its atmosphere. In the ordinary one can find beauty.

Drawing on her own memory of theatre and theatre life, Joan continued piecing together scene after scene: Marie's private life, alternating with music hall scenes performed before a front cloth. That's when you heard her famous songs like 'Oh Mr Porter' and 'My Old Man Said Follow The Van'. The Norman Kay songs were reserved for telling the backstage story.

As usual, research went on simultaneously. Avis listened to records of Marie Lloyd singing. What came from that was how small Marie's voice was and how unemphatic her delivery. She didn't have an accent either. Georgia Brown, not long before, had recorded 'My Old Man', bashing it out in a theatrical cockney, presumably because that's how we think of music hall performers: loud and unsubtle. Think again. Those acts toured for years and years. It gave the artistes time to refine, polish and add detail that could make the acts really subtle. When, at the end of Act One, Avis quietly sang: 'We had to move away, for the rent we couldn't pay. The moving man came round just after dark. There was me and my old man, shoving things inside the van. . .,' the audience went quiet and listened to the story which was not very happy. The words describe a moonlight flit. In that way, the song became new.

Joan wanted a tea stall scene with lots of terrible gags. She delegated the writing of that to Jimmy Perry who was playing Marie's first husband, Alec Hurley:

Toff: What kind of sandwiches have you got?

Stallholder: Any kind you like.

Toff: I'll have an elephant sandwich.

Stallholder: I'm not cutting up a new elephant just for you.

Toff: I'll have a crocodile sandwich then and make it snappy.

Upstairs in his dressing room, Jimmy was also writing the first episode of *Dad's Army*.

Joan remembered that music hall artistes only met up on Sundays, often at the Horns pub in south London near where she was born. It was the only day of the week these get-togethers could happen as artistes were working every other day, often away from London. Joan, following this tradition, used to have Sunday lunch parties now and again at Blackheath. Nearly all her actors past and present were invited. In the show, Marie Lloyd gets to throw such a party. The wretched baby from the first scene is there and so is an old bum, played by Nigel Hawthorne, whose main aim is to eat and drink as much as he can because it's probably the only decent meal he'll have all week. In this way, Dan Farson's artifice was replaced by the believable and the charming. If one looks at the script today, one can see that whatever her feelings about the show – 'a present for Avis' – Joan put a surprising amount of herself into it.

As usual, during rehearsals, actors were added to the company. A young man called Jimmy Winston appeared. He'd been with the group, The Small Faces. It was at the end of a day's rehearsal when he arrived and Joan, right there and then, without going to watch him from the dress circle or even leaving the stage, asked him to mime a champion diver climbing up a ladder and performing a champion dive. Jimmy did this and was given a job on the spot. As he left, Joan said: 'I just needed someone who could move.' And yet that was by no means the only show Jimmy did for Joan.

The company loved the show. This horrified her but, worse, they loved each other. She sent for Pat Tull who'd been the Sheriff in *Macbird*. Earlier in the year, he had been unpopular with his fellow actors and that was just what Joan wanted. Unfortunately, Pat, in between times, had found a new girlfriend, Pam Jones, an actress who had been in the Vanbrugh and she had cleaned him up, slimmed him down and softened his aggression. Joan was most disappointed, particularly as Pat loved the show too.

And The Nutters? Each evening they came in, three quarters of an hour before the company's warm-up, to carry on their improvisations and, by simply being around a show, they picked up stuff. Bright Liz Langan could put many of the cast to shame by learning all the dialogue and all the songs in double-quick time. As a consequence, she could easily stand in when an actor went for a pee.

Geoff Wincott, who was always being sent up because he wore glasses, got to play a callboy who summoned Miss Lloyd from her dressing room. The first time he rushed it, and Joan told him not to anticipate but to think through what would really happen in such a situation. It was a lesson in timing but not a technical one. During a gala charity scene, he and Chris Shepherd, Sam's younger brother, lolloped across the stage as that year's Derby winner. For this they had to wear pink tights and, although their faces were not seen because they were under a horse blanket, they thought they would never live it down. Joan wanted other Nutters to do that horse on other nights but Pat Tull – he still wasn't totally lovable – complained to Equity. Nowadays, children alternate all the time. That's the ruling on their being able to perform.

As part of the set, right at the back of the stage on a diagonal, was a proscenium arch, so for scenes that took place in the music hall wings, you only had to fly in three little wing pieces downstage, also on a diagonal. There, Marie and other performers could gossip while looking upstage at the act, Jimmy Winston and his non-existent performing seal, for example. Obviously this arch had to have a colour and again Joan clashed with a tasteful designer. She came in to find it painted the colour of the Louis Vuitton LV. 'Goose turd green,' she said, and had it painted sparkly silver.

Another example of Joan asking someone to stand in was less of a success than Liz Langan. Max Shaw, playing an important part, was not there. Joan asked an assistant to take his place. The assistant, not wanting to be caught acting, stood absolutely still. No use. 'What are you doing?' asked Joan, 'You're stuck there like a turd on a blanket.'

What the assistant was at least able to learn was the power of the diagonal. The sparkly upstage arch was also used for a sweeping entrance made by Marie and her entourage as they stepped off a train into the main hall of the station. The angle they came on at through the arch added to the force of the entrance.

When Joan started to rehearse this scene, she first had to establish the comings and goings before Marie's entrance. She told everyone to go off and work out who they were – a porter, a little family, a late passenger, it didn't matter, but they had to fix on something. The point was, before they came on, they knew what they had to do so that Joan only had to say: 'Go,' and suddenly there was the scene. With Joan's training in sensitivity, they kept their eyes open as they went. That way, they didn't bump into each other. John Gielgud, in his writing, refers to beautiful groupings. That's what he did. He arranged the actors on the stage to make a pleasing effect. Joan never did that and yet everyone was in the right place, and it looked good too.

The show got quite good notices and even won an award for Best New Musical. Some critics rhapsodised over that first scene and also over a little one in which a small, bedraggled group forms a queue in the rain for cheap seats in the gallery.

This was the scene that Joan remembered from 'late door' at the Old Vic when she was a teenager.

She, herself, sitting in the stalls during a break in rehearsals, said: 'This one is designed to be jet propelled into the West End,' which was unusually cynical of her. The cast, uncynically, looked forward to going into a theatre up West and so, by then, did Dan Farson who had become proud of what was now 'his' show. At least he was smart enough to recognise what Joan had achieved on his behalf.

Winter came. Little throwaway *Mrs Wilson's Diary* was running successfully at the Criterion, and big, commercial *Marie Lloyd Story* was poised to join it in the West End. There were still The Nutters.

CHAPTER TWENTY-EIGHT

THE NUTTERS MAKE A FILM

Ｉt was during the run of *The Marie Lloyd* show that Gerry dropped a bombshell. At least, that's what it felt like to Joan. He rented the theatre out. It was to go to a pantomime starring an old Brothers act that nobody had heard of except Avis Bunnage. Gerry doing the deed without first telling Joan didn't help. Despite her scorn for the place, she was put out. It may have been old-fashioned but the Theatre Royal, if nothing else, provided a space for activities.

It seemed like Gerry was returning the theatre to the days before Theatre Workshop, when it hosted shows like *Soldiers in Skirts*. In later months, this feeling was strengthened by such titles as *Boys Will be Girls* appearing on the billboards. Here was Gerry's argument again: the last thing a theatre could do was go dark. He had a point because, for all its ups and downs, the theatre is still there, still putting on plays.

At No 48 Martin Street, a few streets away from the theatre, was a light industry factory that was only being used for a bit of storage. Christine Jackson acquired it from Newham Council at a peppercorn rent. There, when it grew dark, the playground children could continue making things and The Nutters could carry on improvising.

Joan's constant challenge – ways and means – still faced her. In the old days, Theatre Workshop could go into an unappealing hall and with no money but plenty of will, clean it and make it fresh. Its arrival at Stratford East in 1953 was a good example. However, that kind of effort requires a team and every member of that team must know what the aim is. That is how Theatre Workshop had its ways and means. Joan, though it didn't look like it, was on her own in 1967. It didn't look like it because she could make things happen by the power of her personality. Her problem was maintaining the necessary level of concentrated stamina.

An example of her being out on her own came with the playground. Yes, Joan did make a team. However, the members of that team had not set out to be play

197

supervisors. It was not their aim. They had other interests and, what's more, needed to earn a living. Joan could chip in with small sums of her own money, not with Gerry's approval though, but those sums could never be enough. The team gradually broke up and wandered off in different directions. The one person who stayed was Christine Jackson, but then children and play was her aim.

No 48 Martin Street, dedicated to the children and The Nutters, sounded ideal but as a building it was not that lovely. It needed work. Meetings were held. Reports were made – Joan always insisted on those – and indeed some work was done, like a bit of plumbing, but the place remained shabby and so became a space the children and The Nutters didn't respect. Good heavens, hadn't the Theatre Royal, with its strong identity, been broken into often enough? What chance did No 48 have? At the time, though, it was going to be great.

The Theatre Royal with its clear purpose, its hard but exciting work, its discipline, even its glamour, was a better place to be. The children and The Nutters were guests there and had to show respect, well, a bit. At No 48, they were not guests; it was supposed to be theirs. Joan tried to add formality by making it a club with membership but its identity was never strong. What happened next brought things to a head.

One of the many people who visited the playground during the summer was a young man who dreamed of being a film maker, Barney Platts-Mills. While he was there, he got to hear about The Nutters and decided he wanted to make a documentary film about them. No 48 seemed to be the ideal place to make it. There were lots of meetings about that too.

Shooting started early in 1968. However, it was soon obvious that bringing in a crew of ex-public school boys who had never watched the improvisations, had a bad effect. Each time they had a go, the games rapidly disintegrated. Doug Quant turned into a film star, went upstairs and refused to come down to work.

Barney was not getting his film. Joan, sensing that No 48 was one of the problems, sent the crew and The Nutters out to play football that could then be filmed. It was, but it lacked interest. Then, one night, there was a break-in at No 48 and everything inside was smashed to bits. Barney Platts-Mills was shocked, particularly as he could see that his film could no longer be shot there. He drove out to a boys' club in Essex, taking only a few of The Nutters. It was a dismal place. Even so, the other Nutters followed and the evening fell apart.

Having got very little, Barney and his crew left. He cut together the footage and called it *Everybody's an Actor, Shakespeare Said*, a remark made by one of The Nutters. He showed this film to Bryan Forbes, the film director, who then helped him raise the money to make a feature film, *Bronco Bullfrog*. He cast The Nutters but, except for Roy Haywood and Sam Shepherd, not the really good ones. They had scarpered. In comparison with the improvisations on the theatre stage, which Barney had never seen, the film came across as a bit soppy. But then maybe nobody could see those improvisations. The plays The Nutters came up with existed for themselves.

Shortly after the filming, Joan closed No 48 down, which upset Christine Jackson. Joan found her another playground job elsewhere.

During this unhappy period, some of The Nutters were hailed into court. They didn't care. They knew they would only be given a warning. Joan did care. She knew that it was still a black mark against their names. If they had to show a clean record in later years when applying for something important, like a mortgage, that black mark could come to haunt them. She paid for a solicitor and went to court with them. She wasn't allowed in, though, because The Nutters were minors. A few minutes later, the solicitor bounced out with a big smile on his face. He had not only got The Nutters off but seemed genuinely to believe that Joan had done the right thing.

When the playground children, who were between six and ten years old, did something they should not have, Joan rang the Dean of St Paul's and said they were coming on a pilgrimage to the cathedral, on foot. He, seeing how imaginative this walk was, said that he would be there on the cathedral steps to greet them. Sometimes Establishment figures did understand Joan but then, perhaps he wasn't so Establishment, being Australian.

The closing of No 48 brought an end to the children making things and the end of The Nutters. However, if you talk to any of them today – they're now in their sixties – they will tell you that they have never forgotten 1967 and that, ever so slightly, it changed their lives.

CHAPTER TWENTY-NINE

REACTING TO THE TIMES: RONAN POINT, BUBBLE CITY & INDIA PART TWO

D uring this period, Joan's reputation as a theatre director was still immense and she was still receiving offers. Early in 1968, the Royal Court Theatre asked her to direct the opening production of the Theatre Upstairs. Sam Wanamaker, whom she had known from *Uranium 235* days back in the 1950s, asked her to do *Bartholomew Fair* at the Globe and Oscar Lewenstein – no quitter, he – sent her Joe Orton's last work, *What the Butler Saw*, hoping that she would direct it.

The Royal Court job, she turned down. Her excuse was that she was going to make the film in India she had mentioned late in 1966. She did, however, see one of the Theatre Upstairs's early productions, *Christie in Love* by Howard Brenton, of which she spoke well. Remarkable, really, as she hardly spoke well of any play she went to. The Globe – that's when it was a plastic tent – she nearly accepted. That is, until she discovered she couldn't do the play out in the street.

To Oscar she wrote a letter, written in a playful style she often used when extracting herself from an awkward situation. She disliked saying no and this was a way of avoiding the word.

> Dearest Oscar (Actually I only know two Oscars and the other one isn't dear at all, so it should be just dearer Oscar)
>
> I read the poor Orton's semi-posthumous right away, but have left time for it to settle; and I still think it's rather eccentric of you to be keen on it. It has a super opening and some very good jokes, but how can you be so "King Lear"? I didn't notice any giveaway gestures or the secreting of scented handkerchiefs or suchlike which might have told me that you have gone bent!
>
> Now Oscar the only way to do it is as a TV serial with Lucille Balls and Charlotte Drake and all the men playing women and the women men. One can't be semi-serious, demi-comic about the sex war. *Lysistrata* is the only successful comedy on the theme.

She finished the letter talking yet again about the film she wanted to make in India.

And, of course, there was *The Marie Lloyd Story*. While Gerry dealt with managements, Joan wrote sheets of notes about how to make it better. She sent them to Dan Farson. He tried to put the breaks on. After his early indignation, he thought the show, by its last performance, was not that bad. It went nowhere, though. *The Marie Lloyd Story*, probably the only show Joan aimed at the West End, never reached it. Talks fell apart over Norman Kay's songs. Joan and Gerry wanted to junk them and use only the old music hall ones. Norman Kay and Harry Moore weren't having it. Dan Farson was easy.

Joan did not seem that upset. 'If you were to do it again,' she said over dinner at Blackheath, 'you'd need someone dangerous to play Marie, like Judy Garland.' So Avis Bunnage was vindicated. During rehearsals, she had joked: 'I'm only standing in for Barbara Windsor.' About three years later, Philip Hedley, who was to become Artistic Director of Stratford East, put *The Marie Lloyd Story* on at Lincoln with Jean Boht in the lead. The Norman Kay songs were not in it.

Really, Joan was still thinking about the Fun Palace and how to adapt it to her circumstances which, right then, were no theatre, no other space, nothing. That April, she set up a meeting at the Architectural Association in Bedford Square.

Present, among others, were Keith Albarn, Hazel's husband, James Dyson and Bruce Lacey. Bruce and some musical clowns called The Alberts had put on a show at the Comedy Theatre called *An Evening of British Rubbish*. Joan, when asked to organise a CND rally at the Albert Hall, had sent The Alberts on to interrupt when it grew boring. Among those on the podium that night was JB Priestley and Jolly Jack was rendered a good deal less than jolly. This could have been Joan's revenge for the crushing letter he had sent Theatre Workshop turning down a request for money in its early days. Bruce Lacey and The Alberts meant anarchy and Joan did love interruptions.

But what were Bruce Lacey and Keith Albarn and the others doing at this meeting? Joan, at first, spoke of her journey from the Fun Palace, via the playground and The Nutters to where she was at that point. She had been remembering how Theatre Workshop started, out on the road. So, that's what she was planning to do again. The Mobile Fair, as she would call it, would go to various places round the country and Robert Atkins, an assistant stage manager on *The Marie Lloyd Story* but with much more to give, had found the first space, Woburn Park. Because it had its own strong and commercial identity Joan wasn't crazy about it. Still, it was available.

After this introduction, talk turned to finance, how to raise money for this fair and how visitors would pay. Would there be a fence round it with punters buying one ticket for the whole thing, or would there be no fence with each event charging separately? It was the kind of practicality Joan was not comfortable with. She hated fences, yet paying for each event seemed fiddly.

More fun was the discussion about the events themselves, particularly Bruce Lacey's. He wanted to build a body so huge, people could walk around inside it, a humanoid, not a standing figure but laid out across the ground like Gulliver.

When the others had put forward their ideas, which included an audiovisual tower and a soft wall – more of that later – Peter Cook, not the comedian, but a member of Archigram, a group of architects whose ideas, nutty then but influential today, put forward his proposal. He thought that it was important to have an area where people could smash things up. Joan, with the destruction of No 48 fresh in her mind, agreed. Actually, this idea had occurred to her long before.

Woburn, to her relief, didn't happen. Something better did which got rid of fences, tickets and the dodgy image. The Reverend Eric Saywell of All Hallows, Tower Square sent her an invitation. His church, hard by the Tower of London formed one side of the square, he explained, while office blocks formed the others. The space in the middle, he thought, was deadly dull so, as the City of London Festival was to take place that summer, he wondered if Joan would like to come there with some kind of entertainment. And that is where the fair was to go.

Should Joan not have been directing plays, though? That's what plenty of people were thinking, but she was too busy reacting to the moment. The Fun Palace, the playground and the fair, forms of education and ways to explore, really, were badly needed sparks. On 16 May, vindication came when a side of an East End tower block collapsed, killing four people. For Joan, tower blocks had long been a symbol of soulless living. Ronan Point, as this one was called, would eventually bring her back to the theatre.

A few days later, though, another disturbance, benevolent this time, stimulated her curiosity. The students at Hornsea School of Art, fed up with its teachers using them as serfs for their own projects, voted for a sit-in. They didn't stop work. They did what they wanted to do and, to watch them, came all the world and his wife, among them Joan. There, in the garden, she was able to see what Keith Albarn had previously talked about, a series of brightly coloured, interconnected inflatable tubes in which you could walk, a gently disorientating experience that made you laugh. It would go to the fair in Tower Square.

Hornsea's work-in began on 28 May and lasted over a month. It therefore ran parallel to the events in Paris that had started 25 days earlier. As the Hornsea students, inside their place of learning, used their energy to create, so the Parisian students, locked out of the Sorbonne, used theirs to throw cobblestones, another example of the need to demolish.

The tribunal for Ronan Point to be held at Newham Town Hall, came up. Joan went.

The hall itself was the kind of hall where you take exams. However, nobody was on trial this time. It was an inquiry but, as the days went by, it felt like a trial.

Gradually those present learned that a Mrs Ivy Hodge on the eighteenth floor had risen one morning, put the kettle on, lit the gas, heard a bang and was knocked out. As a consequence of the bang, the whole side of the tower block where the living rooms were situated, collapsed. It was lucky that most of the residents were still asleep at the time. If the explosion had occurred a little later, they would have been in those living rooms and many more would have died.

Before the inquiry got to this moment, witnesses, who had been out in the street at the time of the explosion, gave evidence. Was it a boom they had heard or a bang and, if it was both, was there a five- or a ten-second gap? The cloud of dust they saw, was it brown or grey? And was it dust or was it smoke? This went on for quite some time but, at the end, no one was any the wiser.

The residents, when questioned, revealed how unpopular the building was. They told of the mysterious bad smells that lingered and of the unexplained heat that caused draughts to slam doors. For them, it was like bad magic. For the barristers, it was a way of making working-class people look too stupid to live in a decent new building. 'You mean to say, you slept with nothing on and the window shut?' queried one of these barristers, sounding like Edith Evans and her handbag.

There was one barrister of whom Joan was particularly mistrustful. He started with banal simplicity and curved round to where he wanted to be, or rather where he wanted the witness to be: trapped.

This hearing was Joan's theatre, better than anything she saw on a stage, well, someone else's stage. She didn't pull her hat down over her eyes. She didn't fall asleep and she didn't tear through the paper as she made notes.

Simply by looking and listening, she picked up what she needed to know and, by being there she also picked up the telltale details, the tones of voice, the comedy, the incompetence and the danger.

One day, Mr Hopkins, a barrister, speaking in honeyed but poisonous tones for the gas board, was gently pressing Mr Pike to, frankly, admit that he had fitted Mrs Hodge's stove badly. Life is so much easier if you can pin the blame on one person. The atmosphere was already tense when a trolley was wheeled in, on it the gas pipe in question. Hopkins asked Mr Pike to pick it up. Cobra quick, Justice Griffiths, leant forward. 'Listen to me,' he said, 'Don't touch that pipe!' It had not been inspected for fingerprints.

Actually, all this clever questioning turned out to be irrelevant. What was absolutely relevant was the system by which Ronan Point had been built. Larsen-Nielsen, it was called, prefabricated parts brought to the site, intended for buildings nine storeys high, not 23. Added to that, the work had been slipshod. Some of the concrete was crumbly. Mrs Hodge caused a gas explosion, so what? The kitchen walls should have withstood it. The outward pressure was not that great.

Some weeks later, by roundabout means, Joan got the transcript from the Stationer's Office. Roundabout because she didn't want the Stationer's Office to know the identity of the real recipient.

On looking through it, she noticed that she could no longer hear the superior tone of the barristers or sense their tricks. 'I'm sorry, the sound system doesn't seem to be working very well. Could you repeat that?' This was one of them. Rarely did the witness repeat what they said, not exactly. They were too cowed.

In the transcript, proceedings were smooth. In the hall, they were not. The microphone system really did fail. Witnesses went missing. Those who did appear were sometimes handed the wrong photo or the wrong statement. They still carried on talking, though, until the mistake was discovered.

That barrister Joan thought could not be trusted, arguably, was only doing his job. However, when you realise that his and Hopkins' job was to get the builders, Taylor Woodrow Anglian, and the Borough of Newham off the hook when that's exactly where they belonged, it doesn't seem so admirable.

What happened after the inquiry? Ronan Point and the eight other tower blocks built by the same method were strengthened with glue. Epoxy resin, it was called. Comic as that sounds, it was stronger than the buildings it was there to reinforce. Eighteen years later, all nine tower blocks were demolished. Whatever you did to them, you could not make them popular.

Joan wanted to do a Ronan Point show right away. She even had her eye on a possible performance area, St Paul's Cathedral. Stations of the Cross was her plan, years before promenade theatre. Then she discovered that, even using the transcripts, she could be accused of libel. There was nothing for it but to bide her time.

Immediately it was time to get the Mobile Fair going in Tower Square, except that it was no longer called Mobile Fair but Bubble City.

Bruce Lacey didn't have enough money for a whole body. He had to settle for a head and a stomach. Nevertheless, his was still the main attraction. You climbed up steps to the mouth, clambered over a lusciously upholstered lip and slid, via the tongue, into the stomach. There you found giant tomatoes, carrots and some of the organs you would find in a stomach, nothing revolting, though, just brightly coloured soft toys. When you had had enough, you walked through a fibreglass maze of inner tubing and out the other end.

In fact, apart from the audiovisual tower, soft and squashy was the theme that ran through most of the events, including Keith Albarn's tubes. The soft wall was a row of big, jelly female nudes which you could bounce against as hard as you liked. Who did the bouncing? City gents in their bowler hats, just what Joan wanted.

Good fun as Bubble City was, it did not revert to Mobile Fair and take to the road. Maybe it was the thought of trying to tour something no one had heard of or, maybe, having achieved something, the team felt less strongly about doing it again. The Festival's existing structure plus its time limit, two weeks, had been the perfect spur.

That autumn you could find Joan busy preparing her Indian film. It really looked like it was going to happen. This was a timely satire on shenanigans in India: politicians and businessmen, both American and Russian, moving in to see what they could grab. The story was told in a picaresque way contrasting the old and the new, Smollett with a flavouring of James Bond. Its hero was a Scapino type called Lall. In those days, a Western actor was needed to help raise the finance. Joan mentioned Cliff Richard because he had an Asian antecedent, and Warren Beatty. In fact, for a month, Warren Beatty, a fan of *Oh What a Lovely War*, was often on the phone. Even so, this batting about of famous names sounded odd because Joan didn't know much about any of them. Actors had, for so long, come to her, not vice versa.

She got to India, Gerry too, and met up with their grand and comic producer, Santi Chaudhury. However, once the film was made, no one saw it, certainly not a paying audience. It ended up in a garage, rotting. What's left of it turned up quite recently. There was no luscious French photography as Santi had dreamed of and no big star. It was shot in 16 mm and Lall was played by Max Shaw. What acting could achieve he did, but film is unkind. Lall should have been in his twenties. Elegant and handsome Max was in his 40s and it showed.

As for the film itself, it has a distant charm, like the Lumière brothers' first snatch of film, shot in 1895, the one where you watch passengers getting off a train.

CHAPTER THIRTY

BARRAULT? THE THÉÂTRE NATIONAL POPULAIRE? + POWER CUTS

O n their return from India, Joan and Gerry went, in the autumn of 1969, to see the *Rabelais* show at the Old Vic Theatre which, on this occasion, was acting as host. The Compagnie Renaud-Barrault had brought the show over from Paris.

It was quite an event because, the year before, during the student uprising, students had occupied and desecrated Jean-Louis Barrault's theatre in Paris, the Odéon. Despite Barrault talking to them, saying that he was on their side, he still had his company's costumes pissed on and had to leave. The Compagnie Renaud-Barrault was state subsidised and so represented the Establishment; that was the trouble. It was bad luck that the Odéon was situated on the Left Bank.

Regardless of politics, though, the Odéon productions had grown tired. What had been bubbly ten years earlier was, by then, flat. So when Barrault opened up for business again in a boxing ring to the north of Paris with a lively adaptation of Rabelais's works, it really was the phoenix rising from the ashes.

The Old Vic was obviously not a boxing ring but a special performing area had been constructed that projected into the stalls. Barrault with his slight frame and cawing voice, paced around in brown velvet trousers and soft shoes as the Orator of the Company and when he wasn't doing that, turned into a horse, a piece of mime he'd doubtless been delighting Paris with for decades but which, for London, was new. After all, what actor knight would you find turning himself into a horse?

After the performance, Gerry drove Joan in his Buick, now sprayed red, much to the disgust of Joan who compared it to a London bus, over the river to Jack's Club in Panton Street, a small, dark room where you hardly saw anyone and ate steak and baked potato because there wasn't anything else. It was very exclusive.

The evening that Joan and Gerry had experienced, France amusing in a way that England wasn't, excited them and soon it looked as if Joan was going to direct an English version in London.

But then, another French team, The Théâtre National Populaire of Paris invited her to direct a show at their theatre. They wanted her to do *Entre Chien et Loup* by Isaac Babel, a brilliant short story writer and a slightly less brilliant playwright. He wrote about Jews in Odessa circa 1913, naughtier Jews than the ones in the Sholem Aleichem stories, so more intriguing.

During the spring of 1970, Joan flew to Paris. After the meeting with Georges Wilson, the artistic director of the TNP, she joined up with one of her students from Hammamet, Alain Guémard. He took Joan to a little restaurant in the rue des Canettes the other side of the Boulevard Saint-Germain. As she walked, Joan was unwilling to discuss her talk with Georges Wilson but eventually said that the place had depressed her and the fact that she wasn't offered even a sandwich at one o'clock had put her right off the whole thing. 'A theatre where they rehearse till midnight and don't eat, only drink whisky and Coca-Cola, I couldn't stand that.'

Toward the end of dinner, a large number of noisy fire engines were heard going by but not noticed. For that reason, when the two left the restaurant, the sight of students running down the street by the hundred gave them a shock. They peered round the corner into the Boulevard Saint-Germain. The riots were back on. Thuggish policemen with visors, shields and long truncheons, the CRS (Compagnie Républicaine de Sécurité) were marching down the road as students and bystanders ran before them. The students, when they were at a safe distance, stopped and chanted: 'Libérez Le Dantec!'

Joan and Alain found themselves watching and, occasionally, running on, out of the way of the police. As they pressed themselves into a doorway, Alain told Joan what it was about. Two editors of a Maoist magazine, *La Cause du Peuple*, had been arrested and were on trial, he said. The magazine incited students to violence, advising them to use the same methods as the police.

Shots rang out.

'What's that?' asked Joan.

'Gaz lacrymogène.'

Tear gas. Gradually it drifted their way and their eyes started to sting. 'In the May 1968 riots, they used nerve gas,' said Alain, 'I was sick for a month, couldn't keep anything down.' Little pebbles started to fly. It was difficult to tell who was throwing them, the students or the police. Joan cursed and tut-tutted:

> France, the country of reason. It's worse than anywhere else. Do you see, there are no TV cameras. The police can do what they like. I was here in the 30s during the riots against the Cagoulards, on these streets too, but it was nothing like this. Fuck it. Shit.

By making a detour, they were eventually able to cross the Boulevard Saint-Germain and return to the Louisiane hotel, haunt of famous low-lifers, where Joan was staying. The Cagoulards, Joan remembered, tried to introduce a Nazi system when Hitler came to power.

The next morning, she recounted to a friend what had happened afterwards. 'It went on till dawn,' she said:

> Alain stayed with me most of the time, telling me his life story. I couldn't get to sleep. It was going on all around us. They even thought the police were going to come into our hotel. I saw them get hold of a group of people and cudgel them in a corner. I suppose it's all a game. There was a girl who came in downstairs to hide. Her friend had been hurt and she was making a terrible noise. She was thoroughly enjoying herself. I think that gas kept filtering through because my eyes were stinging all night. I had to give some cotton wool to Alain for his eyes. Well, it was more exciting than a cowboy film.

Wasting nothing, Joan wrote this up and, the following Sunday, it appeared in the *Observer*.

On returning to London, Joan came to the conclusion that she would have difficulty finding enough heavyweight Jewish actors and so, what with one thing and another, that was the end of *Entre Chien et Loup*.

Back on the cards was the London version of Jean Louis-Barrault's *Rabelais* show. However, things with Joan were never straightforward. Despite that depressing visit to Paris, she decided she wanted to do a play called *Murderous Angels* by Conor Cruise O'Brien and that the TNP, despite everything, would be the place to do it.

In this play, O'Brien, Chief of Operations of the UN in Katanga in 1961, says that Dag Hammarskjöld, Secretary-General of the United Nations, with whom he worked closely, was responsible for the assassination in 1961 of Patrice Lumumba, prime minister of the Congo. Not only that, the death of Hammarskjöld himself, was planned. In its form, at that time, it was impossible. The speeches were so long they made Shaw seem like Pinter and there were no characters, just information. It would have lasted five hours too. Still, it was good material for Joan to jump into and, from it, make a show.

In the summer of 1970, Joan went to Avignon to inspect the TNP actors. They were performing in the Palais des Papes, something they did every year. All of them were dreadful, she said, as were the plays, among them Sartre's *Le Diable et Le Bon Dieu*. That one again. The design was dreadful too. There was one actor she did like. That was the elderly Marcel D'Orval. Also there was Maria Casarès but everybody said she was impossible. It was Casarès who played Barrault's wife in the film, *Les Enfants du Paradis*, and in 1958, on the stage of the TNP under Jean Vilar's direction, was the fieriest, most terrifying Phèdre anyone could remember. Still, that didn't really matter because it looked as if Joan would, after all, not go to the TNP.

What about Gerry during all these comings and goings? Every now and again, since *Oh What a Lovely War*, he would find enough money for a season at Stratford East. How that money accrued, he never explained, but there it would be and there it was in 1970.

True to form, he wanted to put on something contemporary and relevant. An ex-secretary, Jane McKerron, mentioned a writer, Ken Hill. She thought he could come up with a comedy about local government, and indeed Ken did. This tall, redheaded Brummie had made a comfortable living writing for TV soaps but was bursting to get out. His show was *Forward, Up Your End*, overlong and packed with gags, too many thought Joan, who was less sympathetic to Ken's writing than Gerry. Even so, it became clear that she was going to direct it. And where did the *Rabelais* fit in to all this? That, after all, had not gone away.

Forward, Up Your End: light, quick and visually inventive – not despite, but because of Joan's lack of interest – opened to the public. *The Sunday Times* critic, Harold Hobson, compared Joan to Charlie Chaplin, which was perceptive, but the other critics thought little of the show. The froth was not up on that evening.

During its short run, Alain Guémard came over. He was in a woeful state. Joan had turned down the *Rabelais* show which was to be presented at the Roundhouse and, on which, he had hoped to work. To really confirm it, he said that her name was up on TNP posters all over Paris as director of *Murderous Angels*, which was to open in the spring of the next year, 1971.

The producer of the *Rabelais* show was – no surprise – Oscar Lewenstein. Joan's excuse for not doing it – she had to come up with something – was the translation by Robert Baldick: she didn't like it. In a letter to her, Oscar made it clear that he thought she had let him down, and not for the first time. Back in 1955, there had been the fiasco of *Mother Courage*, which he had also produced. Oscar must have thought that he was a glutton for punishment but, in his letter, he added that geniuses could get away with that sort of behaviour.

The spring of 1971 was still a few months off and there was another show at Stratford East to do. By this time, Joan had worked out how to get round the Ronan Point libel problem. Her idea was a long-lost eighteenth-century comic opera called *The Projector*, rather like *The Beggars' Opera*.

In it, the projector, a jerry-builder, takes people's money to put up a building that falls down. The gas explosion at Ronan Point was replaced by a fart. Rufus Chetwood was the author, or so the programme said. In fact, it was John Wells who co-wrote *Mrs Wilson's Diary*. His friend, Carl Davis, composed the music and Carl wrote some of the best songs he has ever written and played them in a wig on a twangly piano in the pit. It was a happy coming together of Joan's love for seeking out a period's style and of Gerry's demand for the relevant.

A subplot contained a flamboyant homosexual, Lord Aimwell, who hides when, in a sad but pretty scene, a cartload of sodomites are dragged, in both senses of the word, 'drag', away to be hanged. Soon he is fancying a strapping young lad, Hawthorne, fancied by various women as well. Their mutual lust comes to a climax when, at the end of Act One, on a moonlit night, Aimwell and the women drape themselves round the young man angelically singing 'My Hand, Thy Heart', except it's not his heart on which they place their hands, but his cock.

At the back of her mind, in this doodle so typical of Joan, was her old friend, Tom Driberg. He came but didn't get the point. Tom's approach to young men did not involve songs.

During its run, the show was hit by power cuts, so it was lucky that Joan had agreed to direct some commercials for the production company, Signal Films. As it was a friendly company that knew Joan well, it provided some lights and a generator to keep the show going.

There was talk of it transferring to the West End but on condition that Victor Spinetti play Lord Aimwell. This was grossly unfair to Griffith Davies who had been playing the part. Each night, he had kept Joan in stitches as he'd pranced on to the stage as a milkmaid flinging daffodils in all directions. The daffodils were made of plastic and it was their unromantic clatter to the stage which made Joan's night.

Next, Mrs Sylva Stuart Watson, mistress of the Haymarket Theatre's bricks and mortar, came down. After the performance, she talked to Gerry in the foyer. 'It's not really Glyndebourne, is it? One expects to hear singers with voices like Raimund Herincx,' Raimund Herincx being a bass baritone at Sadler's Wells. Her patronising ignorance was breathtaking. The point of the show had gone straight over her head. Gerry listened politely and, in that moment, you could catch a glimpse of what Joan had had to cope with as a student at RADA and what Gerry had been obliged to put up with when trying to sell Theatre Workshop in its early days. Still, it explained why the Haymarket, London's most beautiful playhouse, which Gerry wanted to own, kept putting on the most stuffy of revivals, thereby keeping real theatre lovers away.

A few days before Christmas 1970, Joan, using actors from *The Projector*, directed the commercials. They were for Lyons Maid ice cream and, on Shepperton studio's freezing back lot, had to appear summery. 'Props! More plastic daffodils.'

At lunch in the canteen, where Ken Tynan was sitting with a team from *Playboy* magazine, all of them wearing paper hats out of Christmas crackers, Edna O'Brien came shuffling towards Joan, literally on her knees. 'This'll be a bad play in the post,' said Joan. Nevertheless, it reminded her of the translation of *Murderous Angels* into French. A Monsieur Jean Paris had been assigned the task by the TNP but she was not happy about it.

A couple of weeks later, she and John Wells sat in her freezing private room at the top of the Theatre Royal and combed through every word of the prologue. John was going to Paris too but as an actor, not as a translator. He may have been an established translator *into* English. Translating *out* of English was another matter, as he was to find out.

Joan had done an adaptation which had been approved by Conor Cruise O'Brien but M. Paris had restored passages of the old version which Joan had been at pains to remove. Also, apart from some mistranslations, he seemed to be showing a bias, spelling Blacks with a small b and Whites with a capital w. John decided that it would be better to criticise Paris for his bias rather than his French and so drafted a cool letter full of subjunctives which was sent to the administration of the TNP. So much for Jean Paris, but now there was no translation and the start of rehearsals was a few weeks off.

Luckily, Joan remembered that the TNP had given her a straight translation of Conor's original play. Perhaps the man who did that could translate her adaptation. She looked it out and read it. Yes, it was plain but it was accurate. The French could be improved later. This did not stop Joan adapting her adaptation.

She went to Paris for casting. The TNP had no proper company, she said, and the actors they offered were all much older than they pretended to be. Their hair was badly tinted and they wore corsets.

Auditioning at the theatre was no good. It frightened people off. So Joan alternated between improvisations in a ballet studio and seeing actors individually in a Quartier Latin bar called the Chaye de L'Abbaye. The ballet studio was a scream because often she found lots of little dancing girls who were obliged to join in the improvisations so as not to be spectators.

A well-known actor, Pierre Vaneck, turned up. Joan mistook him for a dancer. No, he couldn't play Hammarskjöld, he said, because Hammarskjöld was 56 and he, Pierre Vaneck, played 35 at the oldest. This despite him being in his 40s.

Baschia Touré, Paris's most distinguished black actor, got thrown out because he cut off a young girl in the middle of her improvisation and started to direct her.

One young black actress said she wanted a good part:

'Good for who?' asked Joan, 'You or the public?'

'Me,' said the girl.

'What have you been in?'

'*The Blacks* by Genet.'

'Didn't you feel cheapened by appearing in that racist play?' asked Joan.

Back in London, mention of Royal Shakespeare Company actors grumbling because vast amounts were spent on the set and not on them made Joan put an end to the original idea of the TNP set and think of a new one.

At first, there were going to be floating discs, a ramp and a big screen at the back, which would be enveloped in a shiny green jungle. However, Joan didn't like the idea of a row of ladies sewing a jungle in an ill-lit room the other side of Paris, so she asked for the money to be given to the actors and then asked her designers, Guy Hodgkinson and Mark Pritchard, to come up with a new set. This was merely four screens and a two-tone grey, shiny floor with arches and cubes as props.

More casting news came through. Jean-Pierre Aumont, ex-Hollywood French actor, was going to play Hammarskjöld and Wole Soyinka would definitely be playing Lumumba, though he would be flying over from Nigeria a month late. Bernard Farrell, a second unit film director, son of Françoise Rosay, and on-off boyfriend of Nidal Achkar, the Hammamet student who was not allowed to work with Joan in London, seemed to be doing the casting, as the TNP didn't have much to offer.

Not long before rehearsals began, arose the problem of the rehearsal room. Joan detested the TNP one because it was underground and the air was bad. She wanted somewhere large, light and airy, with coffee and tea readily available. Gérard Lorin, actor and assistant director, the perfect Dickens clerk – pinched face, bald on top and hair sticking out all round – had been working on this but with no luck. Space was hard to come by in Paris, even harder than in London. A compromise was reached. Joan and the company would rehearse in the theatre foyer which, at least, had a view of the Eiffel Tower.

On one of Joan's earlier visits, Gérard Lorin took Joan down to the stage. The lift was an enormous, filthy tin box, fit not even for cattle. It had no inside doors. A wall slid upwards before you. As they went down, Gérard explained to Joan that the stage was so far underground the technicians were paid a special miner's wage and, not only that, the air was so bad that they had to have an extra week's holiday to recover from it. The stage itself was enormous. Gérard then told Joan that the seating was not much cop because the angles were wrong for good sightlines. She didn't back out.

CHAPTER THIRTY-ONE

MURDEROUS ANGELS
Part One

On a wet February morning, in the fascist-huge and echoing foyer of the TNP, Joan asked for carpets to be brought and chairs to be arranged in a circle, a magic circle of intimacy and comfort. Tea and coffee were mentioned but not brought.

Conor's play asked for only a handful of black characters to speak. Most of the dialogue was given to characters who were white. In Joan and Gerry's youth, communist thinking asked for plays to be about the people, not just kings and queens. It's fine if you're doing *Fuenteovejuna* or *Henry IV*. The author has done your work for you but sometimes he or she has not, hence productions of *Macbeth* in which silent peasants, not listed among Shakespeare's dramatis personae, stare accusingly at audiences. It also accounts for Stephen Daldry's 1992 production of *An Inspector Calls* where something similar happened.

With that directive at the back of her mind, Joan saw in Conor's play a Congo that was under-represented. She had therefore cast several black actors not requested by him. They came from French-speaking African countries like Mali, Dogon, Cameroun, Senegal and the Ivory Coast. One was from Martinique in the West Indies. None were born in France.

As rehearsals proceeded, they would take part in devised interludes and, so, right the balance. Having decided this, Joan was aware that the black actors, as with her Arab students in Hammamet, were likely, faced with their colonisers, to suffer a sense of inferiority. Colonisers, in this case, were not the white actors themselves but the experience white actors had gained through regular employment, even if that experience only meant the staginess of the Comédie-Française. Her solution was apartheid (her word). There would be two companies, a black one and a white one and the two would rehearse separately, only coming together a month into the nine-week rehearsal period. That first morning was to be devoted to the black company.

Once everyone had sat down, Joan said something that she never said back home. 'I come from the working class.' In the UK, when she heard the words: 'Joan Littlewood does theatre for the working class,' she said: 'Fuck the working class.' What she believed in was a bunch of bright people, whatever their class. Here in Paris, she wanted to convey her understanding of what it was like to be squashed or overlooked. Decorating that line of thought, she gave the Comédie-Française two fingers and, indeed, the whole of Europe. 'A tired old tart,' she called it. Her strategy for building confidence had begun.

After a hurried snack – saying goodbye to the actors took half an hour – Joan settled the white company down to read, not the whole play, but bits of it. As at home, she was keeping things fluid. Various actors read in a low-key, 'I'm not acting' way. Jean-Pierre Aumont stayed out of it. In his skewbald pony coat, he sat and looked serious with his glasses on, just as he does in Truffaut's film, *Day for Night*.

Before everyone went their ways, Joan discussed general arrangements. British hours, mornings and afternoons, was how she intended to work. As she had indicated months before, she did not want French hours, which is afternoons and evenings. Marcel D'Orval whom Joan hadn't forgotten from Avignon, was shocked. 'All my life I have never worked those hours,' he said, 'but for Miss Littlewood, I will.'

Gerry was there and, at the end of the day drove Joan back to the Louisiane Hotel. As he drove, Joan commented on the bad breath of the actors. 'And they will insist on leaning right over you. It's Hogarthian. I bet there are blue flames when they fart.'

The next day, before rehearsals, Joan laid books and pictures on a table, just as she did for any show that required research. These were about the Congo. Then came the question of the word rehearsals itself. In French, it's *répétitions* but Joan hated repetition. She settled on *essais*. However, she did use the word improvisation, which she never used to in England.

With the black company, she did fascism parallels, for instance a strict schoolmaster and his class. What does one do to evade the discipline? One has to act subtly. Towards the end of the morning, Joan left parallels and got on to the play. The scene was soldiers coming into a village. How do you react? It appeared the actors had been seeing too many films. They jumped on the soldiers, got themselves shot, jumped up again and had a fearful fight in which one actor twisted his ankle and another grazed his arm, something that had never happened with The Nutters at Stratford East. Joan told them that they were all being very courageous, fighting the soldiers but, in real life, they'd have to be much cleverer if they wanted to stay alive.

In the afternoon, there was more reading with the white actors. The only scene they liked was the last one, which Joan wrote, not the author. There were cinematic dissolves in it that made it go with a whoosh.

Above: *A Taste of Honey.* Avis Bunnage, Murray Melvin, John Bay, Frances Cuka (Theatre Royal Stratford East);
Below: Brendan Behan on Sean Kenny's set for *The Hostage.*

Above: James Booth, Roy Barnett, Frank Norman, Lionel Bart, Dudley Sutton looking at script of *Fings Ain't Wot They Used T'Be*; *Below:* Joan directing *The Hostage* at the Wyndham's Theatre.

Above: Fings Ain't Wot They Used T'Be. Miriam Karlin, Paddy Joyce, Glynn Edwards, Edward Caddick (Garrick Theatre); *Below: Every Man in his Humour.* Griffith Davies, Michael Forrest, Roy Kinnear, Claire Neilson, Brian Murphy, Maurice Good, Ann Beach, Sean Lynch (Theatre Royal Stratford East).

Left: Fings Ain't Wot They Used T'Be. Edward Caddick, Toni Palmer (Garrick Theatre); *Below:* Joan rehearsing at the Theatre Royal Stratford East.

Opposite: Joan on the stage set of *Sparrers Can't Sing* (Theatre Royal Stratford East).

Above: Sparrers Can't Sing. Griffith Davies, Barbara Ferris (Theatre Royal Stratford East);
Below: Sparrers Can't Sing. Murray Melvin, Frank Coda, Sean Lynch, Bettina Dickson, Brian Murphy, Bob Grant, Barbara Ferris, Amelia Bayntun, Fanny Carby, Griffith Davies, Barbara Ferris (Theatre Royal Stratford East).

Above: Oh What a Lovely War. Myvanwy Jenn, Larry Dann, second soldier from the left, Brian Murphy, third soldier from the left. (Wyndham's Theatre); *Below:* Victor Spinetti, furthest left, George Sewell, fifth from left, Myvanwy Jenn (Wyndham's Theatre).

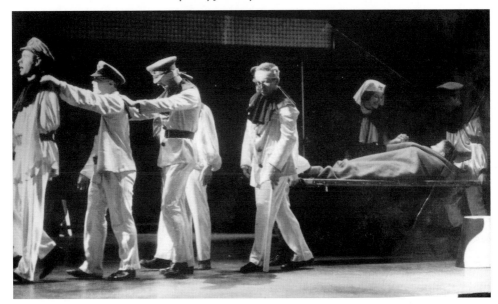

Joan Littlewood presents the FIRST GIANT SPACE MOBILE IN THE WORLD

it moves in light turns winter into summer....toy.... EVERYBODY'S what is it?

Above: Cedric Price's plan for the Fun Palace; *Below: Oh What a Lovely War.* Victor Spinetti, George Sewell, Murray Melvin, and Brian Murphy behind him (Wyndham's Theatre).

Above: Gerry in his office at the Theatre Royal Stratford East.

Above: Shy Joan, adventurous Gerry in New York for *Oh What a Lovely War*; *Left: Mrs Wilson's Diary.* Myvanwy Jenn, Sandra Caron (Theatre Royal Stratford East).

Above: Gerry, Joan, Maxwell Shaw, filming in India; *Below: The Marie Lloyd Story.* Gaye Brown, Avis Bunnage, Maxwell Shaw, Valerie Walsh (Theatre Royal Stratford East).

Above: Conor Cruise O'Brien in the rehearsal room at the Théâtre National Populaire
for his play, *Murderous Angels.*

Above: Joan rehearsing *Murderous Angels.*

Opposite: Joan in the bar of the Theatre Royal Stratford East;

Above: Ken Hill, Joan and Gerry celebrating twenty years of Theatre Workshop at the Theatre Royal Stratford East; *Below:* Lionel Bart, Joan and Peter Rankin rehearsing *The Londoners* at the Theatre Royal Stratford East.

Above: Joan and Guv.
Left: Presenting Bubble City.

In the evening, as Joan started to work out the schedule for the next day, actors crowded round to say that they wanted days off for TV, radio, visits to the doctors and appearances in court. Stratford East it wasn't. During rehearsals at the Theatre Royal, Gerry allowed no time off for anybody. Joan suggested drawing up a huge list marking all the actors' off-days, so that she could work her schedule around it. Would that Gerry had been there that evening.

He returned at the weekend and did what Joan loved. He took her for a drive. They ended up at a restaurant near Versailles, where he said that she had made the right decision in turning down *The Rabelais Show* because, great though Rabelais was, he was not relevant to England. Gerry was that strict.

Later in London, Oscar Lewenstein announced that the English version would be directed by Jean-Louis Barrault. It went ahead but the poor acoustics of the Roundhouse blew the chic away. Years earlier Arnold Wesker, when he had been running the Roundhouse as Centre 42, had tried to get Joan to take an interest but she had said that it would always be a place for turning round engines and that it would never lose the smell of soot.

After the weekend, Gerry returned to England, anxious that Joan might go unfed at lunchtime. He had a point. There was no canteen at the theatre and getting out to the cafés of the Place du Trocadéro, where the TNP was, took ages. If she was lucky, someone would feed her an orange, pig by pig, as she never left the building while she was working.

During the first weeks of rehearsals, casting continued. Originally Joan had wanted an international cast with the Swedish actor, Per Oscarsson, as Hammarskjöld and British actors for three important roles, Bonham, Tamworth and Sir Henry Large White. Added to that, for smaller parts, she wanted Israelis, Arabs and Australians but that was too expensive. She was allowed John Wells for Tamworth, Henry Livings, playwright and French speaker, for Bonham and Willie Rushton for Sir Henry Large White. She got John Wells.

In the event, Sir Henry was played by a big, jovial actor called Jacques David. Jacques came from Roger Planchon of whom he said: 'With Planchon, one can breathe.'

One day, while Joan was explaining how she worked, a burly actor called Hervé Sand took up her theme and embroidered upon it. He looked as if he were going to be a discovery. And to him went the part of Bonham.

It's simplest to say, as far as the play went, that all the white characters were up to no good, except for Hammarskjöld, and even he was ruthless, while many of the black characters, in particular the leaders, were up to no good either, except for Lumumba. The question that always hovered was who was in whose pocket.

During the first week, things went so slowly that Joan cancelled the Saturday walk-through she had planned, convinced she was a week behind schedule.

After a few days of the actors echoing in the Grand Foyer, the administrator, Jean Ruaud – pinstripe suit, nattily coiffed hair, drawn-down face – suggested a move to the foyer of the studio theatre, the Salle Gémier. It was a more manageable space and still had a view of the Eiffel Tower but, even there, the acoustics were bad and not helped by the French actors who did not take easily to listening or shutting up.

Segregation carried on and, in the mornings, Jean Loulendo an actor/student who, some wished had stayed a student, gave history lessons about the Congo. To be fair, those were useful, because, out of them, came 'The History of the Congo' song, exposition made entertaining. Actor-singer-composer, Georges Anderson, took it upon himself to write the music and Dane Bellany, all furs and perfume, was going to sing it. Six young Congolese men called the Echos Noirs formed the backing group. Joan thought they were too Europeanised but was convinced that their electric guitars could be tactfully taken away. The real problem with the Echos was that they either never turned up, or some did one day and others another. Added to that, they had a habit of changing their stage names from day to day, which may have been refreshing for them but made life hard for others. After a month, they settled for Titos, Porthos, Gilbert, Sharif and Fantôme.

With the move into the Salle Gémier foyer, Joan started simultaneous rehearsals. The white actors stayed in the foyer, while the black actors, with nowhere else to go, went to the rehearsal room that Joan disliked so much, but only for an hour at a time.

She started to do improvisations with the white actors, beginning with the last scene where all hell was let loose. After Lumumba's death, the Congo was in chaos. Hervé Sand revealed himself as an inventive improviser as did an actor, who had enjoyed working with the British director, John Blatchley of the RSC, the tall, Jean Mondain. American accents were his thing. Jean-Pierre Aumont stayed out of it.

With Marcel D'Orval and Paul Bonifas, another elderly actor, whom you can see as a stamp collector at the end of the film, *Charade*, Joan did not force it. They stood there clinging to their scripts and, with actors improvising around them, dropped lines in from the script where they thought it was appropriate.

In the early stages of rehearsals, it was difficult to do the Lumumba scenes because Wole Soyinka was not there. Even so, Joan started working with an actor who was in those scenes, the fat, Belgian, Fernand Ghiot. He had a great wide, white face, the biggest in the business and was bone from ear to ear. He too loved doing accents, so Joan cast him as a Russian ambassador.

At an improvisation of a cocktail party, an actor hastily picked up a wide-brimmed straw hat and pretended it was a tray. Every actor understood and mimed taking a drink. Not Fernand Ghiot. He looked puzzled. He looked irritated and finally said: 'You want me to put it on?' Or rather he mimed it because it was a silent scene. In his favour, he played Lumumba's secretary and mistress beautifully with a rose behind his ear.

Philippe Léotard, with a face like a beat-up angel, read in Lumumba. Philippe came from Ariane Mnouchkine, famous at the time for her French revolution show, *1789*. Before that, she had done Wesker's *The Kitchen* which Philippe had

216

translated into French. Actually, he was still playing in *1789* because the actor who should have been in it was always drunk. Again, if you want to know what Philippe looks like, he's the young policeman who, mistakenly, lets the heavily made up Jackal (Edward Fox), through a barrier in the film, *The Day of the Jackal*. If you're a fan of French films, you will know that Philippe became a film star but died at no great age.

After the weekend, Joan and Gerry were walking down the many flights of stairs to the foyer and the Salle Gémier when they were approached by the actor, Roland Bertin. 'I'm exhausted. I can't do it. I'm rehearsing with you. I'm doing a play in the evening. I'm doing another play at midnight. It's too much. I'm leaving.' Gerry was annoyed. Why did Roland have to inflict all this on Joan? Why didn't he just tell Ruaud and piss off. Joan was not to have these emotional upheavals on Monday morning. Roland Bertin is today a sociétaire honoraire of the Comédie-Française.

Joan too was fed up with having snap conferences on the staircases of the TNP. She suddenly found that big decisions were being made as a result of a chance encounter with Ruaud on the staircase. She wanted a proper meeting with all assistants to discuss props and costumes.

And so, six o'clock meetings were instigated at which props that had come up through the day were listed. At the first one, Joan discussed what was going to happen in the foyer. In her original prologue, she had asked for the TNP and the vestibule to be done up like a UN building with guards, flags and an exhibition. The seats of the theatre were to be divided up among delegates. Everybody would be given questionnaires. Half the questions would be serious, the other half, frivolous. All this was scrapped. Joan asked for coloured lights in the foyer and a tape of Conor Cruise O'Brien giving a lecture on the Congo. That didn't happen either. In fact, nothing did. The biggest luxury Joan could have was lighting up flags in the auditorium. What a comedown when she had wanted to change the whole environment.

If your leader is no good then nobody else is any good, right down to the doorman. This held pretty well for the TNP. Even towards the end of the reign of its previous boss, Jean Vilar, the place was on the downhill slope. He was tired. It was so big and unmanageable that you needed a man with fire in his guts to keep it going. Georges Wilson was not that man. Once upon a time, he'd been a good company member but then, as the director of the TNP, nothing. Few saw him. Everyone despised him, including his own secretary, who, when Joan asked where he was, shrugged her shoulders.

Guy Hodgkinson, the set designer, reported a conversation he had with an alcohol-breathing assistant called Alain Wendling.

'The holes in these bobbins are round and the spigots are square,' said Guy.

'Ah,' said Alain.

'Do you think you could get these bobbins changed? Who has them?'

'Monsieur Savaron. I'll ring him . . . Hallo, could I have Monsieur Savaron's office . . . He's not there? Could you put me back to the switchboard? . . . Hallo, could you give me Monsieur Savaron's home number? . . . You don't have it? Could you put me through to Madame Fraenkel? She'll have it . . . Madame Fraenkel isn't there? Could you put me through to someone else in administration? . . . There's nobody in administration . . .'

'Who else has his key?' asked Guy.

'Could you put me through to the doorkeeper? . . . Hallo. Do you have a key to Monsieur Savaron's office? . . . No? . . . Monsieur Savaron keeps them all himself.'

'But what would happen if the theatre were on fire?'

'That's what we're all hoping for.'

On hearing about this, Joan said: 'Peter Brook is cannier than I am. The TNP asked him to come here too but he didn't. He must have known.'

Gerry, who had kindly said that rehearsals were going fine, told Joan not to fight the system but play it the TNP way. What a way, though.

Next to the TNP was the Musée de L'Homme. Joan thought a lecture about the Congo woud be a good idea and so a sweet, timid soul who worked there, Madame Ndaye, offered to show a film and give a talk. Her name is misleading, by the way. She was white but married to an African.

A couple of afternoons later, the actors rolled up. Joan stayed back at the theatre. The film was a rather boring, paternalistic affair made by a Belgian information department. Strictly speaking, not many of the cast needed to see it but a broad view of things is not such a bad idea. Marcel D'Orval didn't see it that way. A row broke out. The actors used the film as a cover to insult each other about personal things that had been bothering them in rehearsals. Hervé Sand implied that there were anti-Joan people in the company, at which point, Marcel D'Orval walked out saying that he would next see Miss Littlewood at rehearsals.

Fernand Ghiot bridled at Hervé's remark but then it was intended for him, as, a few days earlier, he had tried to get Hervé's part by telling Joan that he would never get out of his contract with Marie Bell, she being a famous classical actress who had become a powerful boulevard theatre manager. This had been carefully relayed back to Hervé by Alain Wendling, who had been asked not to repeat it. Madame Ndaye never got to give her lecture.

In the play, Hammarskjöld has a black secretary, Diallo. Joan cast an actor called Gérard Essomba. He had authority. However, when he was taken away from the black company, he felt stranded and went downhill. At first, Gerry was convinced that Joan would get a performance out of him but Gérard became more and more tense, acting badly and unable to do what Joan asked for. Admittedly he wasn't helped a scrap by Jean-Pierre Aumont, who merely put on a pained, weary expression whenever he had to rehearse with him. Jean-Pierre, himself, gave cool, elegant readings in a low voice but nothing else.

He didn't take any interest in what Joan was doing with the other actors either. After a month she brought the two companies together and, during the rehearsal of movement scenes involving the black actors, he never looked up. Instead, he perched his spectacles on the end of his nose, put his nose in his script and ignored all else. As it turned out, he was ignoring the script too because whenever his cue came up, he missed it.

Essomba's disease spread to the rest of the black actors. In the presence of the white company, they became, what Joan had feared, rigid.

On that first day of bringing the two groups of actors together, she rehearsed an airport scene in which Hammarskjöld was mobbed by journalists, false tribal chiefs and finally, the president of Katanga, Moïse Tchombé. It was an improvisation, so no worries about holding scripts, and yet Georges Anderson, playing Moïse turned into a marionette. He was imitating bad French habits, Comédie-Française, as Joan called them, rather like she'd say Old Vic when she was in England. She ticked him off and the others too, saying, once again, that Europe was finished and that they were not to copy tired old white acting habits. This was deliberately said in front of the white actors. It had no effect. When you wanted to needle them, you couldn't.

From the start, the cast had not been pleased with the translation. It was accurate but flat. They wanted a *beau texte*, whatever that meant. Joan simply wanted to do her improvisations and change the script daily. That's why she had brought John Wells. Philippe Léotard could translate what John wrote and together they would make a team.

Jean-Paul Sartre had been offered to Joan. She mentioned this to the company. They swooned. Hervé Sand thought he was great. Joan thought he was a bore and not a dramatist. Sartre was nevertheless, the company's idea of a *beau texte*. Joan calmed the company, temporarily, though every now and again, you could hear Jean Mondain saying: 'These improvisations are all great fun but where's the text?' Hervé Sand, whose part did seem to be diminishing and making less and less sense said: 'If in a week's time, Bonham isn't properly sorted out, I'll just play a mercenary.'

Jean-Pierre Aumont wasn't happy either. He went for dinner with Joan and subtly ran down the company and the text. Joan pacified him, at least for a while, and then, the author, Conor Cruise O'Brien, arrived.

219

Part Two

Joan had asked him to come with a new version of a scene she was stuck with. He arrived in the evening and out they went for dinner. As, by then, Joan had already altered much of her adaptation, she had to explain this. Attack was the best method, she thought. 'You didn't write a Lumumba or a Hammarskjöld,' she said. Conor bridled. 'Well, why are you doing the play?' Joan was going to carry on: 'However, with our hard work, we'll make a play,' but Conor got in first. He had re-written almost the entire play.

The following morning there was a reading of this new play. When the company was assembled, Conor started chatting away in English to Jean-Pierre Aumont. Joan insisted he speak in French and do an instant translation of what he had brought with him. He did, reading with flourish and satisfaction. All he had done, however, was write a series of flowing new speeches which sounded grand without actually getting anyone anywhere. No more was known about Lumumba and Hammarskjöld than had been known before. The cast thought it was super. Conor was even more pleased with himself.

This straightforward round the table reading was appreciated by the company because it made them feel secure. So far, Joan, never keen on security, had managed to avoid this. By it, Conor had won the actors over and put Joan out on a limb, the opposite of her and Barbara Garson on *Macbird*. She had to take a line of defense.

The TNP's administration was so slow, she said, that it would be impossible to do his new version. The set would have to be re-designed. Scenes would have to re-rehearsed. The best they could do was incorporate some of his most important new speeches.

Lunchtime came. John Wells hurriedly whispered to Joan that she should make O'Brien sit down at a tape recorder and do another instant translation. That would keep him out of rehearsals for the next two days and, after that, he had to leave. The three went to lunch. Joan could hardly speak. John did all the work. He flattered Conor, called him 'Sir' and dropped names that would please. It did the trick. Conor was a name snob. All Joan could do was needle him by constantly talking of Brendan Behan, implying that he was someone O'Brien could never be. By the end of lunch, Joan had persuaded him to be flexible on the role of Lumumba, quite a triumph considering his intransigence the night before. He also consented to do the tape-recording.

At a second dinner, Joan hoped to extract from Conor some exciting piece of information about Hammarskjöld that nobody knew. After all, Conor had claimed to have been very close to him. But he just got drunk and pushed Joan's cap down on her face. The play was an obsession for him because, by his own slowness to act in the Congo men had died, so it was some kind of attempt to exonerate himself and, because of that, he couldn't reveal what Joan wanted to know about Hammarskjöld, as that would have meant revealing himself.

There was one new scene, the Congo Club, which explained or purported to explain why Hammarskjöld went to Katanga in the first place but it had a strong and unfortunate resemblance to the last scene where Hammarskjöld sacrificially steps on to the plane that will blow up. So what did that leave you with? A nut, but making a tragedy or, indeed, a conflict out of a madman is not possible. Where was the man?

Joan told Conor and the company that his new script kept her awake all night. Privately, she said that she fell asleep over it and only finished it when she woke up.

Conor, unfortunately, got through his taping rather rapidly and was bouncing into rehearsals once more. So instead of rehearsing, there was another round-table conference, this time about Lumumba.

The black company did not at all appreciate a scene in which Lumumba played around with his secretary and finally went to bed with her, while Hammarskjöld was desperately trying to telephone him to prevent a world war or his own death.

The first person to object was the actor, James Campbell, regarded by Joan as a *voyou*, a rascal, a fixer of women and drugs, but necessary for the company. Given his private life, his distaste for the Lumumba/secretary scene struck Joan as hypocritical. Then, Georges Anderson said that he had mourned Lumumba for three weeks wearing black all the time. 'What boring puritans,' thought Joan. But they wanted their hero straight and clean, so in the end, she agreed, mainly because the writing of the scene was not too great anyway.

None of this had been mentioned to Conor. So, Joan took this opportunity to put him in the hot seat by letting the company have a go at him. 'Franchement je trouve cette scène vulgare' (Frankly I find this scene vulgar), said Dane Bellany. Conor was taken aback, so much so that he instantly said that, when Wole Soyinka arrived to play Lumumba, he could change it as he saw fit. 'Oh, you know Wole?' asked Joan, but he didn't. He had just heard of him and thought he was posh.

The round-table could not go on forever. Rehearsals had to continue. Joan mentioned that Bonham had become French as he was being played by a Frenchman. Also, she didn't see why the French should go unscathed. 'No, Bonham is English,' said Conor. 'There isn't time to change him now,' throwing Joan's argument back in her face.

The scene being rehearsed took place in a private enclosure at a racecourse. In fact, it turned into the prologue of the show. Joan set up an improvisation. Conor took part, playing Bonham and he wasn't bad. The scene was merely one of introductions, getting Bonham known by everyone. It was interesting to see that the way Conor had written the scene made it impossible and he had to admit it. In fact, it was he who discovered the slip-up. One up for Joan and improvisation.

That evening there was another dinner. Conor got drunk again and, while Joan was paying the bill, made a determined physical advance, which she had to resist. Before leaving, he promised to come back next morning to talk to the company.

He didn't. Most people would have thought: 'Thank goodness.' Not Joan. She was furious: 'Here we are, back in the shit.'

Actually Conor had caused damage. He had wrecked the little confidence there was in the company. The white actors went back into their tizzy about the script and started to threaten walkouts. This was a feint: nobody walked out; they just pretended to. However, there were times when Joan wished they would.

The black actors were less affected as few of them had parts, as such. For them, Joan was inventing these interludes which were not in Conor's play but helped to open it out. 'Perhaps it'll be the first black musical,' she said. 'Conor puts Hammarskjöld and Lumumba on the stage but he forgets the most important thing, the Congolese people, who were there before the crisis, during the crisis and after it. In fact they're always there. Lumumba and Hammarskjöld just come and go.' Send for Shakespeare and the *Henrys*.

One of the interludes was 'Les Nouveaux Riches' in which the black troupe came swanking on with huge cigars, gold bowlers, gold waistcoats and gold chainmail for the girls. They were supposed to be black nouveaux riches copying whites. At last, black people poking fun at black people, it was an advance on the prim Lumumba scene.

When Jean-Pierre, who had never looked at anything up until now, saw the first 'Nouveaux Riches' improvisation, he was impressed. 'How long have you been working on this?' he asked Joan. 'It's the first time they're doing it,' she answered. Still, after that, his nose was back in his script.

To get herself shipshape after the Conor débacle, Joan cancelled rehearsals for two days. 'Altogether he's lost us a week,' she maintained, so that was another week lost after that slow one at the beginning of rehearsals, if Joan was to be believed.

During those two days, not having an office, she tucked herself away, at the furthest end of the Grand Foyer, behind a plastic screen that advertised the plays of the season. She thought this to be the safest place to continue re-writing the script. It wasn't.

A chic gorgon with green eyelids, thin red lips and Walt Disney fingernails swooped down. This was Madame Colette Aubriant, Head of Publicity. 'I have two interviews for you, the *Figaro* and the *Daily Express*.' Joan apologised and said it was impossible because she was too busy. 'The *Daily Express*?' reiterated Colette. Joan stuck two fingers up. 'Well, never mind the *Daily Express*,' said Colette. 'What about the *Figaro*?' 'Fuck the *Figaro*,' said Joan who considered it right wing. Madame Aubriant was vexed but at least she left Joan in peace. Not for ages was she seen again. During the rehearsal period, Joan gave no interviews.

Other problems, not to do with the actors, bubbled up. Guy Hodgkinson, the set designer, was having a conference with the TNP's head of design, Jacques Le Marquet. There he was, Le Marquet, in front of a blackboard with Monsieur Van Yen, who supervised all purchases and looked after the budget. Van Yen looked on as Le Marquet leapt backwards and forwards, with a piece of chalk in his hand, making stabs at the blackboard. He was finishing the budget for the set and checking through his figures. When everyone was sitting comfortably, he gave a rapid rundown. He always gave rapid rundowns. It was a way of leaving everybody else behind. In this particular case, he was aiming to make Guy Hodgkinson and Mark Pritchard look silly in the eyes of the rest of the staff.

'Your floor's going to cost you 5,400 francs,' said Le Marquet.

'That's expensive,' said Guy.

'Your arches are going to cost 142,000 francs (£1,000).'

'That's ridiculous.'

'Your lighting up flags are going to cost 67,000 francs.'

'That's impossible.'

'That's France.'

'I'll do it myself in a couple of afternoons – for nothing.'

The reason for this absurd expense was that the TNP farmed out work because their own prop-men were useless. The firms that did these jobs ran what were almost monopolies and, therefore, could charge what they liked. Everybody said Monsieur Van Yen was a toughie who brought the prices down as low as possible but Sarah Hodgkinson, Guy's wife, said that when she was out shopping and mentioned the TNP, shop girls could hardly suppress their giggles.

Le Marquet gleefully suggested cutting something big, like the lighting up flags in the auditorium, though, heaven knows, the set was stark enough. Guy suggested a nipping and tucking of each object's price but that didn't begin to put the set within budget. An executive decision was needed: Joan would have to be called.

Having suspected that Le Marquet was a racketeer who took percentages, she entered the office with a deadly smile. Le Marquet went on chattering to his blackboard. Guy explained the situation to Joan. 'I'll get Sam Spiegel to do it,' she laughed. 'He's cheaper. I'm changing nothing,' and wreathed in smiles, walked out. Le Marquet didn't look particularly perturbed. He merely said that it was time Ruaud was brought in. Ruaud happened to be holidaying in Geneva but that wasn't going to get in Le Marquet's way. He was having too much fun.

The following day, he held a post-mortem on Joan's little number. 'There are two words she used which are understandable in any language: racket and Sam Spiegel. I'm not accustomed to being treated like that. It's a question of standing.'

Ruaud, furious that Le Marquet had rung him, returned from his holiday and fixed everything in a trice. He put the budget up.

About this time, Jean-Pierre Aumont decided that 'Hammarschöltz' was 'derl,' as he pronounced both those words. This was especially annoying of him because he was right. The man had no sense of humour and appeared to have all his decisions made for him by the Americans. 'A cloud in trousers,' said Joan. John Wells was put on the job. He and Jean-Pierre went off to work in cafés. Bit by bit, the role of Hammarskjöld was strengthened, though sometimes Joan was not always in the know about what John was doing. As a result, Bonham's role became weaker until finally Hervé Sand clicked and started insisting on a good text too. As Joan didn't want to lose Hervé, morning sessions with John and Hervé were instigated, while the afternoons were reserved for John and Jean-Pierre.

Weeks before the start of rehearsals, Joan announced: 'It'll be the first time you see me direct a play. You've never seen me direct a play before.'

Usually she rehearsed using games and parallels, saving production and direction for the last few days. With this lot, the games stopped much earlier than usual. What with spending so much time on creating a text and having to cope with actors who couldn't improvise, Joan found herself moving on to a high-class rep style. Two steps to the left, lean on the cube, say the line. It was the kind of work that bored Joan into making remarks like: 'I'll never work in theatre again.' As she left the TNP in the evening, she would say: 'It's like working in a geriatric ward – one hand on the rail dear, lift your leg over the side, that's right. Now the other one.'

Leaving the TNP in the evening was very much a time for post-mortems. Either Mark Pritchard drove Joan home in the back of his van or Gerry did in his hired car when he came over at weekends. It was in these cramped quarters that Mark, Guy and Sarah would talk of their problems with costumes and props. Their chief grumble was slowness. Even the buying of a tassel had to be recorded in quadruplicate and the forms stamped by several different TNP types. When they'd finished their stories, Joan would serve them up with lurid tales about which actor walked out today and who tried to murder whom. It was a sumptuously gloomy ride. When Gerry was around, he would, by his silence, discourage revelling in this morbid talk. In the middle of a tempest of disaster, he would say: 'Come on, it's time for tea,' an interjection which whisked the British team to some kind of well-ordered, non-existent English nursery world. They were very grateful to him and looked forward to his weekend visits.

Considering all the 'Où est le beau texte?' and Gérard Lorin getting in a fluster because he lost the thread of an improvisation, you would have thought that adopting a weekly rep style would make the actors feel more at home. This was not so. Joan gave precise directions and, for the most part, they were precisely forgotten. What were they good at doing, you may well have asked.

Gérard Essomba, who was paying Diallo, was not getting any better. In these cases, Joan usually cut and cut so that the actor had the minimum to say, but, in this particular case, there was almost nothing left. Certainly any sex or love interest with Hammarskjöld, which Joan wanted to imply, had long been jettisoned. Optimistically, she put him on the morning rota for script strengthening and asked him to come in after work for private exercises. It was like being at school in the 1950s, having Radio Malt in the morning and extra maths in the evening, but Gérard did not want to come in after lessons. It put him on Joan's no-no list. Jean-Pierre, for his own reasons, didn't like him either. Nor did he make the slightest attempt to hide his scorn. In private, he said: 'I have two big scenes where I open my heart and they're both with him. He has as much right to be on stage as I have to be pope.' Joan said that opening your heart was bad theatre but she had to admit that Gérard wasn't too hot as an actor.

Jean-Pierre didn't like Hervé, who was playing Bonham, either. 'I am entirely selfish. Only Hammarschöltz's – he could never get that right – problems interest me. Once they are resolved the whole play will be resolved.' He was talking about Bonham's fast-fading role. 'Frankly the man bores me. What he says is so vulgar. I cannot understand why Hammarschöltz would employ a man like this who was against him.' By now, Jean-Pierre was confusing his own feelings with Hammarskjöld's. He just didn't like Hervé, who was a good actor. That, however, was not a bad thing. Joan's answer was that clever men always employ their opposite to get the other point of view.

When Joan was first dreaming of an international cast, she wanted to bring over, from Lebanon, Nidal Achkar, the student from Hammamet and Stratford East days. Having other commitments, Nidal could not come at once and, for a while, it looked as if she would not come at all. Suddenly she was there, part or no part.

Joan switched her on to movement. By then, Joan's own rehearsals were taking place in the theatre. Nidal's were in the rehearsal room where she did dances for a White House scene and for the 'Story of the Congo' song. They seemed to go well but every time she moved the actors from the rehearsal room to the stage, their efforts were dissipated in the vastness of the TNP. This depressed her. Gerry told her that she had to take a firm hand because it was her name out there on the posters as choreographer. He'd fixed it.

The fun part of the show was that it was multi-media: it had slides, film and closed-circuit TV. Mark and Guy were looking after the slides but Joan had to do the film as it involved the actors. A day was set and everybody got into a lovely fuss about what they were going to wear. Half the day would have to be spent at the airport for Hammarskjöld climbing on and off planes and the other half in the rehearsal room because it had the most neutral background for doing things like close-ups of leaders making speeches, the people's reactions and an important telephone call where Hammarskjöld, by saying nothing, seals Lumumba's doom.

A few days before the shoot, the Gérard Essomba problem came to a head. He had to be replaced, but by whom? Essentially, it had to be someone in the company because it was too late for newcomers and, if he was a newcomer, he'd have to be considerably superior to the rest, otherwise they wouldn't take it. Conor had said, before leaving, that he rather fancied James Campbell, the *voyou*, in the part, which had made everyone hoot with laughter. As Jean-Pierre put it: 'Hammarschöltz would razzer ferk a goat zan ferk 'im.'

A princely young actor called Manuel de Kset, who was in the company, looked the part but had a faint voice. Jean-Pierre had liked a young Algerian actor in *Tom Paine*, the previous TNP production, but Gerry had also seen that and knew he was too soft. It was only then that Jean-Pierre noticed Manuel who had been there all the time. 'He is the perfect Diallo.' Joan had to explain the voice problem all over again.

In order to relieve Gérard Essomba of the tensions of rehearsing his role, Joan used to get other people to read in and he would watch. Alain Wendling, often did it and, even in his lazy way, was better. Anybody who happened to be there was liable to be called and in this way, James Campbell found himself reading in. He was cool, relaxed, and intelligent. It was a relief from all those silly arguments and bad acting Joan had been getting from Essomba. She decided to let James read the whole of the first act at the next Saturday run-through. Somehow or other Gérard Essomba had been relieved of his part without being told he wasn't playing it. At one point, Joan was going to divide Diallo into two. Gérard could look after the secretary side, while Philippe Léotard could look after the sex side. It wasn't that you would see Philippe doing anything with Hammarskjöld but the attraction had to be there. It got very confusing, though, and the costume department was in the most trouble because suits had to be made for the filming. There was a moment when everyone was going to be in the play, including Gérard, but not in their proper roles.

On the day of the shoot, those in the bits to be filmed assembled at the theatre to get ready. No one was late. The girls looked happy in Carmen rollers. One actor came just for the ride and, as they all emerged from the theatre, the sun came out. They got on to a coach with the wardrobe ladies and off they went to Le Bourget airport. It was like a school outing.

At the airport, an official counted everybody through customs and, in a glass-covered passage, they waited until a suitable plane was available. Suddenly, a ground hostess led everyone out on to the tarmac because it was not a question of finding an old plane that never did anything. Working Caravelles that came and went had to be used. An Iberia plane had just flown in from Spain. The passengers were in the process of getting off.

The ground hostess climbed the steps and spoke to the Iberia hostess. She was not pleased. This was news to her. In the meantime, the passengers were still getting off but, by now, as they descended, they were posing for the camera and looking for stars in their midst.

There were 25 minutes to do it in. The actors were hurried on to the empty plane to change their clothes. Jean-Pierre Aumont or no Jean-Pierre Aumont, the cleaners inside were disgruntled. Outside, Joan kept saying they'd never get it. Gerry, there because it was a weekend, told the actors to get a move on.

John Wells was the pilot and those getting off were Jean-Pierre, Hervé Sand and James Campbell. As he'd only got the part the day before James was in an improvised suit, rather than a proper one. His hair was a problem: he had a 'rasta' as the French called it and, in those days, it was not *comme il faut* for the secretary of the Secretary-General of the United Nations. By every possible means, Magali, the wardrobe girl, pinned it back, so that, from the front, James looked quite respectable, for once.

It was time to shoot. Everything had to be done four times as on stage there would be four screens. Action! Jean-Pierre came parading down the steps, very dignified. Cut! Back again. They all scrambled back up the steps. Dignified they came down again. As Jean-Pierre made his sixth descent from the front, fresh passengers were climbing in at the back. The 25 minutes were up. Walk, walk, walk, to another plane. There it was, but the steps were very high. Someone suggested focussing the camera on the top few steps so that the actors would walk upwards into the frame but no, the entire flight of steps would be used. This was the scene when Hammarskjöld was ascending to the plane which would blow up. It would be like Katharine Hepburn climbing the scaffold in *Mary Queen of Scots*; she just goes on for ever and ever.

Guy Hodgkinson jumped up the steps, covered all the airline signs with Fablon and slapped up UN signs instead. It was quick. It was ingenious. A thundercloud came up behind the plane, just right for Hammarskjöld's death, if you were into German romanticism. Shoot, shoot, it was all done. Joan was still anxious about all those steps. For safety's sake, another plane was needed. The company waited in the covered passage again. This was jolly. The fresh air and the speed of work had blown away the TNP blues and, just as Jean-Pierre was impressing everyone by saying that he had once met the Kennedys, another Iberia Caravelle landed.

Out on to the tarmac went the team once more. Each airhostess, who opened her door to let out her passengers, became, progressively, more fed up with the onslaught of the ground hostess and the actors. None however said 'No.' After only an hour, it was a wrap. Back through customs everyone went. Yes, as expected there was a hitch. More were going out than had come in. Who slipped up? No, none of the company had their passports. There was irritation on both sides. 'You're the last crew that will film at Le Bourget,' said the official.

Part Three

Parallel to the whirlwind gaiety of filming ran a problem that was becoming increasingly serious: Lumumba, or rather the lack of him. Wole Soyinka was supposed to be arriving on 17 March, already a month late. Joan had given him a big build-up, which was alarming because she had a habit of doing this, only for the person arriving to turn out to be a nice enough person but hardly the Jesus Christ, Napoleon-type genius she had described.

Two days after the day he was supposed to arrive, Wole was not there. Two days after that, a telegram arrived: his passport had been taken away from him at the airport. Joan rang Gerry in London. Gerry rang Tom Driberg who knocked up the High Commissioner, while Jean Ruaud got on to the Nigerian Embassy in Paris. Every day, calls from the theatre were put through to Lagos or Ibadan but soon these calls felt like a hopeless ritual. Then suddenly one morning during one of these calls, Wole's voice could be heard. 'I will know definitely at three o'clock this afternoon whether I can come.' Shortly after that, he was cut off.

At five o'clock another call was made to Wole. Two successful calls to Wole in one day, was that asking a bit much? But there he was. 'I've been given back my passport.' Nidal, who was standing by, took the receiver. She didn't know Wole but she was very much in on the excitement. To keep the line busy while someone fetched Joan, she chatted him up. On stage, Joan was rehearsing and couldn't understand why she was being interrupted. When her rehearsing mind was eventually penetrated, she jumped off the stage like a frog. After a few joyful but guarded words with Wole – the lines were always being tapped – Joan put down the receiver, turned and hugged Nidal: 'And he can't speak a word of French, but I couldn't care less.'

On Thursday, a call from the theatre was put through to Nigeria Airways and British Overseas Airways Corporation (BOAC) but Wole wasn't on any passenger list. He had said that he would probably be on the Friday plane coming via Rome. On Friday evening, after work, Nidal took a taxi out to Orly airport. Wole did not arrive.

This looked like serious trouble because there were only three more weeks of rehearsal. That was apart from Wole possibly being in danger. However, Joan had had enough. 'I give him up. We'll have to find somebody in the cast.'

The next morning, Nidal Achkar was on the telephone in search of a copy of the script. Why? Wole had arrived the night before.

And why was all this going on? Wole was a bright, humorous writer and because of this was considered a threat in Nigeria. He had already been in prison and would have been murdered if literary types in England had not kicked up a fuss. At the time of *Murderous Angels* he was teaching at the University of Ibadan and had recently been on a demonstration with some of his students, three of whom had been shot dead, so he gave evidence at a trial. This did not go down well with certain parties. In fact, it was those parties who removed his passport because they feared he would broadcast in Europe the goings on in Nigeria. It was also they who put him in gaol originally. However, because of Tom Driberg's pressure on the High Commissioner in England, he was given back his passport

Finally, the reason for Wole's late arrival was that he refused to go on a flight which landed on the border of Arab territory. The chances were, he would have mysteriously vanished and the Nigerians would have known nothing about it. So, he took a later direct flight to Rome, got off there and found there wasn't a connection until the following day. Instead, he took a train which he thought would have him gliding into Paris by morning. He'd slipped up on his geography. It took exactly twice as long and, when he did arrive, went straight to bed. So there was Joan writhing around in her bed wondering what to do about Lumumba and there was Wole sound asleep a floor below.

When he had recited his poetry with The Buskers at Stratford East four years earlier, Wole was young, slim with the look of a student. In 1971 at the Louisiane, he was an authoritative man in his 30s with a good, strong voice, which was a relief, even if he didn't speak French. As soon as the script arrived, Joan sent him off with Nidal to study it. This was Joan up to her tricks. Sending Nidal to the airport was also her idea. She detested the influence of Nidal's current boyfriend, whom she had nicknamed the tapeworm, and thought that Wole would be much better for her.

With the help of Nidal, Philippe Léotard and a tape recorder, Wole learned his part in a week. The only problem was that he spoke with a posh English accent and tended to use English intonations which made nonsense of the French. Joan was just thrilled that, as a personality, he came over so strongly on the stage.

The chief problem in his scenes was the actress, Madeleine Vimes, who was playing his secretary, Rose Rose. Right from the first reading, she had poured false emotion into her voice and now she was pacing up and down, rehearsing her inflections and, when Wole tried to loosen her up with jokes, couldn't be budged. A little chat in Joan's room ensued but this little chat went on and on. When Joan emerged, she said that, sweet, sensitive, Madeleine had become surprisingly tough and insensitive:

'It's unfair,' she said, 'Who's going to play my part?'

'It's none of your business,' said Joan.

'Couldn't I sit in and watch?'

'No, we don't want you spreading your misery round the cast.'

'You're all against me. You English, you went out and plotted it last night.'

'No, no dear. Look, you're an attractive woman. Go to Jean-Louis Barrault. Go to André Perinetti [a director, despised by Joan, who worked for the French Ministry of Culture on the Ivory Coast] but don't come to me.'

In a way, it was unfair, as this upheaval came so late in rehearsals. Joan had known, from the off, that Madeleine was no good but had left her in the show because there were bigger problems to face. The arrival of Wole had brought her up against this particular one. However, if Madeleine had been at all sensitive, she would have felt that things weren't going right and that she wasn't catching on. Joan said that when she was sacked as an actress, she had thought what a stupid, talentless person the director was and simply walked out. This wrestling that Madeleine went in for, she found most ungracious. Nor did it finish there.

The second Madeleine was out of Joan's room, she went round stirring up the actors, Hervé Sand, Fernand Ghiot and Jean Mondain, among them. She also threatened to inform the union if Nidal was given her part as she had no card. Jean Ruaud was in a panic. It was OK to fire Gérard Essomba, but Madeleine Vimes, that was another story. The white actors knew she was no good but she had worked at the TNP before and she was one of them.

The next day, the Sand, Ghiot and Mondain delegation demanded a meeting. In fact, they broke into the middle of a rehearsal of the black company. This was a nuisance because the black company then had to become involved, though they had nothing to do with it.

The atmosphere was electric as they sat there waiting for it to start. Hervé began:

'We don't know whether we're coming or going. We don't like this atmosphere of insecurity.'

'Ah yes, reign of terror,' popped in Joan.

'OK, you're the boss but we like to be aware of decisions and not find things done behind our backs. We want an explanation.'

Joan then launched into one of her fabulous 'explanations'. In such situations, she never gave a straight answer. It was always the most lavish, roundabout lecture lasting at least ten minutes. Halfway through this one, Fernand Ghiot walked out, which weakened his case.

Instead of saying that Madeleine Vimes was a bad actress, which was the basic truth, Joan wove a long story about how, at her dear little theatre in Stratford (the dear little theatre she had previously wanted to blow up), they tried things out, dropped them if they didn't work, tried something else and nobody was upset as it was all for the good of the show. *Murderous Angels* was like a milky white set of teeth which was rotten inside and only recently had she discovered that the part of Rose Rose was no good and it wasn't Madeleine's fault that she could make nothing of it. Maybe the part wouldn't exist at all. Maybe she would give it to an actress from the black company. That was her problem and the actors would have to leave that to her. She was not able to realise that Rose Rose was nothing before now because there had been no Lumumba.

When she had finished, Joan turned to Hervé and said: 'Please make her come back and she can play all the other little roles she was rehearsing. I don't want her to leave.'

This cleared the air but then the company had not heard her make a speech like that before. Some of her actors back home had. What a good thing they were not there.

The company for the show was by then fixed but Madeleine still wasn't. She wanted a rendezvous over the weekend. Joan dutifully turned up at the Chai de l'Abbaye accompanied by Gerry with the intention of persuading her to come back but, by then, wishing she wouldn't.

'Where's Georges Wilson and Jean Ruaud?' asked Madeleine, her eyes popping out of her head, 'I asked for a proper meeting with everybody.' Joan couldn't account for Wilson's and Ruaud's movements, so Madeleine had to make do with just her. It didn't go well. In the end, Joan told her that she was badly in need of a psychiatrist. Hervé Sand had previously told Joan that Madeleine was highly strung, not to say neurotic. Even he began to get fed up when she rang him at all hours of the day or night during this affair.

That was Madeleine sort of gone but her ghost lingered on. What was to happen to the role of Rose Rose? As soon as Joan had seen that Madeleine was not going to make it, she had wanted Nidal to play it and, indeed, that is what happened, except she became Arabic, was called Salma and had some of her wetter speeches cut. In some ways, it was a relief for Nidal to drop the choreography and concentrate on a part for herself, except that she didn't like it much.

By then Joan and the entire company had moved out of the rehearsal room and were permanently on the stage, which was healthier but had its own problem as Joan's ideas of time on the stage didn't coincide with those of Philippe Mulon, the stage manager. Rehearsals were from two to six and then from eight to midnight. But if ever she should go five minutes past six o'clock, the hair tearings! The flouncing! 'Blerdy ferking Littlewood. If she loves her Theatre Workshop so much, why does she not go back there?' The English contingency always thought Philippe was their ally and when he first made one of these scenes, they were put out but when they saw him making them day after day: 'I won't be treated like a child,' and at the same time of day, they were no longer ruffled. He never did it in front of Joan, so he was just weak. Once he did but then it was by accident. She wasn't supposed to see and she was quite upset until someone explained to her that it happened regularly.

Because of the technical problems with the timing of the slides and film, Joan decided to have plenty of run-throughs. Georges Wilson, who had not been seen much, apart from one flabby visit to the black company for a head-masterly handshake, let Joan know that he would like to come to one of these run-throughs. Joan's answer was that as soon as she thought it was good enough, she would let him know. Come run-through number one and there he was sitting just behind Joan, uninvited. Joan turned round. 'You mustn't judge this, you know.'

'No, no, I am not here to judge at all.' And to pledge his faith, he played a solo on his saxophone before the start.

As a run-through, it wasn't much cop but that was to be expected as it was the first on the stage. However, what could be seen when it was over? Sitting in a corner, surrounded by some of the white actors was Georges Wilson.

John Wells came over to Joan. 'Do you know what Wilson said? He said: "Frankly, I didn't understand a thing. I mean, Jean Mondain, what are you doing?"' Jean-Pierre Aumont, Hervé Sand, Jacques David, Jean Mondain were all very depressed.

Joan didn't say anything at the time. She merely returned to the Louisiane and, in a white rage, spent the entire night writing a letter to Georges Wilson. It was several pages long and damning. It included such phrases as, 'You are a dead man who shouldn't be running this theatre; you should hand it over to a young man.' Early in the morning, she rang Gerry who advised her not to send this letter as it would completely break off all diplomatic relations and make life utterly miserable for the rest of the rehearsals. Instead this is what went:

Joan Littlewood to Georges Wilson:

> ENTRANCE TO MY REHEARSALS IS BY INVITATION ONLY, SIR. I SAID I WOULD SEND YOU A PLAN DE TRAVAIL [a schedule] AND INDICATE WHEN THE SHOW WOULD BE READY TO BE SEEN. EVEN AFTER 8 WEEKS IN THIS THEATRE I WAS ASTONISHED BY YOUR EXTRAORDINARY DISCOURTESY IN DISCUSSING AND CRITICISING THE SHOW WITH MEMBERS OF THE COMPANY AND I MUST ASK YOU NOT TO COME BACK TILL INVITED.

By the evening of that day, Jean Ruaud was skulking trying to get Joan to go and see Wilson. She refused, saying that the only things she had to say to him were best left unsaid.

Ruaud went through his repertoire of sad smiles, diplomatic shoulder shrugging and sympathetic but useless remarks. The poor man, you could just see him doing exactly the same with Wilson in a few minutes time. Joan kept on saying that Wilson was despicable and 'un con' (con means cunt, though it doesn't have the same power in French as it does in English). Finally Ruaud left whispering: 'There's something I'll tell you in secret. You're not the first one to say that.' Everyone went out to have something to eat. On their return, they found Joan sitting alone at her improvised desk in the auditorium. Her face was pale and she looked whacked.

'I've just done ten rounds with Georges Wilson.'

He had come down to her private room bringing Philippe Léotard to do the translation. Philippe hadn't even had time to get into the room before the yelling started, so, hearing that communication was perfectly adequate, he vanished. It was a fantastic row that started in her room, went out into the corridor and ended up in the theatre. Actually, it wasn't exactly a row as Wilson just kept crawling and moaning: 'Ah Joan, I love you. I was only doing my job.'

Joan, at the same time, recited to him the precise contents of the first letter she had written during the night including the 'dead man' bit and quite a lot else including: 'You are corrupt.' To which he answered: 'I know.'

John Wells found Wole in the lavatory. It turned out that he'd prepared the ground splendidly. Wilson had come up to him and asked for Joan.

'Ah yes, you're Wilson, aren't you?' said Wole, 'You're looking for Joan? I warn you, she's got a hatchet in her pocket to split your head open and I'm going to help her to use it.'

All this was said with the most charming smile. The result of both attacks wasn't bad. There was no more chat out of Wilson for quite a while. This bust-up was coming to him for he was guilty of repeated attempts at sabotage in the past but always involving young directors who couldn't argue back. When he wailed to Joan: 'I have never been spoken to like this before,' he was probably telling the truth.

Looking forward to a quiet night and a peaceful Sunday with Gerry, Joan returned to the Louisiane. From one o'clock onwards, every half hour, a different person rang her, each with a more shocking report. 'Pints of blood!'; 'Internecine war!'; 'Georges Anderson will never play the guitar again.' 'Will you please explain,' Gerry asked Joan. 'No, I can't. I'll get empathy.'

Gerry rang Akonio Dolo, the coolest of the black company and soon the stories of five different people were unravelled.

It was nearly midnight and the black company was exhausted. Someone had noticed Manuel and Georges arguing in the corner but didn't take it seriously. In the scene they'd been rehearsing they'd been porters and an argument had arisen over a piece of business. A few minutes later, they dropped it. Rehearsals came to an end and they went out for a drink. While they were drinking they dug up the argument again, only this time becoming more and more excited. Manuel had been fed up with Georges because of a lot of other things and this was the head of the boil. They decided to finish the argument outside. Georges took a glass. At a point when they were absolutely eyeball to eyeball, Georges hit Manuel across the face with the glass. Manuel bled profusely. Everybody gathered round. The police came. An ambulance came. They all went to hospital. Manuel made a charge and dropped it. Philippe Léotard offered to give evidence but the police told him to keep out of it and that is when the telephone calls started.

Joan sat there, saying it was all her fault.

As by then Gerry knew the name of the hospital where Manuel was and the name of the commissariat where Georges had been taken, he was able to make a couple of calls. The nurse at L'Hôpital Ambroise Paré told him that Manuel had not been seriously injured and the commissariat told him that Georges could not be reached until after three o'clock.

Gerry took Joan out into the sun and it was indeed a beautiful day.

'This kind of energy never destroys a company,' said Gerry as they drove through the streets of Paris, 'It's boredom and apathy that are really dangerous.' And then he took Joan to the Bois de Boulogne where they sipped champagne by a lake and talked of the past, of England, of walks on the moors and anything that took their minds off what they had to do. It was time to go. They braced themselves and got into the car. Of course, the address was wrong. There they were in a quiet road in the 16th arrondissement outside the Nicaraguan embassy. There was no hospital. It was the other side of the Bois de Boulogne. However, it was still a splendid day.

The hospital was a big new place, bare and clinical but airy and clean. Magali, the wardrobe girl, and James Campbell were already there. Magali was waiting for Joan and Gerry in the corridor. 'It's nothing much.' They went in. It was a general ward with six beds in it and a television set. Even if Manuel had not been badly injured, Joan and Gerry still had to walk past patients with gashed faces, non-existent eyes, slashes across the mouth, noses and cheeks and one man in the corner who was completely purple. But then they saw him. There he was, at the furthest end, lying like a prince in mauve pyjamas with a little pom-pom of cotton wool on his temple. His face was untouched; thank the lord because he was a good-looking bloke. He waved and smiled. He could never be less than chic anywhere.

Joan apologised. She felt that she had overworked the company and that that was the reason for the quarrel. She and Gerry talked about money. Gérard Lorin had already been in and suggested that Manuel could claim the costs of the hospital by saying that it was an accident that had happened on the way home from work. As things did not look so bad, Joan and Gerry hurried off to find Georges Anderson who was virtually in the nick.

Actually, his commissariat was in a posh, quiet street and looked more like a hôtel particulier (a house on its own, rare in Paris, as most people live in apartments). The desk was upstairs and a policeman told Joan and Gerry that all was well. That came as a surprise. 'You mean the little boy who was lost, don't you?' No, they did not. 'Ah.' They got shown into a little office where a plain-clothes policeman, stern but with a hint of camp, was off-hand. 'No, you can't see him. What do you want?' Somebody else came into the room. He and the plain-clothes guy whispered together. The plain-clothes guy went out leaving Joan and Gerry sitting there like idiots. Joan looked around and said that it reminded her of the prison where Nidal's father had once been held. The man came back:

'What are you to Georges Anderson?'

'I'm the metteur en scène,' answered Joan.

'Oh, j'adore les metteurs en scène,' he whooped.

Quickly he flicked on his intercom and ordered up Georges Anderson but he used Georges Anderson's African name, reminiscent of Vautrin's real name, Jacques Collin, Trompe-la-Mort, in Balzac's *Le Père Goriot*. Georges was brought in. His hand was bandaged. His trousers were covered in blood. The camp policeman made him sign a document and he was free. If it hadn't been for Joan, he would have had to stay another two hours. It was all red tape. He could have left in the morning. After all, Manuel had dropped the charge. Gerry and Joan were asked to leave by one door. Georges had to leave by another.

As Gerry drove him home, Joan maintained that lots of people must have tried to reach him but the police had put them off. She didn't want Georges to feel less favoured than Manuel who had received a lot of attention. You couldn't say that Georges was the aggressor and that Manuel was the victim because they were both furious with each other. Perhaps if Georges had bled more and Manuel less, it might have been Georges in hospital and Manuel in the commissariat. Still, Wole said they should have used fists and that it was bloody stupid of Georges to pick up a glass.

At Georges's flat, his wife was waiting, pale and tearful. She had been to the commissariat early in the morning where they had been extremely rude to her. Firstly, they had refused to let her see Georges and then they had asked all sorts of impertinent questions. 'How do you earn your living? In which district do you live? How much do you earn?' All this because they wanted to know how a white woman got on being married to a black man.

It was evening by then but still a beautiful day. In a daze and not really appreciating it, Joan and Gerry sat down at Les Deux Magots in the rue Saint-Germain-des-Prés and ordered thé citron (lemon tea).

Part Four

After his first reading of Diallo, which was the best piece of work he did, James Campbell was never as good. At first he pretended to be deferential towards Jean-Pierre but, by the time they'd reached the end of eight days' rehearsal, the knives were out.

They were running through what was always called scene ten, though the number was subsequently changed. In it, Diallo attacked Hammarskjöld for lying to the UN and not preventing the death of Lumumba. There had been many problems in the writing of it and the shape had only just been found. For once, it seemed to be going quite well and then suddenly Jean-Pierre broke off. 'No, no. It's impossible. How can I act a difficult scene like this if he's going to carry on like that? He's had the script long enough.' James, from his side of the stage, started shouting about how it wasn't easy working with Monsieur Aumont.

Joan ran up between them to act as referee. 'My children, my chidren, don't fight,' and she grabbed hold of their hands. 'It was going so well. Poor James, he's only been rehearsing for a week.' What had happened was that James had not come back with a line that was in the rhythm Jean-Pierre wanted. He had made a long pause or perhaps he'd even forgotten it. As a result, it left Jean-Pierre hanging in the air looking a fool. Joan pacified both of them and they started again. With pure hatred between them, it went very well. If they could have been persuaded to do the row every night, the play would have been sure to run as long as *The Mousetrap*.

At the end of the rehearsal, Jean-Pierre called out: 'Diallo,' probably because he'd forgotten James's name and then went up to him. It was kiss and make up time. Wasn't it sweet? Or rather: 'Comme c'est attendrissant,' as Bonham said about the two of them in the play.

Joan quietly promised that this little contretemps would not be the end of it. 'Nine days after the play opens, he'll destroy Jean-Pierre,' she predicted. 'James is so rotted inside, after the first night, he won't care about his own performance. We'll have to start looking around for a replacement.'

In the last week of rehearsal, there were run-throughs nearly every night. These were important in order to seal the joins between scenes. Joan didn't like dropping curtains, having blackouts or shifting huge blocks of scenery. Instead she preferred 'liaisons' and interludes during which the actors, in the course of the action, shifted the few props that were on the stage. This gave a carousel effect. As one scene ended at one side of the stage, another actor would be coming on starting the next scene at the other side. It took ages to explain to actors that they needn't wait till everybody else was off before coming in. At the TNP, the stage was so wide a person could finish his last speech and then take about fifteen seconds to get off. Therefore, it was much better to let the actor in the following scene start speaking the moment the actor onstage finished. In this way cross cuts and dissolves could be achieved as well as the carousel effect. Actually Joan did it in her own little theatre. It was not just a question of the TNP. Of course, it did mean that the actors had to keep their wits about them and know the show inside out. There were members of the black company, particularly les Echos Noirs, who never learned their exits and entrances. They just followed the others or got pushed on by an actor who did know.

This was also technique week, technique for the actors and for the scénographie, which was the posh new word for design. The actors' technique consisted mainly of learning to hold conversations looking straight at the audience and not at the fellow actor. At the TNP, if you turned sideways, you were inaudible to half the house, despite *le renforcing* amplification system. This problem was easy enough for Jean-Pierre to surmount because Hammarskjöld was rather stand-offish and, in any case, preferred to indulge in monologues with God. It meant he could do a Hamlet downstage. Paul Bonifas, on the other hand, couldn't or wouldn't get the hang of it at all. He was the old actor playing Baron D'Auge. It seemed that he had worked mainly in films or little theatres and so preferred a more intimate style. In his first scene he interrogated a black priest. Joan felt he would be much stronger if he just stared out into the blue and asked the questions but old Paul insisted on turning to look at the priest. Joan, in fact, was right. By giving to the priest, Paul weakened himself.

Distances were difficult to judge on the TNP stage. Only someone out front could do it. Onstage you could be diagonally six foot in front of another actor, yet for the audience, you would appear to be standing next to him. Actors were reluctant to take Joan's word on trust when she spaced them out. They felt so awkward. Conversely, she couldn't understand why they always clung together and seemed so stupid when directed to stand apart.

She hated this positioning period. She felt that if actors' minds and bodies were working properly they should be capable of shifting themselves but often a scene would come to a halt and an actor, like Gérard Lorin would wail: 'Where do I go now?' Wearily but effortlessly, Joan would direct him from the stalls. 'Walk over to Jean Mondain, look over your shoulder, circle round Jean. Jean circle round Gérard and walk côté jardin (stage right) together, both looking over your shoulders.' No good. He hadn't a clue.

Often towards the end of a rehearsal period with things getting difficult, Joan's weak chest would play up and she would get bronchitis. At the TNP there was no exception but this time, there was no comforting Gerry to bring her those glasses of hot milk which she would hide behind the proscenium arch. This time she just had a temperature of over a hundred. Even so, with other things on her mind, she dashed up on to the stage and whisked through the movement herself. A beautiful piece of choreography, she was literally doing it in her sleep. Gérard, his forehead screwed up, concentrated as best he could. Still, he mucked it up. Joan pushed him through it. 'You know how I enjoy this sort of thing,' she muttered as she climbed off the stage.

That weekend, Gerry came over with medicine to keep Joan going but he wasn't happy.

Next came the scénographie, the design. The slides came. The film came and so did the closed-circuit TV man. Miraculous. And the film was not bad.

For some weeks, an old man had been pottering around the auditorium, sometimes sitting in on rehearsals, but nobody knew who he was. Eventually Joan turned to him and asked politely. He was the coordinator of the slides and film. No one at the TNP had bothered to introduce him. Well, there he was at his Waterloo and it was a losing battle from the start. Not a single slide came on at the right moment, while snatches of lively film would whirr on to the screens in the middle of an intimate conversation. Night after night, it was the same. Not a jot of improvement. The poor man had no sense of the show or of timing in general. He sat at the back tearing his hair out, panicking, and pushing the wrong buttons – frenzy. Apart from that, there were Marcel D'Orval, Hervé Sand and Jean Mondain who had to time speeches precisely to film and they weren't getting much opportunity to rehearse. Funnily enough when they did do it, Marcel D'Orval was by far and away the best, and he was the oldest.

It was an important scene in which he, as Rajat Asdal, an intermediary, speaks to Hammarskjöld on the telephone begging him to let the UN troops intervene and save Lumumba's life. Hammarskjöld says: 'No,' and it's one of the biggest decisions in the play. In writing it, Conor had muffed the whole thing by not putting Hammarskjöld on the stage. So Joan simply put him on film. You had four close-ups of Jean-Pierre turning round looking heaven-ward and finally walking off; very effective, but Marcel had to time his telephone conversation to finish with Hammarskjöld's face leaving the screen. Amazingly he got it right and never lost it. As it happens, Jean-Pierre had asked him to come in during the filming to say the words while he reacted in close-up. It seemed a bit starry of him to ask an actor to come trailing in on a Saturday afternoon, only to feed him and not be in the film himself, but it paid off.

Jean Mondain, after panicking at first, easily got his right. He thought he wouldn't fit his words in but it was merely a question of starting the film a sentence later and all was well. Hervé Sand detested having the film because he thought it detracted from the actors. He was quite right; it dominated entirely, but variety was much needed. Hervé did not appreciate this and took any slip-up in the film as an opportunity to walk off the stage or play the rest of the scene in a flat voice.

The weekend before the opening arrived and the coordinator man was still no use. What could be done? The actors were becoming impatient. They knew what they were doing but the slides and film were chaotic, not to mention the closed-circuit TV which was utterly hopeless and had to be scrapped. It needed special lighting and a far too expensive camera.

Guy Hodgkinson had wanted to sack the coordinator man much earlier. Mark Pritchard had thought he might improve but by then it was too late. Ruaud and Savaron, head of lighting, were called in. Savaron blamed the equipment but everyone knew it wasn't simply that. Joan snapped his head off but obliquely by saying that slides belonged to YOUNG people not OLD fuddy-duddies with no sense of rhythm. Needless to say, Savaron was an old man. Who could do the job? Joan suggested Fabrice Méchin, an assistant, who had been dragged off the show halfway through rehearsals to work on a play in the Salle Gémier. Ruaud said that Maurice Fourt, head electrician, would do it aided by some young man who was unknown to the company. OK, said Joan and Gerry but he had better be good. And indeed they both were good. The next show was technically spot on. It was the actors who were off. If only the TNP had given them Maurice Fourt in the first place.

Marcel D'Orval was the first to start learning his lines. He'd known them for weeks. Paul Bonifas was the last to start. He had maintained that he was good and quick but the show was getting closer and closer to its first public performance and he hardly knew a word. What's more, when he looked up from the text, he forgot all Joan's direction. In the end, she told him to get a move on and learn his lines. He was quite insulted: nobody had ever told him that before. Over the next weekend, he did mug up but even after that, it was agony to watch him. He kept tripping over his words and clutching his head. It looked as if he wouldn't make it to the first night.

Despite all those run-throughs, the scene change interludes were still very slow. Granted, many actors had quick changes but there did seem to be time. Anyone going backstage and looking into the wings during a performance, would be confronted with this scene: actors chatting audibly, smoking and leaning against the projection towers, making the pictures on the screen wobble. When they had quick changes, they merely dawdled off the stage and climbed at a leisurely pace into their clothes. The quick change girls weren't helping at all, nor were the TNP scene shifters. They stood there getting in the way. It was chaos, and Alain Wendling had said that all was fine.

When Philippe Mulon was informed of this, he and the quick change girls felt insulted, but the next run-through was much quicker. Even so, however good the quick change girls became, a lot still depended on the actors. Quick change is really a way of thinking, a style of show, as at Danny La Rue's. 'No,' Jean Mondain would say, 'I haven't time to change my trousers.' He had minutes. It seemed that the actors thought it was humiliating to change costume and character quickly. They liked one grand role and no doubling.

A telegram arrived. Conor Cruise O'Brien was coming back for what he thought was the first night. Actually it wasn't because the TNP's custom was to open for a week and then have the critics, so there was no proper première. Nevertheless, O'Brien was coming. Joan wrote a memo to Georges Wilson:

J.L. to G.W.

WELL, THIS TERRIBLE EXPERIENCE DRAWS TO ITS CLOSE, SO DO I. CONOR CRUISE O'BRIEN ARRIVES TODAY TO SEE HIS PLAY. IT WOULD HELP ME GREATLY IF HE SAT WITH YOU TONIGHT. IT WOULD HELP ME VERY MUCH IF IT WASN'T TOO NEAR ME AS I HAVE TO CONCENTRATE ON A DOZEN PROBLEMS AT ONCE. IF YOU COULD GIVE YOUR NOTES TO ME* NOT TO THE ACTORS IT WOULD PREVENT THE COLLAPSE OF WHAT LITTLE MORALE THE COMPANY HAS.

I'M AFRAID THEY ARE THE MOST INSECURE PEOPLE I'VE
EVER WORKED WITH. IT'S A GREAT SHAME THAT THE PLAY
WAS SO DIFFICULT TO CRACK.

AS EVER JL

*PREFERABLY LATE TONIGHT OR TOMORROW BEFORE
THE AFTERNOON'S FILAGE [run-through]. THERE IS A
TREMENDOUS LOT OF WORK TO DO ON THE TECHNICAL
SIDE YET.

In Conor Cruise's telegram, he asked, as usual, for hotel arrangements to be
made and implied that he wanted to be met at the airport. He always sent his
telegrams to Joan as if she were head of administration. The first telegram was
acted on. The second one disappeared. Still, come the run-through, there he was
with Georges Wilson and the two sat well apart from Joan. The first act didn't go
too badly. Conor took notes in a little book.

During the interval he talked to Georges Wilson. It must have been an odd
conversation because Wilson knew almost nothing about the show and couldn't
admit to having been thrown out of the theatre.

When Conor wasn't looking, Philippe Léotard asked Wilson what he thought of
the show. 'Don't ask me,' he said, 'Do your own cooking.'

After the performance, John Wells could be seen standing with Conor in the
auditorium. They both looked severe. John asked for a script. As it happened, there
were none, so to speak, because there were only individual scenes in different files.
It would have been handy and not all that dishonest to tell Conor there was nothing
for him to see. Nevertheless one was pieced together and given to him. He asked to
have dinner with Joan. She said yes, at the same time arranging for John and Wole
to be there too.

By then, Joan regretted having involved Conor and his play at all. She would have
preferred to have devised a 'Let's Go Congo' show using research alone but, as she
put it: 'We had to have Conor because he was the only one actually there.' Indeed
his factual book *To Katanga and Back* had been very helpful, more help to Joan than
the play.

At dinner, Conor was in an extremely good mood. He'd only wanted to look at
the script to check the French. Apart from that, he liked the production. 'It's going
fine, you old playbreaker,' he said. In a way, what else could he do? It wasn't his play
but, on the other hand, it was obviously much better because it was quicker, livelier
and more opened out. How could you say no to that? Also you had Wole sitting
there, kindly taking the blame for all alterations, knowing that Conor had entrusted
the script to him on his previous visit and professed to respect him.

The day after the first performance, Jean Ruaud and Georges Wilson appeared
clutching each other like a nervous double act not quite sure whether to go onstage
or not. Approaching the first person he saw, Wilson asked: 'Is Joan here? It's very

urgent we see her. Tell her it's nothing to do with, uh, what happened? The two withdrew.

Joan did go and see them. The government, it seemed, was not too happy about the King of the Belgians appearing as a character in the play. Georges Wilson told her that he liked to keep in with the government because it was dangling a carrot in front of him: a large sum of money for improving the theatre. 'Et je suis putain. What do you say "strumpet"?' 'Putain will do,' answered Joan.

To be precise, the government was anxious about the King in the prologue rather than in his other scene. So, could Joan just alter the prologue? Joan, for the time being, did nothing but when she found Conor in the restaurant that night, she told him about it to take his mind off criticising the play. It worked. 'Not a word will I have changed. Take out the King of the Belgians and they can take the whole play off.'

Joan implied that she could safely leave all that in Conor's hands and off he went to chat with John Wells and Wole Soyinka. What fun he was having; all that scandal. Until now, his productions round the world had created no stir at all. John came over to Joan's table. He was thrilled too. Taking the play off with lots of publicity would suit him perfectly. He could get back to London and carry on with his writing.

It was the strangest scene at the Muniche, the late-night restaurant in the rue de Buci where Joan and Gerry ate. Helpfully, it was round the corner from the Louisiane. Many actors from other shows ate there too, including Delphine Seyrig and Sami Frey. That night, Wole, John and Nidal sat at one table, Joan and Gerry at another and, my goodness, there was Ruaud with his wife at another. Conor was somewhere between the three. He went to Ruaud and told him that he would withdraw the play if anything happened to the King of the Belgians. Ruaud came over to Joan's table. Was he shocked? No. He agreed, of course. It looked as if he would enjoy the publicity too. For the rest of the evening, these characters moved from table to table, getting more and more excited. At 2.30 a.m., they went home feeling extremely pleased with themselves. Actually, John and Wole went off for a drink, which left Wole with a terrible headache when he came to work in the morning.

The next day, Joan was in a totally different mood:

> I'm not going to close the play to please publicity seekers like John and Conor. There are the actors to consider. I don't want Jean Mondain or Hervé Sand or anyone to be out of work. The King of the Belgians is not that important. It's a subsidiary role, not worth taking a stand over.

In point of fact, Jean Mondain and the rest of the cast were already paid up to the end of the month, so, in a way, they would not have lost out but Joan didn't know that. In any case her tradition was, 'The show must go on.'

Overnight, she had devised a gag. Jacques Baillon, another of her Hammamet students, who was playing the King of the Belgians, would step forward and announce himself as the Comte de Guyot, aide to the King, and apologise for the absence of His Majesty. 'He's gone to a conference at the Ministry of Culture but never mind. I write all his speeches anyway.'

Joan was quite pleased with that because she thought it would make a big stir without taking the play off. She asked Jacques to come and see her as soon as possible. When he came, he was thrilled because it gave him the chance to clown about, rather than limit himself to the sepulchral booby he was playing. He would rehearse the prologue in the evening just before the show.

By now the stage had been reached where Joan knew that if the show was to go ahead with the King of the Belgians still in it, the government would take it off. A tricky situation because, conversely, if Conor did not have his way, he would take it off. Joan steered through the day rehearsing other things.

When it was time for the evening rehearsal Jacques David and Hervé Sand were having none of Joan's new idea. They wanted to keep the King of the Belgians and they didn't like the Comte de Guyot. They didn't believe that leaving the King in the show would really close them down because they didn't believe Georges Wilson was telling the truth.

'Have you been shown an actual letter from the government?'

'No,' said Joan.

'Well, there probably isn't one. Georges Wilson's just frightened.'

The freshly Roneo-ed Comte de Guyot scripts were left strewn on the stage – and the company went out for a snack. Hervé and Jacques came up behind Joan. 'We've been to admin. There has been a letter.' Joan cursed. 'I knew I should have rehearsed that scene. You shouldn't trust actors to know things like that.'

She wanted to go back and rehearse. Gerry said that it was too late and that they might as well eat. The two sat in a café but didn't eat much. John Wells came over. Jacques Baillon came over. 'We do? We don't?' Fernand Ghiot came over and started talking about the suit he was going to wear. All of them went back to the theatre. It really was too late; there was nothing anyone could do.

And nothing was exactly what happened; no riots and no tear gas. Conor had met M. Antoine de Clermont-Tonnerre from the Ministry of Arts and settled everything. Jean Ruaud sat in on the conversation and, as an ex-diplomat, was deeply impressed by Conor's performance. Clermont-Tonnerre or Cauchemar-Tonnerre (Nightmare-Thunder) as Joan called him, had said that putting the King of the Belgians in the play would cause uproar and upset French relations with Belgium. Conor answered that the only uproar was in the process of being created by M. Clermont-Tonnerre. The King of the Belgians was a small part that would, otherwise, go unremarked. If it came to it, Conor, had positively white-washed the King. End of argument. M. Clermont-Tonnerre went home.

Conor came on the first night with his wife, Maire, who was all done up for a première, though it wasn't really one at all. Having said that it was terrific, they went off, not to be seen again.

Part Five

After this non-first night, Joan brought in Conor's notes and addenda. They were all fiddly bits which the actors didn't appreciate at all. It showed that Conor really had no sense of theatre. For example, there was a little scene where Tshombé announced on the radio: 'The battle for Elizabethville continues!' followed by a direct cut to the other side of the stage where a girl came wafting on at a cocktail party. Conor wanted to put in a few words of explanation after 'continues!' which ruined the cut. Another load of freshly Roneo-ed sheets lay scattered on the green room floor.

At Stratford East during runs, Joan had warm-ups every evening. If she was not there, somebody else, like the musical director, would take them. When scenes became bad she rehearsed them during the afternoon, sometimes swapping actors around in their parts. This prevented boredom and over-confidence and kept the blood circulating.

At the TNP, although the show was officially open, the critics weren't coming for another week – and therefore it was a good opportunity to do some polishing. Joan rehearsed with Wole and Nidal during the day but two actors also in the scene, Marcelline (who was playing Lumumba's wife) and Sidiki (who was playing a house boy), didn't turn up, thus ruining the evening's performance because they were not in the know. Joan screamed at Marcelline: 'You're paid to come, so come. If you don't, I'll cut the role.' Marcelline took it very coolly. She came the next day but, by then, she was fed up because she thought that Wole and Nidal were arranging things behind her back. Sidiki was also of this opinion.

Hervé blustered. He didn't like being ordered into rehearsals after the show was open. 'If you ask us nicely, perhaps we'll come but you must realise you only have the right to call us twice a week and only then for cast changes or pulling the show up, not for script changes. We don't want any more. We're just beginning to get relaxed and secure in our roles!' 'But I don't want them to be relaxed and secure,' said Joan. 'That's what I always try to avoid. They are babies. The script changes are minute but Hervé goes off the deep end.'

Gerry asked Jean Ruaud whether it was true about only rehearsing twice a week after the opening. 'Not at all,' was the answer. 'Until the critics come, you can rehearse them full-time.' Fernand Ghiot and another actor said they had work elsewhere. All Joan could do was rehearse the members of the black company who turned up but even Georges Anderson, who admitted that rehearsals were badly needed, arrived late the following day. Most of the work had to be done in notes.

Joan had been writing notes for some time, in fact ever since the run-throughs started. She did them during the show, a couple of words per page, without looking down. Then at night or the next morning she wrote them out ready for the typist who, when she had finished, would pin them up on a board. As the typist also had to translate, this didn't work so well. Joan's notes could be very tough but at the same time, lively and amusing; for example, a note to Nidal: 'You sound as if you're wanking a snail.' This one didn't have to be translated as Nidal's English was very good. The rest did and how cold and cruel they looked typed out in humourless French.

One day, Hélène Legrand, a black actress, came rushing into the middle of a rehearsal saying that she wouldn't be publicly insulted. The note on the board said: 'Don't come on like a stupid, boring actress.' Joan was very annoyed with the translator/typist. It should have been a private note. 'I wouldn't write that on the general notes for Jean-Pierre Aumont, so Hélène shouldn't be treated differently.' And it is true that Joan did present her notes in different ways. Some were put in envelopes and this one should have been.

Unable to rehearse, Joan carried on writing notes furiously. Every morning at the Louisiane, there she'd be in her little room, sitting on the floor or on the bed, cross-legged and rather bad-tempered. Gerry would be there too, unable to leave his chair for fear of disturbing the notes which covered every part of the floor. He was desperate to take Joan out but there never seemed to be any time.

To make matters worse, Tom Driberg flew in. Joan would dearly have liked to spend time with him but there were always those wretched notes.

It got very bad one morning. Tom was downstairs in his room waiting to be taken out. Joan was sitting in her pyjamas with acres of notes to do and Gerry was shifting around restlessly:

> Leave me alone, Gerry. Take Tom out. You don't need me. You're old enough to go out on your own. I can't work with you brooding there. You're too big for this room. Get another room. If you'd just leave me alone, I'll get through much quicker.

At about lunchtime, Joan agreed to go out. Tom was sitting down in the hall his impatience aggravated by having recently trapped his foot in a lift door. 'She said she'd be free all day. I suppose this is the penalty for being acquainted with genius.'

Joan came down. It was a dull day. Gerry drove out to the Bois de Boulogne. All the way there, Joan wanted to stop at the first café available but Gerry was looking for better things. 'What's that?' said Joan pointing at a huge posh joint by a lake. It turned out to be a banqueting hall that you hired. 'Well, at least give me my attaché case, so I can get on with my notes while you drive.'

Because of the panic, they ate at Le Grand Cascade, a lone building in the Bois de Boulogne with a huge fan-shaped glass cover to the entrance. It was beautiful, dull and expensive; not at all what Gerry had in mind but panic really had taken hold. All through the meal, Joan was desperate to get away but when she went to fetch her coat, Gerry, slightly drunk, was arguing over the bill. 'He's making a complete fool of himself,' she said, pacing up and down the vestibule absolutely livid.

'Have you noticed the doorman?' asked Tom. 'He's rather nice.'

Nobody, apart from Tom, was in the mood for looking at doormen.

'But you should. You should look carefully at everybody you see.'

'You drunken lout,' shouted Joan. Gerry had just come from paying the bill, 'I'm going to be late for rehearsal. I'll never go out with you again.'

Gerry drove rapidly through the Bois de Boulogne. 'You know I like to be at rehearsals a quarter of an hour early,' said Joan, 'I need time to change my shoes and get myself in the right frame of mind. I'm supposed to be sacking half the black company for turning up late and here I am, late myself.'

Gerry pointed out, quite reasonably, that none of the cast would be there on time as they never had been. Joan realised the truth of this and became a little quieter. 'But there's a whole pile of notes that have to be translated before this evening.' She'd started again. Tom, who had no interest in the matter, tried to soothe her but he soothed irritatingly because he was not involved, nor did he care.

When they arrived at the theatre, they were five minutes late and Gerry was proved right. Not a single member of the company was there. In the evening, Joan was, once more, quite calm.

Over dinner, Joan gave Tom the King of the Belgians story for the papers. He was thrilled but the following day, the story was already in *The Times*. Conor had put it there: such a disappointment and it was only *The Times* Diary. Tom could have got a much better spread in the *Evening Standard*. At the end of Conor's piece, it said that the Belgians had warned the French government not to put in the King but when the Belgian embassy was contacted, it claimed it hadn't said a word. Conor also proudly stated that M. Clermont-Tonnerre had asked him to treat the incident as if it hadn't occurred. He of course had answered no.

It was time for publicity, the ordinary kind. Newspapers wanted to do pre-opening stories while TV and radio wanted to do interviews. Jean-Pierre Aumont was very conscientious and did several articles and interviews, thus helping to make up for the lack of stories from Joan. Others who helped out were Wole, John Wells, Lydia Ewandé (who would eventually go to work with Peter Brook), and Hélène Legrand: a good little team that could be switched on to any spare reporter hanging about the theatre.

Philippe Mulon, the stage manager, would occasionally stun the company by announcing the presence of a TV film crew in the middle of a difficult rehearsal, prompting Joan to say that the TNP paid more attention to publicity than to the actual show. A compromise was reached. Filming could take place in the green room. The Echos Noirs suddenly came very much to the fore by doing half their cabaret act for the cameras. Little did the film crew know that none of these songs were in the show.

One *Figaro Littéraire* journalist managed to sneak into the theatre for ten minutes before being thrown out. Out of his short stay, he made a half-page spread.

The press night, which was not the critics' night but the night the press took photos, was great fun. The actors, cheered by the clicking and flashing all along the front, gave a very respectable performance. For once, there seemed to be some hope for the show. Jean-Pierre was floating in the clouds. He had a handful of monologues downstage centre and so it was very easy for him to pose and lengthen any speech if he thought that the cameramen had missed an angle.

One line, 'Mort, je t'attends avec impatience' (Death I await you with impatience), which he normally threw away, suddenly became three times as long. 'Mort (click, click, click, flash) je t'attends . . . (flash, flash, click) avec impatience.' It is a line any actor would be tempted to make the most of but the way Jean-Pieere had slid elegantly over it had been so admirable in its restraint. Henceforth, he stretched it out every night to the point that anyone watching would think he'd never finish.

Until the last, Joan was still making alterations but only through the notes, so one evening, Fernand Ghiot received a note saying that Jacques Baillon would be coming on with him as the aide to the Russian ambassador. Joan had found that Fernand's ambassador had become slow and unfunny. He needed a boost. Jacques went on, paced up and down, looked critically at Lumumba's house and added weight to Fernand's official statements with the occasional 'Da, da,' or 'Nyet, nyet.' It was outrageous because Fernand didn't know he was going to do it, but it was extremely funny.

Come the interval, Fernand was standing outside Joan's room. She hadn't arrived yet. When she did, he was off: 'If Jacques Baillon comes on stage one more time . . .' Joan answered him good-humouredly but then suddenly Gerry's voice raised itself above both of them. 'How dare you speak to Joan like that. How dare you!' And roaring like a lion, he chased after Fernand who was by then moving quite rapidly and calling for the police. Joan dragged Gerry into her room. 'Gerry, you mustn't get yourself worked up like that. It's not worth it.' She sat him down and smoothed his brow. 'It's been like this all the time we've been here, nothing but rudenesss.' She was delighted.

From the tone of Fernand's voice, it sounded like he would leave if Jacques went on stage again. In fact, he was merely trying to announce that he would be resuming his Russian accent, which Joan had told him to stop doing because he was sounding so artifical. At the end of the show, Joan found Jacques in the green room. With a mischievous smile, she shook his hand. He apologised for what he had done but it really had livened up a dull scene. It might have been even livelier if Fernand had hit Jacques, which is what he'd nearly done as they left the stage together.

The next day, Fernand was still there. Jacques apologised to him and remained in the scene. Joan explained to Fernand that if he had bothered to study a real Russian for his accent instead of doing a comic opera generalisation, maybe he would have been allowed to keep it.

Tuesday night, the night the critics were coming, arrived. During the afternoon, Joan worked as usual, knowing that she would not be seeing the show in the evening. Gerry, who had been wanting to get her away from the TNP ever since the onset of her bronchitis, had booked tickets, to cheer her up, for Robert Dhéry's latest musical, *Vos Gueules les Mouettes!* (*Shut up, you Seagulls!*).

At 7.30 p.m. it was time for Gerry's high tea but Joan spent ages going round the dressing rooms giving personal notes. It was goodbye but she couldn't say it because the cast was expecting her to be there.

Five to eight and she and Gerry were leaving the theatre when she bumped into an actor, Guy Michel, dolled up in a dark suit and carrying a bunch of flowers. 'Isn't it ridiculous? I've heard of flowers for a leading lady but somebody has sent some to me! And I don't know who it is. You're not going, are you?'

'No, no,' answered Joan, 'just for something to eat.' She walked on. 'The lies I have to tell.'

Out in the Trocadéro, Joan caught sight of an old friend, Claude Plançon, who used to be the boss of the Théâtre des Nations at which Theatre Workshop had enjoyed so much success. 'If only we'd had Claude on this job, then we'd have been all right,' Joan had sighed during rehearsals. Well, there he was, a tired, hollow-cheeked little man. Joan and he embraced. 'I never go out to the theatre these days,' he said, 'but I've come out for you.' Again, she said that she would be there after the show, this time, genuinely wanting to be. 'Doesn't he look ill?' she remarked as she and Gerry continued on their way.

Back at the theatre, Wole announced that he was going to make Lumumba severe. What could that mean? The show wasn't very good that night. It was flaccid, but the big disaster was Wole.

Conor, in his original version, had explicitly shown that Patrice Lumumba was having an affair with his secretary. However, after the objection from the black company Joan had shaken things up. She introduced Pauline Lumumba, his wife, who was never in the play. 'I'm sure Patrice could cope with two women. Wole can.' And so, during Wole's three weeks of rehearsal, Joan built up the Lumumba household. Sidiki was the servant. Nidal was the secretary, Salma, and Hélène Legrand was Pauline's companion, while Denis Fleurot, another Hammamet student, played the baby, wailing quite convincingly behind a screen. It was all jolly and cosy. It was also supposed to be sexy with Wole hugging his wife one second and goosing his secretary the next.

When the Russian ambassador arrived, Patrice pretended to be asleep and snored. Nidal fluttered around trying to keep a serious face and wake him. As she faced the ambassador, earnestly pointing out that the prime minister was exhausted by the crisis, Patrice was tickling her bottom with his toe. That Tuesday night, when the Russian ambassador was announced, Wole walked off the stage. There was a long pause during which nothing happened and then he walked on again from behind the screen, wearing a respectable grey jacket. It was boring; all the fun had gone.

That night after the Robert Dhéry show, Joan and Gerry went to the brasserie, La Coupole, on the Left Bank. There, Joan heard what Wole had done. She was very angry. 'And on the first night too. I don't know what's come over Wole since he was in prison. He used to be such fun. And now, he's so puritanical, the hypocrite.' She gave instructions that he should go back to what was rehearsed. 'He's not allowed to change the production,' said Gerry. 'If he doesn't,' continued Joan, 'it means he's just another unruly spade.'

The next day, Joan visited a few art galleries and then, together with Gerry, caught a flight to London.

The reviews were not good. Fortunately for Jean-Pierre, he came out of it well. 'A splendidly sober and dignified perfomance but he has not the text to get his teeth into.' So, it was with a certain amount of equanimity he was able to say: 'I knew it all along. We should have had someone like Jean-Paul Sartre.' Well, whatever people thought about Sartre as a writer, it was difficult to see him sitting in on improvisations and going off to write material based on what he saw.

Some of the reviews were plain chauvinistic like: 'So Georges Wilson decides to have a season of modern plays but why couldn't he choose a French one?' It was almost enough to make one feel sorry for Wilson.

Colette Aubriant, the green-lidded publicity lady, sat in her office surrounded by papers. 'Jamais au TNP un spectacle aussi médiocre,' said one. It got rather boring after that. 'What was it like for *Tom Paine*?' (the previous show) asked an actor, 'Oh, much worse,' said Colette. 'You were lucky to get off so lightly. Last night you had a curtain-call. *Tom Paine* was whistled off the stage.'

Wole, though asked, did not go back to what was rehearsed and the scene remained dull. Paul Bonifas, towards the end of the run, fell ill and was replaced by Philippe Léotard. It all happened so quickly that, for his first performance, Philippe had to go on with the book. It was a Sunday matinee and the company's spirits were low. They had been for some time. But then, who should come round afterwards but the grande dame of the French theatre, Edwige Feuillère. In a natty grey suit, looking not at all the grande dame, she went round every dressing room and complimented every actor. Whether she meant it or not was, by then, irrelevant. She was a tonic, no, a glass of champagne. You wished she could have been there every night.

Murderous Angels brought Joan to a point where she found herself saying something no one had heard her say before. It happened one evening, late in the rehearsal period, when Gerry was driving her back to the Louisiane. 'Everything I have done away from you has failed,' she said. 'The film, *Twang*, and now this.' To that, she added the unrealised Fun Palace of which she said: 'I suppose all I can do is grow a show.'

Given Joan's remark, it's time to reflect on *Murderous Angels*. If one were to list a subject worth investigating, research, Joan's long experience of agitprop in which history is made clear in a dance, and slides projected on to a screen, it sounds like *Oh What a Lovely War*. It also describes *Murderous Angels* but what different outcomes.

Joan's personality was so powerful that she could give the impression that she always knew what she was doing and that she could do everything. All you needed for a show was her. The truth, learned on this show, was not so simple.

Her experience in Paris revealed to those who hadn't realised, that, in order to achieve what she wanted, she needed help and lots of it, specifically protection, organization, and even guidance. At work, she could be tough and ruthless. In the case of *Murderous Angels*, her grit in the face of the actors' eroded concentration, the cause of which was alcohol, drug taking and lack of employment, was enviable, frightening and heart-breaking. At organising she was not bad, but her plans were so exquisitely intricate that people who didn't understand them could easily trample on them. A simpler plan made by someone else could be more effective.

And so the penny drops about the division of labour between Joan and Gerry. It had come about oddly because it had come about through the lack of Gerry. This was a lesson in how an artist, even a great one, cannot do it all by him or herself.

Coming into the echoing foyer during the early days of rehearsals, Joan used to sing: 'Oh bury me not at the TNP.' She nearly was.

CHAPTER THIRTY-TWO

REDEVELOPMENT

While Joan was away in France, Gerry had been going to his office at the Theatre Royal every day, not because he had work to do but because he had to make his presence felt. Plans for redeveloping Stratford, drawn up shortly after the war, were going ahead. It was 1971. The houses opposite the theatre entrance were coming down, as was Angel Lane. The market would be moving into a new shopping mall, when it was built. In the meantime, the land around the theatre was one big building site and, if anything, the theatre, right in the middle of it, was an inconvenience. Gerry was making his daily appearance so that no wrecking ball accidentally on purpose knocked into one of its walls.

This was also the year Philip Hedley directed that other production of *The Marie Lloyd Story*, the one at Lincoln with Jean Boht as Marie. It wasn't all he was doing. Together with Oscar Lewenstein, he was fighting at the Arts Council for the Theatre Royal to receive a proper grant and, where Gerry had been struggling, the two of them succeeded. In fairness to Gerry, he was the first to admit that dealing with the Arts Council was not his forte. As for Joan, on the rare occasions that she attended a Theatre Workshop/Arts Council meeting, she gave the representative two fingers.

The result of Philip's and Oscar's efforts was that Gerry was able to announce a new season starting in 1972. With Gerry and Joan, however, it was unlikely to be plain sailing. Joan couldn't ignore the building site. For her, the summer of 1967 flowed straight into 1971. However, the space she was dealing with was not the unofficial rubbish dump at the end of Salway Road but a much bigger one that started beneath her nose, as she looked down from the window of her office at the top of the theatre.

Enlisting anyone who was interested, her usual way of doing things, she began to organise another playground. Thus, once more, her ability to excite people came together with the youthful enthusiasm of others. This time it was Mike McCarthy – he was thinking of becoming an actor – and Jenny King, who saw Joan's colourful plans as a gauntlet thrown down in the face of Newham's unexciting ones. Today, Mike looks after poets and comedians. Jenny is a theatre producer.

'Oh, not more charity. I had enough of that with my old man.' This was Gerry's attitude to Joan's work on the playground. What with the newly acquired grant, he had the job of dragging her into the theatre to do plays.

Redevelopment being all around and also one of the themes of *Sparrers Can't Sing*, he revived it, this time, with songs. It meant, though, that he had to find someone to write them. Photos had been appearing in newspapers of a comically forlorn figure outside the court in Bow Street with the insides of his pockets pulled out. It was Lionel Bart. He was bankrupt and it was to him Gerry turned for those songs. 'That spell Joan put on me,' said Lionel, 'I have to break it.' It's true too. Joan had said that *Twang* would be the end of him and, indeed, nothing good had happened to him after that.

He didn't quite write the songs. He took old tunes from unperformed shows of his and put new lyrics to them. Even when drunk he could always come up with lyrics. In fact he talked in them and, annoyingly for the less talented, they were perfectly usable. The resulting show pleased Gerry because he felt it had a touch of the old Joan and also because it was a formula. Take a subject that concerns the local people – in this case, high risers versus two-up, two-downs – add songs and you will attract a local audience. *The Londoners*, as the show was retitled, did just that.

Lionel was actually going to be in it, singing Joan's favourite song, 'Mirror Man', but, running down a flight of stairs from the upper part of the set, he panicked, jumped and cracked his ankle. The backstage scene of him lying in the wings crying out: 'Bring me a crutch and I'll go on,' while his new friend, Kirk Douglas, leant over him – Hardy to his Nelson – was a memory that could always cheer Joan up. She particularly liked the moment when the actress, Valerie Walsh, 'Practical Val,' she used to call her, actually went to look for a crutch.

The show that she enjoyed the most that year, at least the rehearsing of it, was a revival of *The Hostage*. Ray Stark, the Hollywood producer, had been round all the people, each of whom thought they had exclusive rights to it, and bought them out. He was ready to start filming. A script had been written by John Osborne but he hadn't got the feel of Brendan, so Joan was going to do it.

Her idea was to build a set that wasn't theatrical, like Sean Kenny's original, but one that was realistic so that filming could take place on it after the show's run. To that purpose, the director, Maurice Hatton, who had helped Joan with her Fun Palace film, brought in Tony Woolland, a set designer accustomed to doing films. As she had done for Joan on Broadway, Patience Collier came back to play Miss Gilchrist. Also taking up their old parts were James Booth and Max Shaw. It was all of this that put Joan in a good mood.

Whereas the 1959 production had been sharp and cartoony, 'a happy jabber of styles' wrote Ken Tynan, this one was Chekhovian and three-dimensional. Copper-bottomed, you might say. Gerry hated it and out again came his comment, 'The dead hand of the British film industry.'

During the run, there were two incidental delights. Continuing Joan's idea of rolling entertainment, Ken Campbell's Roadshow performed outside the theatre before the main show. That was 'Sensation Seekers' invited to watch nails hammered up noses, Marcel Steiner's Smallest Theatre in the World and ferrets going down Sylvester McCoy's trousers. Ken himself was not there at the time but, years later, on hearing talk of no Fun Palace, said: 'It doesn't matter. The Fun Palace was wherever Joan was.'

The second delight, though not the actors' – they were furious – was a surprise appearance by Marty Feldman. He came on as a Russian sailor, picked up Jean Boht playing an old prostitute, flung her over his shoulder and took her to an upstairs bedroom.

Also during the run, Ray Stark went for tea with Princess Margaret. On hearing of the proposed film, she said that it might be considered tactless, given that the Troubles in Northern Ireland, which had gone quiet in 1958, were not quiet in 1972. As it happened, the Theatre Royal had received two bomb threats, not that Ray Stark was aware of that. It was Princess Margaret's observation that put an end to the film.

Joan and Gerry went for a holiday, a better one this time. It was to the Camargue. Even so, Joan climbed on a horse that bolted. The two returned, Joan bubbling over with an idea for a new show: package holidays. So excited was she that she persuaded Gerry to drive straight from the airport to Frank Norman's place. He could write the show and Lionel Bart could write the songs. Gerry, seeing that the subject was topical and believing in package holidays because at least they got the working class out of the UK, had a huge poster put up on the underground, 'Frank Norman and Lionel Bart together again.' Not a word had been written. Not a tune had been hummed and neither Joan, nor Gerry, nor Frank nor Lionel had ever been on a package holiday.

A company was quickly assembled, some old some new, and Frank came to the green room to read out twelve pages of his proposed show, *O Bleedin' Lé*. There was plenty of laughter, except at a joke about turds floating in the sea and some anti-German cracks, but everyone thought those would go in the next draft. They didn't and Frank's script was dropped, not that he was told. Every now and again, he would appear wondering what was going on.

What was going on was Gerry rapidly bringing in Alan Klein who had written the musical, *What A Crazy World*. Gerry, who had produced it, had faith in Alan who, as it turned out, had been on a package holiday. The donkey work on the show that became *Costa Packet* was done by him, both songs and dialogue, with Joan doing her bit as usual. Lionel, his powers of concentration badly eroded, produced one song, 'I Want My Bed', which came from the musical, *Gulliver's Travels*, another of his unperformed works.

The style Joan had in mind was that of the zany revues the French comedian, Robert Dhéry, used to put on. It was one of his shows that she had seen on *Murderous Angels*' press night. Dhéry was the first to have monks yanked up into the air by bell ropes, not Dave Allen. It was a style that proved elusive, however, and no one involved in the show was happy with it. Nevertheless, Joan's sleight of hand had the critics writing good reviews and, as it was a show that fitted the formula, a local audience made it a hit. Gerry was proved right.

Joan's idea for before the show was a tour bus that would take members of the audience around Stratford. A guide would pick out the dreariest of landmarks and talk about them as if they were of great beauty and historical importance. Although it didn't happen, it's worth jumping forward to what goes on nowadays: pop-up theatre, site-specific shows, plays put on in hotel bedrooms and the backs of moving vans. Joan was thinking about those 42 years ago.

Having announced herself as good at explosions, Joan set one up: *The Body Show*. She saw it at the ICA and thought it would be good for Stratford. Janet Street-Porter had thought of it. The person who'd make it happen was Gordon Deighton. Joan introduced a device similar to one she had used before on *The Merry Roosters' Panto* – the double booking.

By accident, George Sewell and Victor Spinetti were booked to appear on the same evening, George to present his wrestlers, Victor to present his model girls. Neither of them was prepared to back down. They put on their shows at the same time. It worked a treat and ended up with the models intertwined with the wrestlers. A mixture of King's Road and East End packed out the house but not before all of them had spent time in the foyer, sampling the cosmetics and scents that were on display there. It was exactly what Joan wanted.

It was, however, for one night only. Organising explosions for several nights in a row was much harder, as Joan found out with a topical revue called *Nuts*.

The idea was to have, first of all, a store of sketches rehearsed by a small group of actors. Then, each day, Joan would choose which to perform and intersperse them with hot news items and guest appearances by celebrities doing their party pieces. The news items were preferably ones that journalists were unable to get into the papers or on to television. These would be backed by pictures, recorded that day, and shown on a huge screen. It was a lot of work because you were making a new show every day. Joan had to spend most of her time on the telephone.

The pictures on the screen were achieved by a gadget called an eidophor. This was a present from Gerry to Joan and she loved it. However, it was huge, hard to move and not easy to operate. On many nights, *Nuts*, which had the unknown Elaine Paige in it, went off like a damp squib.

Joan's happiest memory of it was Myvanwy Jenn, who had driven *The Sunday Times* critic, Harold Hobson, wild with her singing of 'Keep the Home Fires Burning' in *Oh What a Lovely War*, stepping on to the stage to sing 'Vilja o Vilja' and being immediately followed by a man leaping up to say: 'I want to tell you why I became a communist.' It was a perfect cut and a good example of Joan's figure of eight.

By giving Joan the eidophor, Gerry was going along with *Nuts* but, up in the green room, during a rehearsal for the sketches, he insisted that the engine of a theatre was a play. Joan said she wasn't interested in plays. When making a remark like that, she could be so forceful that nobody would argue. John Antrobus, who was not only writing some of the sketches but appearing in them, did argue. He said that he was very interested in plays.

Gerry had other worries. He knew that when the redevelopment of the area was complete, the theatre would be overshadowed. Bearing this in mind, he instructed an architect to come up with designs that would not only improve the theatre's interior, but make the exterior look like The Golden Nugget in Las Vegas. Joan, as with the programme design for *Mrs Wilson's Diary*, was sniffy. She needn't have worried. The Borough of Newham was only interested in knocking the theatre down and putting a new one in an office block.

Fed up, Gerry handed the theatre over to Ken Hill, the author of *Forward Up Your End,* and motored down the rivers of France to Marseilles in his new boat, the ErmeX, a patrol boat. Joan went with him. Four months later, leaving the ErmeX behind, they returned and Joan went back to working on the playground where she created a zoo and held an Easter Fair. For that, Gerry gave her a cherry tree.

In the spring of 1975, it was time for the ErmeX to come back to the UK. Joan didn't want to go but knowing that Gerry, on his own, was not a good idea, asked two people at the theatre if they would accompany him. They couldn't; they were busy. Gerry went on his own. Driving the ErmeX up the Rhône from Marseilles, he didn't feel too great and stopped off at Valence for a check-up. Keen to make progress, though, he discharged himself and carried on up the Rhône. The next day, at Vienne, he disembarked to buy petrol and provisions. Within sight of the garage, he collapsed and died. He was a few days short of his 52nd birthday.

His prediction that he would not live to see old age had come true. Joan's prediction that she would die shortly afterwards, though she heartily wished it would, did not come true. She had a strength that Gerry didn't have.

CHAPTER THIRTY-THREE

KEEPING BUSY

As Gerry died, so did the flat at Blackheath. Only he could keep all those tops spinning. To most people this was not immediately obvious as his memorial was held in a tent in the garden. Joan wrote and directed and so elegant was the flow of it that Harold Hobson wrote a piece in *The Sunday Times*, almost as if it were a show.

While it was taking place, Joan stayed in the kitchen. She had, however, made a recording of John Donne's poem, 'A Valediction: forbidding mourning'. This was played at the end and it brought Joan and Gerry's relationship full circle. Donne was her favourite poet and it was a Nonesuch copy of his verse that she had given Gerry as her first present to him when he was a teenager. Although there was a touch of Agatha Christie about the reading – think of the scene in which a recording of a dead person is played – it was a reminder of how well Joan spoke verse.

Gerry's death knocked the wind out of Joan's sails, knocked her sideways, knocked her flat, turned her into a shadow of her former self, turned her into a ghost, turned her into someone else. She promised herself that she would never set foot inside the Theatre Royal again, and would never direct another play.

Right away, though, she instructed Ken Hill to do the classics. This is why she appeared to turn into someone else. The classics had not been a regular feature at Stratford East since the mid-Fifties. It was a shock. You had to understand that, just as Gerry was a shield for Joan, so were the classics and Gerry wasn't there anymore.

Some months later, Alain Guémard, the young Frenchman who'd been disappointed that Joan hadn't done *The Rabelais Show*, found her a course of talks she could give in Aix-en-Provence. At least they would get her away from the flat at Blackheath which needed to be sold. She went and talked about the use of verbs, how they contained action. No sooner were these talks over, than she went on a pilgrimage to Vienne and stayed there. Gerry had died intestate, so for a while she had very little money. A cleaner at the hotel where she was staying, Odette Estève, invited her to her home.

It was a dark, stuffy little flat that looked out on to a dirty stream at the front and a cliff face at the back. Between the flat and the stream was a narrow, twisting road where lorries changed gear and shone their headlights into the room where Joan was sleeping. Even though she had no money, there was something annoying about her punishing herself like this. Odette had to live there because she was poor. Joan, you felt, didn't and, besides, Odette often said that her dream was to move to Grenoble. But then again, Odette provided what Joan absolutely needed, dinner cooked by someone else and a bed for the night.

Remorse swamped her. Why had she been so selfish, so wilful? Why had she done nothing for Gerry when he had done everything for her? Why had she stayed on the playground which was only a whim, anyway? Why had she not been on the boat with him? Why wasn't she dead? To the last one, Ken Tynan gave an answer:

20 March 1976

> Spinetti says you are going to throw yourself into the Rhône, but I don't believe a word of it, and in any case it would be exceedingly unfair of you: I insist that you go on suffering like everybody else. Why should you be let off school while the rest of us are kept in?

Still, these thoughts would go round and round in Joan's head for many years.

What didn't go round in her head was 'My only talent is to grow a show.' When she remembered the image of Gerry alone in his office staring at a newspaper headline, 'Joan leaves Theatre Workshop', she damned herself for her cruelty. If she had remembered 'My only talent . . .,' spoken while Gerry was driving her back to their hotel in Paris, she would have realised that from 1961 onwards, she had been kicking, not only against Gerry and the Theatre Royal, but against that talent too. She didn't stop either. Her return to the playground was only months after Paris.

The trouble was, she couldn't help her restless mind. Still, at least it was interesting. Ideas she had, like one-off events and rolling entertainment, have filtered through the decades to the present day. A small example came from her scorn and fear of national critics. It made her suggest to Gerry that he invite an authority on the subject of the play, instead of a drama critic. BBC Radio's *Front Row* does that today – not always – but from time to time.

This fear came from something she didn't say until very late. Having spent most of her life pooh-poohing success, she admitted that she wanted it desperately. She absolutely wanted to be the best.

As for Gerry, he'd been stuck holding on to Joan, like Tam Lin holding on to changing and frightening objects, in the hope that she would return to – not so much herself, what on earth was that? – but to what he had believed in all his life, her talent for theatre-making.

When Joan wasn't writing pages and pages of this self-laceration, she sent sharp letters to the theatre. Why was she not being kept informed? Why were minutes of meetings, either late or badly written? When, in one set of minutes, she read that

Clare Venables, whom Max Shaw had appointed Artistic Director, was doing Brecht, she wrote that Brecht, after the war, had returned to Germany, guilt-ridden, to write for a guilt-ridden audience and had consequently produced 'such masochistic plays'.

Some months later, with the theatre close to losing its Arts Council grant, Joan returned, sympathised with Clare Venables over the difficulties of running a theatre and saw to it that she left her post on the spot. Philip Hedley was at that meeting and Joan asked him to take over the running of the theatre. In truth, she just wanted it off her hands and dreaded that it might come back to her because, by then, she had inherited the bricks and mortar so painstakingly bought by Gerry. Philip succeeded in doing precisely what she wanted. He kept the theatre open. It was a great relief.

From Joan's correspondence, during this period, you would have had no idea that anything else was going on in her life, but it was. It started with John Wells spotting the predicament of two friends of his – both had lost their life partners – and bringing them together or, rather he told Philippe de Rothschild about Joan Littlewood.

Philipp de Rothschild, a practical man, who knew that he could not spend the rest of his life alone, motored from Paris to Vienne – not a problem, he'd been a racing driver – and, there, met Joan outside a hotel, bringing his secret weapon, the Elizabethans. His excellent English, which he had learned from his British nanny, had enabled him to translate *Tamburlaine* and the Elizabethan poets into French.

After he and Joan had talked about these, her most-loved writers, he invited her to his country home, Mouton Rothschild. She accepted, eventually, and so she and he found themselves in a coda. Your life's work is done but, there you are, still alive. You have to find a way of keeping yourself amused.

When writing home, Joan said that her new friend lived in a converted stable, surrounded, like Don Quixote, by books. He made wine and was not a banking Rothschild. This was completely true and completely misleading. He did live in a converted stable but it was some conversion. This stable, where oxen used to live, was huge and his late wife, Pauline, an interior decorator, had done it up to the nines. He did have a library but he didn't read the books in it. He dipped into whatever was the latest sensation, which his secretary used to put on a low table at the end of his bed. He was the boss of Mouton Rothschild wine but he didn't make it himself. His particular branch of the Rothschilds were not bankers, no, but his cousins were and his fortune was built on Rothschild money.

Spoilt, selfish and rude, he was all those but clamber past and you could get on with him well enough. Above all, he was energetic. A fortune he may have had but resting on it had not been for him. Taking a nineteenth-century villa, surrounded by tumbledown sheds, and turning it into a place of glamour that people from all round the world came to see, introducing chateau bottling and raising Mouton Rothschild from a deuxième cru to a premier cru were means to make his own mark. He was a man of the theatre – his father had been a playwright – and Mouton was theatre all around. That and the fact that it was a haven where Joan didn't have to be ON and didn't have to be JOAN, was what appealed to her. Step away from

Mouton and the countryside was gentle and unthreatening. It's where she took Rajah, the golden retriever, for walks.

Of course the two argued. They argued from first thing in the morning until last thing at night, at which point, they nodded off looking like two owls. It became the arguing of an old married couple. Once, Philippe, whom Joan – nomenclature being so important – called Guv, stuck his fingers in his ears and drummed his heels against his chair and then, when he had calmed down, said: 'I do sympathise with Gerry Raffles.' The Franco-Soviet Pact, which had so exercised Joan before the war, caused such a heated exchange – actually the heat was coming more from Joan – that 'afters' that evening, remained untouched.

The weight of the Rothschild family and all it entailed did bear down on Joan and, once, after running away, which she did frequently, she wrote to Philippe: 'We are of two different worlds and have been happiest in neutral territory or when working which makes all territory neutral.'

This was true. On Sundays, with no lunch laid on at Mouton, the two ate at a restaurant called Le Moutchiko, opposite the lake at Lacanau. The food was ordinary but, sitting there, with Rajah looking on, hoping for titbits, they were happy.

Work was mostly whatever came into Guv's head, a scenario for a ballet, a booklet about one of his lesser wines, the lighting at night of a new statue. It showed that Joan could turn her hand to anything.

Her favourite wine among all the wines Guv owned was Clerc Milon. It came from a small vineyard nearby that she used to enjoy visiting every now and again. The only thing she didn't like about it was its label. If you looked at it casually, you misread the design. Guv had a wine museum and in it were two little Callot figures. Joan said: 'Why not use those?' In this way, an artist Joan had loved all her life provided Clerc Milon's new label. On her own, she wrote a comedy about a holiday in Italy she and Guv went on together. An old countess says: 'A lonely woman seeks consolation in beauty.'

For Guv, one of the many novelties about Joan was that she didn't want anything. He thought he was popular with women. It didn't occur to him that money might have had something to do with it. Joan never asked for a penny but did complain that he was always borrowing cash off her.

If anything, she thought it was she who owed Guv. Jonathan Cape, the publisher, turned down his autobiography. Joan volunteered to re-write it. The book was billed as 'The Autobiography of Philippe de Rothschild by Joan Littlewood'. Work on it was not easy. First thing in the morning, Joan would sit on the edge of Guv's bed to collect stories, only to be interrupted by the cook wanting to go through the menu and Mouton's managing director wanting his daily business chat.

After Guv had changed his mind once too often about stories, she gave up and had them relayed to her by someone else. The final touches were written in Paris where Guv had a house that looked on to a prison at the back and a morgue at the front. It was August, when all Parisians are out of town, so there really were fewer distractions. When an old girlfriend rang to ask Guv to the pictures, he was able to say: 'I can't possibly. I'm far too busy writing my book.' He wasn't. Joan was but it showed goodwill because, if anything, having nothing to do, he was a little bored.

In the end, it was the book that caused the split between Joan and Guv. Members of the family objected to some of the stories, so it was not published in France where it might have had a decent readership. Joan who in her diaries had never stopped cursing Guv and cursing herself for being with him, used this as the moment to make the break. If the book did one good thing, it gave her the confidence to write her autobiography. This, what with knocking herself out on a storm-tossed Brittany Ferry to Cork and, later, breaking her collar bone merely by falling off a stool in a kitchen, took seven years.

Two honorary doctorates came to her, one from the Open University which, given that it was a university anyone could go to, echoed the Fun Palace. The other was from Adelaide. To pick them up, she travelled, not only to Belgium for the Open University one, but to Australia. For all her complaining, she did love adventure.

To keep her hand in, she went back to her youth, and radio. She acted in some plays. Surrounded by actors, rather than watching them, she became a different person. In between scenes, she chatted away, encouraging her fellow players, which they adored, and rubbishing directors, which they adored even more.

In 1983, The Society of West End Theatres gave her a Lifetime Achievement Award. Thank goodness they did it when they did because the very next year, the SWET Awards became the Olivier Awards and Joan would have had trouble accepting that. Her opinion of Laurence Olivier was well known.

That evening, she thought it would be good to have some flowers but it was Sunday and all the shops were shut. When the announcement of her award came, she got up from her seat in the stalls, noticed some huge canvas daisies lining the front of the stage, plucked one, ran up on to the stage, looked up at the packed Drury Lane Theatre, forgot everything she was going to say, knelt down, kissed the stage, got up and said:

'This is the land where no one dies.'

She didn't have to say any more.

POSTSCRIPT

O f the two promises Joan made, the first, never to set foot inside the Theatre Royal again, the second, never to direct another play, she managed to keep one. Even with the one she broke, she didn't do badly. It was twenty years after making those promises that she came back to the theatre for a special occasion.

During the rehearsals of his show, *Zorro*, Ken Hill died. I, who had been working with him for 23 years, took over the last week of the production. A friend of the theatre, Brian Berry, thinking that Joan needed to mark Ken's death and offer me some support, rang her in Paris where, as Jeanne Petitbois, she was staying in a pied-à-terre leant to her by Philippe de Rothschild who, by then, had been dead fourteen years. Over she came, saw *Zorro* and hated it. Not for two weeks did I hear the last of that.

Joan died here in London in 2002. She had given instructions that her ashes, together with Gerry's be sprinkled into the Rhône from a bridge at Vienne. As this was illegal, it turned into a wartime operation. First her ashes had to be smuggled through customs, then Gerry's had to be collected from the Paris pied-à-terre where they had been kept for several years and, finally, the actual sprinkling, which was from the centre of the bridge, had to take place, with the help of some of Joan's Vienne friends, after dark when no one was looking. Excitement to the very end.

BIBLIOGRAPHY

Correspondence, diaries and playscripts of Joan Littlewood and Gerry Raffles.

de Jongh, Nicholas (2000), *Politics, Prudery and Perversions: The Censoring of the English Stage 1901-1968*. London: Methuen.

Duchartre, Pierre Louis (1966), *The Italian Comedy*. New York: Dover Publications Inc.

Goodman, Pearl (2000), *More Pearls*. Chichester: Belfry Books.

Goorney, Howard (1981), *The Theatre Workshop Story*. London: Methuen.

Goorney, Howard and MacColl, Ewan (1986), *Agit-Prop to Theatre Workshop*. Manchester: Manchester University Press.

Guthrie, Tyrone (1959), *A Life in the Theatre*. New York: McGraw Hill.

Gyseghem, André van (1943), *Theatre in Soviet Russia*. London: Faber and Faber.

Kempson, Rachel (1988), *Life Among the Redgraves*. New York: E P Dutton.

Kops, Bernard (2000), *Shalom Bomb*. London: Oberon Books.

Lewenstein, Oscar (1994), *Kicking Against The Pricks.*
London: Nick Hern Books.

Littlewood, Joan (1994), *Joan's Book: Joan Littlewood's Peculiar History As She Tells It.* London: Methuen.

MacColl, Ewan (1990), *Journeyman.* London: Sidgwick & Jackson.

Murray, David (2004), *Seán O'Casey.* Dublin: Gill & Macmillan.

Norman, Frank (1975), *Why Fings Went West.*
London: Lemon Tree Press.

Soyinka, Wole (2007), *You Must Set Forth at Dawn.* London: Methuen.

Spinetti, Victor (2006), *Up Front....* London: The Robson Press.

Tynan, Kenneth (1961), *Curtains: Selections from the Drama, Criticism and Related Writings.* London: Longmans, Green and Co.

Tynan, Kenneth (1967), *Tynan Right And Left.* London:
Longman, Green and Co.

Articles and recordings:

BBC Radio, Archives

George A Cooper, British Library Oral History, 17.04.07

Guardian, 04.04.08 (article on declassified MI5 documents)

Observer, 05.03.06 (article on declassified MI5 documents)

INDEX